MONTESQUIEU'S IDEA OF JUSTICE

by

SHEILA MARY MASON

MARTINUS NIJHOFF / THE HAGUE / 1975

ISBN 90 247 1670 5

PRINTED IN THE NETHERLANDS

MONTESQUIEU'S IDEA OF JUSTICE

ARCHIVES INTERNATIONALES D'HISTOIRE DES IDEES

INTERNATIONAL ARCHIVES OF THE HISTORY OF IDEAS

79

SHEILA MARY MASON

MONTESQUIEU'S IDEA OF JUSTICE

PREFACE

Part One of *Montesquieu's Idea of Justice* comprises a survey of the
currency in philosophical, ethical and aesthetic debate during the
second half of the 17th century of the terms *rapport* and *convenance*,
which are central to the enigmatic definition given to justice by Montesquieu in *Lettres Persanes* LXXXIII. In this survey, attention is concentrated on the way in which the connotations of these terms fluctuate
with the divergent development of the methodological and speculative
outgrowths of Cartesianism into two schools of thought, materialist and
idealist, often widely at variance in their views of the nature and organization of the universe.

In Part Two, Montesquieu's definition of justice is set against this
background, whose doctrinal conflicts, because of the characteristic associations of its key terms, it may be taken to reflect, just as it may be
held to epitomize, by virtue of its elaboration in the opening chapter of
De l'Esprit des Lois and its close terminological affinities with the definition of law there given, an undoubtedly related conflict between the
implications of causal determinism and the aspirations of idealist metaphysics surviving at the heart of Montesquieu's outlook, and, remaining
unresolved, often said to impair the coherence if not the validity of his
theory of society.

The reconstitution of the philosophical matrix of the definition
which is now undertaken, drawing largely on the fragmentary evidence
of Montesquieu's notebooks and his minor works, demonstrates, however, by clarifying his intellectual allegiances and his methodological
procedures, that, far from internal inconsistency, his idea of justice
represents a fruitful interpenetration of the philosophical currents of his
time. The union within it of the epistemological assumptions of contemporary empiricism contained in the notion of relationship, with the
transcendent, if elusive, ideal of fitness, summarizes in a single formula

his double achievement of dignifying his scientific thesis with serious moral aspirations, while at the same time founding this idealism on a solid empirical groundwork. Montesquieu's idea of justice holds the key to establishing the unity of his thought and also offers his posterity an escape from the blind alley of determinism.

In preparing this work, which began as a thesis for the degree of Doctor of Philosophy approved by the University of London, I have been much helped by the encouragement and advice of friends and colleagues, particularly of Dr. Pauline Smith of Hull. I owe a special debt to Professor J. S. Spink for his generous assistance and his unfailing patience.

TABLE OF CONTENTS

INTRODUCTION

In Letter LXXXIII of the *Lettres Persanes* Montesquieu sets out to define justice:

"La justice est un rapport de convenance, qui se trouve réellement entre deux choses: ce rapport est toujours le même, quelque être qui le considère, soit que ce soit dieu, soit que ce soit un ange, ou enfin que ce soit un homme."[1]

Justice is a relationship of suitability actually existing between two things, a relationship which remains the same whoever considers it, whether God, angel or man.

Justice, a relationship of suitability existing between things? It is difficult to conceive of an odder pronouncement from a trained and practising magistrate, and even odder to discover it in the pages of a work largely devoted to the comparative study of morals and manners. The imposing abstractions of Letter LXXXIII, the soaring metaphysical vision of a necessary geometrical structure of moral relationships linking all beings together, are a far cry from the homespun didacticism of the Fable of the Troglodytes, the allegorical but transparently simple and straightforward answer to Mirza's enquiries into Usbek's thinking on the quality of justice in men. Usbek has now obviously progressed beyond mere human virtue to the contemplation of a justice, which if it is still a quality seems to invest the whole nature of things; but how or why he does not tell us. The Troglodytes' justice consists plainly enough in patriotism and mutual consideration, while the what and wherefore of a relationship of suitability are left disquietingly vague. In *De l'Esprit des Lois* Montesquieu forestalls complaints on a similar score:

"il ne faut pas toujours tellement épuiser un sujet, qu'on ne laisse rien à faire au lecteur."[2]

[1] Nagel I, p. 169; Pleiade I, p. 256.
[2] Bk. XI, ch. 20: Nagel I, p. 249; Pleiade II, p. 430.

It is up to us to fathom Usbek's words and to put his theory into perspective. To do so we must not only investigate the philosophical and moral traditions and related terminology which could have been familiar territory for Montesquieu, but also piece together from the whole body of his works the incomplete and scattered jigsaw puzzle which represents his personal philosophy.

The core of Montesquieu's definition of justice is made up of two elements: the idea of relationship, and the idea of suitability, of which the first possesses structural and cognitive associations, and the second functions descriptively or normatively depending on whichever of two broad philosophical streams, naturalistic or idealistic, is selected as the framework of Montesquieu's thinking. Both elements have a special significance in the context of the history of ideas during the 17th and early 18th centuries, but the origin of their association with justice can be traced back at the same time to some of the earliest Greek thinking on the subject.[3]

Using the analogy of mathematical correspondence between opposite terms, the Pythagoreans produced a theory of limit and proportion in society, thereby moving towards a more refined definition of the ordered relationship between persons that had always been implied in the idea of requital central to the primitive law of talion. In Book V of the *Ethics* Aristotle elaborated and systematized the Pythagorean theory, again drawing a parallel with mathematics. The starting point of his discussion is justice in its general aspect, justice as the sum of human virtue, defined as obedience in every respect to the laws of society. He soon passes to justice in its particular distributive and corrective applications, reaching the conclusion that justice is response to the awareness of proportion in human relationships, a proportion which reflects the degrees of merit in each party. There is no indication in the *Ethics*, however, that such a proportion is necessary or essential in the sense that it corresponds to the pre-ordained order of things. On the contrary, Aristotle emphasizes that men commonly understand a variety of things when they speak of merit, and seems to consider that differences of merit have no qualitative significance, only quantitative:

"Justice is therefore a sort of proportion; for proportion is not a property of numerical quantity only, but of quantity in general ..."[4]

---

[3] See G. del Vecchio, *Justice: an Historical and Philosophical Essay*, Edinburgh University Press, 1952.
[4] *Op. cit.*, Bk. V, ch. 3; translated by H. Rackham, London, Loeb series, 1926, p. 269.

One has to look elsewhere, to the *Rhetorica*, for the association of justice with a principle of universal validity:

"In fact, there is a general idea of just and unjust in accordance with nature, as all men in a manner divine, even if there is neither communication nor agreement between them. This is what Antigone in Sophocles evidently means, when she declares that it is just, though forbidden, to bury Polynices, as being naturally just .... And as Empedocles says in regard to not killing that which has life, for this is not right for some and wrong for others. 'But a universal precept, which extends without break throughout the wide ruling sky and the boundless earth'." [5]

and the precise metaphysical significance of this principle in the wider framework of Aristotelian thought is a matter for speculation in view of his general opposition to Platonic idealism.

As far as the strictly inter-personal bearing of justice is concerned, the Scholastics added little to Aristotle. Aquinas contents himself in the *Summa Theologica* with a generalized restatement of the idea that it expresses proportion:

"(Justitia) importat aequalitatem quamdam, ut ipsum nomen demonstrat: dicuntur enim vulgariter ea quae adequantur, justari." [6]

However they were naturally concerned to endow their theory of justice with the metaphysical dimension lacking in the Master. The proportion which justice expresses had for them a significance beyond mere quantitative distribution of virtue in the social sphere, for it reflected the operation of a transcendent principle. This they represented as the expression and fulfilment of a transcendent and omnipotent will, in which justice was fused with wisdom, and goodness with pity:

"Impossibile est Deum velle nisi quod ratio suae sapientiae habet. Quae quidem est sicut lex justitiae, secundum quam ejus voluntas recta et justa est. Unde quod secundum suam voluntatem facit, juste facit; sicut et nos quod secundum legem facimus, juste facimus. Sed nos quidem secundum legem alicujus superioris, Deus autem sibi ipsi est lex." [7]

Linking justice with such a metaphysical principle opened the way for the kind of definition which Montesquieu was to produce. Once the nature of things is seen to be clearly determined by an omnipotent and omniscient force, then one can begin to represent its moral structure in terms of relationships of suitability which actually exist between things.

[5] *Rhetorica*, 1373b.; London, Loeb series, 1926, pp. 139–141.
[6] *Op. cit.*, IIa, 2ae, Quaest. 57, Art. 1c.
[7] *Ibid.*, Ia, Quaest. 21, Art. 1, ad. 2.

Such relationships are so described because they conform to the norm fixed by transcendent authority.

This is not to say that the large dose of theology which the Scholastics injected into moral thinking immobilized the vigorously positivist strain of juridical theory cultivated by Aristotle. On the contrary, the definitive form that it received at the professionally experienced hands of Roman jurisconsults passed unchanged into the mainstream of European culture. Its basic formula:

"Justitia est constans et perpetua voluntas suum cuique tribuendi,"

remains still today the prototype of most dictionary definitions for example.

Moreover, scepticism towards the universalist doctrine of natural justice which usually accompanied metaphysical conceptions of its source constituted an equally resilient tradition, endorsed by believers and non-believers alike. In the 16th century Thrasymachus is resurrected by Montaigne in the *Essais*,[8] and nearer to Montesquieu's day, by Pascal in his *Pensées:*

"Sur quoi fondera-t-il l'économie du monde qu'il veut gouverner? Sera-ce sur la justice? il l'ignore. Certainement s'il la connaissait il n'aurait pas établi cette maxime, la plus générale de toutes celles qui sont parmi les hommes, que chacun suive les moeurs de son pays. L'éclat de la véritable équité aurait assujetti tous les peuples. Et les législateurs n'auraient pas pris pour modèle, au lieu de cette justice constante, les fantaisies et les caprices des perses et allemands. On la verrait plantée par tous les états du monde, et dans tous les temps, au lieu qu'on ne voit rien de juste ou d'injuste qui ne change de qualité en changeant de climat, trois degrés d'élévation du pôle renversent toute la jurisprudence, un méridien décide de la vérité. En peu d'années de possession les lois fondamentales changent, le droit a ses époques, l'entrée de Saturne au Lion nous marque l'origine d'un tel crime. Plaisante justice qu'une rivière borne. Vérité au-deçà des Pyrénées, erreur au-delà." [9]

Pascal, it is true, not least in his attitude to reason, swam against the tide of the 17th century, a time when the human mind began to assert its self-sufficiency and its independence of divine patronage and guidance in such fields of knowledge as politics and jurisprudence as well as in the physical sciences. Descartes provided it not only with critical weapons for use against authority, but also with a general method suitable for all kinds of research, and the means by which a whole body of rational philosophy embracing mathematics, the natural sciences and

---

[8] In Book III, ch. 13, *De l'Expérience.*
[9] *Pensées* 294 (Brunschvicg numeration), éditions du Seuil, Paris, 1962, p. 63.

metaphysics could be constituted. Mathematics provided him with the clue to this general method: he perceived that science in general could be approached in a similar way as a study of the relationships between things. Baillet, his biographer, recounts how he made his discovery:

"... il abandonna l'étude particulière de l'arithmétique et de la géométrie, pour se donner tout entier à la recherche de cette science générale, mais vraie et infaillible, que les Grecs ont nommée judicieusement *mathesis* ... et ... il jugea qu'il y avait une science générale destinée à expliquer toutes les questions que l'on pouvait faire touchant les rapports, les proportions et les mesures, en les considérant comme détachées de toute matière, et que cette science générale pouvait à très juste titre porter le nom de *mathématique universelle*, puisqu'elle renferme tout ce qui peut faire mériter ce nom de science et de mathématique particulier aux autres connaissances."[10]

The idea of a universal algebra was first expressed in the *Regulae ad Directionem Ingenii*, written about 1628,[11] but Descartes comments upon it directly in the better known *Discours de la Méthode*:

"Mais ce qui me contentait le plus de cette méthode était que, par elle j'étais assuré d'user en tout de ma raison, sinon parfaitement, au moins le mieux qu'il fût en mon pouvoir: outre que je sentais, en la pratiquant, que mon esprit s'accoutumait peu à peu à concevoir plus nettement et plus distinctement ses objets; et que, ne l'ayant point assujetti à aucune matière particulière, je me promettais de l'appliquer aussi utilement aux difficultés des autres sciences que j'avais fait à celles de l'algèbre."[12]

From this insight combined with the application of the criterion of *évidence*, drawn also from mathematics and reinforced by the experience of the *cogito*, Descartes was able to construct a new and purely rational explanation of the physical world. It is true that he did not replace analytical and deductive processes by more empirical procedures, though he was prepared to experiment in order to discover the questions that needed to be answered. He continued moreover to subordinate the natural sciences to metaphysics, in which many arbitrary principles went unquestioned; but the first and greatest step had been taken.

It was in the same spirit of pioneering rationalism that Hugo Grotius asserted a few years prior to the *Regulae* in the preface to his *De Jure Belli ac Pacis* that the propositions of natural law would retain their

[10] *La Vie de M. Descartes*, Paris, 1691; Part I, ch. 2, sec. 6, p. 114.
[11] The *Regulae* were first published in the *Opuscula posthuma physica et mathematica*, Amsterdam, 1701.
[12] *Op. cit.*, (1637), Part II; Paris, Garnier, 1960, p. 52.

validity even if we were to assume that there was no God,[13] an assertion
which could be read as a premature reply to Pascal's scepticism about
justice. And Grotius's substitution of the authority of reason as revealed
in natural law for the authority of divine command as expressed in revelation and orthodox tradition, together with Descartes's contribution
to the philosophy and techniques of science itself, hold two of the keys
to the genesis of Montesquieu's definition of justice. For the essence of
Cartesian method was the application of the idea that all knowledge
consists in the perception of relationships. Since there was never any
doubt that the form of intelligence corresponded exactly to the nature
of reality, it was permissible, not to say perfectly logical to represent its
structure in terms of relationships also. Thus when Montesquieu defines
justice as "un rapport de convenance qui se trouve réellement entre
deux choses," he is treating it as a structural element of moral reality,
and could equally be signalling the belief that ethics can be subjected
to a scientific approach as much as physics, in anticipation of his approach to concrete social phenomena in the *Lois*, where he actually
produces a science of society. When he qualifies his definition, adding
"ce rapport est toujours le même, quelque être qui le considère, soit que
ce soit dieu, soit que ce soit un ange, ou enfin que ce soit un homme,"
he is treading in the steps of Grotius by suggesting that the principle
which informs the moral structure of the world, which determines the
fitness of relationships of justice, while undoubtedly transcendent, is
nevertheless in some way independent of the arbitrary will of any supernatural or intelligent being. The relationships of justice are unalterable
by God, men or angels.

But the nature of their independence is never precisely indicated,
which raises the possibility of a third key to the significance of Montesquieu's definition. Since God is, as it were, made to stand down, and
the relationships of justice are described as really existing between
things, it could be that Montesquieu was putting into necessarily ambiguous words a theory inspired by the kind of rationalistic materialism
usually attributed to Spinoza. The suitability of the relationships between things could amount to nothing more than the compossibility of
phenomena which a doctrine of reason immanent in nature implies.

The viability of this particular interpretation is one of the things
which a study of the significance attached in the works of contemporaries and near contemporaries to the specialized vocabulary used by

[13] The work was first published in Paris in 1625.

Montesquieu in his definition, in conjunction with a reconstruction, as far as surviving texts allow, of his personal philosophy, should help to decide. More generally it is hoped that this double investigation, in showing the extent to which Montesquieu's ideas about justice crystalize the moral thought of a generation, will also reveal how far they surpass it.

PART ONE

MONTESQUIEU'S DEFINITION OF JUSTICE: PRECURSORS AND PARALLELS

CHAPTER ONE

LEXICOGRAPHERS

A detailed examination of dictionary definitions reveals the general significance of the terms *rapport* and *convenance* during the second half of the 17th century. So far we have thought of *rapport* above all as a structural principle and of *convenance* as a normative idea; and in the main these conceptions are shared by the compilers of dictionaries. The meaning of *rapport*, as might be expected with such a basic term, underwent little change over the period, and was consistently associated with the ideas of *convenance* and *bienséance*, the relationship between which will be considered later.[1] At the beginning of the century, the following illustration is given in the *Thresor de la Langue francoyse*:

"Le rapport et bienséance des parties l'une à l'autre, convenance et accordance: convenientia partium."[2]

Convenance and *rapport* are intimately associated in their Latin root; one recalls that *convenio* meant not only to be in conformity with, but also to assemble together. Towards the end of the century, the *Grand Dictionnaire de l'Académie française* defines *rapport* as: "convenance, ressemblance, conformité," and adds the following illustration:

"On dit, 'par rapport du petit au grand, du grand au petit,' pour dire, 'en gardant la proportion qu'il y a de l'un à l'autre'."[3]

Rapport is undoubtedly concerned with the structure or composition of things, but there never seems the slightest doubt in the minds of the compilers, of Jean Nicot or of Thomas Corneille, that relationships are ever anything but proper and symmetrical. Thus Corneille's contemporary and rival Antoine Furetière writes in his *Dictionnaire Universel:*

[1] Below pp. 4–7.
[2] *Thresor de la Langue francoyse*, 1606, edited by Jean Nicot; at "rapport."
[3] *Op. cit.*, 2e édition revue et corrigée, Amsterdam, 1696.

"La proportion n'est autre chose que le rapport que des quantités ont les unes avec les autres ... La symétrie est un rapport que toutes les parties d'un bâtiment ou d'un tableau doivent avoir entre elles et avec leur tout. On dit en ce sens que du fini à l'infini il n'y a aucun rapport ni proportion." [4]

He also goes on to mention the traditional teleological associations of the term:

"... se dit aussi en Morale de la relation des choses à leur fin. Toutes les actions d'un Chrétien doivent être faites par rapport à Dieu. Un mondain ne fait rien que par rapport à lui-même. Le mérite d'une action est considéré par le rapport qu'elle a à sa fin bonne ou mauvaise."

The history of the term *convenance* is more complex, associated as it was on the one hand with *rapport* and on the other with *bienséance*. We have just noted the definition of relationship given in the *Thresor de la Langue francoyse*: "Le rapport et bienséance des parties l'une à l'autre, convenance et accordance." Now the definition of *bienséance* which is given there is almost the same:

"La bienséance et rapport des parties l'une avec l'autre: convenientia rerum, decentia."

As time passed the meaning of *bienséance* became much more specialized; gradually it came to be the simple equivalent of *decentia*, and was no longer the synonym of *rapport*. But these definitions have a common term: *convenance*, which seems almost to combine the meanings of both. It is certainly impossible to talk of conformity without thinking of some kind of relationship, whereas it is not the case that relationship always implies conformity. Similarly, propriety, or *bienséance* always suggests conformity with a certain standard or accepted convention.

The obvious conclusion is that *convenance* was already at the beginning of the 17th century a very general term, almost as general as *raison*, and signifying some widely accepted, but ill-defined criterion. However, this conclusion is not borne out by the entries in the *Thresor*. Related to the Latin verb *convenio* were several nouns: *convenientia*, *conventio*, and *conventum* among them, whose meanings ranged from agreement in the abstract, to a material compact, and even to an actual assembly. Some of these meanings seem to have coalesced in the French word *convenance*, although this sounds closest to the most general of the Latin terms, *convenientia*. Thus, in the *Thresor* particular attention is paid to such definitions as marriage compact, written or verbal agreement: "Il fait convenance et accord avec eux par le moyen d'une gran-

---

[4] *Op. cit.*, La Haye, 1690; at "rapport."

de somme d'argent." The most general significance is attached to the adjective *convenable*, "propre ou sortable à quelque chose"; while the meanings of *convenir* are closer in feeling to *bienséance*: "Cela ne convient pas à un homme de telle dignité que tu es."

The picture has changed considerably by the end of the century. In the Academy's *Grand Dictionnaire des Arts et des Sciences*, there is a long elaboration of Nicot's article in the *Thresor* on the matrimonial significance of the word,[5] but elsewhere the discussion concentrates on its more abstract meanings. Generally speaking, the terms *convenance* and *bienséance* still share common ground, though the latter is becoming more specialized, and *convenance* is moving towards the wider significance of *rapport*. The *Grand Dictionnaire de l'Académie française* gives *bienséance* and *décence* as synonyms of *convenance*, but Furetière in the *Dictionnaire Universel* does not. It is easy to see why their meanings overlap: there is little difference between the ideas of fitting something well and simply fitting; the extra ingredient of *bienséance*, the adverb *well*, since it must ultimately depend on personal judgement, although that judgement may be shared by many people, probably accounts nevertheless for its gradual restriction to areas of experience where personal factors dominate, such as social intercourse and art. It does not necessarily follow from this however, that *bienséance* ceased to be regarded as an independent criterion, just as much as *convenance* was, or that they did not remain closely connected in people's minds.

In Furetière's Dictionary the notion of proper relationship is clearly expressed in his definition of *bienséance:* "ce qui convient à une chose"; nothing could be simpler, but this is modified in such a way as to show the important aesthetic significance that the term had acquired: "qui lui donne de la grâce, de l'agrément," and also its intimate connection with *honnêteté:*

"Il est de la bienséance de se tenir découvert et en une posture honnête devant les Grands et les Dames. La bienséance exige de nous plusieurs devoirs et civilités. Il faut en toutes choses observer les bienséances."

This is the traditional notion that Jean Nicot included in his definition of *Convenir* in the *Thresor de la Langue francoyse*, and there one also finds the notion of utility, which Furetière attaches to *bienséance*. In English we have the word *convenience*, which is obviously similar to *convenance*, and related to the Latin *convenientia*, and which we associate almost

---

[5] *Grand Dictionnaire des Arts et des Sciences*, 2nd. ed., Amsterdam 1696, art. *Convenancer*.

exclusively with material advantage and personal comfort. This is exactly the meaning of *bienséance* in the 17th century:

"... se dit aussi de ce qui est commode, utile et avantageux. Il a acheté cette maison, cette terre, parce qu'elle était à sa bienséance, dans son voisinage. On a dans ce quartier toutes choses à sa bienséance: l'église, le marché etc..."[6]

Or again in the *Grand Dictionnaire de l'Académie française:*

"On dit qu'une chose est à la bienséance de quelqu'un, pour dire qu'il lui conviendrait de l'avoir à cause de quelque convenance particulière; ... telle province est fort à la bienséance de ce Prince-là."[7]

The association which this utiliarian meaning has with purposive activity is basically the same as that which the social significance of the word has with the teleological notion that the individual must fulfil his rôle in society. And this in turn can be reduced to the idea that everything must fulfil its own nature, and the related notion that the attributes of things must accord with their essence. At this point the line of demarcation between *bienséance* and *convenance* is very blurred indeed: it is virtually impossible to distinguish for example between these two illustrations which Furetière gives: "Il est bienséant à une fille d'être modeste, de rougir" and: "L'amour, la galantrie n'est pas une chose convenante à un vieillard." [8] *Bienséant* is perhaps a shade more emotive, and *convenant* a more neutral adjective, but that is all.

A comprehensive review of all the definitions of *bienséance* and *convenance* given in both Furetière and the Academy's *Dictionnaire* tends however to enlarge and underline this distinction. Thus although such illustrations as "Il s'est chargé d'une commission qui n'est point convenable à sa dignité," are connected with the notion of *honnêteté*, in general the simple idea of relationship is more closely associated with *convenance* than with *bienséance*. In Furetière for example, we also find the following definition of *convenance:*

"Terme relatif. Proportion, rapport, ressemblance que deux choses ont ensemble. Le blanc et le noir, le chaud et le froid, n'ont aucune convenance ensemble. Ces deux étoffes ont tant de convenance, se ressemblent si fort qu'on les prend l'une pour l'autre."[9]

The definition of the *Grand Dictionnaire* is similar:

[6] Furetière, *Dictionnaire Universel*, La Haye, 1690; art. *Bienséance*.
[7] *Op. cit.*, art. *Seoir*.
[8] *Dictionnaire Universel*, arts. *Bienséance* and *Convenance*.
[9] *Op. cit.*, art. *Convenance*.

"Rapport, conformité. Ces choses-là n'ont point de convenance l'une avec
l'autre. Quelle convenance y a-t-il entre des choses si différentes? Pour bien
discourir des choses, il en faut observer les convenances et les différences."[10]

And harking back to the old idea of talion there is: "La grandeur du
crime demande une punition convenable," [11] a maxim whose implications escaped the attention of most magistrates of the day. For us however it provides a simple illustration of the idea of *convenance* expressed
in juridical terms; and with regard to the problem of distinguishing between *bienséance* and *convenance*, it shows how much more versatile the
latter is, since it would be strange to talk of "une punition bienséante"
in any context. The *Grand Dictionnaire* is also very explicit on the subject
of *bienséance:*

"Convenance de ce qui se dit, de ce qui se fait par rapport aux personnes,
à l'âge, au sexe, aux temps, aux lieux, etc. Cela choque la bienséance, n'est
pas dans la bienséance, ... garder la bienséance, ... observer les bienséances, les règles, les lois de la bienséance."[12]

Its social significance, and the way it came to be used as an independent abstract criterion, something akin to *politesse* or *honnêteté* are clearly
shown in this definition.

In conclusion we may say then that *bienséance* denotes a standard of
social behaviour, or as we shall see later an artistic criterion; it is not
yet as narrowly defined as in modern French, where it rarely signifies
more than conformity with social convention, although by the end of
the 17th century its development lies clearly in that direction. Thus as
a normative principle it implies reference to something arbitrary rather
than rational; as we mentioned above, it sometimes appears to call
upon factors which we would call affective.[13] *Convenance* on the other
hand is a much wider term implying a relationship of conformity or of
proportion, which may be used in a social context, but is not restricted
to the subject of manners. Indeed, when considered in isolation, its
unlimited nature makes of it a kind of metaphysical entity controlling
every possible relationship in the universe, and as such a criterion superior to *bienséance* or any other.

[10] *Grand Dictionnaire de l'Académie française*, art. *Convenance*.
[11] *Ibid.*
[12] *Op. cit.*, art. Seoir.
[13] See above.

CHAPTER TWO

METAPHYSICIANS

The dictionary compilers of the 17th century were not concerned primarily with the philosophical meaning of *convenance;* for them the term meant little more than a relationship of conformity, something not quite so simple as *rapport,* but that is all. We must look elsewhere for the notion that it is the quality which constitutes the relationship between the real and the ideal, which is the force that it possesses in Montesquieu's definition of justice.

As soon as one begins to consider Montesquieu and philosophy, the name which springs immediately to mind is that of the great Oratorian philosopher Malebranche. This is not just because of the echoes of the *Recherche de la Vérité* or the *Traité de Morale* which found their way into Montesquieu's work; but also because much evidence points to the fact that Malebranche was a considerable influence in his education. Montesquieu was born in 1689, and Malebranche died in 1715: during the whole of the period from the publication of the first volume of the *Recherche de la Vérité* in 1674 until his death, Malebranche was involved in disputes on all sides arising out of misunderstanding and criticism of this work.[1] Although he was by all accounts a gentle and retiring person, his creative activity was almost entirely governed by the bitter attacks which he had to answer. Religious disputes between Protestants and Catholics, between Jesuits and Jansenists continued unabated during the last quarter of the century, but all alike found time to criticize the Oratorian. Perhaps they saw and feared in his work the shadow of Spinoza, and seized the opportunity to attack it where it seemed to be openly published, rather than waste their efforts on the numerous pamphlets and fragments which circulated secretly.[2] But while these

[1] For details of Malebranche's life and controversies, see Le P. André, *La Vie du R. P. Malebranche . . . avec l'Histoire de ses Ouvrages,* publ. by Ingold, 1881, Bibliothèque Oratorienne vol. VIII.

[2] See P. Vernière, *Spinoza et la Pensée française avant la révolution,* 1954, Part I, ch. 5.

did their work slowly and surely, Malebranche and his controversies dominated intellectual discussion during the greater part of the period, and this is important for us because it includes the time of Montesquieu's childhood and youth, and particularly the years he spent from 1700–1705 at the famous Oratorian college at Juilly. Eclecticism was the hallmark of Oratorian thinking, but he could hardly escape the influence of their most famous son, especially when the latter was constantly the subject of public debate. Added to this was the influence of personal acquaintances, such as the mathematician and scientist Dortous de Mairan, who was the pupil of Malebranche, and who later became Montesquieu's colleague in the Academy of Bordeaux; and Father Pierre-Nicolas Desmolets, the librarian of the Paris Oratory, who introduced him to Paris circles while he was studying law there from 1709–1713.[3]

Malebranche's influence was not limited to France; his philosophy was read and discussed in Italy, Holland, Germany, England and Ireland. He corresponded with Leibniz; in Ireland his ideas were taken up by Browne, King and above all Berkeley;[4] Michel Levassor, a former Oratorian priest, translated the *Recherche de la Vérité* into English;[5] and such men as the Abbé Bernado Lama, whom Montesquieu met in Paris during his first stay there, travelled from Italy to sit at the feet of the master.[6] Wherever Montesquieu was to pass later during his travels, the works of Malebranche would already be known and debated.[7]

It is difficult to decide between the impressions which Malebranche's works leave with the reader; on the one hand they are pervaded by a deep religious feeling that amounts almost to mysticism, and indeed there is no question that he was anything but a sincere and orthodox Christian; but on the other, one is conscious, as many of his contemporaries were, that this mysticism arises from the divinization of reason. As the perfection of reason, God loses his personality; he ceases to be the Christian figure of a being of perfect goodness and charity. Like Fénelon's idea of mystical union with God without the support of revelation

[3] For details of Montesquieu's acquaintance with Mairan, see R. Shackleton, *Montesquieu, A Critical Biography*, Oxford, 1961, ch. I, section 5; and P. Barrière, *Un Grand Provincial, ... Montesquieu*, Bordeaux, 1946, part 1, ch. V, section i. And for Desmolets, Shackleton, *op. cit.*, ch. I, section 3.

[4] See A. A. Luce, "Malebranche et le Trinity College de Dublin," in the *Revue Philosophique de la France et de l'Etranger*, 1938, vol. CXXV.

[5] See F. Bouillier, *Histoire de la Philosophie Cartésienne*, Paris 1868, ch. 17.

[6] See Shackleton, *op cit.*, ch. I, section 3.

[7] Montesquieu recorded his travels in the notebooks *Voyages*, published Nagel, vol. II, and Pléiade, vol. I.

or of any external media at all, Malebranche's insistence on the conception of God as pure intelligence undermined in a serious way the whole fabric of traditional dogma and the established authority of the Church. Small wonder that the *Traité de la Nature et de la Grâce* which transformed grace into a kind of general law operating in a way similar to the order of nature, was awarded the not uncommon distinction of being placed on the Index of Prohibited Books in 1690.

The title of his first book, *La Recherche de la Vérité* is most significant. His philosophical career began according to Father André's biography,[8] when he discovered a copy of Descartes's *Traité de l'Homme*, and conceived the notion that the metaphysics of St. Augustine completed Cartesian physics by elucidating certain problems such as the nature of ideas, and of eternal truth. But the *Traité de l'Homme* which introduced him to Cartesian philosophy, is a long mechanical explanation of the human body, and from this he retained above all the idea that truth is mathematical, that it is expressed in the form of a relationship, and that reason consists in the apprehension of this relationship. This was the real starting point of Descartes in the *Regulae ad Directionem Ingenii*, and it remains the starting point of all Malebranche's works too:

"Lorsque tu vois que 2 fois 2 sont 4 et que 2 fois 2 ne sont pas 5 tu vois des vérités: car c'est une vérité que 2 fois 2 sont 4 ou que 2 fois 2 ne sont pas 5. Mais que vois tu alors sinon un rapport d'égalité entre 2 fois 2 et 4, ou un rapport d'inégalité entre 2 fois 2 et 5? Ainsi les vérités ne sont que des rapports: mais des rapports réels et intelligibles. Car si un homme s'imaginait voir un rapport d'égalité entre 2 fois 2 et 5 ou un rapport d'inégalité entre 2 fois 2 et 4, il verrait une fausseté: il verrait un rapport qui ne serait point, ou plutôt il croirait voir ce qu'effectivement il ne voit point. Car il n'y a que le réel qui soit visible, que la vérité qui soit intelligible: le faux ne le fut jamais: il peut être cru, mais prends-y garde, un rapport qui n'est point ne peut être vu."[9]

With Malebranche it is the notion of reason as the vision of real relationship (un rapport qui n'est point ne peut être vu), which becomes, rather than Descartes's *cogito* or the subjective experience of consciousness, the basis of his metaphysics and morals. The vision of God becomes a vision of Reason, of relationships of perfection, which man may comprehend because of their mathematical nature, while his own perceptions remain obscure and confused:

---

[8] See above p. 8 n. 1.
[9] *Méditations Chrétiennes et Métaphysiques*, 4th. ed., Lyon, 1707, IV, para. iv, pp. 54–55.

"Nos sentiments sont confus. Ce ne sont que les modalités de notre âme qui ne peuvent nous éclairer. Mais les idées que la raison nous découvre sont lumineuses: l'évidence les accompagne. Il suffit de les considérer avec attention pour en découvrir les rapports et s'instruire solidement de la vérité." [10]

Since the idea of relationship, rather than the notion of intuition, dominates his conception of reason, the quality of *convenance* which we have seen to be closely linked with the idea of relationship, though less often mentioned, is an active force behind much of his thinking.

Malebranche sees relationship as a structural fact in spatial analysis, but more important, in its rational embodiment, as a metaphysical reality. In his works he calls reason by many names: "le Verbe," "la Sagesse éternelle," "la Loi inviolable," and in his theology, Christ becomes its embodiment, no doubt on sound scriptural grounds. This transcendent Law contains the order of creation and it is consubstantial with God, whose will is subject to it:

"Sache que je suis la Loi éternelle, Loi que Dieu consulte sans cesse, et qu'il suit inviolablement. Car je suis la sagesse de mon Père, et il m'aime non comme un homme aime son enfant, à cause que son enfant lui ressemble, mais il m'aime par la nécessité de sa nature comme un fils qui lui est consubstantiel et auquel il communique toute sa substance." [11]

The eternal law consists in relationships of perfection and relationships of size: the latter constitute eternal, necessary truths, mathematical in nature; and the former universal order:

"Or il y a cette différence entre les rapports de grandeur et les rapports de perfection, que les rapports de grandeur sont des vérités toutes pures, abstraites, métaphysiques, et que les rapports de perfection sont des vérités et en même temps des Lois immuables et nécessaires: ce sont les règles inviolables de tous les mouvements des esprits. Ainsi ces vérités sont l'ordre que Dieu même consulte dans toutes ses opérations. Car aimant toutes choses à proportion qu'elles sont aimables, les différents degrés de perfection règlent les différents degrés de son amour, et la subordination qu'il établit entre ses créatures." [12]

The perfections which are in God represent all possible creatures, and these perfections, though infinite in themselves, are not equal. Thus the conception of a kind of hierarchy of archetypal ideas in the divine understanding emerges. This can be seen as the metaphysical structure of reality.

But what of the question of creation? Aquinas had also seen in the

---

[10] *Entretiens Métaphysiques*, 1688, III, para. 17, pp. 109–110.
[11] *Méditations Chrétiennes*, III, para. 21, p. 47.
[12] *Ibid.*, IV, para. 8, pp. 57–58.

divine being a hierarchy of ideas which were the prototypes of created things, reflecting in their diverse imperfection the manifold perfections of the Creator. However, for him God was not only perfect goodness but also pure act, and therefore order of goodness was also order of being. He did not see reason as the ultimate reality; it entered into the world order only in so far as man was a rational animal; that was his essence and his justification lay in fulfilling his rational nature. For Malebranche the problem is different, since his conceptions are not teleological. The universal order is necessary not arbitrary, and the perfections which subsist in God are absolute although they are unequal, their inequality being demonstrated by comparison with the relationship of inequality which exists between an infinity of single units and an infinity of groups of ten units. How then does creation come about? Malebranche has to link the material order to the order of reason by means of the divine will. Thus the natural law is arbitrary, but dependent on necessary universal law:

"Ainsi Dieu a deux sortes de lois qui le règlent dans sa conduite. L'une est éternelle et nécessaire, et c'est l'ordre: les autres sont arbitraires, et ce sont les lois générales de la Nature et de la Grâce. Mais Dieu n'a établi ces dernières que parce que l'ordre demande qu'il agisse ainsi. De sorte que c'est l'ordre éternel, immuable, nécessaire ... qui est la loi que mon père consulte toujours, qu'il aime invinciblement, qu'il suit inviolablement, et par laquelle il a fait et conservé toutes choses."[13]

Malebranche sees a necessary relationship between the virtual order of perfections in the divine substance and the totality of creation, but unlike St. Augustine, he does not conceive of a distinct correspondence between divine action and purpose.[14] God's will is subject to the norm of universal reason, thus action and purpose, creation and conservation become very difficult to distinguish. This position is far removed from that of Descartes, who like Augustine saw will as the source of universal order:

"... il (Dieu) s'est déterminé à faire les choses qui sont au monde, pour cette raison, comme il est dit dans la Genèse, 'elles sont très bonnes,' c'est-à-dire que la raison de leur bonté dépend de ce qu'il les a ainsi voulu faire."[15]

It was precisely this break with orthodox Cartesianism, and the apparent similarity between Malebranche's conception of universal rea-

[13] *Méditations Chrétiennes*, VII, para. 18, pp. 138–139.
[14] For a detailed comparison of the Malebranchian and Augustinian standpoints, see M. Gueroult, *Malebranche: Les cinq Abîmes de la Providence*, Paris, 1959, Vol. II, ch. 2.
[15] Descartes, *Réponse aux VIes Objections*, 8.

son and the doctrines of Spinoza, which struck his contemporaries.[16] Arnauld seized upon the scarcely comprehensible distinction between the "étendue réelle de l'univers" and the "étendue intelligible" in both the *Traité des vraies et des fausses idées* (1683) and in his *Défense d'Arnauld contre la Réponse de Malebranche* (1684); and it was later the same accusation of spinozism which formed the basis of Malebranche's quarrel with the Jesuits. It appears from his correspondence with his pupil Dortous de Mairan, that he was in fact acquainted with Spinoza's *Ethica*, and it was Mairan who later administered the *coup de grâce*, by declaring himself unable to distinguish between "étendue réelle" and "étendue intelligible" in his master's system:

"Il est clair que votre étendue intelligible n'est autre que l'étendue substance dont l'étendue créée ou matérielle n'est que le simple mode."[17]

In his book on Spinozism in France, Paul Vernière suggests that the ninth *Méditation Chrétienne*, is in fact a refutation of Spinoza, since Arnauld's criticisms had not yet been published, and Malebranche's attempts to defend his position cannot be seen as a reply to them.[18] The *Méditations Chrétiennes et Métaphysiques* were indeed completed in 1682, though the first four were composed by 1676; from the fifth onwards scattered remarks suggest that Malebranche had become conscious of certain disquieting similarities between his doctrine and the dangerous ideas of Baruch Spinoza. In the following passage for example he struggles to define his idea of the will of God, without on the one hand being forced to declare its independence with regard to divine reason, and on the other, striving to exclude the possibility that material extension is simply a mode of this reason:

"Afin que Dieu pût anéantir ce corps, il faudrait que Dieu pût vouloir que ce corps ne fût point: il faudrait que Dieu fût capable d'avoir une volonté dont le néant serait le terme. Or le néant n'a rien de bon ni rien d'aimable. Dieu ne peut donc l'aimer ou le vouloir d'une volonté positive. Dieu peut anéantir son ouvrage, parce qu'il peut cesser de vouloir que cet ouvrage subsiste: car les volontés de Dieu, quoiqu'éternelles et immuables ne sont point nécessaires: elles sont arbitraires à l'égard des êtres crées. *Le monde n'est point une émanation nécessaire de la Divinité.* Dieu peut d'une volonté éternelle et immuable le créer pour un temps. Mais Dieu ne peut avoir une volonté positive et pratique de le détruire ... Ainsi puisque les corps existent

---

[16] See P. Vernière, *Spinoza et la Pensée française avant la révolution*, Paris, 1954; Part I, ch. 5.
[17] Letters from Mairan of Sept. 17, and Nov. 19 1713 in V. Cousin, *Fragments de Philosophie Cartésienne*, 1845, p. 272; 292.
[18] *Op. cit.*, Part I, ch. 5.

à cause que Dieu veut qu'ils soient; puisqu'ils ne cessent point d'être à cause que Dieu ne cesse point de vouloir qu'ils soient, il est évident que la création et la conservation ne sont en Dieu qu'une même action."[19]

One has only to recall the much repeated notion that creation and conservation are effected by means of the eternal and necessary law of reason to realise the fineness of his distinctions. The strikingly intimate connection which exists in his system between the divine substance and the act of creation, between the relationships contained within this substance and their material determination, cannot be overlooked. But over and above the complications arising from his conception of *necessary* reason, the very form of this conception, its exclusively geometrical cast, could not help but draw him towards a philosophy of immanence, as at least one modern commentator has noted:

"Le système des idées ou l'ordre de la raison s'identifie, en effet, chez Malebranche, avec l'essence de Dieu, puisqu'en Dieu la raison est une seule et même chose avec son acte éternel, et que, dans l'homme, la vision des idées est la vision de Dieu même. Mais il y a plus: le système des idées a pour principe non pas l'idée d'un ordre finaliste, mais l'idée de l'infini, exprimant le caractère de relation, qui est la forme immanente du rationnel, relations qui trouvent leur détermination dans l'étendue intelligible. Il est facile de voir que de cette façon Malebranche se rapproche d'un rationalisme de l'immanence."[20]

Clearly, however, whatever the implications of his doctrines, Malebranche himself insisted on the transcendence of reason. Thus, while he maintained that the eternal truths constituting part of the Divine substance could only consist in adequate relationships:

"si un homme s'imaginait voir un rapport d'égalité entre 2 fois 2 et 5 ... il verrait une fausseté: il verrait un rapport qui ne serait point, ou plutôt il croirait voir ce qu'effectivement il ne voit point."

at the same time, he denied the possibility of adequate relationships between the other part of this substance, made up of the archetypal ideas of perfection, and the material creation with which it is nevertheless connected. Where Spinoza saw a necessary identity, Malebranche saw only a virtual relationship, which could be completed only by the action of a creative will:

"le rapport d'égalité entre 2 fois 2 et 4 est une vérité éternelle, immuable, nécessaire: mais les rapports qui sont entre les êtres créés, ou entre ces êtres et leurs idées, n'ont pu commencer avant que ces êtres fussent produits; car il n'y a point de rapport entre des choses qui ne sont point: un néant considéré comme tel, ne peut être double ou triple d'un autre néant, ni même lui être positivement égal."[21]

An adequate relationship exists in creation by virtue of the operation of the divine will, which is in turn dependent on eternal reason.

Malebranche's reasoning goes full circle, but if we disregard the problem presented by his explanation of creation, we see that it is in his vision of the created universe that the idea of adequate relationships, of *convenance* between the real and the ideal, plays its greatest part. An adequate relationship between God who is the sum of perfections, and the finite creation, is established by the mediation of universal reason incarnate in the "Word," controlling the operation of the laws of nature and of grace.[22] Through this agency the universal order of justice is revealed to men, for God is

"la justice même, la loi éternelle, la règle immuable, puisque cette loi éternelle n'est que l'ordre immuable des perfections qu'il renferme dans l'infinité et la simplicité de son essence."[23]

Virtue, he explains in the *Traité de Morale*, consists in recognition and love of this universal order of justice.[24] The idea of a transcendent ideal to which men may conform is essential to his moral thought.

If we and one or two of his contemporaries like Mairan, see in Malebranche the germ of a conception of immanent reason, the majority of his critics were content to make the accusation of Spinozism against him, simply on the grounds of his use of Cartesian geometry; very few of them had anything but a second-hand knowledge of the Dutch philosopher's work, and for most of them he was simply the notorious atheist of the age. They feared most a rejection of traditional standards, and a re-examination of accepted patterns of thought.

Thus the very fact that Malebranche elevated reason to a supreme position in his philosophical system, a position above that of faith or of authority, was sufficient confirmation of their darkest suspicions, and ample justification for the accusation levelled against him.[25] Among the

---

[21] *Méditations Chrétiennes*, IV, para. 5, p. 55.
[22] Doctrine elaborated particularly in the *Traité de la Nature et de la Grâce* of 1679.
[23] *Entretien d'un philosophe chrétien avec un philosophe chinois sur l'existence et la nature de Dieu*, 1708; ed. A. Le Moine, Paris, 1936, p. 81.
[24] First published in 1684.
[25] Malebranche was quite explicit in his attitude to faith: "L'évidence, l'intelligence est préférable à la foi; car la foi passera, mais l'intelligence subsistera éternellement." *Traité de Morale*, II, 11; and in the second part of the *Traité* he writes: "Il ne faut pas forcer les hommes à agir contre leur conscience." (IX, 13.)

critics representing the party of social and religious orthodoxy, and probably most powerful among them, was Bossuet. One of the few things he shared with the Jansenist Arnauld was his dislike for the doctrines of the *Traité de la Nature et de la Grâce*, though his reasons were not so narrowly theological. The following passage taken from a letter to one of Malebranche's disciples is a typical expression of his fears with regard to the Oratorian's philosophy:

"Un autre inconvénient gagne insensiblement les esprits. Car, sous prétexte qu'il ne faut admettre que ce qu'on entend clairement, ce qui, réduit à certaines bornes, est très véritable, chacun se donne la liberté de dire: J'entends ceci, et je n'entends pas cela; et sur ce seul fondement, on approuve et on rejette tout ce qu'on veut sans songer qu'outre nos idées claires et distinctes, il y en a de confuses et générales qui ne laissent pas d'enfermer des vérités si essentielles, qu'on renverserait tout en les niant. Il s'introduit, sous ce prétexte, une liberté de juger qui fait que, sans égard à la tradition, on avance témérairement tout ce qu'on pense. Et jamais cet excès n'a paru, à mon avis, davantange que dans le nouveau système, car j'y trouve à la fois les inconvénients de toutes les sectes, et en particulier ceux du pélagianisme."[26]

A sincere reconciliation took place between the two ecclesiastics in 1697; and, indeed, it would be misleading to represent Bossuet as an outright opponent of Cartesianism as such. He disliked the use of reason as a critical weapon directed against established beliefs and institutions, but he was himself a rationalist in the 17th if not the 18th century sense of the word. Even when attacking the Cartesians he admits that the clear idea, when dissociated from the claims of individualism, is a reliable guide to truth, in some if not all fields of enquiry. The unfinished *Politique tirée de l'Écriture Sainte*, composed for the benefit of his pupil the Dauphin, is a fine example of the deductive method applied in literature; each book is divided into articles, in each of which the opening proposition is clearly demonstrated; "l'ordre qui est observé est géométrique,"observed the Abbé Bossuet in the Preface to the 1709 edition.[27] Not surprisingly, the core of the whole work is the exposition of "maximes de droite raison." As tutor of the Dauphin he also undertook certain anatomical studies, which at some time were incorporated in the treatise *De la Connaissance de Dieu et de Soi-même*. This work, a short introduction to all branches of philosophy which was not published until after his death, also reveals a certain rationalism not totally unrelated to Cartesian thought, at least in its original form. They meet for

[26] *Correspondance*, vol. III, pp. 372–373; Letter of 21 May 1687 to M. d'Allemans.
[27] Bossuet, *Politique tirée de l'Écriture Sainte*, Paris, 1709, Préface, XX.

instance in a common acceptance of reason as a normative principle, which in human experience takes on the rôle of conscience. But whereas Descartes's attitude to social and moral factors, as revealed in the third part of the *Discours de la Méthode*, is temporary and governed by practical considerations, Bossuet conceives of the established social and political structure as something permanent and sanctioned by reason. He is not a relativist in this or anything else; rather, like the great dramatists of the age, he seeks to convey the permanent and universal in human experience. Like most conservative minds however, he found this embodied in the contemporary state of things, although his endorsement of the status quo was limited to a degree by the constant emphasis he placed on the notion of responsibility in public life, a quality which he never failed to demonstrate in his own career as bishop of Meaux. Undoubtedly, his concern for peace and stability was also connected with a realistic appreciation of the unidealistic nature of human motivation: conscience and conscientiousness can moderate the effects of passion and interest, but these remain "les deux grands ressorts de la vie humaine";[28] he felt, like Montesquieu after him, that any change was most likely to be a change for the worse.[29]

These are his concerns then: peace, stability, responsibility in government, moderation in society; our concern is to show how he used the idea of reason and more particularly the criterion of *convenance* to demonstrate their necessity. As we have already mentioned, much of his writing reveals strong Cartesian affinities; here and there one even finds similarities with Malebranche. The treatise *De la Connaissance de Dieu et de Soi-même* opens with a characteristic attempt to define reason and to describe its function. It is "la lumière que Dieu nous a donnée pour nous conduire," and its function is not only, in the form of moral conscience, to turn man from evil, but also to recognize the proportion and order in things, to discover by comparison the relationships binding things together. Bossuet has a very clear understanding of the discursive function of reason in spite of his antipathy to its use as a critical instrument and his conception of it as an intuitive moral faculty:

"Le rapport de la raison et de l'ordre est extrême. L'ordre ne peut être remis dans les choses que par la raison, ni être entendu que par elle. Il est ami de la raison, et son propre objet."[30]

[28] *Sermon sur la Justice*, in *Oeuvres Oratoires de Bossuet*, ed. J. Lebarq, Paris, 1922; vol. V, p. 170.
[29] In *La Politique de Bossuet*, Paris, 1867, ch. III, J. F. Nourrisson discusses the relationship between the principles of reason and utility in Bossuet's thought.
[30] *De la Connaissance de Dieu et de Soi-même*, Paris, 1722, ch. I, section 8, p. 38.

The scientific function of reason could hardly be better expressed, though whether Bossuet understood by *order* an artificial order imposed from without, or the natural order of things is a matter for speculation. Bossuet even goes as far towards Malebranche as to suggest that the eternal truths of reason subsist in God:

"L'intelligence a pour objet des vérités éternelles, qui ne sont autre chose que Dieu même, où elles sont toujours subsistantes et toujours parfaitement entendues"

and also that these truths constitute the eternal law and primordial pattern of the universe:

"Il faut reconnaître une sagesse éternelle, ou toute loi, tout ordre, toute proportion ait sa raison primitive."[31]

Moreover, it is in the contemplation of universal reason that man discovers the moral law:

"Là elle (l'âme humaine) découvre les règles de la justice, de la bienséance, de la société, ou pour mieux parler, de la fraternité humaine, et sait que si dans tout le monde, parce qu'il est fait par raison, rien ne se fait que de convenable, elle qui entend la raison, doit bien plus se gouverner par les lois de la convenance ... C'est sur cela qu'elle fonde les Sociétés et les Républiques, et qu'elle réprime l'inhumanité et la barbarie."[32]

There is no clearer statement of the relationship in contemporary thought between the primitive metaphysical order of reason and the temporal moral and structural criterion of *convenance*. One begins to wonder whether Bossuet did not transform the necessity of writing an introduction to contemporary philosophy, presumably for the benefit of his royal pupil, into an opportunity to rewrite Malebranche's *Recherche de la Vérité* in more orthodox terms, and if the resulting work does not form a hidden link between Malebranche's conception of order which only suggests the idea of *convenance*, and Montesquieu's definition of justice as "un rapport de convenance." [33]

Although what we have seen so far of Bossuet's system suggests that he conceived of reason alone as a sufficient moral criterion, and as the metaphysical principle on which all creation depends, the picture painted by these short quotations is to a large extent misleading. He did indeed see reason as a necessary principle, but he associated it with a teleological view of the universe, and that is the point where he parted

[31] *Op. cit.*, ch. IV, section 5, p. 277.
[32] *Ibid.*, ch. V, section 6, p. 343.
[33] The first part of the *Recherche* was published in 1674, and Bossuet was tutor to the Dauphin from 1670–1681, so there in some possibility of a connection with Malebranche. As far as Montesquieu is concerned it must be borne in mind that the work was not published until 1722, *after* the *Lettres Persanes*.

company with Malebranche. One must take care not to be deceived by the effortless grace of his writing which conceals a fairly superficial presentation of ideas; instead of delving deep, turning them over again and again, constantly checking and qualifying them as Malebranche did, he outlines them smoothly following a single line of thought, so that their full significance is not immediately clear. Thus, although certain passages prompt comparisons with other thinkers he is known to have opposed, they cannot be taken at their face value. A passage from the *Sermon sur la Divinité de Jésus-Christ* might suggest for instance that he had a very similar concepion to that of Malebranche concerning the nature of Christ and the function of revelation:

"Celui-là doit être plus qu'homme, qui, à travers de tant de coutumes et de tant d'erreurs, de tant de passions compliquées et de tant de fantaisies bizarres, a su démêler au juste et fixer précisément la règle des moeurs. Réformer ainsi le genre humain, c'est donner à l'homme la vie raisonnable; c'est une seconde création, plus noble en quelque façon que la première. Quiconque sera le chef de cette réformation salutaire doit avoir à son secours la même sagesse qui a formé l'homme la première fois."[34]

We imagine that Bossuet also had a vision of Christ as reason and mediator between God and his creation, whereas, as a true moralist rather than a metaphysician, he is pointing here to an ideal of human behaviour, *la vie raisonnable*, and using the message of revelation as an indication of the nature of Christ. We cannot even be sure that *la vie raisonnable* does not in fact stand for the old traditional ideal of moderation.

We can be sure, however, by reference to the *Discours sur l'Histoire Universelle*, that Bossuet in no way considered Christ as universal reason to be ultimately responsible for the existence as well as the order of the universe, as Malebranche had done.[35] The creation and maintenance of the universe is totally dependent on the divine will. Bossuet had just as little intention of courting the idea of an immanent reason, as he had of embracing a completely mechanistic interpretation of the operation of natural laws in the physical world. He saw in the rational structure of the world not just the operation of cause and effect, but the ordered development of things towards a given end:

"Ainsi sous le nom de nature nous entendons une sagesse profonde, qui développe avec ordre et selon de justes règles, tous les mouvements que nous voyons."[36]

[34] *Oeuvres Oratoires*, ed. Lebarq, Paris, 1922, vol. V, p. 586.
[35] See above p. 15, note 22 for Malebranche; and Bossuet, *Discours sur l'Histoire Universelle*, Paris, 1681, Part II.
[36] *De la Connaissance de Dieu et de Soi-même*, ch. IV, section 1, p. 250.

Bossuet goes to much greater lengths than many another thinker of rationalist sympathies to accommodate the teleological world view of Scholasticism. Thus, although the whole of the *Traité de la Connaissance de Dieu et de Soi-même* hinges on the notion of *convenance*, it becomes clear that Bossuet is not so much concerned with conformity between a transcendent eternal order of reason and the extended universe, or between physical cause and effect, as with the notion of proportion between the actual state of things and their place in the divine plan:

"Tout ce qui montre de l'ordre, des proportions bien prises, et des moyens propres à faire de certains effets, montre aussi une fin expresse; par conséquent un dessein formé, une intelligence bien réglée, et un art parfait.

C'est ce qui se remarque dans toute la nature. Nous voyons tant de justesse dans ses mouvements, et tant de convenance entre ses parties, que nous ne pouvons nier qu'il n'y ait de l'art. Car s'il en faut pour remarquer ce concert et cette justesse, à plus forte raison pour l'établir. C'est pourquoi nous ne voyons rien dans l'Univers que nous ne soyons portés à demander pourquoi il se fait, tant nous sentons naturellement que tout a sa fin."[37]

As regards the highly controversial question of animal souls,[38] he used this idea of conformity with a given nature to refute those who claimed that the similarities in anatomy and behaviour between man and animals suggested that intelligence was also a faculty common to both. Bossuet stands firmly by the notion that man is an intelligent animal, and that only he is conscious of the conformity in his own actions.[39]

Indeed, man is a creature "d'un grand dessein, et d'une sagesse profonde."[40] Chapter IV of the *Traité de la Connaissance de Dieu et de Soi-même* contains a long section on the beauty, proportion and functional unity of the human body and mind. Just as the human race has its place in the universal scheme of things, so also each individual has his station in life, his rights and his duties, governed by the principle of justice:

"La justice est la vertu principale et le commun ornement des personnes publiques et des particuliers; elle commande dans les uns, elle obéit dans les autres; elle renferme chacun dans ses limites; elle oppose une barrière invincible aux violences et aux entreprises; et ce n'est pas sans raison que le Sage lui donne la gloire de soutenir les trônes et d'affermir les empires, puisque en effet elle affermit non seulement celui des princes sur leurs sujets, mais encore celui de la raison sur les passions, et celui de Dieu sur la raison même."[41]

---

[37] *Ibid.*
[38] See H. Hastings, *Man and Beast in French Thought*, Baltimore, 1936; and L. C. Rosenfield, *From Beast Machine to Man Machine*; New York, 1941.
[39] *De la Connaissance de Dieu et de Soi-même*, ch. V, section 1, pp. 301–5.
[40] *Ibid.*, ch. IV, section 1, p. 249.
[41] *Sermon sur la Justice*, 1666; *Oeuvres Oratoires de Bossuet*, ed. Lebarq, vol. V, p. 161.

The established structure of society is as much part of the divine plan as are the universal laws of motion; but this sanction of authoritarian government and of an hierarchical society is tempered in Bossuet by an insistence on the universality and evidence of the principles of natural law. The laws of primitive reason are accessible to all through the medium of moral conscience.[42] In addition, Bossuet associates the restraining influence of conscience with the classical ideal of moderation:

"Que chacun, en se tenant dans ses limites, s'exerce de tout son pouvoir dans la vaste étendue de la charité."[43]

Not only is man's station in society regulated by the laws of justice, but within that station he must strive to conform to an ideal of mediocrity. According to the *Sermon sur la Justice* this is the quality which distinguishes the just man; in this way the general idea of *convenance* links Bossuet's abstract ideal of justice, which is in itself an expression of the grand universal plan, to the social concepts of *bienséance* and *honnêteté*. The most important point however is that Bossuet's notion of *convenance* is linked above all with a teleological view of the universe.

Like Malebranche, Bossuet was one of the figures of Montesquieu's early years, whose general outlook must have been familiar to him. The future author of the *Considérations sur la Grandeur et Décadence des Romains* would know of him not only as one of the ablest ecclesiastics of his day and a prominent figure in political and social life, but was surely acquainted at least with his *Discours sur l'Histoire Universelle* if not with other of his works.

Yet another outstanding contributor to the philosophical and scientific discussions of the end of the century was Leibniz, although his influence was perhaps not as widespread. There is some evidence to suggest that Montesquieu was acquainted with the *Théodicée* before the writing of the *Lettres Persanes*, and among his friends, the Abbé Antonio Conti was a correspondent of Leibniz.[44] Montesquieu relates his opinion of certain of Leibniz's historical theories in a letter to the Baron de Stain, and his esteem for the philosopher does not seem very great:

---

[42] *Politique tirée de l'Ecriture Sainte*, Paris, 1709, I, iv, 2–4.

[43] *Sermon sur nos Dispositions à l'égard des Nécessités de la Vie, Oeuvres Oratoires*, ed. Lebarq, Paris, 1916, vol. III, p. 308.

[44] See Shackleton, *Montesquieu*, p. 62. The influence of Leibniz in Letter LXIX of the *Lettres Persanes* which deals with the problem of divine foreknowledge and human liberty, was suggested by Elie Carcassone in his edition of the work (Belles Lettres, 1929). We shall deal later with Leibniz's influence on Montesquieu's theory of justice in Letter LXXXIII, proposed by A. S. Crisafulli in "Parallels to ideas in the *Lettres Persanes*," *Modern Language Association of America*, Sept. 1937, p. 773 seq.

"J'ai toujours regardé cette idée de M. de Leibniz comme une chimère d'un homme dont l'esprit accoutumé aux systèmes en trouve partout, et même dans les choses qui en sont le moins susceptibles, à peu près comme les graveurs voient des figures sur toutes les murailles."[45]

During his travels, Montesquieu was also presented in Vienna to Prince Eugene of Savoy, at whose request Leibniz had composed the *Monadologie*.[46] Leibniz's influence in France during the first half of the 18th century may have been limited, but it seems unlikely that Montesquieu, in spite of his opinion, entirely escaped it; and we certainly cannot afford to disregard his contribution to the vast pool of philosophical ideas which was formed at this time, and from which Montesquieu was later to draw extensively.[47]

To the many Leibniz was at the end of the 17th century a great name; and to the few who themselves aspired to some standing in the learned world, he was a scholarly genius who had mastered every field of study from historical research to physics, pioneering new techniques, and formulating new theories in most of them. He was also a man of vision and humanity. During this period of violent religious conflict, he inspired and led a movement for reunion between the Catholic and Reformed Churches, entering after 1691 into prolonged and difficult negociations with Bossuet, which continued almost until the latter's death.[48] With Malebranche he debated the question of the laws of movement, and succeeded in pursuading him to abandon the principles of Descartes in favour of his own. Indeed his correspondents were many and distinguished, although his philosophical ideas were less widely known and argued than his discoveries in the field of mathematics and his research in diplomatic history and jurisprudence. The *Monadologie* for instance, remained unpublished for several years after his death; when he was, so as to speak, rediscovered in mid-century, it was often through the medium of Wolff that his theories were examined, and sometimes through the medium of hearsay. Pope, for instance, had never read anything by Leibniz when he embarked on the *Essay on Man*, but had worked from a patchwork of ideas presented to him by

[45] *Correspondance*, Nagel III, p. 934; Montesquieu au Baron de Stain, 17th October, 1729. Montesquieu possessed the 2nd edition of the *Théodicée*, 1714; *Catalogue de la Brède*, p. 32, No. 405. He later acquired P. Desmaizeaux's *Recueil de Diverses Pièces sur la Philosophie* containing Leibniz's critical essays on Shaftesbury; Catalogue, p. 112, No. 1532.
[46] See J. B. de Secondat, *Mémoire pour servir à l'éloge historique de M. de Montesquieu*, publ. in L. Vian, *Histoire de Montesquieu d'après des documents nouveaux et inédits*, Paris, 1879, pp. 399–400.
[47] For the extent of Leibniz's influence, see Barber, *Leibniz in France*, Part II, ch. 6.
[48] See Barber, *op. cit.*, Part I, ch. 1; and P. Hazard, *La Crise de la Conscience Européenne*, Paris, 1935, Part II, ch. 5.

Bolingbroke; yet its optimistic view of life was often attributed to Leibniz's influence.[49] It is no wonder that such misrepresentations and second-hand versions of his system eventually provoked the bitter satire of *Candide*.

However, these later discussions are of less importance to us than the actual contribution which the *Théodicée* made to contemporary thought, and in particular to the elaboration of the notion of *convenance*. One of the inadequacies which Leibniz found in Cartesianism was its attempt to explain the whole of experience in terms of geometry: this not only failed to account fully for the nature of substance by reducing it to simple extension, but also ignored the complexity of perception. This does not mean that he rejected Cartesianism in its entirety; on the contrary there is some ground for arguing, as Brunschvicg does, that Leibniz presents us in some ways with "un dogmatisme de la raison." [50] In the *Discours sur la Conformité de la Foi avec la Raison* he does indeed write:

"La raison consistant dans l'enchaînement des vérités a droit de lier entre elles celles que l'expérience lui a fournies, pour en tirer des conclusions mixtes, mais la raison pure et nue, distinguée de l'expérience n'a à faire qu'à des vérités indépendantes des sens." [51]

But he opens the Discourse with a statement which sets him clearly apart from the kind of rationalism expounded by Malebranche:

"Je suppose que deux vérités ne sauraient se contredire: que l'objet de la foi est la vérité que Dieu a révélée d'une manière extraordinaire, et que la Raison est l'enchaînement des vérités, mais particulièrement (lorsqu'elle est comparée avec la foi) de celles où l'esprit humain peut atteindre naturellement, sans être aidé des lumières de la foi." [52]

The different spheres of reason and faith are then distinct though complementary, and there is no question of reason displacing faith in the perception of religious truth. Equally significant is the place which Leibniz gives to experience in the discovery of what he calls positive truths, namely those relating to the physical world. His empiricism is by no means complete; indeed he would probably have found a method which rejected all data except that accessible to the senses as much a betrayal of reality as the abstractions of geometry. But he does allow experiment some rôle in the processes of science, and this enables him

[49] Barber, *Op. cit.*, Part II, ch. 7, and A. W. Evans, *Warburton and the Warburtonians*, Oxford, 1932, ch. 5.
[50] L. Brunschvicg, *Le Progrès de la Conscience dans la Philosophie Occidentale*, Paris, 1927; ch. 10, p. 248.
[51] *Op. cit.*, para I.
[52] *Op. cit.*

to make a bold distinction between the physical and supernatural orders, so avoiding the equivocations into which Malebranche was forced when obliged to define exactly his concept of an all-embracing reason. Thus, while he does guarantee the validity and independence of that order of truth found in mathematics, affirming its metaphysical necessity, and dissociating it from the action of the divine will, he is able to take up a position somewhat closer to that of St. Augustine, where the connection between the transcendent and the created orders is provided by the operation of will without the sanction of necessary reason.

Absolute metaphysical necessity does not condition God's choice, for necessary truths depend solely on his understanding, and are its inner object;[53] but moral necessity does. Leibniz conceives of an infinite number of possible universes existing as archetypal ideas in the divine intelligence; now of these only one can be actual, and therefore he must ask what principle determines divine choice. The answer is the principle of *convenance*. The only sufficient reason he can find is in the degree of perfection that each of the possible worlds possesses; thus, assuming that each has the right to aspire to existence in proportion to its potential perfection, the best among them becomes the object of the divine choice. God can do everything; but he wills to do the best, to create a world which as one harmonious system is best.[54]

The idea of fitness is again linked to the notion of hierarchy; but unlike Malebranche, Leibniz conceives of a scale of archetypes, differentiated by their relative degrees of perfection, not a scale of relationships of perfection, absolute in themselves, and unequal in a mathematical sense only. In this, although he is dealing in worlds and not in things or persons, Leibniz is much closer to the Scholastic conception of an hierarchical order in creation, and obviously less disposed to found his system on geometric concepts. His notion of conformity is teleological: for *convenance* consists in the measure of perfection that links the possible with the actual, the final cause with creation. It is the world which best conforms in the harmony of its organization, in its parts and as a whole, to the divine intention, which is brought into existence. Thus in Leibniz's system the principle of *convenance* operates on two levels: there is conformity between the possible and the actual; and there is conformity between the constituent parts of the whole. It is associated with compossibility as well as with possibility.

To all intents and purposes then, the principle of *convenance* is for

[53] *Théodicée* (1710), arts. 180–184.
[54] *Monadologie* (1714), arts. 53–54.

Leibniz the same thing as the principle of sufficient reason, and both are distinct from the principles of mathematical reason. They depend on certain qualitative considerations to do with perfection, which are partly inaccessible to the human mind, although we may with justification associate them with the infinite goodness and wisdom of God. There is a distinction between the order of eternal truths and the order of contingent truths, between the principles of mathematical reason and the principles of sufficient reason, just as, on the human level, the principle of contradiction is distinct from the principle of reasoned action.[55] In the *Discours de la Conformité de la Foi avec la Raison* Leibniz highlights this distinction:

"Or les vérités de la raison sont de deux sortes. Les unes sont ce qu'on appelle les vérités éternelles, qui sont absolument nécessaires, en sorte que l'opposé implique contradiction; et telles sont les vérités dont la nécessité est logique, métaphysique ou géométrique, qu'on ne saurait nier sans pouvoir être mené à des absurdités. Il y en a d'autres qu'on peut appeler positives, parce qu'elles sont les lois qu'il a plu à Dieu de donner à la nature, ou parce qu'elles en dépendent. Nous les apprenons, ou par l'expérience, c'est-à-dire *a posteriori*; ou par la raison, et *a priori*, c'est-à-dire par des considérations de la convenance qui les a fait choisir. Cette convenance a aussi ses règles et ses raisons; mais c'est le choix libre de Dieu, et non pas une nécessité géométrique, qui fait préférer le convenable et le porte à l'existence. Ainsi on peut dire que la nécessité physique est fondée sur la nécessité morale, c'est-à-dire sur le choix du Sage, digne de sa sagesse; et que l'une aussi bien que l'autre doit être distinguée de la nécessité géométrique. Cette nécessité physique est ce qui fait l'ordre de la nature, et consiste dans les règles du mouvement et dans quelques autres lois générales qu'il a plu à Dieu de donner aux choses en leur donnant l'être."[56]

Thus the reason of things, and the reason of divine action is more closely associated through the principle of moral necessity with the conception of God as a being of infinite goodness and reason, than as the repository of metaphysical truth. And when the contrast of the natural order with this perfect goodness accentuates the problem of evil, this too is seen to possess its *convenance*, and to contribute to the ultimate perfection of the divine plan. Writing of William King's *Essay on the Origin of Evil*,[57] Leibniz explains his view of the relationship between evil and divine wisdom:

"Je m'imagine que l'habile auteur de cet extrait, lorsqu'il a cru qu'on pourrait résoudre la difficulté, a eu dans l'esprit quelque chose d'appro-

[55] *Monadologie*, arts. 31–32; *Théodicée*, arts. 44, 196.
[56] *Op. cit.*, para. II.
[57] See below pp. 82–84

chant en cela de mes principes; et s'il avait voulu s'expliquer dans cet endroit, il aurait répondu apparement comme M. Régis, que les lois que Dieu a
établies, étaient les plus excellentes qu'on pouvait établir; et il aurait recon-
nu en même temps, que Dieu ne pouvait manquer d'établir des lois et de
suivre des règles, parce que les lois et les règles sont ce qui fait l'ordre et la
beauté, qu'agir sans règles serait agir sans raison; et que c'est parce que
Dieu a fait agir toute sa bonté, que l'exercice de sa toute-puissance a été conforme aux lois de la sagesse, pour obtenir le plus de bien qu'il était possible
d'atteindre: enfin, que l'existence de certains inconvénients particuliers qui
nous frappent, est une marque certaine que le meilleur plan ne permettait
pas qu'on les évitât, et qu'ils servent à l'accomplissement du bien total." [58]

Evil is a purely human experience; in the universal scheme of things it
disappears into the order and beauty of the best of all possible worlds.

Spinoza had seen evil as a perception arising from the limitations of
human judgement; for him it was a false notion that tended to disappear with the development of scientific knowledge. For Leibniz however, the link between the scientific and the metaphysical orders is less
straightforward: it is true that we may discover the natural law by experiment or by considering the structural conformity of things; but the
nature of the principles determining the act of creation, though deemed
to constitute a sufficient reason for action, is ultimately inaccessible to
human thought:

"Une vérité est au-dessus de la raison quand notre esprit ne la saurait
comprendre: et telle est, à mon avis, la Sainte Trinité; tels sont les miracles
réservés à Dieu seul, comme par exemple, la création; tel est le choix de
l'ordre de l'Univers, qui dépend de l'harmonie universelle, et de la connaissance distincte d'une infinité de choses à la fois." [59]

The main guarantee we have of the goodness of the natural order is in
fact the goodness of God; this is the force which determines and supports all created things, and its principles are not to be discovered solely
by the application of mathematical analysis, as the principles of divine
reason are in Malebranche's system, but by probing beyond the sequence of mechanical causation in a search for internal teleological
forces.

For this reason, it is hardly surprising that Leibniz does not formulate
an exclusively mathematical doctrine of justice. As a jurisconsult, he
naturally produced works dealing specifically with jurisprudence, discussing its problems under the particular headings of commutative and

---

[58] *Théodicée*, art. 359; Leibniz actually refers to an extract of King's work in the *Journal des Savants*.

[59] *Discours de la Conformité de la Foi avec la Raison*, para. XXIII.

distributive justice, seen as right in the narrow sense of the strict ground of a jural claim, and right as equity.[60] But as regards the philosophy of law he was strictly on the side of the rationalists; that is to say he followed the path marked out by Grotius, whose declaration in the Preface of *De Jure Belli ac Pacis* that the propositions of natural law would remain valid even if one were to assume there was no God, published the determination of political science to free itself from the apron strings of theology. Like Grotius, he likened jurisprudence to mathematics, on the grounds that both were deductive sciences, independent of experience, whose principles embodied eternal and necessary truth:

"Il en est de même de la justice. Si c'est un terme fixe qui a quelque signification déterminée, en un mot, si ce n'est pas un simple son, vide de sens, comme blitiri, ce terme ou ce mot justice aura quelque définition ou notion intelligible. Et de toute définition on peut tirer des conséquences certaines, en employant les règles incontestables de la logique. Et c'est justement ce qu'on fait, en fabriquant les sciences nécessaires et démonstratives qui ne dépendent point des faits, mais uniquement de la raison, comme sont la logique, la métaphysique, l'arithmétique, la géométrie, la science des mouvements et aussi la science de droit, qui ne sont point fondées sur les expériences et faits et servent plutôt à rendre raison des faits et à les régler par avance, ce qui aurait lieu à l'égard du droit, quand il n'y aurait point de loi au monde." [61]

This being the case, he reasoned that the justice of God was essentially the same as the justice of men, though of course differing in its degree of perfection, and that it was not simply the expression of the divine will. Those who stubbornly described it as purely arbitrary, might as well declare baldly that might is right, that if the devil were to succeed God in Heaven, his law would be as just, or worst of all, that God and his angels would not recognize that 1, 4, 9, 16, 25 are the squares of 1, 2, 3, 4, 5![62]

But although Leibniz drew this general parallel between justice and mathematical proportion, he chose to define it, not in structural but in dynamic terms, as "ce qui est conforme à sagesse et bonté jointe ensemble," [63] in terms of the perfection which must be the object of the mind and will of intelligent substances. This definition conforms to the teleological character of his metaphysics in general. Thus as far as morals are concerned, beyond the *jus strictum* of doing no harm to others, be-

---

[60] See for instance the Preface to the 1st vol. of the *Codex Juris Gentium Diplomaticus*, trans. R. Latta, in his critical edition of the *Monadology*, Oxford, 1898, pp. 281–296.

[61] *Méditation sur la Notion commune de la Justice*, published in *Mitteilungen aus Leibnizens ungedruckten Schriften* by G. Mollat, Leipzig, 1893, p. 47.

[62] *Ibid.*, pp. 40–47.

[63] *Ibid.*, p. 48.

yond the demands of equity and equality, of giving each his just deserts, all of which can be reduced according to Leibniz to the status of mere political strategies nourished by fear and self-interest, there exists another level of justice.

Since it is impossible to conceive of God standing in any relationship of equity or equality with his creatures, perfection alone is the principle and rule of divine justice:

> "On ne peut envisager en Dieu d'autre motif que celui de la perfection ou, si vous voulez, de son plaisir. Supposé selon ma définition que le plaisir n'est autre chose que le sentiment de la perfection, il n'a rien à attendre de dehors, au contraire tout dépend de lui. Mais son bonheur ne serait point suprême, s'il ne se portait au bien et à la perfection autant qu'il est possible."[64]

and the imitation of this perfection in accordance with the limitations of human attributes, is the highest level of human justice, the level at which it contains all other virtues.

> "On peut dire que cette sérénité d'esprit qui trouverait le plus grand plaisir dans la vertu et le plus grand mal dans le vice, c'est-à-dire dans la perfection ou imperfection de la volonté, serait le plus grand bien dont l'homme est capable ici bas, quand même il n'y aurait rien à attendre au delà de cette vie. Car que peut-on préférer à cette harmonie intérieure, à ce plaisir continuel des plus purs et des plus grands dont on est toujours le maître et dont on ne se saurait laisser?"[65]

Similarly, since the perfection of divine justice is expressed in the sum of universal harmony, human injustice or wrongdoing can be seen as an infraction of this harmony, which is redressed partly by the distribution of rewards and punishments.[66] This is the idea which reappears in the *Théodicée*, in a passage which some scholars have isolated as a possible source of Montesquieu's definition of justice,[67] where Leibniz uses the phrase *rapport de convenance*, recalling the terminology of his theory of sufficient reason, to describe the basis of divine justice:

> "Il y a pourtant une espèce de justice et une certaine sorte de récompenses et de punitions, qui... n'a point pour but l'amendement, ni l'exemple ni même la réparation du mal. Cette justice n'est fondée que dans la convenance, qui demande une certaine satisfaction pour l'expiation d'une mauvaise action. Les Sociniens, Hobbes et quelques autres n'admettent point cette justice punitive, qui est proprement vindicative, et que Dieu s'est ré-

---

[64] *Ibid.*, p. 60.
[65] *Ibid.*, p. 61.
[66] *Ibid.*, p. 64.
[67] See below pp. 178–179.

servée en bien des rencontres: mais qu'il ne laisse pas de communiquer à ceux qui ont droit de gouverner les autres, et qu'il exerce par leur moyen, pourvu qu'ils agissent par raison, et non par passion. Les Sociniens la croient être sans fondement; mais elle est toujours fondée dans un rapport de convenance, qui contente non seulement l'offensé, mais encore les sages qui la voient, comme une belle musique ou bien une bonne architecture contente les esprits bien faits. Et le sage législateur ayant menacé, et ayant, pour ainsi dire, promis un châtiment, il est de sa constance de ne pas laisser l'action entièrement impunie, quand même la peine ne servirait plus à corriger personne. Mais quand il n'aurait rien promis, c'est assez qu'il y a une convenance qui l'aurait pu porter à faire cette promesse; puisqu'aussi bien le sage ne promet que ce qui est convenable. [68]

The introduction here of the notion of relationship might lead one to believe that his theory of justice did after all depend on a geometric conception of the order of reality; and it is indeed true that Leibniz never rejected mathematical analysis as the essential tool of science. But the juxtaposition here of intelligence of the relationship of fitness to the notion of the object and purposes of the wise legislator, in fact brings us back yet again to a conception of *convenance* as the final cause of things.

Among Montesquieu's friends, Maupertuis, although primarily a mathematician and scientist, brought out a criticism of Leibniz in the form of Letters published in Dresden in 1752. Here the theory of monads is scrutinized and attacked from an empiricist standpoint. [69] In the Academy of Berlin, of which he was President, Maupertuis was a leading opponent of the Wolffians; nevertheless, in other works he shows a much deeper understanding of Leibniz than most of his fellow countrymen evinced, and a definite commitment to metaphysical optimism. Two of these works, the *Essai de Philosophie Morale*, and the *Essai de Cosmologie*, came to the notice of his friend Montesquieu,[70] who, writing to Cerati, describes the first with some amusement at the author's paradoxical behaviour:

"M. de Maupertuis, qui a cru toute sa vie, et qui peut-être a prouvé qu'il n'était point heureux, vient de publier un petit écrit sur le bonheur. C'est l'ouvrage d'un homme d'esprit et on y trouve du raisonnement et des grâces." [71]

[68] *Théodicée*, art. 73.
[69] See W. H. Barber, *Leibniz in France from Arnauld to Voltaire*, Oxford, 1955, part II, ch. 9, ii.
[70] See *Correspondance*, Nagel III, letter 515, Montesquieu to Mgr. Cerati, 11 Nov., 1749; and letter 622, Mme. d'Aiguillon to Montesquieu, 1 Nov. 1751. There are many letters between Montesquieu and Maupertuis in the *Correspondance*, (283, 294, 297, 304, 354, 366, 380, 381, 515, 536, 583), and Maupertuis paid tribute to the President in his *Éloge de Montesquieu*, Berlin, 1755.
[71] Nagel III, p. 1265.

The question of influence does not arise here, for these works date from the middle of the century and the end of Montesquieu's life; but it is interesting to examine Maupertuis's optimism, not only because it expresses his acceptance of Leibniz's idea of the best possible world, but also because, like Montesquieu, Maupertuis seems also to have been influenced in his thinking by Malebranche. They both drew on a common pool of ideas, and we find in these works more examples of the ever changing combinations in which the notion of conformity plays a basic part.

The *Essai de Philosophie Morale* sets out to prove that the chief spiritual pleasures of life are the practice of justice and the contemplation of truth. Like Montesquieu in the *Traité des Devoirs*, Maupertuis equates the former with the performance of one's duties; while the latter consists in the feeling of satisfaction induced by the clarity of one's perceptions. Reacting strangely against materialism, he claims that liberty is the inalienable possession of man, and his weapon against natural forces. Maupertuis's conception of God has Malebranchian affinities: "Dieu est l'ordre éternel, le créateur de l'univers, l'être tout puissant, tout sage et tout bon." [72] And again like Montesquieu, he undertakes a comparison of Stoicism and Christianity.

The *Essai de Cosmologie* represents a much more serious attempt to formulate a complete system; and here the notion of *convenance* enters into its own. In his Preface, Maupertuis again rejects the position of the materialists and followers of Spinoza, this time declaring his support for a teleological conception of the universe. His debt to Leibniz is evident in his determination to avoid geometric proofs of the existence of God, on the grounds that they are basically indifferent to man; if proof is necessary, then it is found in the conformity of the whole of nature:

"C'est ainsi que, malgré quelques parties de l'univers dans lesquelles on n'aperçoit pas bien l'ordre et la convenance, le tout en présente assez pour qu'on ne puisse douter de l'existence d'un Créateur tout puissant et tout sage." [73]

Maupertuis thinks it best to look beyond the unity of the species, or the obvious design of certain parts of the body to fulfil certain needs, for proof of a divine plan however, since the powerful argument of spontaneous natural combination can be brought against such theories:

[72] *Essai de Philosophie Morale*, Berlin, 1749; in *Oeuvres Complètes de Maupertuis*, Lyons, 1768, vol. I, p. 235.
[73] *Op. cit.*, Avant-propos; in *Oeuvres Complètes*, vol. I, p. xx.

"...ne pourrait-on pas dire que dans la combinaison fortuite des productions de la nature, comme il n'y avait que celles où se trouvaient certains
rapports de convenance, qui pussent subsister, il n'est pas merveilleux que
cette convenance se trouve dans toutes les espèces qui actuellement existent?"[74]

Accordingly, he joins to the idea of the order and fitness of universal
design, a theory which is related to Malebranche's doctrine of the
"simplicité des voies," or the simplicity of the laws involved in the
creation and conservation of the universe. In mechanics he enunciated
the theory of least action; and applying this to metaphysics he produced
the theory of economy of means in creation. Thus the idea of fitness, of
convenance, is associated in his thought not only with structural harmony,
as it was with Leibniz, but also with the idea of economy in design; and
the laws governing the harmony and simplicity of the design are held to
constitute the natural laws known to man:

"Chaque espèce, pour l'universalité des choses, avait des avantages qui lui
étaient propres: et comme de leur assemblage résultait la beauté de l'univers, de même de leur communication en résultait la science."[75]

This idea of economy represents a new utilitarian application of the
notion of *convenance*.

It is interesting to note in passing that Maupertuis uses the phrase
"rapport de convenance" in his exposition of the materialist argument
against the idea of fitness in things as proof of a divine plan; possibly he
remembered the phrase from the *Théodicée* or even from the *Lettres Persanes*; but on the whole it seems much more likely that it was a topical
phrase, much used in scientific and philosophical discussions by materialists and theists alike, both sides admitting that there was a conformity in nature, but modifying the precise significance of the term to
suit their philosophical standpoint.

We have already seen that the place occupied by the notion of *convenance* differs widely from system to system, even in a small group of
thinkers of similar persuasions. In Leibniz and Bossuet it is associated
primarily with a teleological view of the universe; for both of them, the
pattern of things is invested with the quality of fitness, and this pattern
is the expression of a final cause. But while Leibniz makes fitness the
equivalent of the principle of sufficient reason, thus linking it with the
ideas of intention and of creative action, rather than with a mathematical interpretation of rational truth, Bossuet on the other hand, content

[74] *Ibid.*, part I, p. 10.
[75] *Ibid.*, part I, p. 73.

with broader outlines, continues to associate it with a quasi-geometrical interpretation of reason, and simply subjects rational truth to the operation of the divine will. Malebranche differs from both his contemporaries. Mathematical reason as the expression of eternal truth dominates his whole vision: hence the idea of absolute relationships between the essences of things is stressed, rather than the notion of fitness in the material structure of the universe; although, in the field of morals, the ideal of perfection which the abstractions of spatial analysis are said to represent, is put forward as the moral criterion to which men must conform.

CHAPTER THREE

MORALISTS AND OTHERS

The majority of thinkers at the turn of the 17th century were more concerned with the problems of human behaviour than with metaphysics, although the search for moral criteria often led them to formulate some kind of system, more or less coherent. Although for reasons of the influence he exerted, we have put Bossuet in the august company of Malebranche and Leibniz, he is really a case in point. His flights in the realm of systematic theology were mostly undertaken for practical ends: to bolster up the political regime, or to persuade his aristocratic readers that privilege entailed responsibility. He was not primarily concerned with definitions of justice for instance, but with its execution in the social framework of the day; thus the notions of *honnêteté* and *bienséance* have a very important part to play in his thinking, and the idea of fitness in the structure of things is an essential but secondary concept.

To the moralist it was also always abundantly clear that it was never sufficient to analyse the nature of things, and then to content oneself with characterizing this nature as fitness or *convenance*. Conformity as such might mean a lot within the framework of an abstract system: that 2 plus 2 equals 4 constitutes a relationship of equality is all very well in mathematics, but the problem is to interpret this conformity in the terms of human relationships. Unless one has a ready made set of precepts, a table of the law, or an accepted code of behaviour at hand to build into the abstract framework, one is bound to invent some subjective answer to the question of the nature of this conformity. One is brought face to face with the problem of what constitutes the natural law, and the related difficulty of deciding how we apprehend its precepts, whether reason alone is sufficient, or whether one must introduce the notion of conscience.

For the thinker who adopts an a priori system based on mathematical abstractions, this problem can be particularly acute; the difficulties are less obvious if one starts from more empirical bases. If for instance, pleasure and pain are established as moral principles, one may go on to affirm that the moral code consists in performing those actions which are pleasurable, and avoiding those that are not; although the burden of proving that what one enjoys doing is what one ought to do remains. The energies of the 18th century were to be almost completely devoted to debating the relative merits of rational and non-rational criteria, and to evaluating the kind of behaviour which they seemed to authorize. We are mainly concerned with those moralists who inherited the notion of *convenance* and its various mechanistic and teleological associations, and used it to demonstrate what in their view constituted honest action and social behaviour. We must examine how they answered the question "which actions are fitting, and how is this fitness revealed?"

So far we have dealt with three major figures of the close of the 17th century: Malebranche, Bossuet and Leibniz, all of whom utilized in some way the idea of fitness, and helped to establish its position as a basic notion in the thought of several generations. Montesquieu was likely to have had some acquaintance with the work of all three. There were however innumerable writers of lesser standing, some perhaps also familiar to Montesquieu, who used the idea, and whose works confirm its wide acceptance as a moral and aesthetic criterion.

Moralists are essentially concerned with the relationships of people in society, and to a lesser degree with their attitude to their material surroundings, the way in which they exploit them. This second concern is aggravated by scientific progress, a phenomenon scarcely familiar to the 17th century, but whose potential contribution to human happiness was certainly appreciated by Descartes.[1] The main ethical concerns of the 17th century were, however, social; and beyond the normal problems of distributive justice, or the attitudes of epicureanism, material factors were most involved where such considerations touched the sphere of aesthetics. Today it is platitudinous to remark that art and society are inseparable: every age and social group has expressed its pattern of existence and its ideals in material form or in the artificial worlds of literature, though not all have produced an accompanying body of aesthetic theory. France in the 17th century produced both art and theory. Because ethics and aesthetics both reflect social values, they naturally employ similar criteria; while the concrete problems of artistic expression: questions of medium, form and technique are also

---

[1] *Discours de la Méthode*, part VI. The Cartesians also introduced the problem of vivisection into the debate on animal souls.

directly affected by subject matter. This study must therefore take into account at least some aspects of the field of aesthetics in the 17th century, where it throws light on the notion of *convenance*.

Looking at morals first, we can see that certain standpoints are already implied by the philosophical attitudes to reason which we have examined. Where it is associated with a teleological view of the universe, the established social structure is likely to be a major criterion governing human relationships; where an immanentist conception of reason is put forward, then the fulfilment of natural forms is likely to be the accepted norm, though both these criteria may depend upon the respective sanctions of the divine will or the divine reason. In the first case one will talk of the fitness of things, or the fitness of human behaviour, as part of the perfection of all creation; in the second, one will think of conformity with nature as one's only ideal.

Not surprisingly, the 17th and early 18th centuries produced an enormous number of variations and combinations of these two basic attitudes, and very few of them were supported by a consistent philosophical outlook. They were usually an amalgam of traditional ideas, Christian ethics, and borrowed philosophical theories. Nevertheless, certain broad trends can be discerned in the evolution of the idea of what constitutes honesty and goodness. Generally the *honnête homme* of the mid 17th century is regarded as the epitome of the *homme raisonnable*.[2] But whether the characteristic of reasonableness conferred on him the quality of goodness, and conversely, whether this same characteristic necessarily implied recognition on his part of the sophisticated arguments of philosophers, are different matters. For care must be taken not to confuse reasonableness with rationality: very often it signified respect for good sense, and affection for the ideal of moderation, rather than a willingness to submit to the findings of discursive reason. The real rationalists, as is often pointed out, were those like Fontenelle and Bayle who took the method of Cartesianism and used it rigorously to destroy the tissue of prejudice and ignorance blinding men to the real nature of things.[3] Nor was the gentleman's idea of reason necessarily the same as Descartes's, although he might sympathize with the philosopher's pragmatism in morals, his acceptance of the middle course as a rough guide and so on. In some ways Descartes's idea of intuitive

[2] M. Magendie, *La Politesse mondaine et les théories de l'honnêteté en France*, Paris, 1925, part V, ch. 9, p. 791.
[3] They are the "rationaux" of Hazard's *Crise de la Conscience européenne*: the men whom Bayle himself opposes in the *Réponses aux questions d'un provincial*, ch. CXXXIV, to the "religionnaires."

reason was in fact very close to the 18th century notion of *sentiment intérieur*; while Pascal more obviously, rejected and despised reason as a tool of morals, preferring sentiment.[4] The *mondain* was probably unfamiliar with the notion of sensibility as such, but it was equally part of his ideal, if we are to believe the Chevalier de Méré, that he should be unfamiliar with the actual processes of reasoning:

"Le bon goût se fonde toujours sur des raisons très solides, mais le plus souvent sans raisonner."[5]

Reason in the 17th century was a signpost pointing in a dozen different directions: the path of the aristocrat was different from that of the bourgeois, and both of these were different again from those of the philosopher or the theologian.

Yet a major and a fairly reliable distinction can be made between the religious and the non-religious moral traditions, both of which were continuous. The difference between the *honnête homme* and the *homme de bien* in the mind of the later 17th century is summarized in the definitions which La Bruyère provides in *Les Caractères*:

"L'honnête homme tient le milieu entre l'habile homme et l'homme de bien, quoique dans une distance inégale de ses deux extrêmes.

La distance qu'il y a de l'honnête homme à l'habile homme s'affaiblit de jour à autre, et est sur le point de disparaître...

L'honnête homme est celui qui ne vole pas sur les grands chemins, et qui ne tue personne, et dont les vices enfin ne sont pas scandaleux...

L'homme de bien est celui qui n'est ni un saint ni un dévot, et qui s'est borné à n'avoir que de la vertu."[6]

The religious conception of the good man is clearly far removed from the mixture of pessimism and vanity which informed the outlook of some of the *mondains* when they set themselves to moralize. La Bruyère is disillusioned, but he is on the side of Christianity and of virtue; he does not conclude like La Rochefoucauld that:

"Les vertus se perdent dans l'intérêt comme les fleuves se perdent dans la mer."[7]

And he is also obviously far removed from the ideals of the Chevalier de Méré:

[4] *Pensées*, 282.
[5] *Discours de la Conversation.*
[6] "Des Jugements," para. 55.
[7] *Maximes*, ed. F. C. Green, Cambridge, 1945, No. 171.

"A mon sens la plus grande preuve qu'on a de l'esprit, et qu'on l'a bienfait, c'est de bien vivre et de se conduire toujours comme on doit. Cela consiste à prendre en toutes les rencontres le parti le plus honnête, et à le soutenir; et le parti le plus honnête est celui qui paraît le plus conforme à l'état de vie ou l'on se trouve."[8]

There is some truth in the claim that the moral ideal of the 17th century represented a reconciliation between Classical pagan and Christian traditions, but it often seems that it is the notion of the *homme de bien*, with its echoes of the ideal of moderation, which embodies this reconciliation. There is very little ground for arguing that the ideal of charity was a prominent motive in the behaviour of the *honnête homme*, the fashionable aristocrat, or that it figured largely in the written theory that grew up around this ideal type.[9] The aristocrat's prepossession with status and prestige, his delicate appreciation of the susceptibilities of the ego would seem difficult to reconcile with a sincere concern for the good of others. It is possible to argue on the contrary that these traits are more closely connected with an aesthetic than with a moral criterion, if by moral criterion we mean a rule of virtuous behaviour. The simplest conclusion is that the moral code connected with the figure of the *honnête homme* had little to do with Christian conceptions. The renunciation for self, rather than of self, which is preached in the *Princesse de Clèves* for example, has a closer connection with the Stoic than with the Christian conception of virtue.

The notion of the *honnête homme* belongs to the secular tradition in morals, and as Magendie points out, this was an ideal subscribed to by two classes in society. Side by side with the aristocratic interpretation and equally inspired by Classical concepts, was a middle-class interpretation.[10] In Méré the gentleman guards his honour and his self-esteem; in Charron, he pursues the ideal of probity, with a scrupulous concern for the just evaluation of personal merit, and an equal conviction that happiness is an end in itself.

It is this naturalistic tradition which begins to dominate at the end of the 17th century, as the bastions of doctrinal orthodoxy break under the onslaught of critical reason. The psychological pessimism which characterized the attitudes of polite society tended to disappear, and disguised in treatises on oracles and comets or hidden among the erudite notes of Bayle's dictionary, the new ideals were published. The nat-

---

[8] *Discours de l'Esprit*, Paris, 1677, p. 31.
[9] D. Parodi suggests, however, in an article, "L'honnête homme et l'idéal moral du 17e at du 18e siècle," *Revue pédagogique*. LXXVIII, that the *honnête homme* is profoundly Christian.
[10] *La Politesse mondaine*, p. 892.

ural instincts are good; pleasure not virtue is the object of existence; freedom of conscience not doctrinal conformity is the moral basis of the state; self-interest is the cement of society; reason is the tool of progress. Where the *mondains* had been content to conform, if not to believe, the new men actively dissent. They have a materialistic ideal of happiness, and a mechanistic view of nature. They wish to clear away the confusion and lethargy created by centuries of superstitious respect for tradition and legend, and by rigorous application of rational methods, to cure the evils of society, rectify the injustices of a rigid class system, and gain material benefits with the development of scientific knowledge. The new rationalists reject the possibility of metaphysical knowledge, and seek a compromise with empiricism. In the *Pensées diverses sur la Comète*, Bayle declares that a society of atheists would be as virtuous as a society of Christians; and in the Preface to his translation of Pufendorf's *Droit de la Nature et des Gens*, the jurisconsult Jean Barbeyrac affirms the superiority of secular ethics; thus it is not just physics but also morals which are severed from theology.[11]

But the claims of religion did not lack defenders, although the religious camp was split by internal conflicts. Pamphlets and treatises poured through the presses in defence of Christianity, coming from the hand of Catholics and Protestants alike. Some shared common ground, a willingness to reconcile reason with revelation, and an equal debt to Malebranche. At all costs the ethics of the Gospel, if not the details of miracles and the workings of providence, must be reconciled with the dictates of natural reason, so that the ground might be cut from beneath the feet of the libertines and atheists. What ingenuity was displayed by the Abbadies, the Jaquelots, the Lamys and the Thomassins in inventing rational explanations and justifications for textual discrepancies and unlikely happenings, which in the light of the critical treatment of Spinoza and Simon, now seemed to litter the Bible! Even Bossuet, while uttering salutary warnings about the dangers of falling over backwards to accommodate rationalism, threw his weight behind the idea of a natural Christianity, consisting in a universal natural law, accessible to reason and prevailing before the advent of revealed religion.[12] There were a few dissenters in both factions, the Catholic bishop Huet, and the erudite orientalist Veyssière de la Croze, an ex-Benedictine converted to Protestantism, who understood more fully the

---

[11] *Pensées diverses sur la Comète*, 1682, vol. II, art. 161; Barbeyrac, translation of Pufendorf's *Droit de la Nature et des Gens*, Amsterdam, 1706.
[12] *Discours sur l'Histoire Universelle*, Part 1, 4th. epoch.

nature of the illusion under which the rational apologists laboured. They perceived the essential conflict between the rational demonstration of religious truths and their content, between a logical method and the *a priori* notions which it sets out to justify, but must eventually reject. They turned instead to the ideas and methods of Pascal, founding religion on sentiment and questioning rational speculation. Like the English critics of Samual Clarke, who in the *Essay on the Being and Attributes of God* did for Newton's system what Malebranche had done for Cartesianism, they realised that to demonstrate how closely rational precepts coincided with Christian ethics, was the best way to prove that revelation was superfluous.[13]

The weakness of the Christian party lay not only in their line of defence however, but also in their internal divisions. The crushing of Jansenism, and the revocation of the Edict of Nantes left the Catholic and the Reformed Churches at each others' throats; orthodox apologists were as concerned with eradicating heresy as with combatting free-thought, while the Calvinists, in exile and embittered, not unnaturally regarded their persecutors as an equally dangerous enemy. Bossuet and Jurieu not only attacked Bayle, but each other; and there were countless doctrinal disputes within each separate faction, especially among the Protestants, who by their very nature were less closed to radical ideas, and who now, by the fact of their exile in Holland, England and the non-Catholic states of Germany, were coming into close contact with new and disturbing trends of thought. There were men like Jean Le Clerc, Élie Saurin, and Jean La Placette in Holland who moved away from orthodox Protestantism, disputing the authority of those parts of Scripture in conflict with reason, and declaring moral conscience to be the basis of faith, and who were consequently accused of Socinianism and other heresies by their Reformed brethren. In England, Pierre Coste and Pierre Desmaizeaux were the friends and translators of Locke and Shaftesbury and many other prominent figures in scientific and philosophical circles; they played an outstanding part in the dissemination of English thought, of Deism and the ideas of the Latitudinarians, in France.[14] This state of ideological conflict was accompanied not surprisingly by an increase in mysticism, ever a sure

---

[13] For a detailed study of Christian apologetics during this period, see A. Monod, *De Pascal à Chateaubriand*, Paris, 1916, chaps. 1–7, from which most of the details of this outline have been taken. Also A. Sayous, *Histoire de la Littérature française à l'étranger*, vol. I, bk. 1, chaps. 5, 6; bk. 2, ch. 5.

[14] See Paul Hazard, *La Crise de la Conscience européenne*, Part I, ch. 3.

retreat from the problems of belief or action.[15] Add to these divisions in belief and purpose, the fact that Bayle and other leading thinkers were at least nominally adherents of one or other religious body, together with the failure of the eirenic movement in the face of Bossuet's intransigence, and the picture of insecurity and confusion among the defenders of Christianity is completed.[16]

This great upsurge of discussion and re-evaluation of the relative merits of the religious and secular traditions in ethics laid the foundations of a new conception of the *honnête homme*, the conception which in the middle of the century, Diderot crystallizes in the *Encyclopédie*:

"Il me semble que *l'homme de bien* est celui qui satisfait exactement aux préceptes de la religion; *l'homme d'honneur*, celui qui suit rigoureusement les lois et les usages de la société; et *l'honnête homme*, celui qui ne perd de vue dans aucune de ses actions les principes de l'équité naturelle ... *l'honnête homme* rend la justice même à son ennemi. L'honnête homme est de tout pays; *l'homme de bien* et *l'homme d'honneur* ne doivent point faire des choses que *l'honnête homme* ne se permet pas."[17]

The *honnête homme* is still the ideal type, but no longer the gentleman, rather the honest man in the fundamental sense of the word. The term does not change, but its significance is completely transformed. It is still strictly dissociated from the ideal of the good man, but has clearly lost its class connections, is thoroughly secularized, and plainly held to denote the most admirable kind of human being.

During the period which saw this reorientation of attitude, there was, however, a renewal of interest in the old idea of the gentleman, a kind of reactionary movement apparently led by religious interests, and centering round the republication of the works of Balthazar Gracián, a Spanish Jesuit who had died in 1658. Between 1637 and 1657 he had brought out several works, in which he attempted to construct the perfect model of the hero, a kind of Spanish and to some extent desecularized version of the *Cortegiano*, which had earned him the disfavour of his order. Yet after years of obscurity, these works were suddenly translated and published all over Europe. Paul Hazard, examining this phenomenon, describes how as many as fifteen different versions of Gracián appeared in France alone between 1685 and 1716.[18] The republication

---

[15] For an outline of some of the mystical works published at the end of the 17th century, see E. R. Briggs, "Mysticism and Rationalism in the debate upon eternal punishment", in *Studies on Voltaire and the 18th century*, XXIV/XXVII, 1963.

[16] For the eirenic movement, see Hazard, part II, ch. 5.

[17] *Encyclopédie*, vol. II, p. 244.

[18] *La Crise de la conscience européenne*, part III ch. 7.

of Gracián was accompanied by a whole new body of literature concerned with the idea of the *honnête homme*, and not just with the current moral disputes. The debate on the incompatibility of the qualities of the gentleman, notably the quality of probity, with the Christian ideal of charity is renewed and continued in a spate of works between 1680 and 1700. On one side men like Jacques Esprit and the Jesuit Bourdaloue condemn the purely negative quality of the aristocratic ideal, the moral inadequacy revealed in such remarks as that of Méré:

"il est plus aisé de dire les choses qu'il faut fuir que celles que l'on doit suivre."[19]

On the other side there are those like Jean Pic in his *Devoirs de la Vie civile*, who attempt to reconcile the pagan and the Christian ideals by falling back on St. Paul and St. Augustine as authorities, and again utilizing the idea of reason as moderator of the passions. The main participants in the debate seem to have been men of religious convictions, although works were produced during the period by representatives of the aristocratic tradition proper, the Chevalier Trotti de la Chétardie's *Instructions pour un jeune seigneur*, for example.[20]

This is, in outline, the pattern of moral debate during the last decades of the 17th century. As regards the particular part played in its literature by the special notion of *convenance*, the positions of the theist on the one hand, and the atheist on the other, immediately suggest two possible attitudes to the idea of conformity or fitness. The theist will see the purpose of life as striving to fulfil the Christian moral code, in the pursuit of eternal happiness. His ideal is that state of fitness that is achieved by conformity with God-given laws. The deist or the atheist meanwhile will understand the attainment of earthly happiness as the purpose of life; his ideal will be the fulfilment of his own nature, though his concern with the laws governing the organization of matter and the life of men in society will be no less, in spite of the fact that he sees their origin, not in the arbitrary will of God, but in an independent supernatural reason, or simply in the nature of matter itself. His ideal will be conformity with nature. Are these generalizations born out in detail?

One of the disciples of Malebranche whose works may at some time

---

[19] *Lettres*, 1682, vi. J. Esprit was a former Oratorian, and wrote *La Fausseté des vertus humaines*, 1678, while Bourdaloue attacks the ideal of probity in the sermon *De la religion et de la probité*. For details of further works, see A. Lévêque, "L'honnête homme et l'homme de bien au XVIIe siècle", in P. M. L.A., Sept. 1957, vol. LXXII, pp. 621–632. Lévêque pays particular attention to the period following 1660, which Magendie does not cover.
[20] Paris, 1683.

have come to the notice of Montesquieu, was Henri Lelevel. He was an Oratorian and tutor to the Duc de Saint-Simon, and he wrote several works on philosophy, morals, history and education. He appears to have been a major figure in the defence and dissemination of Malebranchian ideas, seconding Malebranche in his disputes with Arnauld and Régis, and giving a series of lectures in Paris, some of which were collected and published as *Conférences sur l'Ordre Naturel et sur l'Histoire Universelle*, (Paris, 1698).[21] Montesquieu is most likely to have seen his *Philosophie Moderne par demandes et par réponses*, (Toulouse, 1698), which is a complete manual of Malebranchian philosophy set out in question and answer form, and intended for use in schools and in fashionable circles, and which may have penetrated as far as Juilly.[22] It is clear from his works on philosophy that he had very little new to offer, though he does move away from Malebranche a little, by presenting God as the final cause, and describing the relationships established in the universe as contributing to the proposed object of the Creator.[23] As far as ethics are concerned, his Malebranchianism is correct down to the last word: Law and Order are identical; reason is the common bond of men, and so on. Everything is straightforward, and in one passage he sets out very clearly the basic terms of the religious ideal of behaviour: conformity with the divine law.

"On peut considérer la sagesse de Dieu ou comme la lumière sur laquelle il forme tous ses desseins et règle toute sa conduite, comme une lumière par laquelle il nous éclaire et le reste des intelligences; ou comme l'ordre même qui se trouve dans sa manière d'agir. Nos devoirs en conséquence de la conduite que Dieu tient dans le gouvernement du monde, sont d'y accommoder la nôtre, de ne rien négliger pour éviter les maux qui nous menacent, de travailler pour avoir les choses nécessaires à la vie, de voir sans émotion la prospérité des méchants, et les adversités des gens de bien."[24]

One of the best known arbiters of taste and good breeding during the

[21] See F. Bouillier, *Histoire de la Philosophie Cartésienne*, Paris, 1868, vol. II, ch. 13.

[22] Lelevel makes some interesting points with regard to the relationship between the character of a nation and its laws, which bring to mind Montesquieu's theory of the "esprit général" set out in Book XIX of the *Lois*. The following is the most striking: "Comme le bon effet des lois dépend de la proportion qu'elles ont avec le génie de ceux à qui on les impose, il faut consulter ce génie dans toutes celles qu'on fait; et même en certains cas il faut, comme si l'on n'avait point de raison à consulter, n'avoir égard qu'à la faiblesse des hommes." *La Philosophie Moderne*, III 14, p. 176.

[23] *Conférences sur l'Ordre Naturel*, Paris, 1698, VIII.

[24] *La Philosophie Moderne*, Toulouse, 1698, III, p. 97. The Stoic note sounded in this passage is misleading. Lelevel did not share the Oratorian enthusiasm for Greek philosophy; he belonged in fact to the group mentioned above. p. 41, who opposed any reconciliation with pagan ideals, and he wrote a work against them, *Le Discernement de la vraie et de la fausse morale, où l'on fait voir le faux des Offices de Cicéron*, Paris, 1695.

second half of the 17th century was Father René Rapin, the author of *Réflexions sur la Poétique d'Aristote*. Together with Bouhours, Fleury, and Ménestrier, he was a frequenter of the salon of Guillaume de Lamoignon, President of the Parlement de Paris. This group was generally conservative in outlook, they combined a moderate eclecticism with a firm conviction in the value of the *Anciens*, of classical models in literature, and of Aristotle in philosophy. Thus, while Lelevel was a partisan of the *Modernes*, Rapin may be taken as a representative of the older, less critical, conformist branch within the religious tradition. He was a Jesuit, a member of the order which had long cared for the education of the aristocracy, and his works are for the most part designed for their consumption. They aim to present an easy digest of the subject in question, mixed with lighter touches, "maximes de morale et traits d'histoire," to make for greater enjoyment. They are the kind of works which Montesquieu would certainly have known from an early age.[25] For us, their contribution to aesthetics is perhaps most important, but where Rapin deals with morals he does reflect certain widely accepted values. In the *Réflexions sur la Philosophie ancienne et moderne*, (Paris, 1676), he deals in the section on morals, with the ideal of "convenance à la nature." While he condemns Stoicism in general, from which he claims, this ideal has been borrowed by contemporary society, he suggests that it may be interpreted for practical ends as "conformité à la droite raison." We have here then the idea that the dictates of right reason are immediately intelligible to each individual; that reason is an independent moral criterion, and that conformity with it must be the aim of the *honnête homme*. All this in a work which condemns Descartes for his geometric method, and proclaims that the utility of philosophy lies only in the support that it affords religion. In the matter of morals, every man is, at least nominally, a rational idealist.

However, further investigation reveals a modified picture. It is not really an ideal of true honesty which lies closest to Rapin's heart, but the old aristocratic and individualistic ideal of the hero, the remnant of feudalism and Italian influence.[26] It is an ideal in which the manner of an action counts more than its intrinsic value: the ideal of *politesse* where morals and aesthetics overlap to a large extent. But the notion of fitness has its place here also, as we shall see.

For the same ideal is to be found in Gracián, the Spanish moralist

---

[25] Montesquieu refers to Rapin's *Réflexions sur la Philosophie ancienne et moderne* in an early entry in the *Spicilège*, 205, see Nagel II, p. 743.
[26] See particularly Rapin's *Du Grand et du Sublime dans les Moeurs*, Paris, 1686.

who suddenly achieved popularity at the end of the century, and whose work Montesquieu may also have known.[27] Here the idea of *politesse* is actually advanced as an artistic criterion; it corresponds to the ordered disposition of the parts of a painting, or to the ordered way in which any work is executed. Gracián talks of the "liaison convenable" which must be established between the objects depicted in any artistic creation, and which results in "l'élégant assemblage, d'où résultent la Politesse et le bel Ordre qui charme dans tous les ouvrages de l'art."[28] This criterion of *politesse* corresponds in the sphere of social behaviour to the idea of *manière*: the proper way in which all actions must be executed. This is the quality which dominates all other considerations:

"La Vérité a de la force: la Raison a du pouvoir: la Justice a de l'autorité. Mais que tout cela perd de son avantage, s'il n'est revêtu de la Manière qui convient; et si la Manière qui convient est jointe à tout cela, qu'elle en rehausse le prix."[29]

Here the emphasis is on order, which may be regarded as the material expression of reason, although this is probably not the way that Gracián would have looked at it. In art as in social relationships there must be conformity between the object and the manner in which it is depicted, or between the action and the manner in which it is performed; to borrow Montesquieu's words, there must be a "rapport de convenance," whereby the demands of order are given tangible expression.

As might be expected, very similar notions are to be found in the works of the abbé Jean Pic, one of the moralists who contributed to the renewed debate on Classical ideals of behaviour which took place at the end of the 17th century.[30] Without adopting completely Gracián's heroic and individualistic creed, Pic likewise stresses that virtue in society consists in more than simple conformity with a moral code. The rules of good manners and of *bienséance*, must be observed.[31] So far so good; it seems that his main object in the *Devoirs de la Vie Civile*, is simply to establish what Montesquieu was later to advance in a fragment of the *Traité des Devoirs*, namely that in a civilized society, the

[27] A copy of Gracián's *L'Homme Universel* is listed in the Catalogue of the library at La Brède, No. 2389, p. 170. See also Montesquieu's Discourse, *De la Considération et de la Réputation*, Nagel III, p. 206. Graciàn is mentioned briefly.
[28] *L'Homme Universel*, trad. J. de Courbeville, Rotterdam, 1729, ch. 18, p. 175.
[29] Graciàn, *L'Homme Universel*, ch. 22, p. 225.
[30] See above, pp. 37–41.
[31] *Les Devoirs de la Vie Civile*, Amsterdam, 1687, part III, ch. 5, "Le parfait mérite ne dépend point de l'observation des lois rigoureuses que les hommes ont établies. C'est de l'observation des devoirs de la société."

rules of convention serve to make life more agreable.[32] Pic contends, moreover, that the code of *honnêteté* must not be restricted to one particular social group; an equal consideration is every man's due. And he attacks prejudice and interest as the sources of anti-social behaviour.[33] But if we turn to another of his works, the *Discours sur la Bienséance* (Paris, 1688), we find that *bienséance* denotes something more than a standard of social behaviour. It does not signify simply conformity with accepted social conventions; its definition goes beyond Rapin's suggested ideal of conformity with right reason, and comes closer to the notion of *decorum* found in Cicero's *De Officiis*: the individual must strive to fit his outward person to his inner being. Thus, *bienséance* here signifies conformity with nature in its fullest sense: conformity of behaviour with personality, with social condition, as well as with the dictates of reason:

"La bienséance consiste en des actions et en des manières où l'on ne remarque rien qui ne réponde précisément à ce que l'on est, et ce n'est point assez pour en remplir tous les devoirs, que de conformer nos actions à la raison et à l'honnêteté; mais il faut encore conformer notre air et nos manières aux actions que la raison et l'honnêteté nous font faire."[34]

For Pic *bienséance* is the sum of all virtue and the source of the good life:

"La bienséance ne préside pas seulement sur toutes les autres vertus en nous les faisant pratiquer; elle contribue encore à les perfectionner en nous les faisant pratiquer exactement et avec application. Je ne parle point ici de cette bienséance du monde qui ne nous porte à nos devoirs que pour sauver les apparences, et pour surprendre l'approbation des hommes; je parle de celle qui nous fait être vertueux, et non de celle qui nous le fait paraître; de celle qui vient des sentiments; qui ne nous engage pas moins à être honnêtes et vertueux pour nous-mêmes, qu'elle nous y engage pour les autres; et qui ne nous fait pas tant consulter, pour nous déterminer à bien faire, les agréments qui nous en peuvent revenir du côté des hommes, que le témoignage secret de notre conscience."[35]

Clearly the ideal of charity is also at the back of his mind. Pic writes of *bienséance*, as Montesquieu writes of *justice*, or even Rousseau of *amour-propre:* he is looking for a source of inspiration, a motive force, as well as for an ideal of conduct.[36]

---

[32] See *Pensée* 1270, (Bkn. 619). M. possessed 1682 ed. of Pic's *Devoirs*; Catalogue No. 669, p. 50.

[33] *Les Devoirs de la Vie Civile*, part III, chaps. 6, 8, 13.

[34] *Discours sur la Bienséance*, Paris, 1688, p. 11.

[35] *Ibid.*, p. 76.

[36] Although propriety seems a far less subjective basis for moral theory than self-respect, the idea of esteem is common to both, and it is interesting to compare what Rousseau has to say in *Émile*, IV: "Étendons l'amour-propre sur les autres êtres, nous le transformerons en vertu, et il n'y a point de cœur d'homme dans lequel cette vertu n'ait sa racine .... Plus

All these theoreticians set out to formulate their ideal of individual behaviour with the notion that man must conform to a universal criterion already firmly implanted in their minds. This is also eminently characteristic of the Protestant apologists during this period; their moral theory emerges, not in limited attempts to portray a model type of man, but through the two great debates with Catholicism and with naturalism. They are rather more concerned with ethics as a subject bordering on philosophy and theology, with combatting aspects of one system by borrowing points from another, than with a narrow treatment of the individual. Most of them were rationalists, at least in the sense that Rapin and Pic may be considered rationalists. In his book on apologetics Monod calls them *rationaux* or *hommes de juste milieu*, in order to distinguish them from the rationalists proper, like Bayle and Fontenelle; but some, Jean Le Clerc springs immediately to mind, were far more radical than this implies, refusing to accept the primacy of faith when it conflicted with reason, or, if allowing any small part to mystery, insisting that reason alone could provide adequate proof of the truth of religion.[37]

The readiness with which Protestantism in general accepted Cartesianism has often been noted. As we have already mentioned, there were many historical and political factors which encouraged such a development.[38] They were linked by a common rejection of traditional authority among other things; and although the main Protestant bodies subscribed to the canons of orthodoxy laid down by the Synod of Dordrecht in 1618, from the middle of the century onwards, there was a growing number of sects, Arminians, Cocceians, Socinians and the like, especially in the Low Countries, who, inspired by theological currents from Eastern Europe, proclaimed the necessity of a continuing reformation based on the inalienable freedom of the individual conscience guided by reason.[39] Cartesianism to them was a welcome ally, and circumstance fostered the relationship when Descartes and his disciples, themselves the victims of orthodox intolerance, were driven from France to work and teach in Protestant countries. Thus it was that as early as 1638 courses in the new philosophy were being held in the University

---

on généralise cet intérêt, plus il devient équitable; et l'amour du genre humain n'est autre chose en nous que l'amour de la justice."

[37] Monod, *De Pascal à Chateaubriand*, ch. V, p. 158. For Le Clerc see also A. Barnes, *Jean Le Clerc et la République des Lettres*, Paris, 1938.

[38] See above, pp. 39–40.

[39] For the influence of Cartesianism on theology in Holland, see C. L. Thijssen-Schoute, "Le Cartésianisme aux Pays-Bas," article in *Descartes et le Cartésianisme Hollandais*, C. Serrurier etc., Paris, 1950.

of Utrecht; and Holland became with the growing tide of repression in France, the power-house of rationalism in Europe.

Geneva, where theologically the situation was more stable, was later to follow the same path into the rationalist fold. In both centres philosophical liberalism paved the way to a revolution in theological attitudes. In Geneva it was the teaching of Robert Chouet which was perhaps most important in bringing this about. Though orthodox in matters of religion, he applied the methods of Cartesianism rigorously in the field of natural science; and it is significant that several of the outstanding Protestant contributors to the religious debate studied with him. Bayle, Basnage, Le Clerc and Bernard all followed his courses in Geneva.[40] So it was that philosophy began to break down the doctrinal bonds which had held Protestant consciences in check, just as the Casuists had loosened those of Catholicism.

In Geneva, Chouet's mantle was inherited by J. A. Turrettini, professor of ecclesiastical history and later of theology at the university. Utilizing the main features of Cartesian doctrine: the self-evidence and simplicity of first principles and so on, and many of the ideas already put forward by jurisconsults like Grotius and Pufendorf, he taught that the first principles of morals constitute a universal natural law known to all men and revealed in Scripture. All points of dogma which conflict with this fundamental law, or are not clearly related to it, are superfluous, if not positively harmful.[41] The natural law is the law of reason; and in demonstrating his theories Turrettini almost inevitably fell back upon the notion of *convenance*, the idea that the rational order behind the universe is expressed in the visible fitness of its parts, which in the mind forms the basis of the rules governing conduct:

"Nihil sunt igitur Leges Naturales, nisi Rationis ipsius dictamina, quae ex ipso rerum ordine et convenientia tamquam ex fonte deducuntur, suamque secum demonstrationem et confirmationem ferunt."[42]

This short formula is a classic expression of the belief of the rational idealists. But its concision saves it from the pitfalls which awaited many of the rationalist theologians as soon as they began to elaborate their theories. The most dangerous of these was that into which Malebranche

---

[40] See A. Sayous, *Histoire de la Littérature française à l'étranger*, Paris, 1853, p. 158, and A. Barnes, *Jean Le Clerc et la République des Lettres*, Paris, 1938, p. 38.

[41] Turrettini's main theological work was the *Traité de la Vérité de la Religion Chrétienne*, trans. J. Vernet, Geneva, 1730. Volume II of this edition contains the *Pensées sur ta Religion*, which outline the main points of his doctrine.

[42] "De Theologia Naturali," in *Cogitationes et Dissertationes Theologicae*, Geneva, 1737, dissertatio VIII, part I, sec. II, art. 18, p. 252.

almost fell, namely of formulating theories of reason and of nature
which add up to a philosophy of immanence, and thereby earn the
stigma of Spinozism.[43] We have already mentioned in our brief discussion of his disciple Henri Lelevel, how the idea of God as final cause
is here introduced.[44] The most likely reason for this departure from the
main tenets of Malbranchianism, was a desire to avoid at all costs any
suggestion that the material universe is simply a mode of reason. Now
one of the Protestant disciples of Malebranche who showed less caution
than Lelevel, was Élie Saurin.

Saurin, pastor of the Walloon church in Utrecht, was at the centre
of the main dispute that split the Reformed churches in Holland. He
was Jurieu's opponent in the battle over religious tolerance which
spread into the very ranks of those whom persecution had driven from
their homeland. Like Isaac d'Huisseau he was as concerned to find a
middle ground in religious doctrine, upon which there could be general
agreement, as to establish the political conditions in which civil and
religious freedom could flourish.[45] To this end he was prepared to sacrifice less important dogmas, and this earned him the accusation of
pelagianism from Jurieu.[46] The quarrel was only ended by the inter-
vention of the États-Généraux in 1696. While Jurieu's accusation of
pelagianism seems unfounded, his concern at the implications of some
of Saurin's doctrines is more understandable. The pastor of Utrecht
was undoubtedly a thoroughgoing rationalist and perhaps even a latitudinarian. For in the *Traité de l'Amour de Dieu*, which he declared to be
an exposition of his metaphysics, he openly admitted the influence of
Malebranche and of Geulinx in his thinking. The latter was almost
unknown outside the Low Countries, but it is perhaps significant that
he is now generally regarded as the intermediary between Malebranche
and Spinoza.[47]

Disregarding the kind of precautions taken by Lelevel, Saurin boldly
declares God to be reason, justice, power, virtue, and wisdom, the first
and only cause of the natural order.[48] Virtue like reason is an inde-

---

[43] See above pp. 12–14.

[44] See above p. 42.

[45] Saurin's political thought is contained in the *Réflexions sur les Droits de la Conscience*,
Utrecht, 1697; for an outline of this aspect of the quarrel see G. Dodge, *The Political Theory
of the Huguenots of the Dispersion*, Columbia, 1947. Isaac d'Huisseau was a leading figure in
the eirenic movement; his *La réunion du Christianisme*, 1669 was a major contribution to its
literature.

[46] Jurieu attacked him in his *Défense de la Doctrine de l'Église*, 1695, and *La religion du
Latitudinaire*, 1696.

[47] See Van der Haeghen, *Geulinx, étude de sa vie*, 1886, II, 6.

[48] *Traité de l'Amour de Dieu*, Amsterdam, 1701, I, 2.

pendent and transcendent force. The Decalogue is the sum of revealed law, but its principles may be discovered by the operation of reason alone, for the relations between men are governed by the eternal law, which consists in the relations of perfection between essences that are seen in God.[49] Law is defined as a relationship. So far we are given a plain account of Malebranche's main doctrines; but soon divergences begin to appear. In the *Ethica*, Geulinx had seen God as the sole cause of all things, and logically this included evil; Malebranche however had gone to great lengths, elaborating his theory of the simplicity of the laws involved in the creation and conservation of the universe, and carefully distinguishing between these natural laws and the eternal laws of reason, in order to avoid this conclusion. But Saurin leans towards Geulinx; he makes no distinction between the eternal law of reason and the natural law:

"Dieu est la première Raison et la première Loi. Son essence est la règle du droit naturel, et sa volonté est la règle du droit positif."[50]

If natural law is to be seen as the essence of God, it is quite possible to deduce from this that the extended universe is simply a mode of that essence. Saurin has no hesitation in positing a necessary correspondence between the real and the ideal, even in the moral order; in his system the existence of God is not required as a guarantee of the order of reality, as it was for the orthodox Cartesian.[51] Indeed reason and love of reason are before God,

"... l'amour de la raison et de la Justice, de la vertu et de la perfection est le premier amour, l'amour primitif, le principe et la règle de tout autre amour, même de l'amour de Dieu."[52]

Virtue is love of reason, and charity love of justice. This is no more than Geulinx advanced: "virtus est rectae rationis amor unicus";[53] but whereas he is prepared to reject the pursuit of happiness and the demands of *amour-propre* as contrary to the fulfilment of the dictates of reason, emphasizing the virtues of humility and self-forgetfulness,[54]

[49] *Ibid.*, III, 6.
[50] *Ibid.*, I, 8, p. 98.
[51] *Op. cit.*, I, 5: "Si ce que nous appellons vertu, mérite, perfection n'était rien de réel, on ne pourrait s'en former aucune idée; comme on n'aurait aucune idée de l'étendue, si l'essence de l'étendue était un pur néant." cf. *Discours de la Méthode*, part IV, "Cela même que j'ai tantôt pris pour une règle, à savoir que les choses que nous concevons très clairement ... sont toutes vraies, n'est assuré qu'à cause que Dieu est ou existe."
[52] *Traité de l'Amour de Dieu*, I, 8.
[53] *Ethica*, I, ii, 4.
[54] See Van der Haeghen, *Geulinx, étude sur sa vie, sa philosophie, et ses ouvrages*, part II, ch. 6.

Saurin on the contrary, declares that virtue is love of that which is in accordance with our nature, since that nature is ordained by reason.[55]

Thus we are again presented with the ideal of *convenance à la nature*, arrived at this time by taking the premises of rationalism to their logical conclusion, in a way reminiscent of Spinoza. Of course, whether this phrase continues to signify conformity with a rational ideal, or really implies the fulfilment of one's capacities as a human animal, depends largely on the interpretation of the term *nature*. Clearly in the 17th century, it could be almost synonymous with reason; while the 18th century witnessed a weakening of this sense, and a movement towards a more empirical definition: nature as personality in a human context, or nature as the world of material things.[56] The dispute between the naturalistic ideal and the rational or religious ideal is as old as western philosophy itself, and sometimes it is difficult to draw a clear line between them; but as we have already mentioned, the notion which throughout the period of rationalism, carries with it the strongest naturalistic associations, is probably that of self-respect or probity, as far as ethics are concerned.[57]

Now when Saurin, whose rationalism taken to extremes has brought him face to face with naturalism, comes to deal in his *Traité de l'Amour du Prochain* with moral rather than metaphysical problems, it is the ideal of justice based on self-respect or *amour-propre*, which he advances. Love of reason involves love of nature, and love of nature includes self. For if God loves the perfections contained in his rational essence, will not man also love those that are reflected in his own being?[58] In this case *amour-propre* is the logical outcome of a rational conception of the divine nature. Saurin has no hesitations on the score of original sin; on the contrary, *amour-propre* is the necessary natural basis of the justice which one renders to one's fellows; and if one perceives more perfection in oneself than in any one else, then it follows that one's self-respect will outweigh one's altruism.[59] Here there is a certain similiarity with Spinoza's idea that the more being embraced by a thing, the higher it is in the scale of reality, and the less dependent it becomes: this idea is in direct opposition to the rationalist viewpoint that between things of the same kind there is a constant relationship of equality, which forms the

[55] *Traité de l'Amour de Dieu*, III, 6.
[56] See R. Mercier, *La Réhabilitation de la Nature Humaine*, Villemonble, 1960; also F. Gohin, *Les Transformations de la langue française au 18e siècle*, Paris, 1903.
[57] See above p. 37.
[58] *Op. cit.*, I, 1.
[59] *Traité de l'Amour du Prochain*, Utrecht, 1704, I, 2; 13. *Traité de l'Amour de Dieu*, IV, 6.

basis of abstract justice, the position which Montesquieu later adopted. Indeed it is easy to suggest that by natural perfection, Saurin could mean little else but being or reality, since he cannot intend to prove the validity of an independent rational criterion when he denies the existence of actual relationships of equality between men, and stresses the importance of material circumstances in determining moral judgements.[60] The scale of values which he draws up to regulate moral conduct is exactly the reverse of that advanced by Malebranche for example, and later made famous by Montesquieu:[61]

"Les voisins, les concitoyens, les compatriotes, les sujets d'un même souverain, les membres d'une même république se doivent quelques degrés particuliers d'amour et d'affection, et certains offices qu'ils ne doivent pas à des étrangers, à des inconnus, à des ennemis. Ils vivent sous les mêmes lois, ils ont en partie les mêmes intérêts; ils sont à portée de faire les uns pour les autres, mille choses qu'ils ne peuvent pas faire pour ceux avec qui ils n'ont pas les mêmes liaisons.[62]

It is conformity with nature, with the actual relationships between things, which forms the basis of Saurin's ethical system; not conformity with a transcendent ideal. He adopts in fact the standpoint of immanent rationalism, rather than that of rational idealism; a position which is close to naturalism, and which is open to anyone who unreservedly associates reason with the nature of things.

Saurin's work, though uninspiring in itself, provides a very good example of the remarkably similar effects which casuistry and extreme rationalism could have on moral attitudes. It also illustrates the use of Classical pagan ideals – probity and moderation, by Protestant writers, once their idea of the nature of things has undergone transformation.

So far we have dealt with writers of the second or third rank, whose works reflect well established ideas or the beginnings of their modification at the end of the 17th century. With Saurin we have seen the weakening of the idealist approach to morals, in favour of the attitudes derived from a conception of immanent reason. The position from which he has moved is essentially one in which the pattern of things is seen to emanate from a design of ultimate perfection: beyond the created universe, there is a transcendent ideal with which the fitness of things is

---

[60] *Traité de l'Amour du Prochain*, I, 9.

[61] Malebranche, *Traité de Morale*, "Il faut être homme, chrétien, Français avant d'être grammarian, poète, historien, étranger." part II, ch. 10, para. xiv. cf. Montesquieu, *Traité des Devoirs*, Nagel III, p. 160; *Pensées* 350 (Bkn. 10), 741 (Bkn. 11); *Histoire Véritable*, Nagel III, p. 355.

[62] *Traité de l'Amour du Prochain*, I, 9, pp. 69–70.

connected, and to which, we, being part of creation yet endowed with freedom, must aspire, in order that our lives will also possess the quality of fitness. To this end a code of laws is evolved, not necessarily based on natural tendencies, but said to stem from the transcendent ideal, often the will of God in association with reason. Against this, the standpoint of naturalism is that organized matter exists we know not how, that we are part of it, and must therefore aim only to fulfil our natural tendencies in so far as these do not conflict with the demands of society. In between lies the position of the immanentist doctrine: the natural structure of things expresses the rational order, and therefore, by conforming to nature, one realizes the ethical demands of reason.

This is a simplified outline, but it enables us to see three points more clearly. First, immanentist rationalism does not necessarily imply a rejection of rational ideals; it simply weakens their position, by emphasizing the necessity of fulfilling natural forms; if nature is the expression of reason, why look beyond it? Secondly, for the rational idealist, the idea of *convenance* signifies more than mere conformity; it is better translated as fitness, since it calls up several secondary notions, such as harmony, unity, perfection. It necessarily implies the existence of a relationship of some kind, but that relationship is invested with a quality of greater meaning than simple correspondence between terms. We may ourselves regard this quality as the simple projection of our own response to the perception of congruence in things, grafted on to a basic idea, and lacking any true counterpart in reality; but generally it is taken to signify participation of the material in an ideal order. Another way of seeing it is as a holist conception: when *convenance* is used to describe an object it indicates a quality that is more than the sum of the object's attributes. It could be described as a term which links theology and physics. The third point is that the idea of a structural correspondence between things is common to all three viewpoints: the idealist, the immanentist and the naturalist. The 18th century may have embraced materialism, but it did not abandon the idea that the pattern of nature was very reasonable, even on those occasions when it rejected the notion that this pattern indicated the existence of a supernatural intelligence.

As regards those thinkers who were instrumental in ensuring the dominance of the naturalistic tradition in morals, the two most outstanding, Fontenelle and Bayle, did not, despite their radical rationalism, make any great use of the notion of *convenance*, even as an extension of the idea of correspondence between terms fundamental to mathematics.

Fontenelle is justly regarded as the pioneer of what for want of a better English equivalent must be called the philosophic movement in French thought. Often described as the first example of the "type philosophe," rather than the "type honnête homme," the perpetual secretary of the *Académie des Sciences* was probably known to Montesquieu at the time of the latter's first visit to Paris between 1709 and 1713.[63] He himself was certainly acquainted with all the outstanding men of science and letters of the day, and he made his own special contribution to the development of thought, as a propagandist of science, and a determined if cautious enemy of religion.[64] But this is not to say that Fontenelle rejected outright the existence of God; he did not. On the contrary, he saw the universe as the expression of the divine intelligence: "la physique suit et démêle les traces de l'intelligence et de la sagesse infinie qui a tout produit";[65] but he denied the possibility of metaphysical knowledge: the ultimate wisdom of God, the purpose and meaning of the world are for ever beyond our reach. Thus in the *Éloge de Leibniz* he questioned the validity of theories like that of pre-established harmony; and he even regarded Newtonian attraction as some kind of occult force out of keeping with a mechanist interpretation of the universe. The structure of things was the proper sphere of human inquiry, for everything was founded on order; even chance vanishes with the growth of knowledge: it is simply "un ordre que l'on ne connaît point."[66]

What happens to the idea of conformity in all this? One would expect Fontenelle to propound a system of ethics founded on the scientific function of reason; if reason is capable of penetrating the structure of the physical world, it can surely analyse the relationships binding the moral world together. But not so; like most thinkers who associated reason with nature, Fontenelle saw the application of rational methods in the moral sphere as a simple waste of time. Man is part of nature; and although the individual may use his natural faculties in the achievement of happiness, his thought is insignificant in the cosmic pattern of things:

"Il y a une raison qui nous met au-dessus de tout par les pensées, il doit y en avoir ensuite une autre qui nous ramène à tout par les actions; mais à ce compte-là même, ne vaut-il pas presque autant n'avoir point pensé?"[67]

[63] See Shackleton, *Montequieu*, I, p. 10.
[64] For a detailed study of Fontenelle, see J. R. Carré, *La Philosophie de Fontenelle*, Paris, 1932, and J. F. Counillon, *Fontenelle, écrivain, savant, philosophe*, Fécamp, 1959.
[65] *Préface sur l'Utilité des Mathématiques et de la Physique*.
[66] *Dialogues des Morts*, Morts modernes II, Charles V et Érasme.
[67] *Ibid.*, V, Parménique et Théocrite de Chio.

Conformity with reason or rather with nature comes about without the operation of our rational faculties.

Fontenelle believed moreover that human nature was fixed, and dominated by self-interest:

"La politesse ou la grossièreté, la science ou l'ignorance, le plus ou le moins d'une certaine naïveté, le génie sérieux ou badin, ce ne sont là que les dehors de l'homme, et tout cela change; mais le coeur ne change point, et tout l'homme est dans le coeur. On est ignorant dans un siècle, mais la mode d'être savant peut venir; on peut être intéressé, mais la mode d'être désintéressé ne viendra point." [68]

Thus although in his essay *De l'Origine des Fables*, he clearly considers that some progress has taken place during the course of history, and emphasizes the importance of overcoming prejudice and superstition, this progress is connected not so much with increased virtue, as with scientific knowledge. The only truth is scientific, and progress in science comes about necessarily, hence all hope of moral improvement is tied to this:

"Avec une bonne logique et une bonne médecine, les hommes n'auraient plus besoin de rien," [69]

that is Fontenelle's conclusion.

How did the other pioneer of scientific rationalism, Pierre Bayle, approach moral questions? Like Fontenelle, Bayle exercised a profound influence on succeeding generations, not least upon Montesquieu.[70] Bayle's outlook on life, in spite of a ruthlessly logical and ultimately destructive approach to revealed religion, was dominated by a thirst for truth, and for moral security in the face of seemingly overwhelming evil.[71] His thirst for truth was the thirst of the sceptic, of a man whose vision of the accumulated errors, abuses and delusions of centuries is so

---

[68] *Op. cit.*, III, Socrate et Montaigne.

[69] *Éloge de Tschirnhaus.*

[70] See Shackleton's article, "Bayle and Montesquieu," in *Pierre Bayle, le philosophe de Rotterdam*, ed. P. Dibon, Amsterdam, etc., 1959.

[71] Bayle's attitude to truth is that of a positivist; although he was obviously always aware of the contradictions between facts, his scepticism was directed above all towards metaphysical speculation and the doctrines of revealed religion. The Article *Maldonat* in the *Dictionary* contains the assertion that even first principles of logic must be verifiable by experience to be valid; similarly, the attacks mounted on doctrine, Cartesian and religious, in the articles *Pyrrhon* and *Manichéens*, are too penetrating, and the conviction that human judgements are the only ones which can be applied to speculative beliefs, is too deep, for the assertion that Bayle was a rational fideist to hold water. This assertion has, however, been frequently made by recent criticism; see E. D. James, "Scepticism and Fideism in Bayle's *Dictionnaire*," *French Studies*, 1962; and R. H. Popkin, "Pierre Bayle's place in 17th. century Scepticism," in *Pierre Bayle, Le Philosophe de Rotterdam*.

acute that he cannot rest until he has shaken his fellow men out of their stupor, and armed them against themselves. Reason, discursive reason, is the tool which, by painstaking research and comparison, can establish the concrete facts of past and present, and right the distorted visions of those who take refuge in fables or in metaphysical speculation:

"Je vous avoue encore qu'en examinant l'enchaînure de plusieurs faits, en considérant le génie des auteurs, en pesant toutes les circonstances, en comparant ensemble ce qui a été dit par les uns et par les autres, on peut découvrir bien des impostures, réfuter bien des calomnies."[72]

But this is a mere declaration of intention; the whole of the *Dictionnaire Critique* is devoted to the thankless task of clearing away confusion, and laying the foundations of positive fact upon which men might base their actions.

For although Bayle undoubtedly loved knowledge for its own sake, he saw in it a tool of progress also. Fontenelle put his faith in scientific progress, Bayle in moral education; but Fontenelle really expresses a common approach to the kind of historical knowledge which preoccupied Bayle when he writes of the purpose of history:

"Comme nous ne saisissons presque jamais les principes généraux si parfaitement que notre esprit n'ait besoin d'y être soutenu par des applications particulières ..., il est bon que l'histoire accompagne et fortifie la connaissance que nous pouvons avoir de l'homme. Elle nous fera voir, pour ainsi dire, l'homme en détail, après que la morale nous l'aura fait en gros ... Ce n'est point l'histoire des révolutions des états, des guerres ... qu'il faut étudier, mais, sous cette histoire, il faut développer celle des erreurs et des passions humaines."[73]

It is the knowledge of human abberation, which holds the key to reform. Bayle makes a moving declaration of his conviction in the article *Mâcon*, note D, when writing of the wars of religion, he pleads, as some today remembering the horrors of concentration camps plead, that the atrocities of past ages should not be forgotten, but kept alive as a constant warning.

Bayle had as few illusions about human nature as Fontenelle; and he realised that conformity with the basic tendencies of this nature is the only real footing on which life can be lived. Thus he accepted that instinct and vice could play a beneficial role in society.[74] Yet there is also a place for conscience, if it is given a positive basis. In the *Commen-*

---

[72] *Critique générale de l'Histoire du Calvinisme, Oeuvres Diverses,* 1727, vol. II, p. 13.
[73] Fontenelle, *Sur l'Histoire, Oeuvres,* Paris, 1790; vol. V, pp. 434–435.
[74] *Dictionnaire,* arts. *Hélène, Melanchthon.*

taire Philosophique, he declares that the natural understanding is capable of coming to clear conclusions in ethical matters;[75] however, the theory of conscience as a sincere act of will as regards belief, and as an intention to secure the greatest social good where secular affairs are concerned, usually lumped together under the heading "doctrine de la conscience errante," and developed in the famous digression of the *Pensées Diverses sur la Comète*, "Si les athées sont capables de bonnes moeurs," fits in better with his approach to truth and his appreciation of human weakness. The good must be pursued when it is seen and understood; but the fallibility of human nature must be admitted, while, at the same time, its essential dignity, and individual freedom must be safeguarded. Bayle's theory of the right of the conscience to err was criticized on the grounds that it laid the way open to the kind of intolerance that it was supposed to prevent. In the *Traité des Droits des deux Souverains*, Jurieu for instance, pointed out that it justified the worst persecutions of the religious fanatic. But this kind of criticism was surely founded on a mistaken conception of what Bayle set out to do; his aim was not to formulate an ideal, founded on a rational conception of truth, rather to elaborate a viable principle for action, that would take into account certain fundamental needs, and certain undeniable facts. His scorn for the rational idealist, for the deist, was as great as his despair for the orthodox believer.[76] Bayle's doctrine of conscience certainly reflects the same positive approach as characterized his attitude to truth.

So the erudite critic and the propagandist of science laid down the foundations of the new materialism. At its heart was the recognition that nature is good, which gave rise to the conviction that behaviour should follow instinctive models, and renounce the pursuit of transcendent ideals. The idea of conscience was difficult to throw overboard, without jeopardizing the health of society, but it could conveniently be linked with self-interest or put forward as a natural moral instinct. Innate ideas were dismissed, and so was the idea of fitness associated with teleological design in the universe. No longer could reason, disembodied, abstract from the perfect order of things a guide for righteous living. Discursive reason, laboriously unravelling the relationships of the physical world, now had the upper hand. If one spoke of conformity, it was of conformity with nature or of conformity be-

[75] *Op. cit.*, I, 1, i.
[76] In the *Réponse aux Questions d'un Provincial, Oeuvres* vol. III, 1727, ch. 128, he upbraids them for attempting to demonstrate the existence of God by reason.

tween perception and the external object. In sensationalist epistemology, such conformity was the basis of sound judgement. What is truth? –
the disciple of Locke has his answer ready, "une conformité de notre
pensée avec son objet." [77] It is not long before the moralist declares, "le
crime est toujours un faux jugement." [78]

But the revolution in philosophical attitudes was by no means a rapid
or complete process. Well established theories, that of Natural Law,
among them, continued to command the respect owing to their antiquity, and were duly incorporated into new systems. Indeed many of
the leaders in philosophical progress preferred a modicum of respecta-
bility to the kind of notoriety which might have accompanied a franker
expression of their views. Locke for example, may have enshrined the
principle of property ownership in his political system, a principle
which may be considered to run counter to the demands of natural
justice, though it had a very respectable ancestry in the English Common Law; but he never abandoned the theory of Natural Law, and, had
he lived long enough, would undoubtedly have been shocked by Man-
deville's outright rejection of virtue as a positive enemy of the state.[79]

In France, much more than in England, circumspection was the
order of the day. Fontenelle's elegant prose, and Bayle's erudition
served to screen some of their more radical propositions from the cen-
sor. Similarly, more minor writers seem to have been able to insinuate
most unorthodox ideas into apparently conventional treatises. The
abbé Edmé Mariotte is a good example. Largely uninfluenced by any
particular system, he simply applied the tools of mathematics and observation to the solving of ethical problems, while nonetheless con-
triving to incorporate many of the theories and much of the conventional terminology of rational idealism into his essay. Thus his work
may be read as a critique of the currently fashionable position.

Mariotte died in 1684, but enjoyed a reputation as one of the outstanding physicists of his day, and as a leading exponent of empirical
methods in science. His observations on rainfall are mentioned in one
of the early entries in the notebook which Montesquieu borrowed from
Desmolets and copied out at the beginning of the *Spicilège*,[80] and it is

[77] Claude Buffier, *Éléments de Métaphysique*, Paris, 1725, IV, p. 59. Buffier, like G. L. Le
Sage, was an early disciple of Locke; in his works he attempts a synthesis of Cartesianism
and of empiricism, and several of his theories were utilized by Montesquieu. See below, and
also Heikki Kirkinen, *La Conception de l'Homme Machine*, Helsinki, 1960.
[78] C. P. Duclos, *Considérations sur les Moeurs de ce Siècle*, 1750, ch. I.
[79] See *Two Treatises of Civil Government*, ed. P. Laslett, Cambridge, 1960, introduction, IV,
pp. 82–84.
[80] *Spicilège*, 8. Montesquieu possessed the 1717 edition of Mariotte's *Oeuvres*, see *Catalogue
de la Brède*, No. 1499, p. 110.

not unlikely that his theories on volume in gases were among the many
scientific topics discussed by the Academy of Bordeaux. His ideas on
ethics were probably less well known. In the *Essai de Logique* he makes
considerable use of the notion of conformity and appears at least at
first sight, to take up an idealist position. He there suggests that in
morals as in mathematics certain self-evident principles exist:

"Il y a de ces propositions qui sont reçues sans qu'on en puisse douter,
comme 'il faut faire ce qui est le mieux'; on les appellera propositions morales premières, ou principes du devoir." [81]

Besides self-evidence, principles such as doing the best, giving to those
in need, or respecting another's property, possess the quality of *convenance*. Mariotte does not define *convenance*, but he implies that these
first principles reveal an inherent orderliness or justice in the actions
they describe. Action in accordance with them constitutes virtue. However, in spite of the fact that virtue is its own reward, it also brings
respect and personal advantage.[82] This element of personal satisfaction,
which is quite distinct from the spiritual pleasure derived from virtue,
holds the key to the other side of Mariotte's theory. For although *convenance* is established as a moral criterion, it is formally associated with
aesthetic satisfaction rather than with reason:

"Il y a deux sortes principales de plaisirs de l'esprit: ceux de l'honneur,
comme d'être loués et aimés, d'être plus parfaits et d'avoir plus de pouvoir
que les autres; et ceux de convenance, comme celui qu'on reçoit de la lecture d'une belle poésie, de la vue d'une maison bien faite suivant les règles
de l'architecture." [83]

A virtuous action is *bien faite* rather than rational, in spite of the self-
evidence of moral principles. Thus pleasure is taken to be the strongest
motive in human conduct, and when the individual is faced with a
choice between the duties arising from the principle of *convenance*, and
those which Mariotte sees as the consequences of natural self-interest,
the latter dominate, since they give greatest satisfaction.[84] This being
the case, Mariotte concludes that practical ethics must be placed on a
purely pragmatic basis. Experience and the practical wisdom of the
proverbs are the surest guides for the individual; and for society, legislation must ensure that natural duty and moral duty coincide, by establishing harsh penalties against self-interest.[85]

[81] *Op. cit., Oeuvres de Mariotte*, Leyden, 1717, part I, art. lvii, p. 625.
[82] *Ibid.*, part I, arts. lxxvi–lxxxii.
[83] *Ibid.*, part I, art. lxxv.
[84] *Ibid.*, part II, section 2, art. iii, pp. 666–668.
[85] *Ibid.*

Thus, in effect, Mariotte's systematic theory of morals based on the ideal criterion of fitness or proportion is superfluous. Once this notion is dissociated from reason, or from something that may be regarded as both transcendent principle and human faculty, it looses all meaning. Pleasure may provide a strong motive, but it is a law unto itself. Within the framework which Mariotte provides, *convenance* could have practical as well as theoretical relevance, only if he were to advance the ludicrous proposition that pleasure is associated exclusively with the contemplation of proportion in things and with nothing else. This of course, he had no intention of doing. His theories are given no real development in the *Essai de Logique*; but we may interpret them as anticipating in some ways those that Locke advances in the *Essay concerning Human Understanding:* independent moral principles do exist, but man has no innate knowledge of them, and does not necessarily pursue them.[86] Alternatively, we may suggest that he presents a naturalistic psychological analysis, and positivist solutions, which are more closely related to Hobbes's theories, or to those of his countrymen who were prepared to affirm, at least in private, the relativity of moral values.

For clandestine pamphlets and tracts were most often the vehicle for the most outspoken criticisms of established ideas and institutions. Among them, Nicolas Fréret's *Lettre de Thrasibule à Leucippe* has some interest for us. Fréret, a learned sinologist, whose advanced views earned him a short stay in the Bastille, was one of Montesquieu's earliest acquaintances among the learned circles of Paris. Montesquieu was probably introduced to him by their common friend Father Desmolets, librarian of the Paris Oratory, and Fréret's old schoolmaster.[87] Like Boulainviller, his close acquaintance, Fréret drew many of his ideas from Spinoza, and although neither of them ever progressed beyond an elementary exposition of his philosophy, they helped to spread the influence of the critical methods employed in the *Tractatus theologico-politicus* throughout French thought. The *Lettre de Thrasibule à Leucippe* was circulated anonymously, but there seems little doubt of its authorship.[88]

[86] See *op. cit.*, I, iii, 6.

[87] See Shackleton, *Montesquieu*, I, pp. 10–12. Shackleton bases himself on a letter from Montesquieu to Desmolets, of April 4th, 1716.

[88] The case against the assignation of the *Lettre* to Fréret is presented in considerable detail as far as documentation is concerned, by Renée Simon in her work, *Nicolas Fréret*, published in *Studies on Voltaire and the 18th. century*, ed. Bestermann, XVII, 1961. She suggests in ch. XIII that the publication of this work and of the *Examen critique des apologistes* under Fréret's name was arranged by the Holbach group, with Voltaire's connivance; and that its real author was Naigeon. However, she brings no conclusive evidence to disprove Fréret's authorship of the *Lettre*, rather than of the *Examen critique*; and she does not comment at any length on the claim that Rousseau knew the *Lettre* before the composition of the

In it we find the basic Spinozistic conception of God as the totality of things set out, and Fréret follows this up with an explanation of what the universal law consists in. If God is the universe, then this law must be based on the relationships between things:

"Cette loi nécessaire qu'est-elle elle-même? Est-elle distinguée de lui et des êtres, ou des perceptions qu'il en a? N'est-ce que la perception des rapports de convenance ou de disconvenance qui sont entre les choses, ou leurs idées?"[89]

If evidence were available to show that Montesquieu actually examined the *Lettre de Thrasibule à Leucippe*, this definition of law would be of considerable importance for the study of his ideas. As it is, we are in a position to make only one definite statement, namely that Montesquieu knew Fréret by at least 1716; it is possible that if Fréret was in fact contemplating the composition of the *Lettre*, he may have discussed some of its theories with his friends. The dating of manuscript copies is uncertain, and no published version dating from before 1762 is extant, so that the likelihood of Montesquieu's coming across the *Lettre*, at least before the composition of the *Lettres Persanes*, is somewhat remote.[90] Nevertheless the idea here presented, that law is associated with relationships of conformity, may be of some importance for the definition of law given in the *Esprit des Lois*.[91] This mention of law suggests another possibility; Maupertuis, as we have already seen, also used the phrase "rapport de convenance" in his *Essai de Cosmologie*.[92] Now, although this is a much later work, it is significant that Montesquieu, Fréret, and Maupertuis knew each other, and during the 1720s frequented much the same society in Paris. Maupertuis and Fréret were, along with Duclos, La Motte and Saurin, frequenters of the Café Procope. We may therefore assume that this and similar notions were often used in their discussions of scientific and philosophical topics.

Both Fréret and Maupertuis use the phrase in relation to natural phenomena, as part of their demonstration of cosmological theories

---

Discours sur l'inégalité, 1754, the claim examined by J. P. Free in *Rousseau's use of the "Examen de la Religion" and of the "Lettre de Thrasibule à Leucippe,"* Princeton, 1935. Circulation of the manuscript before 1754 would cast doubt on the attribution to Naigeon.

[89] *Lettre de Thrasibule à Leucippe*, *Oeuvres complètes*, London, 1775, vol. IV, p. 97.

[90] The dating of all 18th century editions is given by R. Simon, *Nicolas Fréret*, ch. 13. One of the first London editions contains a prefatory note dating the composition of the Letter as 1722, but no confidence can be placed in this.

[91] *Lois* I, 1. It was Montesquieu's definition of laws as "rapports nécessaires qui dérivent de la nature des choses," which most worried contemporary commentators, see Shackleton, *Montesquieu*, ch. XI. It is therefore interesting that Fréret also talks of necessary law and of the relationships between things in the same breath.

[92] See above, p. 31.

which reject the idea of a transcendent order. It is true that in the *Essai de Cosmologie*, Maupertuis himself embraces a teleological view of the universe; but when he actually mentions "rapports de convenance", he is setting out the materialist theory which he wishes to refute,

". . . ne pourrait-on pas dire que dans la combinaison fortuite des productions de la nature, comme il n'y avait que celles où se trouvaient certains rapports de convenance, qui pussent subsiter, il n'est pas merveilleux que cette convenance, se trouve dans toutes les espèces qui actuellement existent?" [93]

We are back again with the conviction of 18th century scientific rationalism, that, whatever its provenance, there is a necessary structural pattern in things, an order which will yield to human intelligence.[94] Stripped of its philosophical associations, it is the basic mathematical notion of correspondence between terms, upon which the whole of modern physics is built. It could then be the starting point for a definition of scientific law (though it hardly enters into the modern conception of scientific laws as descriptive summaries based on statistical evidence); and it is noticeable that Fréret's idea of necessary law is quite unconnected with any theory of universal justice. Depending on one's point of view, one may regard Spinozism proper, as the ultimate in rational idealism; but it admits no transcendent forces, no sanctions except those operating through natural limitations. This was the kind of point that nascent materialism could utilize, without swallowing the corpus of metaphysical theory at the same time. And indeed Fréret's moral theory is founded on the law of natural inclinations, of observed tendencies. Moral attributes are only comprehensible in the light of human pleasure or pain; they have no absolute value. Thus we are again presented with the ideal of conformity with nature, in its sensible rather than its rational form.

"Quant au coeur, c'est-à-dire, au sentiment et à la volonté, il est vrai que j'y vois une loi gravée dès le premier instant de son existence, c'est-à-dire, l'amour du plaisir et l'aversion de la douleur; cette loi est généralement observée par tous les hommes... Cette loi a attaché le plaisir aux actions propres et même nécessaires à notre conservation; elle a attaché la douleur à

---

[93] *Essai de Cosmologie*, I, *Oeuvres complètes*, Lyons, 1768, vol. I, p. 10.

[94] The "Discours préliminaire" of the *Encyclopédie* provides an authoritative statement of this conviction: "L'usage des connaissances mathématiques n'est pas moins grand dans l'examen des corps terrestres qui nous environnent. Toutes les propriétés que nous observons dans ces corps ont entr'elles des rapports plus ou moins sensibles pour nous: la connaissance ou la découverte de ces rapports est presque toujours le seul objet auquel il nous est permis d'atteindre, et le seul par conséquent que nous devions nous proposer.", vol. I, p. vi.

celles qui y sont contraires; et par un instinct naturel, l'amour du plaisir nous porte nécessairement à faire les unes, et l'aversion de la douleur à éviter les autres."[95]

Instinct is the principle of the moral law, not reason. The latter is limited to a comparative function; its role is to compare and choose between impressions. The reasonable man may be described as agreeing with the majority opinion of what constitutes pleasure and pain; the prudent man is he who shares common conceptions with his neighbour.[96] Normality, not virtue, is the bond of society, and social utility is the measure of justice. It could only be founded on equality if all men were reasonable; but, declares Fréret, this is not the case. So it is that laws are relative to the society that makes them, and conceptions of virtue and vice, purely a matter of habit.[97]

But although reason as an independent criterion of belief and action has been banished from the scene, it is interesting to see that the old ideal of moderation, given a slightly different interpretation, is still to be found.

"Ceux-là passent pour raisonnables qui s'accordent avec les autres hommes dans ce qu'ils regardent comme le plus grand plaisir et la plus grande douleur, comme ceux-là passent pour sensés et pour prudents qui paraissent apercevoir les objets de la même manière dont les voient les autres hommes";

in essence, this is simply a materialist's version of the 17th century idea that for the sake of self-respect as well as common comfort, it was necessary to observe certain conventions. As we have already noted it is the naturalistic elements of the 17th century moral outlook which survive into the 18th. But the important change, important for our own organic conception of society and for the emergence of social psychology, as well as for the development of primitive theories of environment already present in the work of Fénelon, Du Bos and others, and perfected by Montesquieu, is the linking of ideas of moderation and of social convention, with the broad-based notion of group consciousness.[98] The 17th century thought of ethics in terms of an individual creed sup-

[95] *Lettre de Thrasibule à Leucippe, Oeuvres Complètes*, IV, pp. 108–109.
[96] *Ibid.*
[97] *Ibid.*, pp. 115–116.
[98] For the history of the evolution of the theory of environment, see K. S. Laurila, *Les Premiers devanciers français de la théorie du milieu*, Helsinki, 1928, published in the annals of the Finnish Academy of Science, series B., vol. XXII. He deals with Bodin, Chardin, Fontenelle, Fénelon and Du Bos. Similar theories, arising out of the study of religion in relation to political development, were put forward in England by Warburton. In the *Alliance between Church and State*, 1736, he establishes the existence of a national personality distinct from the aggregated personalities of its members.

ported by universal conceptions; the 18th began to regard them as the product of society, determined by particular circumstances and characteristics. As regards our present study, this change of attitude involved explaining the notion of *convenance*, conformity or convention in terms of phenomena not of ideals.

The transformation of the idea of *convenance* is best illustrated in the work of another curious figure of the first half of the 18th century. Like Fréret, Saint-Hyacinthe was a propagandist of philosophic ideas, a writer of pamphlets and short discourses, where theories derived from a variety of sources, but mainly from Spinoza were boiled down to make new and sometimes indigestible systems. In temperament however, Saint-Hyacinthe was the diametric opposite of the erudite historian and orientalist. He was a soldier of fortune who left his native France, embraced Protestantism, and settled more or less permanently in England, where, during his visit from 1729–31, Montesquieu made his acquaintance.[99] The President was in due course presented with a copy of his *Letters giving an account of several conversations upon important and entertaining subjects*, a kind of 18th century *Canterbury tales* where in an account of a journey through Holland, serious philosophical discussion rubs shoulders with licentious anecdote.[100] In this and a later work, materialist tendencies come slowly to fruition. The strongest impression they give is of a mind crowded with conflicting theories, each cancelling the other out, which finally takes refuge in materialism, as the only view of the world answering the practical demands of living. Sensationalist epistemological theories seem to have acted as a catalyst in this process, for a typical feature of the second work, the *Recherches philosophiques*, is the fitting of notions drawn from Locke into existing Cartesian formulae.[101] The following definitions are typical examples of this procedure: *évidence* is defined as "le sentiment d'une chose si nécessaire que le contraire est impossible"; and knowledge of truth as "la conformité du jugement avec la nature des choses."[102]

The *Letters giving an account of several conversations* are still ostensibly the

[99] See Shackleton, *Montesquieu*, VI, p. 134.

[100] London, 1731, 2 vols.; *Catalogue de la Brède*, No. 2304, p. 164.

[101] This procedure is characteristic of eclectics in the first half of the century; we have already mentioned Claude Buffier (see above, p. 57, n. 77). The marquis d'Argens's *La philosophie du bon sens*, 1737, provides other typical examples: "on peut aussi bien prouver l'existence, en disant 'je sens, donc je suis,' qu'en disant, 'je pense, donc je suis' ", edition of 1747, The Hague, p. 211.

[102] *Recherches philosophiques sur la nécessité de s'assurer par soi-même de la vérité, sur la certitude de nos connaissances et sur la nature des êtres*, Rotterdam and the Hague, 1743; Book II, ch. 3, para. 79; Book II, ch. 1, para, 54.

work of a deist; the second volume is almost entirely taken up by an exposition of the basic tenets of deism, and we find again such characteristics as the submission of religious dogma to the criterion of *évidence*, the rejection of miracles, the idea of the necessity of a first cause, and the associated proof that nothing can produce nothing, that it possesses no properties.[103]

But in spite of these features, there is a disturbing section in the second volume, allegedly designed to refute Baylien ideas on the virtues of atheism, which in fact does just the reverse, and which sketches in the main lines of the materialist argument developed in the later work. Saint-Hyacinthe's declared intention in Letter x is to prove that without supernatural sanctions, there is no basis for morality or justice; and the argument centres around the notion of fitness, against which he measures the materialist claim that happiness is the sole concern of ethics:

"One thing, which has the most contributed to their error, who have maintained that independent of the positive will of God, and of future rewards and punishment, justice and injustice, our rights and duties, were founded upon the fitness of things, is the not observing that there is no obligation to act one way rather than another, so long as there is no inconvenience for him that is to act, to act one way more than another; that things require no conforming to them, farther than as they are fitting for him who is to act: and that he who is to act, in order to act according to reason, ought to act no farther, than as he makes himself the happier; because well-being is the only thing necessarily fitting and suitable to being."[104]

In this passage, the three main conceptions of *convenance*, which we may roughly describe as the 17th century teleological, the 18th century naturalist/materialist, and the intermediary immanentist, are brought together, and the essential weakness of the latter is effectively described.

This line of argument, characterized in the text as relativist, is taken up much more vigorously in the *Recherches Philosophiques sur la nécessité de s'assurer par soi-même de la vérité, sur la certitude de nos connaissances et sur la nature des êtres*. Here the pretence of proving the necessity of a transcendent will disappears, and the influence of Spinoza appears more pronounced.[105] Saint-Hyacinthe's moral theory is now reduced to the proposition that, because the nature of things is necessarily determined,

---

[103] *Op. cit.*, vol. II, letter XVI; vol. I, letter V; vol. II, letter XV.

[104] *Op. cit.*, vol. II, Letter X, pp. 291–92.

[105] In the *Letters*, Saint-Hyacinthe actually attempted a refutation of Spinoza, following lines similar to that made by Montesquieu in the unused fragment of the *Traité des Devoirs*, *Pensée* 1266 (Bkn. 615): "We are going to confound same with like, and shall presently say the Emperor of China is a chimney sweeper; a rock is a snail, etc." Letter 14, p. 451.

and happiness consists in the fulfilment of the demands of one's relative nature, then to act in accordance with reason and truth is to pursue satisfaction and the perfection of one's nature.[106] The attainment of happiness is the only true motive in human behaviour, and the only end of existence.

"J'entends par vertu, le courage de pratiquer ce que la raison exige, c'est-à-dire, la conformité des sentiments et des actions selon ce qui est le plus convenable au bonheur";[107]

there is no longer any question of the *convenance* of things being related to any transcendent principle: "*convenance* à la nature" is the only moral ideal which may be admitted, and one may only talk of *convenance* in things if they make a positive contribution to the attainment of natural ends:

"L'effet que font les choses selon ce degré auquel elles contribuent ou nuisent au bonheur, est ce qu'on appelle leurs convenances ou leurs disconvenances, et en ce sens on peut dire que les choses ont plus ou moins de convenances eu égard à l'état auquel elles conviennent."[108]

Thus conformity is now related to immanent, not cosmic teleology, and it is a relative quality. However, since the pursuit of happiness is synonymous with virtue, it follows that law and justice will continue to be founded on the relationships of conformity between things:

"C'est sur ces convenances ou ces disconvenances, et sur la nécessité que le bien être soit le but de l'être, que sont fondés ce qu'on appelle le bien et le mal moral ... l'ordre et le désordre, la vertu et le vice, le juste et l'injuste, les droits et les devoirs d'un être ... C'est ce qui fait que ces droits et ces devoirs ont été appelés naturels et que la raison sur laquelle ils sont fondés, c'est-à-dire cet amour du bonheur, cette tendance de l'être à sa perfection, a été nommé loi de nature, car on entend par nature, l'essence des choses, c'est-à-dire, les propriétés nécessaires à leur existence et ce qui en résulte nécessairement, et c'est de là qu'on a dit que les droits et les devoirs naturels étaient inaltérables et inviolables, parce qu'ils résultent des propriétés nécessaires à un être capable de bonheur et de perfection, d'une tendance nécessaire à se procurer tout le bonheur et la perfection dont il est capable et à s'y conserver s'il y était parvenu."[109]

The influence of Spinoza is indisputable, as a brief comparison of this passage with the most distinctive section of the *Tractatus* shows:

[106] *Recherches Philosophiques*, Bk. III, paras. 158–160.
[107] *Ibid.*, para. 154, p. 244.
[108] *Ibid.*, para. 160, p. 249.
[109] *Recherches Philosophiques*, Bk. III, para. 161, pp. 249–50.

"By the right and ordinance of nature I understand nothing but the conditions of the nature of each individual thing in accordance with which we conceive each individual thing to be determined by nature to live and act in a definite way...."[110]

The *Ethica* was less well known in France, but although Spinoza's moral theory is there more highly developed, its basic message remains unchanged: there is no moral law as distinct from natural law, the good for each thing is that which helps it to exist, and the ability to secure this good is virtue.[111]

The change of emphasis which has taken place in the *Recherches Philosophiques*, by comparison with the *Letters giving an account of several conversations*, is so great that one might even begin to suspect a change of author, were it not for certain identical phrases in the two works, and their characteristically repetitive style. There is also a brief mention in the *Recherches*, of the idea that justice is invariable if it is related to a transcendent force, but this is now plainly reduced to the level of a doubtful hypothesis. If this were so however, and celestial happiness was to be attained, then one might speak of "convenances invariables"; but the truth is more likely to be that legislators proclaim the existence of eternal punishments and rewards, in order to enforce their own laws. Natural law is necessary in origin; but its content is always relative to the individual condition, just as the particular laws and customs of a state are variable and relative to the nature of its people.[112]

Thus the transformation is complete. Fitness in things is a relative quality; it does not witness to divine creation, nor to the ultimate goodness and perfection of the universe. It is the basis of justice, but of a justice which is relative only to the individual nature, condition and needs. The ideal of conformity with nature has been taken to its logical extremity, and there is no longer cause for reason, equity or charity to moderate the spontaneous striving of the individual towards fulfilment.

[110] *Tractatus Theologico-Politicus*, XVI, 175.
[111] *Ethica*, IV, 20.
[112] *Recherches Philosophiques*, Bk. III, para. 161.

CHAPTER FOUR

ENGLISH THINKERS

A study of the part played by the idea of *convenance* in the elaboration of moral theories in the opening years of the 18th century, could hardly pretend to be complete without mention of the English. The political upheavals which mark the period: the war of the League of Augsburg running into the war of the Spanish Succession; religious persecution and economic depression in France; bitter mercantile rivalry between England, Holland and France; the revolution of 1688 in England and the establishment of William of Orange on the English throne, followed by Louis XIV's espousal of the Stuart cause; all this, and the inevitable refugee movements that accompanied it, led to a weakening of cultural barriers and an exchange of ideas, in which English influence began to play an increasingly dominant role.[1] In matters of political philosophy, natural science, and economic theory, matters which closely affected the state of France, her men of science and letters began to look across the narrow seas to the country hitherto regarded by popular opinion as barbaric, but which now gave proof of the prosperity and political vigour so manifestly lacking at home. In the preceding chapters we have tried to examine the contribution made to moral philosophy by a few outstanding figures in French literary circles, and to gauge the extent to which certain ideas became embedded in the national consciousness by reference to the works of several other relatively obscure writers. But from the last decade of the 17th century onwards English ideas and theories are a factor to be considered in major as well as minor works. Of course, these theories spring from a common European tradition, and although they may be regarded as instrumental in establish-

---

[1] George Ascoli's *La Grande Bretagne devant l'opinion française aux 16e et 17e siècles*, Paris, 1927, 1930, is invaluable in assessing the extent of this influence up to this period. P. Hazard's *La Crise de la Conscience européenne*, Paris, 1935, deals with English influences in various fields; see especially part I, ch. 3; part III, chs. 1, 4, 5, 6. C. A. Rochedieu's *Bibliography of French translations of English works 1700–1800*, Chicago, 1948, is a useful guide to later periods.

ing the dominance of empiricism in philosophy and science, it is often difficult, in view of the fact that some of them result from parallel developments in thought in which French influences have played their part, to estimate the extent to which they innovate as opposed to merely complementing or reinforcing notions already well established.

The notion of *convenance* undoubtedly possessed a long history in French thought, and the English moral treatises which drew on the idea of conformity or fitness were probably influenced by similar classical models if not also by French works. We have already mentioned the influence of Malebranche in England; and we should not forget the great esteem in which French aesthetic theories were held also.[2] Perhaps it is also significant that several English philosophers of the 17th century had occasion to travel in France, either in the course of their duties as tutors to young noblemen or as a result of political changes which conflicted with their sympathies. Although he can scarcely be called an idealist, Hobbes made several visits to France for both of these reasons, became the close friend of Gassendi, and there acquired the main outlines of his general philosophy. This naturally included an enthusiasm for geometry, which is perhaps reflected in his conception of natural law. Even Hobbes is ready to associate reason with certain "convenient articles of peace," although the great obstacle to their observance is the combination of natural passions and a lawless state:

"The passions that incline men to peace, are fear of death; desire of such things as are necessary to commodious living; and a hope by their industry to obtain them. And reason suggests the convenient articles of peace, upon which men may be drawn to agreement. These articles, are they, which otherwise are called laws of nature: whereof I shall speak more particularly."[3]

John Locke likewise spent his years of exile travelling in France and Holland, and there met at first hand the disciples of Gassendi and Descartes. But whatever the provenance of English ideas of fitness and conformity, and as regards the Cambridge neo-platonists, the main representatives of rational idealism in moral philosophy, we are ill equipped to suggest formative influences other than those implied by their designation, it is important that the works of Cudworth, Locke, and Locke's pupil Shaftesbury were among the first to make a widespread impression on French thought at the turn of the century.

The English works were put into French, analysed and reviewed by

---

[2] For the influence of Malebranche in England, see above p. 9.
[3] *Leviathan*, 1651, I, 13.

the French Protestant exiles in the Low Countries and in England. First among these was Pierre Coste, the translator and friend of Shaftesbury and Locke, colleague of Newton in the Royal Society, and translator of the *Optics*. His translation of Locke's *Essay concerning Human Understanding*, the version possessed by Montesquieu, was one of the most important works of the first half of the century; and he was also responsible for the translation of Locke's *Reasonableness of Christianity* in 1696. Of Locke's other works, the *Two Treatises of Civil Government* were reviewed by Jean Le Clerc in volume 19 of the *Bibliothèque Universelle*,[4] and the second was translated by a Huguenot pastor, David Maazel, also living in Holland.[5] Jean Le Clerc was a friend of Coste and of Shaftesbury, as well as a correspondent of Fontenelle, Leibniz and Vico; the *Bibliothèque Choisie*, one of his other periodicals, also carried important reviews of Shaftesbury's *Letter Concerning Enthusiasm*, which appeared in translation at the Hague in 1708.[6] Shaftesbury's *Essay on the Freedom of Wit and Humour* was translated by both Coste and J. van Effen in 1710 and the complete edition of the *Characteristics* published in 1711, was reviewed by Leibniz in his *Jugement sur les Oeuvres de Shaftesbury*, which appeared in London in the same year, and again later in the *Recueil de Diverses Pièces sur la Philosophie*, another major publication containing essays by Newton and Collins, brought out by another eminent Frenchman in London, Pierre Desmaizeaux.[7] The *Recueil de Diverses Pièces* also contained the correspondence between Leibniz and Samuel Clarke, disciple of Newton and rationalist theologian. His famous Boyle lectures of 1704 and 1705 were translated by Ricotier in 1717.[8] The sermons of yet another noted English latitudinarian, Archbishop Tillotson, were translated by no less a person than the jurisconsult Jean Barbeyrac.[9] These are only a few of the English works that found their way into French libraries during the first quarter of the 18th century, as a result of the labours of Coste, Desmaizeaux and others like them.

Some of them quite naturally found their way into Montesquieu's library at La Brède. He possessed for example the *Recueil de Diverses*

[4] Amsterdam, 1691, pp. 559–573.
[5] *Du Gouvernement Civil*, Amsterdam, 1691.
[6] *Bibliothèque Choisie*, vol. XIX, 1709.
[7] Amsterdam, 1720; a detailed account of the reviews and translations of Shaftesbury is given by E. Casati in "Hérauts et Commentateurs de Shaftesbury en France," *Revue de Littérature comparée*, XIV, 1934; p. 615.
[8] *De l'Existence et des Attributs de Dieu*, Amsterdam, 1717.
[9] Amsterdam, 1713–1718.

Pièces,[10] and the inventory of his Paris library lists Shaftesbury. More surprising, considering that Montesquieu seems unlikely to have read much English before his visit in 1729, are the number of works which he possesses in the original English version in editions published before that date. It is of course probable that he acquired earlier editions during his visit, however. Shaftesbury's *Characteristics* he had in the edition of 1714;[11] and the Catalogue of La Bredè also lists a copy of Clarke's *Discourse on the Being and Attributes of God* in the London edition of 1728.[12] The influence of Steele and Addison's *Spectator* was strong in France,[13] and Montesquieu was obviously attracted by the ideal of good-humoured modesty which it presented, for the Catalogue lists at least two editions, and it appears again in the Paris inventory.[14] Steele's *Le Philosophe Nouvelliste* also appears in the Catalogue.[15] Apart from details given in the Catalogue however, Montesquieu's references are an invaluable source of information.[16] Thus a reference to Cudworth in the *Dissertation sur la Politique des Romains dans la Religion*, read at the Academy of Bordeaux in 1716, reveals a very early acquaintance with the English philosopher's work.[17] In the *Spicilège* Montesquieu describes the works of Tillotson as being good examples of English style.[18] And the use made in both the *Discours sur la Transparence des Corps*, and the *Essai d'Observations sur l'Histoire Naturelle*, of Newton's theories of reflection and refraction of light, shows a sound knowledge of Coste's translation of the *Optics*.[19] He was by no means unprepared for his visit to England two years after the death of Newton, and for his meetings, not only with the leading members of the learned world, but also with those same Frenchmen, Pierre Coste, the secretary of Lady Masham, Ralph Cudworth's daughter, and Pierre Desmaizeaux, whose labours had helped in this preparation, and whose wide and influential contacts

[10] *Catalogue de la Brède*, ed., Desgraves; art. 1532, p. 112.
[11] *Ibid.*, No. 696, p. 52.
[12] *Ibid.*, No. 432, p. 34.
[13] See G. Ascoli, *La Grande-Bretagne devant l'Opinion française au XVIIe siècle*, vol. II, Bk. iii, ch, 5, section v, d.; and P. Hazard, *La Crise de la Conscience européenne*, part III, ch. 7.
[14] *Catalogue*, p. 52, Nos. 701, 2, Amsterdam ed. of 1717, and 9th. London ed. 1729; Inventory of the Paris Library, Appendix I of the Catalogue, No. 34.
[15] *Catalogue* No. 652, p. 49.
[16] Lists of authors cited in Montesquieu's main works are given by P. Barrière in *Un Grand Provincial, Montesquieu*, part I, ch. v, section 3, pp. 199–201.
[17] Nagel III, p. 44.
[18] *Op. cit.*, 560.
[19] *Discours sur la Transparence des Corps*, 1720, Nagel III, p. 96; *Essai d'Observations*, 1719–1721, Nagel III, p. 100. Montesquieu also possessed Coste's translation of Lock'e *Essay* in the Amsterdam ed. of 1700, and the 1710 Rotterdam ed. of the *Oeuvres Diverses*, Catalogue, Nos. 1489, 1490, p. 109.

now contributed to the consolidation of his knowledge of English thought and customs.[20]

Bearing in mind that Montesquieu probably possessed considerable knowledge of the major English works on moral philosophy produced at the end of the 17th century, and in the early years of the 18th, long before his visit to England,[21] we must now examine the place which the notion of fitness occupies in some of them.

Locke is often regarded as the father of sensationalism, and at least as far as French thought is concerned, the prophet and high priest of materialism. It commonly happens that the intellectual climate of one country will tolerate only those elements of an alien doctrine that appear to favour a current of thought which is already beginning to rise above conflicting streams, and needs only a little reinforcement to sweep home in flood. Perhaps too many in cultured circles preferred Voltaire's introduction to M. Locke in the *Lettres Philosophiques*, to Pierre Coste's fine translation of 1700; and Voltaire himself, exercising his journalistic flair in decanting from a considerable treatise, only those elements which served his own opinions and were likely to satisfy the particular curiosities of his audience, provides us with a prime example of the way in which philosophical systems are naturally distorted in the process of absorbtion by a foreign culture. Voltaire channels his reader's attention to three aspects of Locke's doctrine: the rejection of innate ideas, the possibility that matter may be endowed with the faculty of thought, the effect this has on the hotly debated question of animal souls; and all this in the cause of pouring scorn on the theologians.[22] As Paul Hazard points out, Locke became a materialist in spite of himself. True, he rejected the doctrine of eternal torment; and he reduced the articles of faith to a minimum; but his real object in *Reasonable Christianity*, was to reconcile to revealed religion those alienated by the spectacle of warring sects and quibbling theologians. Whatever his tentative suggestions in the *Essay concerning Human Understanding*, Locke was not even a Deist properly speaking, let alone a materialist.[23]

It is therefore not surprising to learn that Locke began his career as a

[20] For an account of Montesquieu's visit, and details of his encounters, see Shackleton. *Montesquieu*, ch. VI.

[21] In his critical edition of the *Lettres Persanes*, Paris, Garnier, 1960, Paul Vernière gives complete lists of Montesquieu's sources, both certain and probable; it appears from these that Thomas Burnet was an influence in Letter 113, and Shaftesbury in possibly four letters, 10, 83, 94, 104; see *op. cit.*, Introduction p. xxiv. Shackleton sees the influence of Samuel Clarke in the vestiges of the lost *Traité des Devoirs*; see *Montesquieu*, ch. IV, p. 71.

[22] *Lettres Philosophiques*, 1734, Letter 13.

[23] See Paul Hazard, *La Crise de la Conscience européenne*, part III, ch. 1.

philosopher of the idealist school. This was not known in his own day
outside his immediate circle of acquaintances, although of course, passages on natural law, and on the finitude of the material universe in the
Essay on Human Understanding, were proof enough of an unwillingness to
undermine the validity of transcendent criteria.[24] Locke's early essays
on natural law, the product of his idealist period, were not published
until our own day,[25] although they date from the years 1654–1664.
They are interesting from several points of view: for the ideas presented
in them, and for the ways in which they anticipate the Essay of 1690.
For instance, in the fifth essay of Van Leyden's edition which deals with
the argument from general consent, there is a long account of the comparative customs and laws of various nations, barbaric and civilized,
where Locke attempts to establish factual evidence for the standard
rule of morality which he has posited. Besides breaking entirely new
ground, the position adopted by Locke in this embryonic study of comparative law, anticipates in some ways that of Montesquieu in the *Esprit des Lois*: one recognizes the strange marriage of observational science and idealism; with regard to the *Essay concerning Human Understanding* however, it represents the start of a gradual transformation
leading to a complete reversal of attitude. For in the Essay of 1690,
Locke argues that the great variety of customs among nations is positive
proof that no universal, innate principles exist.[26]

Yet although the early essays grew out of a discussion with his friend
Gabriel Towerson on the question whether the law of nature,

"can be evinced from the force of conscience in those men who have no
other divine law to square their actions by,"[27]

it is not really true to say that Locke ever embraced the nativist standpoint. He maintains consistently throughout his works, that man attains to the knowledge of God and of natural laws by the exercise of his
natural faculties, that is, the senses and reason; but the implications of
this conviction are not fully worked out in the early essays, whereas in
the definitive work, he has come to realise the length and complexity of
this exercise. On the basis of Locke's chiefly consistent attitude to the
processes of knowledge, and his agreement in this with his friend Arch-

---

[24] *Op. cit.*, Bk. I, ch. 3; bk. IV, ch. 10.

[25] The manuscripts of the Lovelace collection were edited by W. van Leyden, and
published at Oxford, 1954.

[26] *Op. cit.*, Bk. I, ch. 3.

[27] Letter from Towerson to Locke c. 1661–65, quoted in Van Leyden's Introduction to
the Essays.

bishop Tillotson, who, while contending that the principles of natural religion could be ascertained by reason alone, interpreted reason not as innate perception but rather clear ratiocination,[28] it might be possible to suggest that English idealism generally relied on a very different epistemological foundation from its French counterpart. But this is beyond the scope of our study. We must press on to consider the place of the idea of fitness in Locke's treatment of natural law.

Locke's reasoning with regard to the relationship between God and the universe rests on a teleological basis similar to that of Leibniz. While the design apparent in the universe is presented as a proof of the existence of God, the proposition that God is accordingly omnipotent, and omniscient, is put forward as evidence that the universe was built with a purpose, and that all its parts are endowed with a rule or pattern of life appropriate to their nature. Whatever the logical defects in this argument, it is clear that Locke wished to emphasize the conformity he saw between the nature of man and his divinely appointed role in the scheme of things. Of all creatures, man alone has the faculty of reason; it is therefore obvious that God requires him to live according to reason. Following the well trodden Aristotelian path, Locke goes on to affirm that the special function of the rational creature is to worship God and to live in society with other men. But, and in relation to the main stream of rational idealism, this is a very important but, the natural law which these special functions imply, is not so-called, and neither is it self-enforcing, because it derives from supernatural reason; on the contrary, it partakes of the nature of law, because it satisfies the requisite of any and every law established by reason and sense experience; that is to say, it emanates from the positive will of a superior power, to which man is subject. Locke calls it a natural law, because knowledge of it is acquired by the joint exercise of man's natural faculties, it is a law promulgated by God in a natural way rather than by revelation; because it conforms to the natural constitution of the universe, and with the nature of man; and because its precepts are universally binding; that is to say, that like the laws governing natural phenomena, and unlike statutory laws, they do not vary from place to place.

Thus it is clear that the notion of conformity fulfils two important functions in Locke's moral thought: the conformity which is posited between human nature and the content of the natural law is essential to

---

[28] This interpretation of Tillotson's conception of reason is given by D. Brown in *An edition of selected sermons of John Tillotson*, a thesis presented for the degree of M.A. at London University, 1956.

the epistemological argument: by the combined operation of natural faculties man attains to knowledge of the existence of moral law and of its dictates. Secondly, this conformity plays a vital role in the exposition of the nature and extent of obligation, which Locke presents in the seventh of his early essays. Here the idea of *convenientia* is put in its proper perspective. The primary or formal cause of obligation, that is of the binding force of natural law, is purely arbitrary; it consists in the divine will. But at a secondary level, and here again the resemblance to Leibniz's notion of a "nécessité de convenance" is noticeable,[29] obligation derives from the conformity which exists between God's will and its creation, between man's nature and his purpose as a rational being. Thus, taking a short view, one may derive obligation from a material cause: the nature of man. The suitableness of moral values to the essential nature of man provides law with a natural foundation, and makes human reason a self-dependent source of obligation. But when it comes to isolating the ultimate source of moral determination, one must look beyond the teleological interpretation of human nature, beyond the notion of fitness, to the inexplicable will of God.

In his introduction to Locke's *Essays on the Law of Nature*, Van Leyden suggests that Locke took the term *convenientia* from Culverwel's discussion of the notion of harmony between human nature and law, and of the origin of natural obligation, in the *Discourse of the Light of Nature*.[30] Culverwel, he adds, took it from Scholasticism, and in particular from a treatise by Vasquez.[31] Thus Locke at least cannot be associated with any resurgent interest in Stoicism. The seventh essay does however contain a comparison between mathematical necessity and moral obligation. Locke here declares that it follows from the nature of man to observe the law of nature, just as it follows from the nature of a triangle that its three angles are equal to two right angles. This was a very common procedure in philosophical argument; Descartes used the same analogy in the fifth *Méditation* to demonstrate the existence of God; and not surprisingly, it had appeared in Aquinas's discussion of the universal validity of natural law;[32] so too much importance cannot be attached to its presence in Locke's essay. He is in fact rather more concerned with showing that by the proper use of their mental faculties men can arrive at certain knowledge of the order of absolute truth,

[29] See above, p. 24.
[30] *Op. cit.*, pp. 49–52. Van Leyden gives the following reference to Culverwel: *Discourse of the Light of Nature*, ed. Brown, 1857; ch. VI, pp. 71–77.
[31] G. Vasquez, *Comment. in Sum. Theol. Thom. Aquin.*, I, 2, disp. 150, c. 3.
[32] *Summa Theologica*, Ia, IIae, quest., 94, art. 4.

than with demonstrating the generic unity of mathematical and moral principles.

Indeed, in the later *Essay concerning Human Understanding*, Locke's main concern in Book I, is to emphasize the different means by which one comes to a knowledge of these principles:

"the doubt of their being native impressions on the mind is stronger against these moral principles than the others. Not that it brings their truth at all in question. Thy are equally true, though not equally evident. Those speculative maxims carry their own evidence with them; but moral principles require reasoning and discourse, and some exercise of the mind to discover the certainty of their truth." [33]

The core of the work is epistemological, and metaphysics and morals take second place; accordingly, the debate over the arbitrary or necessary nature of the rational order becomes a matter of relative insignificance. Firmly convinced from the outset, of the part played by sense experience in the acquisition of knowledge, Locke had no time for the kind of distinctions which Cudworth and his fellow ethical rationalists were at pains to make. Nevertheless, in the course of his criticism of innate ideas, Locke does develop his moral theories. As compared with the earlier essays, his attitude to ethics becomes more scientific than philosophical. Summarizing the significance of the Essay of 1690, Van Leyden describes it as an attempt, using the historical plain method, to define different kinds of moral evaluation, rather than to consider morality as the embodiment of absolute standards of truth. Locke's aim, concerning ethical matters, is to consider ideas of moral relations, that is, the range and varieties of moral rules to which men refer their actions.[34] Without abandoning the idea of an absolute ethical criterion, he concentrates his attention upon the notion, properly scientific, of adequate relationship between perception and its object, or in the moral sphere, between action and the rule to which it is subject, so leaving the notion of *convenientia* in its special philosophical sense, that developed in the *Essays on Natural Law*, on one side. Discussing in Book II, the various kinds of relationship, which a theory of knowledge must account for, he writes simply,

"There is another sort of relation which is the conformity or disagreement men's voluntary actions have to a rule to which they are referred, and by which they are judged of; which I think, may be called moral relation, as being that which denominates our moral actions." [35]

[33] *Op. cit.*, Bk. I, ch. 3; 5th. ed., London, 1706, reprinted London, 1961, pp. 25–26.
[34] *Essays on the Law of Nature*, Introduction, pp. 76–77.
[35] *Essay concerning Human Understanding*, Bk. II, ch. 28; p. 295.

There is a constant tension throughout the *Essay* between the idea of independent ethical standards and the scientific aim of description and definition of laws. Thus the rules of justice are characterized as "rules of convenience," as the "common ties of society," without which any community disintegrates; they are necessary practical principles, but neither the laws of the country, nor the code of behaviour within any particular group or corporation, always conform to them. Thieves and outlaws may behave justly to their own kind, notes Locke, but their actions towards honest people are dictated by interest not equity.[36] Idealism in ethics is scrutinized for any evidence it may give of power to enforce its own dictates. In the early essays Locke had talked of the necessity of a law-giver with power to enforce his will, but he had also tied the law of nature to the rational nature of man, so that reason became a self-dependent source of obligation. The Essay of 1690 presents a different picture: practical or moral principles, derived from nature, must produce conformity of action, otherwise they cease to be moral principles; but reason has ceased to operate as a motive force, and its place has been taken by the "innate practical principles," desire for happiness, and aversion to misery.[37] These are the real forces behind all action; and conscience is simply our personal judgement of the merit or demerit of our actions in accordance with a rule, which may or may not embody the principles of justice, but which is, whether it be the law of God, of the state, or of fashion, in origin essentially arbitrary, and supported by sufficient sanctions:

"Good and evil, as hath been shown, are nothing but pleasure or pain, or that which occasions or procures pleasure or pain to us. Moral good and evil, then, is only the conformity or disagreement of our voluntary actions to some law, whereby good or evil is drawn on us from the will and power of the law-maker; which good and evil, pleasure or pain, attending our observance or breach of the law by the decree of the law-maker, is that we call reward and punishment."[38]

We might ask what has become of the absolutes of right and wrong, related to the primitive ideas of fitness in the universe, and purpose in the rational essence of man. There seems very little to salvage once moral values are harnessed to subjective judgement on the one hand, and the arbitrary will of the legislator on the other. Yet Locke is at pains to defend his belief in natural law:

[36] *Ibid.*, Bk. I, ch. 3; p. 26.
[37] *Op. cit.*, Bk. I, ch. 3; p. 27.
[38] *Op. cit.*, Bk. II, ch. 28; pp. 295–296.

"And I think they equally forsake the truth who running into contrary extremes, either affirm an innate law, or deny that there is a law knowable by the light of nature, i.e. without the help of positive revelation."[39]

Nowhere does Locke actually deny or set out to disprove the existence of a natural moral law. In the *Recherches Philosophiques*, Saint-Hyacinthe uses Locke's argument that innate moral principles would necessarily suppose the existence of innate conceptions of God, of obligation, of punishment, and of life after death, to demolish the notion that *convenance* is an adequate basis for ethical theory.[40] Locke does not openly reject his own earlier theories however: in this case he simply applies his long-held conviction that moral ideas are valueless unless they are expressed in the form of a command or prohibition which has the support of superior power, to the business of disproving the doctrines of nativism. One can only assume that he held to the conviction that those necessary practical principles, the rules of justice binding society together, were in conformity both with the natural inclinations of man, and with the will and purpose of God. It is a conviction which evades the problem of possible conflict between natural inclination and the demands of justice, by assuming that the operation of rewards and punishments will automatically prevent such conflict. Perhaps too great a reliance is also placed on the proper operation of men's natural faculties in the discovery of natural law: variable factors are obviously a weak basis for an invariable law. But this criticism must be weighed against the fact that Locke's object in the *Essay* was to vindicate empirical philosophy rather than to provide a logical analysis of the concept of natural law. One thing is clear however, namely, that in spite of Locke's efforts to salvage the idea of a law "knowable by the light of nature," it was no impossible task for an aspiring *philosophe* to piece together from the arguments of the *Essay* a doctrine of pure ethical naturalism, proclaiming the sole ideal of "convenance à la nature."

The evolution of Locke's ethical thought reflects the tensions of the philosophical "climate" of the day. Beginning with a theologically legislative ethic, basing right and wrong on God's commands and punishments, he soon adopted a hedonistic ethic as well, of a Hobbesian variety, with pain and pleasure as the springs of action. Meanwhile he passionately believed in the possibility of demonstrating ethics mathematically, but perpetually complicated everything with an anthropological relativism, founded on the observation of the variety of ethical

[39] *Essay concerning Human Understanding*, Bk. I, ch. 3; p. 35.
[40] See above pp. 63–66.

values among the world's peoples, which implied that vice and virtue
were simply customary. Many of these tensions were still unresolved
when Montesquieu came to write the *Esprit des Lois*. But although the
moral testament of the *Essay concerning Human Understanding* is confused,
we must bear in mind that it was not the sole vehicle for Locke's ideas.
The second *Treatise on Government* was translated into French some ten
years before the *Essay*, and here Locke's moral ideas are essentially the
same as those advanced in the early *Essays on the Law of Nature*. The
existence of a body of natural law is an essential presupposition of his
political theory, and he continues to understand that law as being at
one and the same time a command of God, a rule of reason, and a law
in the very nature of things as they are. It may be that in spite of the
disappearance of the early works, the Locke known in the early years
of the century was the idealist Locke, who combined belief in an immutable moral law based on the essential fitness of things, with great
confidence in the natural inclinations and natural faculties of man. This
confidence survives and is intensified in the *Essay* of 1690, but rather
at the expense of his metaphysical idealism.

Locke never embraced the theories of the ethical rationalists of the
Cambridge school, like Cudworth, who in such works as the *True Intellectual System of the Universe*, and the *Treatise concerning Eternal and Immutable Morality*, attempted to found good and bad, justice and injustice
on the necessary and immutable relationships between the eternal essences of things, and declared that this original and independent moral
standard determined the will of God. For Locke, the source of moral
values remained the arbitrary will of a superior being. But his pupil,
Anthony Ashley Cooper, earl of Shaftesbury, combined his master's
confidence in the natural affections of man with the rational idealism
of the Cambridge Platonists. The resulting combination, not without
affinities to Spinozism, but unsupported by any developed philosophical structure, exercised considerable influence on European thought. It
is almost certain, although Montesquieu does not mention him by
name, that some of his ideas found their way into the *Lettres Persanes*,
and into the *Traité des Devoirs*.[41] Cudworth, as we noted at the beginning of this chapter,[42] is cited by Montesquieu, but in connection with

[41] Parallels between Shaftesbury's works and certain theories put forward in the *Lettres Persanes* are discussed in an article by A. S. Crisafulli, "Parallels to ideas in the *Lettres Persanes*," *Modern Language Assoc. of America*, Sep. 1937, p. 773 seq. See below p. 159; p. 243.
[42] See above p. 70.

pagan religions, one of the President's earliest interests.[43] Montesquieu clearly does not regard him in the same light as Shaftesbury however, and his theories were probably overshadowed by the already powerful influence of Malebranche. It is in the elevated company of the Oratorian father and Plato that Montesquieu places Shaftesbury:

"Les quatre grands poètes: Platon, le père Malebranche, milord Shaftesbury."[44]

All Shaftesbury's works are concerned in some way with morals or aesthetics; but the *Inquiry concerning Virtue and Merit* deals particularly with the idea of virtue as a natural characteristic of the social being, and as an essential condition of happiness. In the elaboration of this conception Shaftesbury makes much use of the idea of proportion and harmony in things, a notion with clear affinities to that of *convenance* or conformity.

Paul Hazard describes Shaftesbury as the prophet of humanity; and indeed, his confidence in the natural goodness of man, and of creation in general seems unshakable.

"Whatever the Order of the World produces is in the main both just and good";[45]

the influence of Locke seems present in his refusal to look beyond natural conditions for a standard by which moral judgements may be fixed:

"where can we fix our standard, or how regulate ourselves, but with regard to nature, beyond which there is no measure or rule of things? Now nature may be known from what we see of the natural state of creatures, and of man himself, when unprejudiced by vicious education."[46]

The case for ethical naturalism seems to be accepted without a murmur of opposition. But we find, Shaftesbury is really concerned with finding a ground for morality within the limits of natural constitution. Like Spinoza he saw goodness as the spontaneous fulfilment of natural disposition, not as submission to coercion, human or divine:

"A good creature is such a one as by the natural temper or bent of his affections is carried primarily and immediately, and not secondarily and accidentally, to good and against ill."[47]

[43] Apart from the reference to Cudworth in the *Dissertation sur la Politique des Romains dans la Religion*, Montesquieu refers to him indirectly in another fragment on pagan religions, *Pensée* 1946, (Bkn. 673).
[44] *Pensée* 1092, (Bkn. 2095); Nagel II, p. 296; Pléiade I, p. 1546.
[45] *Inquiry concerning Virtue and Merit*, 1699, Bk. I, part iii, section 3.
[46] *Inquiry concerning Virtue and Merit*, Bk. II, part ii, section 2.
[47] *Ibid.*, Bk. I, part ii, section 2.

The moral sphere may be said to embrace all things, since all things tend to fulfil their natural dispositions; but man alone is endowed with a natural disposition governed by reason, and therefore man alone possesses the special quality of virtue. Life in society is the necessary concomitant of the faculty of reason, and accordingly, recognition of the public interest, and the ability to form ethical concepts, are the characteristics that distinguish the virtuous man from other creatures and from his fellows, if they are lacking in reason.[48] Thus Shaftesbury rejects the conclusion implicit in the simple idea of conformity with nature, that all natural tendencies are good and virtuous. As far as man as a rational being is concerned, the first principle of his constitution is his natural, i.e. rational sense of right and wrong; he is in fact careful to distinguish between natural and sensible affections:

"should the sensible affections stand ever so much amiss, yet if they prevail not, because of those other rational affections spoken of, 'tis evident, the temper still holds good in the man; and the person is with justice esteemed virtuous by all men."[49]

Having established an identical self-dependent basis for both obligation and motivation: ethical behaviour is spontaneous and its reward is the satisfaction of self-fulfilment, Shaftesbury goes on to examine the notion of virtue in itself. For the quality in man corresponds to a transcendent order of reason,

'the eternal measures and immutable independent nature of worth and virtue",[50]

which is unaffected by any arbitrary law or custom. The universe is the material expression of harmony and proportion; and the fulfilment of natural dispositions is virtuous because it contributes to the order of the whole. Here Shaftesbury joins the ethical rationalists, in their persuasion that moral attributes depend on a divine order of necessary justice and truth. Not for him the relativism in ethics which could be drawn from Locke's admission of the variability of human conceptions, or from the metaphysical determinism of Spinoza. The atheist, as much as the wicked man, propagates evil by deliberately rejecting the harmony of the universe: his refusal to co-operate in the work of building this harmony on earth brings unhappiness to himself and to others. For the conformity existing between the supernatural order and the constitu-

---

[48] *Op. cit.*, Bk. I, part ii, section 3.
[49] *Inquiry concerning Virtue and Merit*, Bk. I, part ii, section 3.
[50] *Ibid.*

tion of things means that happiness depends on harmony and proportion being reflected in the individual disposition, and that it is enhanced by an appreciation of cosmic unity. The virtuous man takes

"A natural joy in the contemplation of those numbers, that harmony, proportion and concord, which supports the universal nature, and is essential in the constitution and form of every particular species or order of beings." [51]

And this

"admiration and love of order ... is naturally improving to the temper, advantageous to social affection, and highly assistant to virtue; which is itself no other than the love of order and beauty in society." [52]

Virtue and beauty in fact go hand in hand in Shaftesbury's moral theory: he talks of a "moral kind of architecture," and the "inward fabric" of a personality. Indeed, he understands conscience above all as an aesthetic sense, the sense of difformity in an action which is odious because it impairs the social order – the social order because man is a social animal and the pursuit of self-interest is contrary to his true nature. [53] The situation created by the stifling of natural affections contrasts sharply with the state of harmony enjoyed by the animal world:

"it is hard to find in any region a human society which has human laws. No wonder if in such societies 'tis so hard to find a man who lives naturally and as a man." [54]

Shaftesbury was deeply concerned with human happiness, but the contrast between his interpretation of the ideal of conformity with reason, and the conclusions of those budding materialists like Saint-Hyacinthe who saw in it no more than the pursuit of individual well-being, could hardly be more complete.

As Montesquieu's description of Malebranche and Shaftesbury in the *Pensées* as great poets implies, it is in the works of these two men that idealism in France and England achieves its most perfect expression. Yet this idealism rests on widely differing assumptions, and answered the needs of different generations. Shaftesbury had no time for orthodox doctrines of original sin, no sense of the tragedy of human existence, nor did he see in natural law the working of forces apparently divorced from the order of reason. Conversely, he laid less emphasis on the mathematical nature of truth and justice; virtue has more to do

[51] *Op. cit.*, Bk. II, part ii, section 1.
[52] *Ibid.*, Bk. I, part iii, section 3.
[53] *Ibid.*, Bk. II, part ii, section 1.
[54] *Ibid.*, Bk. II, part i, section 3.

with natural disposition, with essential character, than with metaphysical speculation. If there is virtue and beauty in the world, then it is in ourselves and all around us, not hidden in transcendent obscurity which only the deepest meditation will penetrate. Shaftesbury is the idealist of the 18th century, the century of humanity.

We pass now from Locke and Shaftesbury, two of the dominant figures on the English scene, to an obscurer thinker, and a theologian, William King. King belonged to the group of Anglican theologians centred on Trinity College, Dublin, whose most outstanding representative was George Berkeley; but although King did not make an original contribution to philosophy in the way that Berkeley did, his main work, the *De Origine Mali*, was much discussed by his contemporaries. This essay, an attempt to answer one of the most burning philosophical questions of the age, not unnaturally received considerable attention from both Bayle and Leibniz, champions of opposing factions in the debate.[55] The question of the origin of evil does not concern us directly, but the essay is an interesting example of the kind of latitudinarian thinking, as optimistic in outlook as Shaftesbury's, that put man at the centre of the universe, and drew arguments from a wide variety of contemporary sources to justify this radical change in theological approach. King made considerable use of the idea of conformity, in the development of his thesis.

King bases his definition of truth and his conception of the structure of the universe on the idea of a system of relationships. Here we see the influence of Malebranche combining with that of Locke. King is no Cartesian; he is careful to distinguish the notion of matter from that of space or extension, and he affirms the validity of sense experience; but he takes from Malebranche the notion of a universal system in which things are related to each other and to God by the degree of perfection that they embody. This is the basis for his explanation of evil: it arises from necessary natural imperfection, an imperfection without which the infinite variety of things in the universe would have been unrealizable; and from the operation of natural laws, necessary to hold the world together, and a source of benefits which far outweigh the occasional disaster. If we ourselves were not of necessity finite and contingent beings, then, says King, we would be able to comprehend the perfect harmony of the universe:

---

[55] Bayle attacks King in the *Réponse aux Questions d'un Provincial*, ch. LXXIV; Leibniz discusses the Essay in the *Theodicée*, art. 359.

"if we could view the whole workmanship of God: if we thoroughly understand the connections, subordinations, and mutual relations of things, the
mutual assistance which they afford each other; and lastly, the whole
series and order of them; it would appear that the world is as well as it
possibly could be; and that no evil in it could be avoided which would not
occasion a greater by its absence." [56]

Following from his interpretation of the structure of the universe, King
defines truth as the reason of things, the relationships binding them
together. But it is here that he parts company with Malebranche and
joins Locke; for he does not mean the essential relationships of things
which constitute divine reason, rather the observed relationships between things, which, when there is an exact correspondence between
human judgement and its object, go to form scientific truth. He implies
the immanence of reason, but there his rationalism ends.

For neither does his moral theory depend on the notion of natural
laws derived from a transcendent reason; on the contrary, it owes a
great deal to the epistemology of the *Essay concerning Human Understanding*, and can only be described as naturalistic in tone, if not in
intention. King begins with the usual teleological interpretation of the
universe: the end of creation was to exercise the power and to commu-
nicate the goodness of the deity; there can be no doubt, since God is
both infinite and perfect, that the world is the best possible world, and
so on.[57] Hence the "convenience" and perfection of the universe depends ultimately upon the will of God. But the expression of divine
goodness necessarily involved the existence of man, and it therefore follows that the human constitution, man's reason and his appetites are in
conformity with the divine will. They thus provide a perfectly sound
basis for ethics. This natural teleology, similar in some respects to that
found in Locke's early *Essays on the Law of Nature*, leads to an unusual
interpretation of the fitness of things. The idea that human nature is in
conformity with God's will leads to the proposition that human happiness, that is, the preservation and satisfaction of natural inclinations, is
equally the object of divine concern. Therefore, that which is good and
as King terms it, "convenient," is that which satisfies the "appetites" of
the creature:

"There are certain appetites implanted in us by nature, which are not to be
esteemed useless, but contributing toward our preservation; ... and some
things are naturally agreeable, some contrary to these appetites: ... the

---

[56] *Essay on the Origin of Evil*, translation by Law of the latin work of 1702, London, 1731
ch. IV, section 8; p. 144.
[57] *Essay on the Origin of Evil*, ch. I, section 3.

former when present, please and impress a delightful sense of themselves; the latter displease and create uneasiness. These therefore are called incommodious, troublesome and evil; and those, commodious, convenient, and good." [58]

This reasoning lies behind the two main propositions of King's *Preliminary Dissertation*: that the criterion of the will of God is the happiness of man; and that the happiness of man is the criterion of virtue. Pleasure and pain determine this happiness, and accordingly, it is from a study of those things which cause desire or aversion, namely of the relations of fitness or unfitness between things, that all virtues and vices may be deduced. The function of reason is of course to carry out this study, and it constitutes a moral sense which is acquired by experience and observation. [59]

So it is that in King the idea of relationships of fitness as the basis of virtue becomes associated with a teleological view of the universe, and with what amounts to the naturalistic moral ideal of conformity with nature. Of course, in later chapters of the *De Origine Mali*, King is concerned to emphasize the moderating influence of reason, and to establish the essential freedom of man to choose between various courses of action; it would therefore be inaccurate to describe his thought in terms of materialism proper. Like Locke, some of his roots went deep into Scholasticism; yet, again like his more eminent contemporary, he made a worthy contribution to the cause of re-establishing the integrity of human nature.

It may have been from King that both Leibniz and Samuel Clarke took their idea of the fitness of things. We have given little attention to King's metaphysics, but it is fairly clear that for him fitness was the attribute denoting the compossibility of things in the universe, which in so doing pointed to the ultimate perfection of its design. Leibniz, as we have seen, [60] associated the principle of *convenance* with the principle of sufficient reason, which he saw as determining the relationships of material things in the created universe. Now Samuel Clarke's conception of fitness or conformity is remarkably similar. Clarke is particularly important for our study because of the likelihood that Montesquieu knew his *Discourse on the Being and Attributes of God* before the composition of the *Traité des Devoirs* and perhaps even before the *Lettres Persanes*. [61]

---

[58] *Essay on the Origin of Evil.* ch. V, section 1, p. 151.
[59] *Ibid.*, Preliminary Dissertation, I, xix–xxii.
[60] See above pp. 24–25.
[61] Shackleton suggests the early influence of Clarke on Montesquieu in his *Critical Biography*, ch. IV, p. 71.

As we noted above, Montesquieu possessed the *Discourse* in the English edition of 1728, but it was translated into French by Ricotier in 1717, and there are enough similarities between the arguments used by the two writers, for Clarke's influence at least on the *Devoirs* to be reasonably certain. The precise details of these similiarities will be the subject of later discussion, but they range from the proof of the intelligence of the first cause given in the *Traité des Devoirs* and the first chapter of the *Lois*, to the arguments which on various occasions Montesquieu advanced against Hobbes. Montesquieu seems to have been attracted to Cudworth through his early interest in pagan religions, and this interest, continuing in the form of a deep admiration for the ethics of Stoicism, may also have drawn him to Clarke, who in the second part of the *Discourse*, makes considerable use of Cicero, and, in spite of his declared aim of proving the insufficiency of ancient philosophies for the reformation of humanity, cheerfully begins one chapter by declaring that paganism was blessed with excellent moralists.[62]

In fact, the chief shortcoming of the work in the eyes of contemporaries, was that the excellent account it gave of the principles of natural religion served to justify Deism, rather than to prove its inadequacy in comparison with Christianity. It enjoyed the same reputation as Locke's *Reasonableness of Christianity* in this, although Clarke set out to refute Spinoza and prove the necessity of revelation, working from Newtonian conceptions of the order of the universe. The attack against Spinoza is mounted on a large scale, and Clarke actually goes as far as quoting the *Ethica* in footnotes, a rare occurrence among such refutations. The argument centres around the idea of necessity: against the notion of a unique and necessary substance, Clarke advances the theory of necessary fitness, or as Ricotier's translation puts it, of "une nécessité de convenance." The universe is the creation of a free and intelligent agent, as its orderly design proves:

"Je prouve ... que l'être existant par lui-même, et à qui toutes choses doivent leur origine, est un être intelligent, par la beauté, la variété, l'ordre et la symmétrie qui éclate dans l'univers, et surtout par la justesse merveilleuse avec laquelle chaque chose se rapporte à sa fin."[63]

The only kind of necessity to which such a perfect and omniscient being can be subject is the necessity which proceeds from perfect will: the creation must be worthy of its creator; God must act in accordance with his perfect wisdom. In this sense his will and its creation are subject to

[62] Part II, ch. 10.
[63] *De l'Existence et des Attributs de Dieu*, Amsterdam, 1717; part I, ch. 9, p. 89.

the principle of fitness, and perfect liberty becomes perfect necessity:

"Quelque grande que soit la liberté d'un être qui est tout ensemble infiniment intelligent, infiniment puissant et infiniment bon, il ne se déterminera jamais à agir d'une manière qui soit contraire à ses perfections. De sorte que le libre arbitre, dans un être revêtu de ces perfections, est un principe d'action aussi certain et aussi immuable que la nécessité même des fatalistes."[64]

Subsequent to creation, the order brought into being by the will of God but according to the principle of fitness, obliges even the Creator. It constitutes an order of reason and justice, which is eternal and immutable; here Clarke, in spite of his finalism, joins the ethical rationalists.

Unaware apparently of the inherent contradiction between a created order and an eternal, immutable order, he goes on to found his moral theory on the relationships of fitness in things, which correspond to this order and which contribute to the perfection of the universe. Man, being a rational creature, is capable of perceiving these relationships, and therefore they form the basis of natural law, that is of a law independent of divine command or of positive revelation. It is worth quoting the passage where Clarke sets out this theory, for the echoes it contains of the opening chapter of Montesquieu's *Lois:*

"... il y a de certaines circonstances qui conviennent à de certaines personnes, et qui ne conviennent pas à d'autres, le tout fondé sur la nature des choses et sur les qualifications des personnes, antécédemment à aucune volonté, ou à aucun établissement arbitraire ou positif. C'est de quoi il faut convenir malgré qu'on en ait, à moins qu'on ne s'avise de soutenir, que dans la nature des choses et dans l'ordre de la raison, il est tout aussi convenable qu'un être innocent soit plongé dans une misère éternelle, qu'il est convenable, qu'il en soit affranchi. Il y a donc dans la nature des choses des règles de convenance, et ces règles sont éternelles, nécessaires et immuables. ... Or c'est sur cette connaissance que les êtres intelligents ont des relations naturelles et nécessaires des choses, qu'ils règlent constamment leurs actions, à moins que quelque intérêt particulier ou quelque passion dominante ne vienne à la traverse séduire la volonté, et l'entraîner dans le dérèglement: et c'est ici, pour le dire en passant que je trouve le vrai fondement de toute morale."[65]

[64] *Op. cit.*, part I, ch. 13, pp. 182–183.
[65] *De l'Existence et des Attributs de Dieu*, part I, ch. 13, pp. 174–175 cf., the English of the *Discourse concerning the Being and Attributes of God* in the 1728 edition: "Further, that there is a fitness or suitableness of certain circumstances to certain persons, and an unsuitableness of others, founded in the nature of things and the qualifications of persons, antecedent to will and to all arbitrary or positive appointments whatsoever; must unavoidably be acknowledged by every one, who will not affirm that 'tis equally fit and suitable, in the nature and reason of things, that an innocent being should be extremely and eternally miserable, as that it should be free from such misery. There is therefore such a thing as fitness and unfitness, eternally, necessarily and unchangeably, in the nature and reason of things .... And by this understanding or knowledge of the natural and necessary relations of things,

Reason perceives the relationships of conformity between things, relationships both necessary and eternal, and this perception forms the basis of duties to which conscience obliges, independently of positive law, or of the hope of reward or fear of punishment. No wonder Clarke's fellow clergymen feared that he had argued the case for natural religion far too cogently. Indeed, if the evidence and necessity of these moral relationships is, as Clarke declared it to be, identical with that of mathematical relationships, and God's perfect freedom is no more than perfect necessity, what becomes of the refutation of determinism? If God's nature determines his will, and consequently the form of the universe, it is possible to deduce that the material world is no more than a mode of the divine substance. Thus there were reasonable grounds for complaining that Clarke was setting up his argument on the flimsy basis of nice verbal distinctions, and that, like many of those who set out to refute Spinoza, he had in reality succumbed to his insidious influence. Leibniz certainly took care when he embarked on the same enterprise, to make a clear distinction between the principles of fitness and mathematical necessity, and to subject the former to the arbitrary will of God, clearly and unequivocally.

Yet Clarke's very failure to grapple successfully with Spinoza is important for us, in as much as the main features of his thought anticipate some of the things that Montesquieu had to say on the score of metaphysics, and it is possible that they both stumbled unwittingly into the trap of immanentism.

In view of the innumerable contexts in which the term *convenance* appeared, and the diversity of purposes which the idea of fitness fulfilled in aesthetic and philosophical thought, it would be difficult, not to say foolish, in the absence of certain textual evidence, to try to pinpoint the exact source of Montesquieu's definition of justice, even if one isolated works in which the key phrase *rapport de convenance* is used. But the reading of Clarke probably furnished him with some conceptions to support such a definition, supplementing the influence of Malebranche. Shaftesbury was another possible influence, this time on his moral thought; and Shaftesbury and Clarke were in turn indebted to thinkers like Locke and King. In addition, all of them contributed something to the vast pool of ideas, from which both Montesquieu and his contemporaries drew the raw material of their works.

the actions likewise of all intelligent beings are constantly directed; (which by the by is the true ground and foundation of all morality) unless their will be corrupted by particular interest or affection, or swayed by some unreasonable and prevailing lust." Part I, Proposition XII, pp. 111–112.

CHAPTER FIVE

AESTHETIC IDEAS

We come finally to the examination of aesthetic theory during the second half of the 17th century. In many ways aesthetics and morals occupy the same position in relation to metaphysics: their common principles may be deduced in part from a body of systematic speculation; but on the other hand they may be considered as both the product and the reflection of a particular age and society. They share a common tension between the ideal and absolute and the empirical and relative. Indeed from the point of view of the sociologist or historian, they reflect to an equal degree the character and consciousness of the national or social group.

Their ideals lie parallel: the good beside the beautiful. Care for the cohesion and just equilibrium of the elements of society preoccupies the moralist; harmony of structure, balance of figures or movements concern the aesthetician. The genius of both is normative rather than descriptive, for both make constant reference to absolute criteria. Judgement is of their essence. The moralist makes a direct analysis and evaluation of interpersonal relationships according to his conception of the meaning of things, and draws certain conclusions concerning the justice of motivation and purpose in behaviour; while the aesthetician deals in the same context with the representation of interpersonal and person-object relationships, and with man's reaction to it.

We are concerned with the mind of the 17th century and with those notions proper to its idealism which were shared by ethics and aesthetics. Their common ground is the form of life, and an optimistic and systematic approach to this subject produces certain characteristic ideas. Thus, just as the moralist is concerned with the harmony and equilibrium of society, so the aesthetician looks for balance and proportion in the work of art. This reflects a common realisation of the necessary mechanical coherence of any structure, whatever its scale and kind, and from it are derived theories of compossibility on a cosmic level, or principles of structural unity, or scientific notions of causal determinism. It is as legitimate to talk of relationships of conformity between the elements of an artistic composition, as it is to define moral values in such terms. Similarly, the ethical notion of conformity with reason or with nature seen as the expression of reason, variously interpreted as sincerity, or as conformity between the outward appearance and the inward creature, or as conformity with an established order of things, is parallelled in aesthetics by the idea that the style and medium of a work should fit its subject, and that the whole should fulfil its purpose, either of persuasion or of decoration, or of edification. This brings us to epistemological similarities. Just judgement, or the clear perception of moral relationships, or of regularities and irregularities of composition, is the essential prerequisite of both virtue and taste; and consequently the moral and aesthetic attributes of *justice* and *justesse* arise.

Such words as *convenance*, *bienséance*, *ordre*, *rapport*, and *raison*, are the very stuff of 17th century aesthetic thought, as they are of moral theory in the same period. Their attendant definitions and applications build a mainstream conception of beauty which depends on rules and reason and a strong belief in the inherent order of things. But it was an ideal restricted to the privileged classes whose polished manners were deemed to entail sophisticated taste. *Honnêteté* was an aesthetic as well as a moral quality. Towards the end of the century, with the growing strength of scientific rationalism, there was some weakening of the aristocratic associations of aesthetic theory, as a result of a tendency to emphasize the individual, subjective elements in the process of artistic appreciation. The influence of Locke's *Essay concerning Human Understanding* was dominant here as in other spheres, and the sensationalist theories adopted by Du Bos in his influential but rather uneven *Réflexions Critiques*,[1] were later to receive concise and systematic treatment in the work that Montesquieu prepared for the *Encyclopédie*, the *Essai sur le Goût*.[2] But the rate of transformation in aesthetics, which until the mid 18th century was hardly thought of as a separate branch of thought, was slower than that in the hotly debated field of ethics, if articles by Diderot and Marmontel in the *Encyclopédie*, and the *Supplé-*

---

[1] *Réflexions Critiques sur la Poésie et sur la Peinture*, Paris, 1719.
[2] Published posthumously, *Encyclopédie*, vol. VII, 1757. Montesquieu began thinking about this subject much earlier; he discussed Du Bos's work in a letter to his friend J.-J. Bell, dated 29 Sept. 1726 (Nagel III, p. 862).

ment à l'Encyclopédie [3] where theories originating in the previous century still receive considerable attention, are given any authority.

The primary object of this study is however to demonstrate the way in which the terms that we have already mentioned, in particular *convenance*, and the ideas that accompanied them, were used in a wide variety of works contributing to the elaboration of aesthetic theory during the second half of the 17th century, and the opening years of the 18th, although of course, certain changes will have to be taken into account.

In the earlier discussion of dictionary definitions, certain general notions attached to the terms *bienséance* and *convenance* were reviewed.[4] *Convenance*, we decided, emerged as the more general of the two terms, possessing strong links with ideas of proportion and symmetry; whereas *bienséance*, once almost synonymous, and still dependent on the notion of proper relationship, developed specialized meanings within the sphere of manners and aesthetics. We have already mentioned the affinity between moral and aesthetic ideas, particularly during this period; the association arose from a common intellectual attitude, whose special manifestation was the cult of reason and order, that is of supernatural reason and superimposed order. Once the mind was convinced of the virtual if not actual existence of a correct order of things, and respect for proper manners and deportment in social relationships was firmly established, what was more logical than to insist that the same order should be introduced into the artistic pursuits of the cultured. The critics who voiced this requirement, fully conscious of the connection between art and manners, saw no need to create new words where *honnêteté* and *politesse* would do. Accordingly, they were imported into aesthetics, along with useful multi-purpose words like *bienséance* and *convenance*, whose social significance was accompanied by the general idea of proportion and fitness, and the new socio-aesthetic theory emerged.

By 1610, the French critic Deimier, following paths laid out by Italian critics like Vida in the preceding century, was writing:

"La raison est si étroitement nécessaire en la poésie que sans elle toutes les autres qualités... seraient toujours vides de bonté ... Toutefois il se trouvera quelques-uns qui s'imagineront quelque raison à m'opposer, qu'il est permis au poète de dire tout ... parce que le poète peut se servir de toutes sortes d'opinions pour embellir son sujet. Mais je répondrai là-dessus ... que

---

[3] *Encyclopédie*, vol. II, 1751; *Supplément*, vols. I, II, 1776: articles, "Beau," "Bienséances," etc.

[4] See above pp. 3–7.

en ce terme de tout, on doit entendre toute chose honnête et raisonnable ...
C'est une maxime inviolable que toute mesure et raison est nécessaire aux
écrits poétiques."[5]

Good taste and good breeding go hand in hand, an obvious truth according to La Mesnardière:

"tout ce qu'il y a de bien né, de raisonnable et de savant dans les états bien
policés, est séparé d'avec le peuple, qui n'a pour toute connaissance que
celle des arts mécaniques, qu'il exerce par usage plutôt que par théorie."[6]

Such generalisations are far removed from the clear-sightedness of La
Bruyère where fashionable taste was concerned, and from Montesquieu's conviction that "les gens du monde jugent ordinairement mal";
but they must have reflected only the established social conceptions of
the age.

Similar assumptions underlie the theories of the Spanish apostle of
good manners, Balthazar Gracián, writing in the middle of the century.[7] Gracián did not achieve widespread popularity in France until
much later, but the terminology used in the translations of his work,
and the emphasis found there upon the idea that everything has a
proper place in the scheme of things, and that elegance depends on the
observation of the preordained pattern, is not without significance:

"qu'est-ce que la politesse à l'égard de tout ouvrage en général que l'art produit et dirige? C'est une élégante disposition des choses qui doivent avoir du
rapport les unes aux autres. La perfection d'un tout consiste dans la belle
ordonnance des parties. Un homme serait un monstre de la nature, s'il
avait la tête où doivent être ses pieds; et dans un ouvrage d'esprit, ou de mécanique, si le commencement se trouve à la fin, ce sera un monstre de l'art.
Chaque chose dans l'ordre de l'art, aussi bien que dans celui de la nature, a
sa place marquée: ne l'y mettez pas, elle choque .... Que les mêmes choses
soient ramenées chacune à leur place, chacune comme à leur point de vue:
la justesse et l'élégance de cet arrangement, ajoutées à la beauté des choses,
nous charmeront."[8]

The establishment of a proper relationship between constituent parts
will ensure the perfection of nature, of society and of art.

It is necessary however to distinguish between the actual association
of social class and artistic pursuits in the minds of contemporary writers, and the natural similarity between moral and aesthetic theory,
which arose from a common outlook on life. This outlook we have de-

---

[5] *Académie de l'Art Poétique*, pp. 489–490.
[6] *Poétique*, Paris, 1640, Discours, p. S.
[7] See above pp. 43–44.
[8] *L'Homme Universel*, trans. J. de Courbeville, Rotterdam, 1729, pp. 171–172.

scribed as a firm belief in the existence of a metaphysical entity combining reason and order in its essence; rectitude in everything is the
main aspiration of the believers, and their first duty to bring orderliness or perfection to all their works. René Bray saw the "culte de la
raison" as the mainspring of classical doctrine;[9] Henri Peyre, in a later
work on Classicism, insisted on the diversity of attitudes hidden behind
such an all embracing title, some of them diametrically opposed to each
other; and he suggested instead that the common characteristic of the
age was a penetrating intellectualism, directed towards psychological
analysis.[10] They are both really concerned to show that the rationalism
of the 17th century had more to do with the kind of beliefs implied by
Cartesian metaphysics, than with the reasoned processes of Cartesian
method. If cult there was, it was a cult of intuition, of certain knowledge which, but for its alleged universality, was not unlike inspiration;
a cult which finally manifested itself in Quietism. Such rationalism was
not incompatible with art: it simply demanded a renunciation of individualism in favour of universal themes. Simplicity, unity, symmetry,
the qualities bestowed by reason, became the watchwords of criticism;
as La Bruyère explained in the *Caractères*, all that smacked of barbarian
complication or Gothic obscurity was banished from art:

"On a dû faire du style ce qu'on a fait de l'architecture. On a entièrement
abandonné l'ordre gothique, que la barbarie avait introduit pour les palais
et pour les temples; on a rappelé le dorique, l'ionique, et le corinthien: ce
qu'on ne voyait plus que dans les ruines de l'ancienne Rome et de la vieille
Grèce, devenu moderne, éclate dans nos portiques et dans nos péristyles. De
même on ne saurait en écrivant rencontrer le parfait et, s'il se peut, sur-
passer les anciens que par leur imitation.

Combien de siècles se sont écoulés avant que les hommes, dans les sciences
et dans les arts aient pu revenir au goût des anciens et reprendre enfin le
simple et le naturel."[11]

Nature was in vogue, but the enthusiasm of the 17th century was
not for wild and solitary places. The natural resolved itself into the
regular and well-proportioned, that which avoided excess; like the
truth, especially the historical truth, it consisted in that part of experience, or those qualities, which persons or objects possessed in common. It was the essential being, the embellished product, the artificial.
To arbiters of fashionable taste like Father Bouhours, this presented no
contradiction:

[9] *La Formation de la doctrine classique*, Paris, 1927; part II, ch. 4.
[10] *Le Classicisme français*, New York, 1942; ch. IV.
[11] "Des ouvrages de l'esprit," 15.

"... il y a bien de la différence entre la fiction et la fausseté: l'une imite et perfectionne en quelque façon la nature; l'autre la gâte, et la détruit entièrement."[12]

In short, nature, that is perfection, furnished the ideal of all artistic enterprise, and the criterion of all aesthetic judgement; and conformity with nature, with the archetypal idea fixed in the preordained pattern of the universe, was the guarantee of authenticity.

Accordingly, the would-be poet, painter, architect, or dramatist was exhorted to bear several things in mind: to avoid the deformed and irregular by the observance of certain necessary and permanent rules, corresponding to the essential character of the subject and ensuring a result of perfect and permanent beauty; to create an authentic work by establishing within it a perfect correspondence between its subject, the means employed, its purpose, and its public. Success depended on giving tangible expression to certain links in an invisible pattern:

"Cet art merveilleux des bienséances consiste principalement à ne rien souffrir qui ne soit parfaitement conforme au caractère de celui qui parle, à ceux à qui il parle, et à la manière dont il parle, selon Quintilien. C'est cette harmonie secrète, et ce rapport parfait de toutes les parties, qui fait cette bienséance que nous cherchons, dont le détail serait infini;"[13]

such is the secret of eloquence according to Rapin. But although, as he goes on to explain, authenticity depends on the careful consideration of circumstances: time, place, subject, person, etc., it is not to be considered a relative quality. For it expresses the eternal core of truth in things, that part of them that is subject to immutable general principles, and therefore it too is absolute.

"Il y a dans l'art un point de perfection, comme de bonté ou de maturité dans la nature. Celui qui le sent et qui l'aime a le goût parfait; celui qui ne le sent pas, et qui aime en deçà ou au delà, a le goût défectueux, il y a donc un bon et un mauvais goût, et l'on dispute des goûts avec fondement."[14]

La Bruyère, we find is in general agreement. After this, it is no surprise to read his definition of taste:

"Entre le bon sens et le bon goût il y a la différence de la cause à son effet."[15]

Taste is directly related to that quality in man by which reason manifests itself.

[12] *La Manière de bien penser dans les Ouvrages d'Esprit*, 1687, 1er Dialogue; 2nd. edition, Amsterdam, 1692, p. 9.
[13] *Traité des Bienséances*, Paris, 1686, art. xxii, pp. 119–120.
[14] *Les Caractères*, "Des Ouvrages de l'Esprit," 10.
[15] *Les Caractères*, "Des Jugements," 56.

The same point is made by Bouhours in his *Manière de bien penser dans les Ouvrages d'Esprit:*

"La sublimité, la grandeur dans une pensée est justement ce qui emporte, et ce qui ravit, pourvu que la pensée convienne au sujet: car c'est une règle générale, qu'il faut penser selon la matière qu'on traite; et rien n'est moins raisonnable que d'avoir des pensées sublimes dans un petit sujet qui n'en demande que de médiocres." [16]

The recognition of relationships of just proportion is the main factor in appreciation as well as composition, and it is intimately connected with reason. It comes as no surprise to find Henri de Lelevel, the faithful disciple of Malebranche, describing the sublime and the natural in his treatise on eloquence, as the

"juste rapport que toutes les pensées ont les unes aux autres, toutes se soutenant mutuellement, et l'une servant toujours de preuve à l'autre." [17]

Indeed, as far as the principles governing taste and composition were concerned, there was little to distinguish the majority of theorists from each other during the second half of the century. Conformity was the central criterion to which all factors involved in the creation and judgement of a work of art were ultimately subjected.

But this central notion possessed, as we shall see, two distinct applications, one absolute, and the other relative, which sometimes determined the choice of the term used to express it. The difference between the absolute and the relative significance lay between the idea of conformity as the right relationship of the subject and its expression, and the idea of conformity as the right relationship of the finished work and its audience. Bray groups the whole theory of conformity under the heading *Bienséance*, and characterizes these two related notions as *bienséances internes* and *bienséances externes*,

"harmonie à l'intérieur de l'oeuvre d'art et harmonie entre l'oeuvre d'art et le public." [18]

The first of these is related to the idea of *vraisemblance*, and the principles of authenticity and universality; and the second depends on the accepted moral and social standards of the contemporary public. However, Bray's choice of terminology does not altogether reflect that of the theorists in question. Rapin, as we saw above, [19] does write of the

---

[16] *Op. cit.*, 2e Dialogue, p. 79.
[17] *De la Vraie et de la Fausse Éloquence*, Toulouse, 1698, ch. V, p. 245.
[18] See *La Formation de la Doctrine classique en France*, part III, ch. 2, p. 215 ff.
[19] Above p. 93.

"art des bienséances," and includes under this heading all the particular conformities that the aspiring orator must observe. Similarly, Fénelon declares in his "Projet de Rhétorique" in the *Lettre à M. Dacier sur les Occupations de l'Académie*,

"Il y a une bienséance à garder pour les paroles comme pour les habits",

and goes on to expound a theory based on the principle enshrined in the *Logique de Port-Royal*,

"La vraie raison place toutes choses dans le rang qui leur convient." [20]

Indeed the great Jansenist writers provide much of the theory attached to the term *convenance*, rather than *bienséance*, and it is perhaps significant in this respect that their account of aesthetic theory is more scientific in character, and that less regard is paid to the variable factor, the demands of public taste, which do in fact seem worthier of the title *bienséances*. The importance of this group lies in the stress they place upon the idea of conformity between the artistic work and the nature of man, rather than the conventions of a particular age. Nicole dismisses the beauty which results from the application of the latter principle as transient and superficial.[21] Clearly, their conception of the nature of man will not be that of the post-Lockian era; but their theories anticipate in some measure the introduction of the principle of sensibility, and the criterion of subjective judgement, into aesthetics. Pascal, for example, combines predictable comments with an outright rejection of judgement by rule and reason.

"Ce n'est pas assez qu'une chose soit belle; il faut qu'elle soit propre au sujet, qu'il n'y ait rien de trop ni rien de manque",[22]

is an opinion which could have come from the pen of any of the writers that we have so far examined. But he follows this with the idea that aesthetic appreciation depends to a certain extent on individual dispositions:

"Il y a un certain modèle d'agrément et de beauté, qui consiste en un certain rapport entre notre nature, faible ou forte, telle qu'elle est, et la chose qui nous plaît." [23]

[20] *Lettre à M. Dacier sur les Occupations de l'Académie*, Paris, 1714, IV. *Logique de Port-Royal*, 1662, Ier Discours.
[21] In the *Traité de la Vraie et de la Fausse Beauté*, introduction to the *Epigrammatum delectus*, Paris, 1659, trans. Richelet, 1698; ch. V.
[22] *Pensées*, (Brunschvicg) 16.
[23] *Ibid.*, 32.

Conformity is considered a necessary attribute, but its imposition by rule under the sanction of reason is excluded not only by the introduction of subjective elements into the definition of beauty, but also by a definite negation of the efficacity of reason:

"Ceux qui jugent d'un ouvrage par règle sont à l'égard des autres comme ceux qui ont une montre à l'égard de ceux qui n'en ont point. L'un dit: 'Il y a deux heures que nous sommes ici.'; l'autre dit: 'Il n'y a que trois quarts d'heure.' Je regarde ma montre; je dis à l'un: 'Vous vous ennuyez'; et à l'autre: 'Le temps ne vous dure guère'";[24]

and more briefly: "Tout notre raisonnement se réduit à céder au sentiment." [25]

No doubt Pascal was the exception in a generation particularly susceptible to the attractions of rational idealism; and it is always possible to weigh his anticipation of the 18th century revolution in aesthetic thinking against his debt to the scepticism and mysticism of earlier centuries. The ideas of Pierre Nicole are perhaps more moderate and more characteristic of the age, while possessing clear similiarities with those of Pascal. Just as Pascal's rhetoric was based on a deep psychological penetration, so Nicole's aesthetic theories stemmed from his pedagogic activities and his equal concern with the processes of persuasion. This common psychological interest was perhaps one of the reasons for the new emphasis in their work on human nature, and the need to consider it when theorizing about art. Nicole's *Traité de la Vraie et de la Fausse Beauté* was in fact conceived as the introduction to a school anthology, the *Epigrammatum delectus*. It sets out very concisely a theory built around the idea of conformity between human nature, seen undoubtedly as something universal and invariable, and the work of art, where beauty takes on the universal and eternal characteristics of that reason which brings it into being.

"Un des principaux avantages de la vraie beauté, c'est qu'elle n'est ni variable ni passagère; mais qu'elle est constante, certaine et au goût de tous les temps."[26]

True beauty, as opposed to the transient elegance that results from the observation of fashionable tastes, is not to be created nor appreciated, by applying the principle of pleasure and following the faulty judgement of sentiment:

[24] *Pensées*, 5.
[25] *Ibid.*, 274.
[26] *Op. cit., Recueil des plus belles épigrammes*, trad. Richelet, Paris, 1698; vol. I, ch. 1, p. 5.

"Si l'on veut donc éviter cet embarras de décisions équivoques, il faut avoir recours à la lumière de la raison. Elle est simple et certaine, et c'est par son moyen qu'on peut trouver la vraie beauté naturelle . . . . Elle nous conduira d'abord à la nature; elle nous apprendra pour règle générale qu'une chose est belle, lorsqu'elle a de la convenance avec sa propre nature et avec la nôtre." [27]

Reason is understood as the clear perception of an objective body of truth revealed in nature; it depends on the conformity of thought and object:

"Nous allons présentement traiter des pensées qui, comme nous avons déjà dit, doivent convenir aux choses et aux personnes. Elles conviennent aux choses lorsqu'elles sont vraies, propres et tirées du fond du sujet; et aux personnes lorsqu'elles s'accommodent aux mouvements que nous a donnés la nature." [28]

Nicole develops his theory of *convenance* by examining the constitution of the human mind, and deducing the particular rules that the writer must follow from his conclusions. Since we are for example, incapable of prolonged effort on a high level, variety is an essential ingredient in all works.[29] These beginnings of an empirical approach seem to have influenced the method adopted by Montesquieu in the *Essai sur le Goût*. Although Montesquieu works on the principle that pleasure determines aesthetic judgements, and the metaphysical trappings of Nicole's theory are entirely absent from his essay, the whole work consists of a development of the insight that art should satisfy the needs and nature of the human mind; he examines in turn the pleasures of order, the pleasures of variety, the pleasures of symmetry, and so on. An entry in the *Pensées* makes Nicole's influence even more possible:

"Pour bien écrire, il faut sauter les idées intermédiaires, assez pour n'être pas ennuyeux; pas trop, de peur de n'être pas entendu. Ce sont ces suppressions heureuses qui ont fait dire à M. Nicole que tous les bons livres étaient doubles." [30]

Nicole's theory of *convenance*, however, and his conception of reason as a metaphysical entity reflected in nature, seem more relevant to Montesquieu's theory of justice than to his aesthetic theories.

One of the first apart from Pascal to suggest that feeling and pleasure were more important in aesthetic appreciation, than reason and rules,

[27] *Traité de la Vraie et de la Fausse Beauté*, ch. 1, p. 5.
[28] *Ibid.*, ch. 8, p. 28.
[29] *Traité de la Vraie et de la Fausse Beauté*, ch. 6.
[30] *Op. cit.*, 1970 (Bkn. 802); Nagel II, p. 604; Pléiade I, p. 1220.

was the ever controversial Malebranche. And Malebranche even went as far as to incorporate his ideas into one of the major themes of his philosophical work, the theory of occasional causes, thus giving it the support of a whole body of metaphysics. In the *Connaissance de Dieu et de Soi-même*, Bossuet wrote at length of the beauty and economy of the universe, of the harmony of every part within the pattern of the whole, and of its perfect correspondence to the end of creation. Similar terms were also used to describe and explain the nature and function of the human constitution.[31] But reason is presented as the only faculty capable of appreciating a beauty which consists in order and proportion:

"Connaître les proportions et l'ordre, est l'ouvrage de la raison, qui compare une chose avec une autre, et en découvre les rapports .... La beauté ne consiste que dans l'ordre, c'est-à-dire, par l'arrangement et la proportion."[32]

As we have seen in most of the theorists of style and taste, although considerable emphasis is placed on the duty to please, it is always assumed that the artist must satisfy the intellectual appetites of his public. Now Malebranche, much more of a metaphysician than Bossuet, conceived of a universal economy that would include and utilize every aspect of human nature; feeling and pleasure, "amour naturel," as opposed to "amour de choix," received the theoretical justification that their obvious dominance in judgement and motivation would appear to demand. Taking care to safeguard the definition of beauty as order and proportion, Malebranche achieved a careful reconciliation of reason and sentiment, by transforming the latter into the natural cause bringing man to a knowledge and love of this order. Pleasure is not seen as a barrier to aesthetic appreciation, but as the actual and only cause of human happiness:

"La lumière et le sentiment sont en général les deux principes des déterminations de la volonté. Afin que tu aimes l'ordre, il faut que tu en voies la beauté, et que tu la goûtes. Tu ne peux ni voir ni goûter cette beauté, si Dieu ne t'éclaire de quelque lumière, et ne te modifie ou ne te touche de quelque plaisir: et, afin que Dieu agisse en toi, et donne la connaissance et le goût de la beauté de l'ordre, il faut que tu détermines l'efficace de la volonté par la cause occasionnelle qu'il a établie pour te sanctifier, et pour former son ouvrage d'une manière sage."[33]

---

[31] *Op. cit.*, ch. IV : "L'homme est un ouvrage d'un grand dessein, et d'une sagesse profonde .... C'est ce qui se remarque dans toute la nature. Nous voyons tant de justesse dans ses mouvements, et tant de convenance entre ses parties, que nous ne pouvons nier qu'il n'y ait de l'art, etc."

[32] *Op. cit.*, ch. I, section 8.

[33] *Méditations Chrétiennes et Métaphysiques*, XIII, para. 10.

that is by

"la Grâce de sentiment, ou cette délectation intérieure qui fait aimer aux hommes, comme par instinct, une beauté qu'ils ne devraient aimer que par raison." [34]

Remove the theology, and couch the whole passage in the plain language of sensationalism, and one is left with Montesquieu's definition of taste:

"La définition la plus générale du goût, sans considérer s'il est bon ou mauvais, juste ou non, est ce qui nous attache à une chose par le sentiment; ce qui n'empêche pas qu'il ne puisse s'appliquer aux choses intellectuelles, dont la connaissance fait tant de plaisir à l'âme .... L'âme connaît par ses idées et par ses sentiments; elle reçoit des plaisirs par ces idées et par ces sentiments: car, quoique nous opposions l'idée au sentiment, cependant, lorsqu'elle voit une chose, elle la sent; et il n'y a point de choses si intellectuelles, qu'elle ne voie ou qu'elle ne croie voir, et par conséquent qu'elle ne sente." [35]

Strangely enough however, the aesthetic theories which drew their inspiration from Malebranchian philosophy in general, like Père Roche's *Traité de la Nature de l'Âme*, and Père André's *Discours sur le Beau*, remained strongly idealist, advancing the theory that truth is beauty, and beauty truth against the oncoming tide of sensationalism. Shaftesbury's works likewise injected a strong dose of Platonic idealism into the aesthetic thought of the early 18th century. Not unnaturally, the prophet of virtue proclaimed beauty to be identical with truth and goodness, external beauty being nothing more than internal beauty in a material form.[36] In fact, much of the aesthetic thought of the 17th century survived intact, for the main reaction of sensationalism in favour of sensibility as the ultimate criterion of taste, was directed not so much against it, as against the scientific rationalism which prompted such comments as that made by Terrasson in the Preface to the *Dissertation critique sur l'Iliade d'Homère:*

"Tout homme qui ne pense pas sur toute matière littéraire comme Descartes prescrit de penser sur les matières physiques, n'est pas digne du siècle présent .... Rien ne prépare mieux que les mathématiques à bien juger des ouvrages d'esprit." [37]

The first concerted attack was made by the Abbé Du Bos in his *Ré-*

---

[34] *Ibid.*, XIV, para. 14.
[35] *Essai sur le Goût*, "Des Plaisirs de notre Âme."
[36] For a full account see W. Folkierski, *Entre le Classicisme et le Romantisme*, Crakow, 1925, part I, ch. 2.
[37] *Op. cit.*, Paris, 1715; p. 65.

flexions critiques sur la Poésie et sur la Peinture. Du Bos was a friend and disciple of Locke, and his aesthetic theory was founded on observation rather than speculation, and on the doctrine that the senses determined man's vision of the world. Accordingly the artist's main concern became the provision of pleasurable experience; the academic shortcomings of a work mattered little unless they greatly hindered this purpose. On this basis Du Bos classified works according to their "intérêt de rapport" and their "intérêt général"; the first heading indicated a limited appeal, relative only to certain groups at certain times, and the second, an appeal to basic human sensibility. Both qualities were essential to the successful work.[38] In this way, Du Bos modified the idea of "bienséances internes" and "bienséances externes," to fit his terms of reference. Similarly he retained the notion of authenticity or *vraisemblance*, and many of the rules associated with it. Imitation remained a factor of primary importance in composition: the painter for example must observe the natural order of things, and also ensure that the emotions he portrays are fitting to his subject. Some apparent or hidden order in the structure of the composition is necessary for ease of comprehension.[39] Yet excessive regard for proportion and fitness leads only to disaster by creating monotony and consequently boredom. Du Bos introduces a new term into the discussion: *le merveilleux,* a quality far more important than *convenance.*

"Les sentiments où il n'y a rien de merveilleux, soit par la noblesse ou par la convenance du sentiment, soit par la précision de la pensée, soit par la justesse de l'expression, paraissent plats."[40]

This quality characterizes the work of genius, which satisfies the demands of *vraisemblance,* avoids the absurd, and yet at the same time continually surprises and delights.

But Du Bos's new term is essentially descriptive; it is characteristic of a work full of energy and ideas, which nonetheless restricts itself to describing methods and examples, and suggesting reasons for appreciation of beauty in terms of psychology, environment, climate and so on. Though it utilizes many notions proper to the previous century, simply dressing them up in different clothes, it proffers no metaphysical definition of beauty, fully integrated into a systematic, rational view of the universe; and this empirical approach to the subject of aesthetics, made in the cause of human sensibility, is the true measure of its originality.

---

[38] *Réflexions sur la Poésie et sur la Peinture,* Paris, 1719; part I, ch. xii.
[39] *Réflexions sur la Poésie et sur la Peinture,* part I, ch. xxxi.
[40] *Ibid.,* part I, ch. xviii, p. 227.

The terms *convenance* and *bienséance* continued to hold their own however in aesthetic theory, if the evidence of the *Encyclopédie* is anything to
go by. In his article *Beau*, Diderot examines at length the theories of
Nicole and Le Père André, and sets out his own system founded on the
idea of harmonious relationships existing between the members of the
object, between the object and other objects and so on:

"J'appelle donc beau hors de moi, tout ce qui contient en soi de quoi ré-
veiller dans mon entendement l'idée de rapports; et beau par rapport à moi,
tout ce qui réveille cette idée." [41]

Yet Diderot makes it clear that he is dealing only with the idea of the
beautiful, or rather with the perception of certain elements in an object
which may be said to constitute an impression of beauty; he does not
associate them with an objective body of reason, but with human intelligence. He remarks in passing for instance: "Ces notions sont experi-
mentales comme toutes les autres." [42] Thus, while conserving the idea
of relationships of fitness or proportion as a kind of independent objective standard by which the beauty of things could be judged, Diderot
took care not to confuse attribute with essence, by assuming that the
quality of harmony pointed to the existence of a metaphysical entity
called beauty.[43] In later works he went on to examine the place of feeling
and the idea of utility in aesthetics.[44]

The articles in the *Supplément à l'Encyclopédie* devoted to *Convenances*
and *Bienséances* were written by Marmontel, and provide us with a
perfect summary of the aesthetic thought of the preceding century.
Everything is to be found in them: the association of fitness with the
idea of eternal beauty and of natural law; the precise distinction of
convenance and *bienséance* according to the universal or relative significance of the conformity in question; their relationship to historical
authenticity and so on. In poetry and drama the 18th century tended
to be backward looking and this perhaps helps to explain Marmontel's

[41] *Op. cit.*, vol. II, 1751; p. 176.
[42] *Ibid.*, p. 175.
[43] The avoidance of this error preoccupies Montesquieu in the early entries of the
Pensées: "Substance, accident, individu, genre, espèce, ne sont qu'une manière de concevoir
les choses, selon le différent rapport qu'elles ont entre elles . . . ." (156, Bkn. 2061); and, "Les
termes de beau, de bon, de noble, de grand, de parfait, sont des attributs des objets, lesquels
sont relatifs aux êtres qui les considèrent . . . . Il faut bien se mettre ce principe dans la tête:
il est l'éponge de la plupart des préjugés. C'est le fléau de toute la philosophie ancienne,
de la physique d'Aristote, de la métaphysique de Platon..." (410, Bkn. 2062). On the
whole his own aesthetic theory as presented in the *Essai sur le Goût* observes the principle;
but the idealism of the moral theory of the *Lettres Persanes* and the *Traité des Devoirs* would
seem to run directly counter to it.
[44] See W. Folkierski, *Entre le Classicisme et le Romantisme*, Part II, ch. 3.

remarkable fidelity to the theories of the 17th, although surprisingly in his article *Beau* he took issue with Diderot, pointing out that such ideas as order and regularity were only relative to intelligence, which was neither the first nor the only cause of the admiration inspired by beauty.[45]

His other contributions amount nevertheless to a definitive statement of idealism in aesthetics, and furnish a useful conclusion to this part of our study. In the article *Convenances*, the sphere of conformity is carefully separated from that of propriety:

"Il y a dans les objets de la poésie et de l'éloquence des beautés locales et des beautés universelles: les beautés locales tiennent aux opinions, aux moeurs, aux usages des différents peuples; les beautés universelles répondent aux lois, au dessein, aux procédés de la nature, et sont indépendantes de toute institution."[46]

The entry on *Bienséances* elaborates the difference between these two criteria, and demonstrates their relationship to truth:

"Dans l'imitation poétique, les convenances et les bienséances ne sont pas précisément la même chose: les convenances sont relatives aux personnages; les bienséances sont plus particulièrement relatives aux spectateurs: les unes regardent les usages, les moeurs du temps et du lieu d'action; les autres regardent l'opinion et les moeurs du pays et du siècle ou l'action est représentée. Lorsqu'on a fait parler et agir un personnage comme il aurait agi et parlé dans son temps, on a observé les convenances: mais si les moeurs de ce temps-là étaient choquantes pour le nôtre, en les peignant sans les adoucir, on aura manqué aux bienséances .... Ainsi pour mieux observer la décence et les bienséances actuelles, on est souvent obligé de s'éloigner des convenances en altérant la vérité. Celle-ci est toujours la même, et les convenances sont invariables comme elle: mais les bienséances varient selon les lieux et les temps."[47]

So it is that *convenance*, conformity with the original and universal essence of things, emerged as a central notion in aesthetic as well as moral thought; and as a notion that in this sphere at least, survived into the mid 18th century.

In earlier chapters, we have tried to show how moral values, particularly justice, were connected with the idea of relationships of conformity in things. Now in aesthetics, one of the main values, and one which has a close formal connection with *justice*, is that of *justesse;* and it is interesting to find out whether it too was commonly associated with the

---

[45] *Op. cit.*, vol. I, 1776.
[46] *Ibid.*, vol. II, 1776; p. 586.
[47] *Op. cit.*, vol. I, p. 888.

idea of *convenance*. Clearly, if *justice* depends on the correct assessment of moral relationships, then *justesse*, which is defined in the *Dictionnaire Universel* as "précision, exactitude, régularité," [48] is its near relation. Considered as a human attribute, just judgement is its primary ingredient; applied to objects, it denotes exact proportion, structural perfection, and is almost synonymous with conformity. Voltaire certainly saw *justice* and *justesse* as intellectual and moral counterparts when he wrote of the Duchesse de Choiseul, "Je sais qu'elle a outre les grâces, justesse dans l'esprit, et justice dans le coeur." [49]

But their relative significance was not always so clearly defined. Combining so closely the ideas of right proportion and just judgement, *justesse* possessed a certain moral significance in addition to its intellectual and aesthetic meaning. For in the century of La Bruyère if not in that of Voltaire, proportion and judgement were generally associated, as we have already mentioned more than once, with an all embracing metaphysical reason. La Bruyère's conception of *justesse* clearly implies a connection between intellectual attribute and value judgement:

"La même justesse d'esprit qui nous fait écrire de bonnes choses nous fait appréhender qu'elles ne le soient pas assez pour mériter d'être lues. Un esprit médiocre croit écrire divinement; un bon esprit croit écrire raisonnablement." [50]

And Bossuet, in an eloquent appeal to reason, is quite happy to use *justesse* where one might have expected *justice:*

"Ô justesse dans la vie! ô égalité dans les moeurs! ô mesure dans les passions, riches et véritables ornements de la nature raisonnable, quand est-ce que nous apprendrons à vous estimer?" [51]

The 17th century endowed all judgements whatever their object with a certain moral significance; thus *justesse* tended to imply "ce qui doit être," or the ability, acquired or innate, to perceive what is necessary. As might be expected, the Chevalier de Méré had a word to say on this subject. Addressing his Essay *De la Justesse* to a certain noble lady he writes:

"... vous parlez et jugez de tout également bien, et j'admire principalement cette extrême justesse que vous avez à penser et à dire ce qu'il faut sur tout ce qui se présente."

[48] *Dictionnaire Universel français et latin*, Trévoux, 1704; vol. II.
[49] Lettre à Mme. du Deffand, 13 July, 1768.
[50] *Les Caractères*, "Des Ouvrages de l'Esprit", 18.
[51] *Sermon sur l'Honneur, Oeuvres Oratoires*, vol. V, p. 52.

But this extreme nicety of judgement with regard to changing circumstance, though it might be presented as reasonable and invested
with the authority of right and truth, relied far more on the quality of
sensibility than on the faculty of rational thought. In this respect as far
as aesthetic appreciation is concerned, it seems more closely connected
with the indefinable but essential ingredient "le je ne sais quoi"; and as
regards moral judgements, with the kind of natural charity founded on
"amour-propre," which J.-J. Rousseau later isolated as the foundation
of justice.

Both Méré and Pascal were at pains to distinguish "l'esprit juste"
from "l'esprit géométrique." Méré groups both these qualities under
the heading *justesse*, but when describing the second type, he plainly has
in mind a much more rigid and scientific outlook:

"Il y a deux sortes de justesse; l'une paraît dans le bon tempérament qui se
trouve entre l'excès et le défaut. Elle dépend moins de l'esprit et de l'intelligence que du goût et du sentiment; et quand l'esprit y contribue on peut
dire... que c'est un esprit de goût et de sentiment: je n'ai point d'autres
termes pour expliquer plus clairement, ce je ne sais quoi de sage et d'habile
qui connaît partout la bienséance, qui ne souffre pas que l'on fasse trop
grand, ou trop petit, ce qui veut être grand ou petit: et qui fait sentir en
chaque chose les mesures qu'il y faut garder .... Il est impossible d'en donner des règles bien assurées, car outre qu'elle s'occupe sur des sujets qui
changent de moment en moment, elle dépend encore de certaines circonstances qui ne sont quasi jamais les mêmes. Il me semble que pour l'acquérir
il faut être d'abord extrêmement docile, et consulter le plus qu'on peut ceux
qui en jugent bien. Ensuite on s'achève par l'expérience du monde et dans le
commerce des personnes qui la savent pratiquer."[52]

Adaptability, sensibility and experience are the prerequisites for this
type of *justesse:* they alone will cope effectively with the demands of
bienséance and moderation, always subject to the changing scene. The
other kind, one suspects, will be associated with the perception of the
eternal verities, with the unchanging nature of things, with what critics
and moralists usually called *les convenances:*

"L'autre justesse consiste dans le vrai rapport que doit avoir une chose avec
une autre, soit qu'on les assemble ou qu'on les oppose; et celle-ci vient du
bon sens et de la droite raison: pour peu qu'on y manque ceux qui ont le
sens net y prennent garde, ou du moins ils en sont persuadés sitôt qu'on les en
avertit. C'est que cette sorte de justesse s'exerce sur la vérité simple et nue,
et qui n'est point sujette au plus ni au moins, et qui demeure toujours ce
qu'elle est. Je crois que pour y faire du progrès et pour en trouver la perfection, il faut essayer premièrement de connaître les choses, ensuite mettre à

---

[52] *De la Justesse, Oeuvres de M. le Chevalier de Méré*, Amsterdam, 1692, I, p. 153.

part celles qui ne veulent pas être ensemble, et surtout prendre bien garde de ne pas tirer de mauvaises conséquences."[53]

"Le vrai rapport que doit avoir une chose avec une autre," is indeed nothing more than "la convenance des choses"; and Méré could have called the quality he is describing simply "la raison," or as Pascal preferred "l'esprit de géométrie." It was for this kind of mental constitution that works like Terrasson's *Dissertation Critique sur l'Iliade d'Homère*, later claimed, in the cause of progress and philosophy, supremacy in the field of aesthetic appreciation as well as physics and mathematics. Calling for nothing more than "conformité avec la droite raison et la belle nature"[54] it proscribed sentiment and admiration in art. Pascal in his day was a clear sighted opponent of all that was arid in art as well as religion; and he draws in the *Pensées* a definite line between *justesse* and *géométrie*, the first characteristic of the sensitive, intuitive nature, and the second describing the method of the rigorous thinker:

"Il y a donc deux sortes d'esprit, l'un de pénétrer vivement et profondément les conséquences des principes, et c'est là l'esprit de justesse; l'autre de comprendre un grand nombre de principes sans les confondre, et c'est là l'esprit de géométrie."[55]

A century later, in spite of the recognition of sensibility as a major force in aesthetics, the geometric conception of *justesse* dominates. Vauvenargues defines taste as

"une aptitude à bien juger des objets du sentiment .... Le bon goût consiste dans un sentiment de la belle nature; ceux qui n'ont pas un esprit naturel ne peuvent avoir le goût juste";[56]

but he presents *justesse* as the essential characteristic of the erudite mind:

"Savoir bien rapprocher les choses, voilà l'esprit juste. Le don de rapprocher beaucoup de choses, et de grandes choses, fait des esprits vastes. Ainsi la justesse paraît être le premier degré, et une condition très nécessaire de la vraie étendue d'esprit."[57]

Its moral significance seems to have disappeared almost completely:

"Ceux qui veulent tout définir, ne confondent pas le jugement et l'esprit juste; ils rapportent à ce dernier l'exactitude dans le raisonnement, dans la

[53] *De la Justesse*, pp. 153–154.
[54] Terrasson, *Op. cit.*, 1715; Preface, p. 4.
[55] ed. Brunschvicg, 2.
[56] *Introduction à la Connaissance de l'Esprit humain*, Paris, 1746; Book I, p. 23.
[57] *Réflexions et Maximes*, 215; in *Oeuvres complètes de Vauvenargues*, 3rd ed., Paris, 1797, vol. II, p. 59.

composition, dans toutes les choses de pure spéculation; la justesse dans la conduite de la vie, ils l'attachent au jugement."[58]

The kind of insight acquired by experience, which Méré had associated with the criterion of *bienséance* and the ideal of moderation, Vauvenargues preferred to call *bon sens* and not *justesse;* and although it still consisted:

"à n'apercevoir les objets que dans la proportion exacte qu'ils ont avec notre nature ou avec notre condition",

such conformity was associated not with a quasi-aesthetic approach to manners, but with concern for present utility and advantage.[59] We are reminded again that moral conceptions had changed; that reason was often now considered as a scientific tool not a metaphysical absolute; that idealism in morals and aesthetics had given way to something more nearly approaching empiricism which tended to treat good and bad, beautiful and ugly as relative values.[60]

Yet, while bearing in mind the change in conceptions of reason and the growth of sensationalist psychology, it is clear that the conception of *justesse* that undergoes least modification is that associated with the fixed relationships of things: with the irreducible elements of intelligence, and with the necessary conformity of structural relationships in the universe, whatever their cause. It is this conception, combining the ideas of just judgement and of conformity in things, that is most closely connected with a definition of justice as "un rapport de convenance."

[58] *Introduction à la Connaissance de l'Esprit humain*, Paris, 1746, Book I, p. 11.
[59] *Op. cit.*, pp. 13–14.
[60] Significantly, Vauvenargues tied moral values to the good of the community, and recognized only one natural law, that of violence and coercion of the weak by the strong: "les abus inévitables sont des lois de la nature," *Maximes* 26; cf. nos. 164, 184, 187.

CONCLUSION

We have attempted to review the fortunes of the notion of conformity, more particularly of the notion of *rapport de convenance*, in the fields of philosophical and moral thought during the second half of the 17th century and the early years of the 18th. It might be objected that studies of this kind are in many respects unsatisfactory, since they must aim for a compromise between the comprehensiveness of the encyclopedia, and the narrow limits of the dictionary definition; and in dealing with so general a term, the danger of over-dilution is the greater. But some broad categories have been isolated in which the idea of relationships of fitness or conformity plays a major role, and some main trends in the development of the notion described. For the purpose of the study is not a critical biography of Montesquieu, but an account of the particular area of his cultural heritage which would appear to have most relevance to the terms and ideas incorporated in his moral theory. Thus, although some possible sources have been indicated, attention has not been restricted exclusively to them; and indeed, in the case of major figures like Malebranche, Bossuet and Bayle, there is little need to demonstrate the possibility of influence since they determined to a large extent the shape of philosophical discussion during the period, and it is above all a question of ascertaining the directions in which this influence exerted itself.

One of the most important developments of the 17th century as a whole was the consolidation of the Copernican view of the universe as an harmonious system supported by mathematics. This revival of Pythagorean and Platonic theory not only accounted adequately for the factual knowledge in the possession of contemporary scientist-philosophers, but also established a scientific method dominated by mathematics, that permitted further investigation and systematization. The notion of harmony, the method associated with it, and the theories be-

longing to the ancient tradition from which it stemmed, spread quite
naturally to fields other than astronomy, physics and metaphysics,
embracing among other things, ethics and jurisprudence. Now harmony is above all an aesthetic notion: it expresses the apparent coherence
of organized substance; we feel that there is pattern and purpose in
nature, that the perfection of the whole depends on the proportion of its
parts. These parts must in fact stand in a relationship of fitness to each
other. This primary organizational necessity was recognized by Plato
in the *Timaeus:*

"God, in the beginning of his fashioning, made the body of the universe out
of fire and earth. Now two terms cannot be brought together without a
third: there must be a bond between them to bring them together. There is
no better bond than that which makes of itself and the terms it joins a single
and complete whole. Now such is the nature of proportion ...";[1]

and it was still recognized in the 17th century. Whitehead has expressed the opinion that the safest general characterization of the European
philosophical tradition is that it consists in a series of footnotes to Plato;
this is certainly true of works like Bossuet's *De la Connaissance de Dieu et
de Soi-même*, which is built around the idea of conformity as the essential
characteristic of structure in every part of the universe. Indeed, even
when chance was substituted for God or reason as the cause of organization, the apparent existence of conformity could not be disputed,
since the factual knowledge to destroy the notion was not available.
Even when Maupertuis posed the question in his *Essai de Cosmologie* in
the middle of the following century:

"... ne pourrait-on pas dire que dans la combinaison fortuite des productions
de la nature, comme il n'y avait que celles où se trouvaient certains rapports de convenance, qui pussent subsister, il n'est pas merveilleux que cette
convenance se trouve dans toutes les espèces qui actuellement existent?"[2]

the fact of conformity is not disputed, as it would be now that the
mechanisms of organization and evolution are better understood. Moreover, the mathematical process involved in the analysis and comprehension of the structure of things, by which matter was reduced to a
system of spatial and causal relationships, naturally lent support to the
idea of universal harmony.

Thus the idea of relationships of fitness in things, associated with
mathematical reason, was central to the 17th century world-vision: it

---

[1] *Op. cit.*, 31B–32A.
[2] See above p. 31.

permeated their thinking on physics, metaphysics, ethics and aesthetics, and was for them the foundation of truth and right and beauty. This was the tradition in which Montesquieu's mind was formed and from which he drew his theoretical material; and he himself recognized that originality lay in the reappraisal and reapplication of old ideas:

"Nos pensées roulent toutes sur des idées qui nous sont communes; cependant, par leurs circonstances, leur tour et leur application particulière, elles peuvent avoir quelque chose d'original à l'infini comme les visages."[3]

Spicilège, 265; MS, 210; Nagel II, p. 758; Pléiade II, pp. 1281–1282.

PART TWO

MONTESQUIEU'S IDEA OF JUSTICE:
ITS BACKGROUND, MEANING AND SIGNIFICANCE

CHAPTER ONE

BIOGRAPHICAL ORIGINS

> "Cicéron est, de tous les anciens, celui qui a eu le plus de
> mérite personnel, et à qui j'aimerais mieux ressembler; il n'y
> en a aucun qui ait soutenu de plus beaux et de plus grands
> caractères, qui ait plus aimé la gloire, qui s'en soit fait une
> plus solide, et qui y ait été par des routes moins battues."
>
> *Discours sur Cicéron.*

"Le droit politique est encore à naître .... Le seul moderne en état de créer cette science eût été l'illustre Montesquieu. Mais il n'eut garde de traiter des principes du droit politique; il se contenta de traiter du droit positif des Gouvernements établis. Et rien au monde n'est plus différent que ces deux études. Celui pourtant qui veut juger sainement des Gouvernements tels qu'ils existent est obligé de les réunir toutes deux: il faut savoir ce qui doit être pour bien juger de ce qui est." [1]

Rousseau's judgement of Montesquieu in *Émile*, which, once due consideration is given to his debt to the author of the *Lois*, may be seen to disguise not a little of the same self-esteem as prompted the President to add the epigraph "Prolem sine matre creatam" to the title of his own masterpiece, continues nevertheless to lend authority to those criticisms which deny the *Lois* any serious moral content.[2] Yet many among those who acclaim Montesquieu as the founder of the science of comparative law and the precursor of modern sociology are ready

---

[1] J.-J. Rousseau, *Émile*, Bk. V; édition Garnier, Paris, 1961, p. 584.
[2] The object of Georges Davy's contribution to the bi-centenary of the *Esprit des Lois*, "Montesquieu et la Science Politique" (in *IIe Centenaire de l'Esprit des Lois de Montesquieu*, Conférences organisées par la ville de Bordeaux, Delmas, Bordeaux, 1949) is for example to disprove the existence of any *a priori* elements in the *Lois*. Similarly, P. Martino claims in his article "De quelques résidus métaphysiques dans l'Esprit des Lois" (*Revue d'Histoire de la Philosophie*, Fasc. 43, July–Sept. 1946, pp. 235–243) that the first book was intended only to "endormir des défiances irritables"; and L. Althusser's recent study restates this opinion most firmly: "Refus de soumettre la matière des faits politiques à des principes religieux et moraux ... voilà qui introduit aux grandes révolutions théoriques de Montesquieu," *Montesquieu, La Politique et l'Histoire*, P.U.F., Paris 1959, p. 22.

to acknowledge the existence in his works of certain vital elements, moral in inspiration, that owe more to his intellectual heritage and his cast of mind than to the calm rellections of an impartial observer. In his thesis on Montesquieu's contribution to sociology, Émile Durkheim conceded that the conclusions of the *Lois* were sometimes determined by criteria other than scientific:

"ce ne sont pas seulement les lois, mais les règles de la vie humaine qui sont étudiées dans son livre; ce n'est pas seulement la science, mais aussi l'art." [3]

Meinecke describes the President as a "Januskopf" in the evolution of political and historical thought. In his work on the origins of Historicism Montesquieu's importance is seen to lie in his success in combining the naturalistic and rationalistic attitudes as far as was historically possible:

"Montesquieus Tat war es, dass er, von jenen Bruchstellen der beiden Denkweisen, die wir ihm beobachten abgesehen, sie mit weit ausgreifenden Armen miteinander zu vereinigen und zu durchdringen strebte – den empirischen Sinn für die Mannigfaltigkeit der menschlichen Dinge und ihrer unendlich vielen besonderen Verursachungen, und den Sinn für die vernunftgemässe Einheit, die diese Mannigfaltigkeit beherrscht und letzten Endes erklärt, für oberste Gesetze, aus denen man alle Mannigfaltigkeit wie aus einer Quelle fliessen sehen möchte. So dass zuletzt, wie es im Eingang des *Esprit* heisst, jede Verschiedenheit Uniformität, jede Veränderung Konstanz wird. Die kühnste philosophische Absicht, die immer nur sein kann, dem Sein und dem Werden gleichzeitig gerecht zu werden, regt sich dahinter, aber freilich noch gebannt in das mechanistische Denken der Zeit." [4]

These are judgements of Montesquieu as a thinker and of the purpose of his work, but they inevitably prompt a closer look at certain cultural influences which may have helped form this enigmatic mind that leapt the gap between the universalism of the Renaissance and the universalism of modern scientific determinism.

Shackleton's critical biography is of course mainly devoted to the identification and evaluation of such influences throughout Montesquieu's lifetime, while Barrière's biography pays special attention to the people and institutions of Bordeaux and their importance in the life and thought of the President.[5] Levin's *The Political Doctrine of*

[3] *La Contribution de Montesquieu à la Constitution de la Science Sociale*, published in *Montesquieu et Rousseau, précurseurs de la Sociologie*, Libraire Marcel Rivière, Paris, 1953, p. 45.
[4] F. Meinecke, *Die Entstehung des Historismus*, R. Oldenbourg, München u. Berlin, 1936; vol. I, ch. 3, p. 153.
[5] R. Shackleton, *Montesquieu, A Critical Biography*, Oxford University Press, 1961; and P. Barrière, *Un grand Provincial: Charles-Louis de Secondat, baron de la Brède et de Montesquieu*, Delmas, Bordeaux, 1946.

Montesquieu's "Lois": its Classical Background,[6] is an exhaustive study of
Montesquieu's debt to Antiquity. In their respective fields these works
are authoritative, and the effort involved in reworking the ground
which they cover would be for the most part wasted. In the first part
of this study however, some attempt has been made to illustrate
through the semantic fortunes of the word *convenance* the fluctuating
relationship of naturalism and rationalism in European thought at the
end of the 17th century, and the gradual emergence of the former as a
dominant intellectual current as the 18th century progresses. The
object of the exercise was to place Montesquieu's definition of justice
in the *Lettres Persanes* in its general philosophical context and to throw
its ambivalence into relief against the background of intellectual up-
heaval into which their author was born and which reached its climax
during his formative years. This inevitably leads to the question of
what particular pressures Montesquieu was subject to during his education, and of the measure in which they reflected the general movement of ideas.

Both Barrière and Shackleton devote sections of their works to
Montesquieu's formal education at the Oratorian college at Juilly from
1700 to 1705. Their main concern is to outline the curriculum and
describe the discipline at this model establishment, the testing ground
for some of the most advanced educational theories of the age. They
both emphasize the erudition and the forward-looking liberalism of
its teachers, and note the solid factual basis of the Oratorian education
in contrast to the attention paid by the Jesuits to formal rhetoric and
stylistic elegance. The hallmark of the Oratorian tradition was concern
for the development of the individual personality rather than the
grooming of brilliant Classicists.[7] These general details may perhaps
throw light on the President's subsequent efforts to collect and classify
materials for the *Lois*, on his liking for abstract ideas, and on his
tolerance in questions of religion and manners; but in an article discussing Montesquieu's concept of progress, René Hubert also makes
the point that his education made no radical departure from the
traditional humanism of the Renaissance: it presented him with a
view of an unchanging nature, of man as a universal type at the centre
of the universe.[8] In any discussion of the progressive features of the
President's education this factor must be kept in mind, for the latent

[6] L. M. Levin, *op. cit.,* Columbia University Press, New York, 1936.
[7] See Barrière, *op. cit.,* part I, ch. 1, iii; and Shackleton, *op. cit.,* ch. 1, ii.
[8] See "Le Devenir historique chez Montesquieu," *Revue de Métaphysique et de Morale,* année 46, 1939, pp. 588–610.

conflict between this Classical concept of man, and the relativism encouraged by the more liberal studies of history and geography which were included in the Oratorian curriculum, could account in part for the later tension in Montesquieu's thought between rational idealism and scientific relativism.

The discernible influence of Montesquieu's stay at Juilly on his subsequent literary activity is limited. Apart from early indications of an interest in Roman history provided by a school notebook entitled *Historia Romana* which is preserved in the library of La Brède,[9] we can be certain only of an enthusiasm for tragedy revealed by fragments of a youthful dramatization of La Calpranède's novel *Cléopatre*, renamed *Britomare*, which Montesquieu reproduced in the *Pensées*.[10] Barrière sees in these fragments of verse a taste for the *roman galant* which expressed itself later in such works as *Le Temple de Gnide* and *Arsace et Isménie*; and he adds the more ambitious suggestion that La Calpranède's reputation as an historian over and above his actual achievements as a novelist may have inspired in the young Montesquieu a curiosity for the origins of the French nation. Besides these tangible vestiges of Montesquieu's schooldays, his early participation in the activities of the Academy of Bordeaux may have been encouraged by the existence at Juilly of a literary Academy in which the students were expected to play full part.

Nevertheless, a closer investigation of the methods and spirit of Oratorian education, and of the contribution made by some of its members to scholarship and the theory of education, reveals factors which could be of considerable significance for the development of Montesquieu's thought and for his later works. The period of intense intellectual agitation, of reassessment and rejection of traditional ideas and attitudes, during which Montesquieu spent his schooldays, could not be entirely unconnected with a new approach to the subject of education, even though this approach was made by a body normally associated with the unwavering conservatism of the Church. Indeed the general phenomenon of renewed intellectual activity over a broad European front, and the particular actions of this religious body, resulted from similar, sometimes identical forces, slowly transforming the vision of the Classical age. The prophets of revolution were often as not, whether by choice or accident, themselves clerics of one denomination or another: one thinks immediately of such outstanding

[9] See Pléiade II, pp. 1443–5.
[10] *Pensée* 359 (Bkn. 477); Nagel II, pp. 142–146; Pléiade I, pp. 1027–1031.

figures as Malebranche in the Oratory itself, or of Bayle in the Protestant camp. Thus although the Oratory as an association attempted to remain aloof, in a way that contrasted completely with the involvement of the Jesuits, from political and doctrinal disputes, the activities of its member priests as philosophers, scholars and teachers made of it an instrument of change.[11] Indeed, among ecclesiastical establishments, the Oratory, by virtue of its voluntary and non-monastic institution and its dependence not on Rome but on the French episcopate, was open as few others were to absorb and to propagate new ideas.

It is true that its members were with a few brilliant exceptions such as Richard Simon and Malebranche, men of the second rank as far as their importance for the history of ideas is concerned; but although they failed to provide the brilliant hypotheses which form the raw material of intellectual progress, they contributed to the work of consolidation without which such hypotheses remain in the realm of fantasy. The combination of genius and erudition found in a Leibniz is a rare occurrence; even the depth of intellect found in Bayle expressed itself in criticism rather than creation; and for one brilliantly dexterous manipulator of ideas like Fontenelle there were dozens of obscure but patient scholars. Thus when Monod reviewed the progress of historical studies in France for the first number of the *Revue Historique*,[12] the work of the religious orders, in particular of the Benedictines, in the publication and criticism of documents concerning the origins of feudalism and of the French monarchy received particular attention. Similarly, the Oratorian historians, Lecointe, Lelong and Thomassin gained an honourable mention beside the greater names of Saint-Évremond, Voltaire, Du Bos and Boulainviller. The necessity of a cultural process in which imaginative thought and solid research complement each other is exactly illustrated by Monod's judgement of Montesquieu as a historian:

"Montesquieu fut au XVIIIe siècle le représentant le plus éminent de cet esprit nouveau à la fois philosophique et politique appliqué à l'étude de l'histoire et des lois. Il y apporte une élévation de pensée et une pénétration supérieures, mais ses oeuvres sont propres plutôt à stimuler et à féconder l'esprit qu'à l'éclairer et à le guider avec certitude."[13]

---

[11] Barrière notes (*Un grand Provincial*, p. 13) Le Tellier's reproach to the Congregation for their republicanism, and their spirit of independence and liberty; also their enthusiasm and support a century later for the Revolution.
[12] "Du Progrès des Études historiques en France," R. H., vol. 1, 1876; pp. 5–38.
[13] *Op. cit.*, p. 25.

What was true of historical studies also held good for the law. As Ilbert pointed out in his lecture on Montesquieu, the President was in the vanguard as far as the philosophy of law was concerned, but he had no part in the scholarly work of the French jurists under the leadership of D'Aguesseau and Pothier, of codifying and modernising the existing elements of French law.[14]

From the time of its foundation by Pierre de Bérulle in 1611 for the purpose of instructing the priesthood, the Congregation maintained a tradition of liberal piety. The *Bulle d'Institution de la Congrégation de l'Oratoire*,[15] emphasizes the dignity of knowledge, and associates this with the idea, which runs like a continuous thread through the works of the Oratorian teachers, the philosophy of Malebranche, and the moral writings of Montesquieu, that God is supreme intelligence, and the Law of Reason. Cardinal Bérulle was a friend of Descartes and favoured the adoption of the new philosophy by the priests of the Oratory; but even in this, no rigidity was allowed to hamper their thinking, and Saint Augustine and Plato exercised an equal influence. Indeed, the spirit of Oratorian philosophy is in many ways reminiscent of the Platonic humanism of Erasmus: a spirit of tolerant eclecticism, convinced that the true philosophy is never opposed to genuine Christianity, more concerned with the discovery and interpretation of its sources than with dogma, but, while critical of the antiquated forms of Scholasticism, hostile towards scepticism. Similarly, Oratorian discipline seems to have been inspired by the notion that the sense of Scripture must be understood from the central point of the moral and personal life of the individual. Knowledge of God, Bernard Lamy declares in the *Entretiens sur les Sciences*,[16] is not dependent on erudition:

"La science (de Dieu) est facile; le ciel et la terre nous instruisent mieux que les livres et sans une profonde connaissance de la théologie, on peut aimer Dieu plus que ne font les plus savants."[17]

Although the Oratory had been set up for the purpose of instructing the priesthood, in 1630 it took over the Collège de Troyes, and that was the beginning of its pedagogic interests. The compilation of a *Ratio Studiorum* was begun in 1634 by a team of priests under the

[14] Sir Courtenay Ilbert, *Montesquieu*, the Romanes Lecture, 1904, Oxford.
[15] Reproduced in Appendix to A. Perraud's *L'Oratoire en France au XVIIe et au XIXe siècle*, Paris, 1865.
[16] Bruxelles, Fricx. 1684. This small Oratorian manual exercised a considerable influence in the 18th. century, and has a special significance for both Montesquieu and Rousseau studies.
[17] *Entretiens sur les Sciences*, I.

supervision of Le père de Condren.[18] They set out with the firm conviction that the basis of education should remain the study of the Humanities, but that all method should be taught in French, starting from a groundwork provided by the grammatical study of the French language.[19] This departure from the traditional methods employed by the Jesuits and in the colleges of the University was their first innovation and the basis of all those that followed.[20] Their testing ground was the collège de Juilly.

The study of history followed naturally upon that of French. It was introduced by order of the first assembly of the Congregation of the Oratory and came to occupy a special place in the curriculum. In the senior classes particular emphasis was laid upon French history and a library was provided for pupils to pursue their own research. In his *Notice sur le Collège de Juilly*,[21] le père Adry recounted:

"Lorsque notre langue se fut perfectionnée, il (le professeur d'Histoire) donnait lui-même ses leçons en français, et de vive voix, dans la Chambre des Grands, et l'histoire de France en était toujours l'objet. Dans les cinq autres chambres, il remettait des cahiers d'histoire aux préfets de pension. On voyait l'Histoire Sainte dans les deux dernières chambres où étaient les plus jeunes écoliers: et dans les trois chambres suivantes, on faisait apprendre l'Histoire grecque et l'Histoire romaine."[22]

In all Oratorian colleges use was made of le père Lecointe's notebooks; the regent at the collège de Vendôme was also the author of the *Annales Ecclesiastici Francorum* (1665–1683), a work which Montesquieu

[18] The first part was inserted in the acts of the General Assembly in 1634, but dealt only with discipline; the second part, completed in 1643, and embodying the principles practised at Juilly was published in 1645 under the title: *Ratio Studiorum a magistris et professoribus Congregationis Oratorii Domini Jesu observanda* (Paris, Vitré), but apparently no text remains extant. A résumé by le père Adry is however to be found in the *Mémoire sur le règlement des études dans les lettres humaines par M. Arnauld*, publ. by Ingold in the *Annales de l'Oratoire*, April and May 1885, and also in the *Revue Internationale de l'Enseignement*, July and August, 1886.

[19] Le père de Condren himself compiled a *Méthode en langue française, à l'usage de l'Académie de Juilly, pour apprendre avec facilité les principes de la langue latine, où sont expliqués les genres, la syntaxe et la quantité dans un ordre clair et concis tout ensemble*. See Ch. Hamel, *L'Histoire de l'Abbaye et du Collège de Juilly*, Paris, 1868, part IV, ch. 1, p. 211.

[20] There is some disagreement as to whether the Oratorians were influenced by the methods of the Jansenists in the Petites Écoles de Port-Royal, or vice-versa. Jansenist influence was first suggested by Sainte-Beuve in his *Histoire de Port-Royal*, and A. Théry reproduces the notion in his *Histoire de l'Éducation en France*, Paris, 1858, part II, Bk. 9. But G. Compayré in *Histoire Critique des Doctrines de l'Éducation en France depuis le 16e siècle*, Paris, 1879, Bk. II, ch. 2, inclines to believe that both institutions carried out similar reforms at the same time but independent of each other, while Hamel in his *Histoire de l'Abbaye et du Collège de Juilly*, Bk. IV, ch. 1, on the evidence of the *Ratio Studiorum*, puts forward the case for the influence of Juilly on the Petites-Écoles.

[21] *Notice sur le Collège de Juilly par un Ancien Élève de cette Académie*, Paris, à l'Institut des Sourds-Muets, 1807.

[22] *Ibid.*, p. 13.

later used.[23] Le père Bertault's *Florus Francicus*, an abridgement of French history, which went through 78 editions between 1632 and 1660, was their other main textbook.

History in the Oratory was complemented by geographical studies, which had been originally encouraged by le père Eustache Gault, a friend and contemporary of Bérulle.[24] The syllabus appears to have been unusually full, comprising not only the study and drawing of maps, but also research into social and political factors, such as government, manners and customs, language and natural resources.[25] The course is outlined in the programme of the college at Le Mans, dating from the beginning of the 18th century:

"Nous n'avons point borné la géographie à une nomenclature sèche et aride. Nous avons mêlé à la connaissance du globe un précis des religions, du commerce, du gouvernement, des moeurs des peuples qui l'habitent, des révolutions, des curiosités historiques, des productions en tout genre. Jaloux d'avoir une connaissance exacte de notre patrie, nous nous sommes étendus sur la France. Comment se gouverne la France? Qu'est-ce que le grand conseil, le conseil souverain, le parlement, un président, un baillage, une généralité, la chambre des comptes? On donne aussi un aperçu sur les provinces, avec un résumé des révolutions qu'elles ont éprouvées."[26]

There is no reason to suppose, since Juilly was the model establishment among Oratorian colleges, that its geography syllabus differed greatly from that of Le Mans. The breadth of the course, ranging from cultural background to economics, is obviously not without significance for Montesquieu's practical observations during his European travels, not to mention the sociological preoccupations of the *Lois*. The surprisingly modern spirit in which these new studies were conceived, contrasting strongly with Classical attitudes, is revealed in Lamy's *Entretiens sur les Sciences*; of history and geography he wrote that they go to form a man

"de tous les siècles et de tous les pays, ce que la nature n'a pu faire."[27]

The physical sciences were also given a place at Juilly. In his *Entretiens*, Lamy enthuses over the current fashion for laboratory ex-

---

[23] See *Pensées* 189 (Bkn. 1581).

[24] Cloyseault wrote of le père Gault: "Il aimait passionnément la géographie, à laquelle il s'était toujours attaché avec tant de soin et de curiosité," *Recueil des Vies de quelques prêtres de l'Oratoire*, Bibliothèque Oratorienne, ed. Ingold, vol. I, Paris 1880, p. 339.

[25] Lallemand bases this outline partly on the *Exercices publiques d'Effiat*, (1785) and partly on the syllabus of the college of Le Mans (c. 1700). See *Histoire de l'Éducation dans l'Ancien Oratoire de France*, Paris, 1888, p. 254.

[26] *Programme à la Bibliothèque municipale du Mans*, 408c, quoted by Lallemand, *op. cit.* p. 254, note 1.

[27] *Op. cit.*, I, p. 21.

periments, which may indicate that the idea of utilizing knowledge derived from observation was also introduced to the college's pupils, alongside standard Cartesian physics.[28] Thus the President's willingness to study the effects of climate on physical disposition by experiments with a sheep's tongue may have stemmed from a much earlier acquaintance with the natural sciences than the early activities of the Academy of Bordeaux.[29]

Experiment within the discipline of Cartesian philosophy must have long been part of the Oratorian tradition. Malebranche himself devoted considerable time to physics and wrote a *Traité des lois de la Communication du Mouvement* (1669); while entomology, botany, chemistry and astronomy also claimed his attention. Montesquieu was to make several explicit attacks in the *Pensées* on the epistemological foundations of Malebranchian metaphysics,[30] yet there remains, as we shall see, plentiful evidence to suggest that the President's moral thought was at least partly inspired by the spirit of the great philosopher, and beyond this, that he also approved of the Cartesian method in science.[31]

Yet the influence of Malebranche's thought should be seen in the context of the philosophical tradition of the Oratory. Its founder, Pierre de Bérulle, was as we have already mentioned, a close friend of Descartes, and favoured the dissemination of Cartesianism throughout the Congregation. Generally speaking it combined with a strong Platonic tradition which was basically hostile to dogmatism. Thus although Bernard Lamy was driven from the chair of philosophy at the college at Angers for his Cartesian sympathies, his works in fact reveal a tolerant eclecticism.[32] The college at Juilly used a manual specially composed by le père Fournenc to direct philosophical studies along the paths of Plato and the early Fathers, and, at least according to Hamel,[33] to divert the attention of the official defenders of Scholasticism from the Cartesian elements which had found their way into the syllabus; for Adry describes the manual as a work,

28 *Ibid.*, VI.
29 Montesquieu describes his experiments in the *Lois*, Bk. XIV, ch. 2.
30 *Pensées*, 156 (Bkn. 2061), 410 (Bkn. 2062), 157 (Bkn. 2066).
31 See *Essai d'observations sur l'histoire naturelle*, Nagel III, p. 112; and Pléiade I, p. 39.
32 In the *Entretiens sur les Sciences* one finds on the one hand an unmistakably Cartesian emphasis on the importance of mathematics in the training of the mind, and an adherence to certain Cartesian doctrines such as that of innate ideas, and on the other a remarkable exposition of the critical techniques of an historical method. In an article, "De la Composition de l'*Esprit des Lois*: Montesquieu et les Oratoriens de l'Académie de Juilly," (Revue d'Histoire littéraire de la France, 1952, pp. 440–450) H. Roddier has pointed out the significance of Oratorian eclecticism, in particular that of Lamy, for the political and historical thought of Montesquieu, and for his method of research and composition in the *Lois*.
33 *Histoire de l'Abbaye et du Collège de Juilly*, part IV, ch. 1, p. 223, note 3.

"dans lequel ce Père, en substituant l'autorité de la raison à celle d'Aristote, préparait la voie aux ouvrages plus parfaits qui ont été donnés depuis."[34]

Thus the teachers at Juilly escaped the censure which stifled Cartesianism in the other Oratorian colleges, and continued unmolested to instruct their pupils in the beliefs of a liberal idealism, based on a grounding in Cartesian method drawn mainly from Descartes's *Principes de la Philosophie* and modified by certain rudimentary forms of a comparative method.

In this way, the teaching of philosophy in the Oratory complemented on the one hand the growing relativism of its historical and geographical studies, and on the other the humanism of its Classical studies. These centred on the teaching of Latin authors, among whom, for stylistic reasons quite naturally, and for Montesquieu's moral ideas most significantly, Cicero held pride of place. Cloyseault notes in his biographies of outstanding Oratorians, that le père du Condren, superior of the Congregation at the time of the composition of the *Ratio Studiorum*, had a special liking for Cicero,[35] and this predilection seems to have been widespread throughout the colleges. Lamy reproduces it in his outline of Classical studies in the *Entretiens sur les Sciences:*

"Il faut joindre à la lecture des poètes celle des orateurs, et de tous les ouvrages de Cicéron, car je n'en excepte aucun. Il n'y a point d'Auteur dans l'Antiquité Payenne dont l'étude soit plus utile pour la solidité des pensées, pour les maximes admirables, pour la Latinité et la belle manière de mettre une vérité en son jour, et de la faire connaître avec tant de variété et de fécondité, que les esprits les plus distraits soient contraints de l'apercevoir.[36]

Similarly, Cicero's *De Officiis*, and the *De Natura Deorum* figure prominently in the programme of the college at Le Mans at the end of the 17th century.[37] Seneca was also included in the syllabus, and it therefore seems possible that Stoicism claimed considerable attention in the teaching of moral philosophy, and that Montesquieu's enthusiasm for its ideals of justice and moderation was contracted during his years at Juilly. It is true that the influence of Cicero is usually associated with the *Traité des Devoirs* composed in 1725, some twenty years after Montesquieu left Juilly; indeed, in a letter to Fitz-James

[34] *Notice sur le Collège de Juilly*, p. 15.
[35] Le Père C. E. Cloyseault, *Recueil des Vies de quelques Prêtres de l'Oratoire*, Bibliothèque Oratorienne, ed. Ingold, vol. I, Paris, 1880; Book V.
[36] *Op. cit.*, IV, p. 122.
[37] See P. Lallemand's outline of the curriculum in Oratorian colleges based on the Le Mans programme, in *Histoire de l'Éducation dans l'Ancien Oratoire de France*, pp. 362–371.

referring to a passage on Stoicism in the *Lois*,[38] he names the *De Officiis* and Marcus Aurelius's *Réflexions Morales* as his main inspirations for the *Traité*.[39] Nevertheless, even a rapid glance at the President's earliest literary enterprises, the *Discours sur Cicéron*, dating from about 1709, and the *Dissertation sur la Politique des Romains dans la Religion*, a more mature and serious work read to the Academy of Bordeaux in June 1716, reveals the esteem in which he already held the Roman moralist.

The first of these short essays, the *Discours sur Cicéron*, is nothing more than a straightforward eulogy, in which enthusiasm obscures critical appreciation. The opening paragraph sets the tone:

"Cicéron est, de tous les anciens, celui qui a eu le plus de mérite personnel, et à qui j'aimerais mieux ressembler; il n'y en a aucun qui ait soutenu de plus beaux et de plus grands caractères, qui ait plus aimé la gloire, qui s'en soit fait une plus solide, et qui y ait été par des routes moins battues." [40]

and Montesquieu later added a footnote which reveals not only an awareness of this deficiency, but also a growing interest in the fortunes of the Roman republic itself, not just its great protagonist:

"J'ai fait ce discours dans ma jeunesse. Il pourra devenir bon, si je lui ôte l'air de panégyrique. Il faut outre cela, donner un plus long détail des ouvrages de Cicéron, voir les lettres surtout, et entrer plus avant dans les causes de la ruine de la République et dans les caractères de César, de Pompée, d'Antoine." [41]

Yet Montesquieu already emphasizes in the *Discours* the greater importance of Cicero's moral philosophy compared to his rhetoric, and outlines the content of the *De Officiis*. Besides this, he pays considerable attention to the other work which appeared in the programme of Le Mans, the *De Natura Deorum*, and to a related treatise, the *De Divinatione*. Significantly, the only other moral philosopher mentioned in the essay is Seneca, and not Marcus Aurelius, perhaps because Greek was comparatively neglected in the Oratorian schools; but for Montesquieu at least, Seneca's brand of Stoicism pales before the stouter virtues of his hero.[42]

---

[38] Book XXIV, ch. 10.
[39] Montesquieu to Mgr. de Fitz-James, Paris, Oct. 8, 1750, (Nagel III, p. 1327).
[40] *Op. cit.*, Nagel III, p. 15; Pléiade, I, p. 93.
[41] *Ibid.*
[42] "Qu'on lise ses ouvrages, et on sera dégoûté pour toujours de Sénèque et de ses semblables, gens plus malades que ceux qu'ils veulent guérir, plus désespérés que ceux qu'ils consolent, plus tyrannisés des passions que ceux qu'ils veulent affranchir." *Ibid.*, Nagel III, pp. 17–18; Pléiade, I, p. 95.

Thus in this early work two of the President's main preoccupations, and two which at once reflect both the curious mixture of Classical humanism and historical relativism in Oratorian teaching, and the tension in his own thought between rational idealism and scientific determinism, are already beginning to emerge. The first of these is concern for the dictates of reason, the ideal of justice, and the duties of society. Cicero is

"le premier, chez les Romains, qui ait tiré la philosophie des mains des savants, et l'ait dégagée des embarras d'une langue étrangère. Il la rendit commune à tous les hommes, comme la raison, et, dans les applaudissements qu'il en reçut, les gens de lettres se trouvèrent d'accord avec le peuple . . . . Il nous apprend ce que c'est que l'honnête et ce que c'est que l'utile; ce que nous devons à la société, ce que nous devons à nous mêmes; ce que nous devons faire en qualité de pères de familles ou en qualité de citoyens."[43]

The second preoccupation, and possibly the one which was uppermost in his mind during this early period, is not totally unrelated to his admiration for Cicero's rational ethics however; for the interest in paganism which underlies his brief discussion of the *Traité de la Nature des Dieux* and the *Traité de la Divination* goes hand in hand with an obvious desire to use critical reason in the service of tolerance as well as of science:

"Quel plaisir de voir, dans son livre *De la Nature des Dieux*, faire passer en revue toutes les sectes, confondre tous les philosophes, et marquer chaque préjugé de quelque flétrissure! Tantôt il combat contre ces monstres; tantôt il se joue de la philosophie. Les champions qu'il introduit se détruisent eux-mêmes; celui-là est confondu par celui-ci, qui se trouve battu à son tour. Tous ces systèmes s'évanouissent les uns devant les autres, et il ne reste, dans l'esprit du lecteur, que du mépris pour les philosophes et de l'admiration pour le critique.
Avec quelle satisfaction ne le voit-on pas, dans son livre *De la Divination*, affranchir l'esprit des Romains du joug ridicule des aruspices et des règles de cet art, qui était l'opprobre de la théologie payenne, qui fut établi dans le commencement par la politique des magistrats, chez les peuples grossiers, et affaibli, par la même politique, lorsqu'ils devinrent plus éclairés."[44]

The use of discursive reason in the criticism of pagan superstition, which Montesquieu here admires in Cicero, was precisely the weapon used by some of his contemporaries, scientific rationalists like Fontenelle in their attempt to undermine the blind enthusiasm of the Classicists

---

[43] *Discours sur Cicéron*, Nagel III, pp. 16–17; Pléiade I, pp. 94–95.
[44] *Discours sur Cicéron*, Nagel III, p. 17; Pléiade I, p. 94.

and to destroy the intolerant dogmatism of established religion, by introducing the notion that the value of beliefs, practices and superstitions lies not in their literal meaning – often absurd – but in their relation to the origin and development of social organisation. Thus his admiration has its roots in contemporary intellectual movements, which, while pursuing the immediate ends of overcoming religious intolerance and of freeing science from the yoke of the Church, and whilst retaining some connection with a rational idealism whose supreme values were justice and law, eventually gave birth to the new science of sociology; and it is accompanied by an indication of his own later contribution to the founding of that science: the notion, one of the unifying themes of all his works, that religions are natural products, and religion an essentially social phenomenon.

Montesquieu's interest in paganism spanned much of his lifetime and can be examined from various aspects. But it was not a purely pedantic interest, since paganism was a central topic in contemporary literary and philosophical discussion. It produced in Montesquieu one startling and original idea, that religion is a social phenomenon and as such should foster the State's ends, which after a brief indication in the *Discours sur Cicéron*, is further developed in the *Dissertation sur la Politique des Romains dans la Religion*. Here again extensive use is made of quotations drawn from Cicero, from the *De Divinatione* in particular, although the central theme:

"Ce ne fut ni la crainte ni la piété qui établit la religion chez les Romains, mais la nécessité où sont toutes les sociétés d'en avoir une .... Je trouve cette différence entre les législateurs romains et ceux des autres peuples, que les premiers firent la religion pour l'Etat, et les autres l'Etat pour la religion",

where a germ of the new scientific determinism lies next to a grain of old Machiavellianism, is now more closely related to St. Augustine's account in the *De Civitate Dei* of the political wisdom of Scaevola in matters of religion.[45]

St. Augustine's writings were highly favoured by the Oratorian teachers, but it has also been suggested that Montesquieu drew on Bayle's *Continuation des Pensées diverses sur la Comète* for much of the material used in quotations in the *Dissertation*.[46] They have in common references to the *De Civitate Dei*, to Cicero's *De Natura Deorum*, and to the English Platonist Cudworth. This may be true; it is sufficient to

[45] See Nagel III, p. 44; Pléiade I, p. 86.
[46] In Shackleton's "Bayle and Montesquieu," in *Pierre Bayle, le Philosophe de Rotterdam*, ed. Dibon, Paris, 1959; ch. VII, p. 142.

comment that Montesquieu uses his quotations as illustrations, almost as proofs: like his Oratorian masters he consistently regarded a well established text as valid empirical evidence; Bayle on the contrary used them as the critical weapons of scepticism. It is also certain that Montesquieu's attitude to religion in the *Dissertation* was already quite different from Bayle's,[47] as the remarks made there about Cudworth show. In the *Continuation des Pensées Diverses* (1705), Bayle put forward the objection to Cudworth's *True Intellectual System of the Universe*, that it was in reality a concealed defence of atheism, not a plea for the establishment of religious tolerance on the basis of a liberal attitude to dogma.[48] Montesquieu on the other hand takes up Cudworth's point that in spite of the plurality of gods in pagan religion, the most enlightened of pagan thinkers were in fact deists; he responds to the rational idealism of the Cambridge Platonist, and himself adds a sympathetic outline of Stoic pantheism:

"M. Cudworth a fort bien prouvé que ceux qui étaient éclairés parmi les païens adoraient une divinité suprême, dont les divinités du peuple n'étaient qu'une participation. Les païens, très peu scrupuleux dans le culte, croyaient qu'il était indifférent d'adorer la divinité même, ou les manifestations de la divinité; d'adorer, par exemple, dans Vénus, la puissance passive de la nature, ou la divinité suprême en tant qu'elle est susceptible de toute génération; de rendre un culte au soleil, ou à l'être suprême en tant qu'il anime les plantes et rend la terre féconde par sa chaleur. Ainsi, le stoïcien Balbus dit dans Cicéron, que Dieu participe, par sa nature, à toutes les choses d'ici-bas; qu'il est Cérès sur la terre, Neptune sur les mers .... Comme le dogme de l'âme du monde était presque universellement reçu, et que l'on regardait chaque partie de l'univers comme un membre vivant dans lequel cette âme était répandue, il semblait qu'il était permis d'adorer indifféremment toutes ces parties, et que le culte devait être arbitraire comme était le dogme.
Voilà d'où était né cet esprit de tolérance et de douceur qui régnait dans le monde païen: on n'avait garde de se persécuter et de se déchirer les uns les autres; toutes les religions, toutes les théologies, y étaient également bonnes; les hérésies, les guerres et les disputes de religion y étaient inconnues; pourvu qu'on allât adorer au temple, chaque citoyen était grand pontife dans sa famille."[49]

Thus Montesquieu's approach to the question of religious tolerance is based on the notion that all cults may be tolerated, because they all

---

[47] At some date Montesquieu was particularly concerned to refute Bayle, as the fragments, *Quelques réflexions qui peuvent servir contre le Paradoxe de M. Bayle, qu'il vaut mieux être athée qu'idolâtre*, (Pensée 1946, Bkn. 673) show; Shackleton dates this refutation after 1731, and Montesquieu's return from England however.
[48] See L. P. Courtines, *Bayle's Relations with England and the English*, New York, 1938, p. 47 ff.
[49] *Dissertation sur la Politique des Romains*, Nagel III, pp. 44–45; Pléiade, I, pp. 87–88.

possess a certain validity, namely the way in which they express the idea of a universal reason, or a world soul; it is not based as Bayle's was, on the idea that religion is profoundly indifferent for the fortunes of the State, since from a social point of view at least, atheism is to be preferred to paganism. For Montesquieu man is both a social and a religious creature.

In relation to this passage it is also worth noting that the Stoic idea of a world soul is not far removed from the notion of immanent reason; a predisposition in Montesquieu towards this concept would help to reconcile the determinism implicit in the idea that the establishment of religion follows from social necessity with his rational idealism: for if it is assumed that all religious phenomena are valid in that they express in some way the cult of immanent reason, it follows logically enough that any given religion may be regarded as necessary.[50]

Montesquieu's interest in paganism is directly related in the *Dissertation sur la Politique des Romains dans la Religion* to the concept of religion as a social phenomenon and to the political implications of this idea; the question of religious tolerance is only a secondary theme in the essay. But there is little doubt that Montesquieu desired to use his notion that all religions express something of the religious nature of man, in the contemporary debate on inter-sectarian tolerance which was stimulated by historic events such as the persecution of the Huguenots in France, the emergence of the eirenic movement, and by the dissemination of rationalism and the accompanying growth of natural religion. One of the most hotly debated topics was the question of eternal punishment: it was becoming more and more difficult to reconcile the orthodox dogma concerning heretics and pagans with the notion of a God of reason and justice; and not surprisingly therefore, another of Montesquieu's early works seems to have had as its aim to prove

"que l'idolâtrie de la plupart des payens ne paraissait pas mériter une damnation éternelle."[51]

Other works mentioned in the *Pensées*, but long since disappeared: *Les Prêtres dans le Paganisme*,[52] and a *Discours sur l'idolâtrie en général*,[53]

[50] For Montesquieu and the idea of immanent reason, see below, pp. 164–166; pp. 248–253.
[51] This is referred to by D'Alembert in his *Éloge de Montesquieu*; see Nagel I, p. iii, note a.
[52] Mentioned in *Pensée* 2004 (Bkn. 591); Nagel II, p. 617; Pléiade, I, p. 1082.
[53] *Pensée* 1946 (Bkn. 673); Nagel II, p. 584; Pléiade I, p. 1172. Other entries in the *Pensées*, nos. 112(446), 420(2119), 421(2184), were also possibly connected with this or a similar work.

were also probably the outcome of a combination of sociological interest and rationalist conscience.

The interesting point here in relation to the influence of the Oratorians is indeed the fact that Montesquieu's scientific interest in paganism is inseparable from his rational idealism. For it seems certain on the one hand that both originated in the study of Cicero; and on the other, the concern which he shows to salvage man's spiritual nature while at the same time answering in full the demands of scientific relativism, has more in common with the spirit of religious liberalism found in the works of a Classicist like Thomassin, than with the rational scepticism of Fontenelle, whose influence Montesquieu nevertheless also experienced.

Montesquieu probably met Fontenelle during his first stay in Paris from 1709–1713,[54] and he certainly came to know him well in later life. There is evidence in the *Pensées* that he was in the habit of discussing matters concerning the origin of certain beliefs and customs with Fontenelle, and the account of one of these discussions provides the key to the difference in their attitudes to religion, and also throws light on his lengthy refutation of Bayle's opinions on atheism.[55]

Fontenelle remained faithful to Cartesian physics but not to Cartesian metaphysics; he preserved the positivist-mechanist elements of the new philosophy, emphasizing the importance of a method dependent on doubt and evidence, and his application of it to questions of belief led quite naturally to scepticism. In spite of his rather uncritical adulation of Descartes in early scientific essays like the *Observations sur l'Histoire Naturelle*, Montesquieu was apparently aware quite early of Fontenelle's attitude; his early criticisms of Malebranchian metaphysics in the *Pensées* were most likely inspired by Fontenelle; and at least one judgement of Descartes which he records there recalls his friend's attitude:

"Descartes a enseigné à ceux qui sont venus après lui, à découvrir ses erreurs mêmes.

Je le compare à Timoléon qui disait: 'Je suis ravi que, par mon moyen, vous avez obtenu la liberté de vous opposer à mes désirs.'"[56]

Many years before, in the *Digression sur les Anciens et les Modernes*, (1688) Fontenelle had written:

[54] See Shackleton, *Montesquieu*, ch. I, iii, p. 10.
[55] The account is given in *Pensée* 1677 (Bkn. 2147); Nagel II, p. 499; Pléiade I, p. 1556, and probably dates from the period 1746–1750, though this is not a sure indication of the date of the conversation itself. The refutation of Bayle is of course *Pensée* 1946 (Bkn. 673).
[56] *Pensée* 775 (Bkn. 2105); Nagel II, p. 231; Pléiade I, p. 1548.

"C'est lui (Descartes) qui a amené cette nouvelle manière de raisonner, beaucoup plus estimable que sa philosophie même, dont une bonne partie se trouve fausse ou incertaine, selon les propres règles qu'il nous a apprises."

Nevertheless, Montesquieu perseveres in acclaiming Descartes's contribution to religious thought; in the record of his conversation with Fontenelle he mentions that Descartes was the first to establish a real distinction between the soul and the body, and the same point recurs in the refutation of Bayle:

"Il est même certain qu'avant M. Descartes la philosophie n'avait point de preuves de l'immatérialité de l'âme: car l'âme ne se peut connaître que de deux manières, par l'idée ou par sentiment."[57]

Montesquieu never rejected Descartes's rational spiritualism, though he was prepared to consider the possibility that thought was an attribute of matter.

Fontenelle however was consistent in his outlook. As a partisan of the *Modernes*, he set out to demolish the arguments of those who supported the cause of Classical learning against that of the modern age, by subjecting the fables of antiquity to a comparative interpretation. It little mattered that the critical method used here was equally well suited to reducing all speculative belief to natural, nonreligious origins. The work of demolition began with the *Digression sur les Anciens et les Modernes*, and was continued in the *Histoire des Oracles* (1686), a translation and re-arrangement of Van Dale's *De Oraculis Ethnicorum Dissertationes duae*, and in the *De l'Origine des Fables* (1724).[58] In their enthusiasm for Antiquity, the *Anciens* made spectacular claims for the historical importance of its literature. Rapin's estimation of Homer's significance is typical:

"Les législateurs y ont pris le premier plan des lois, qu'ils ont données aux hommes: les fondateurs des monarchies et des républiques ont dressé leurs états sur le modèle qu'il s'en était formé: les philosophes y ont trouvé les premiers principes de la morale qu'ils ont enseignée aux peuples..."[59]

Claims such as these, however absurdly exaggerated, did however skirt, without ever grasping it, an important truth: namely that the legends of antiquity reflected certain basic characteristics of primitive social organisation. Fontenelle seized on the relationship between

---

[57] *Pensée* 1946 (Bkn. 673); Nagel II, p. 585; Pléiade I, p. 1173.
[58] In his critical edition of the work (Paris, 1932), J. R. Carré suggests that it was probably written before 1680, and drawn from a larger projected work on history.
[59] *Réflexions sur la Poétique d'Aristote*, Muguet, Paris, 1674; iv, p. 7.

fables and religious cults, and developed the thesis that all primitive belief is essentially anthropomorphic:

"Cette philosophie des premiers siècles roulait sur un principe si naturel, qu'encore aujourd'hui notre philosophie n'en a point d'autre; c'est-à-dire que nous expliquons les choses inconnues de la Nature par celles que nous avons devant les yeux, et que nous transportons à la physique les idées que l'expérience nous fournit. Nous avons découvert par l'usage, et non pas deviné, ce que peuvent les poids, les ressorts, les leviers; nous ne faisons agir la nature que par des leviers, des poids et des ressorts. Ces pauvres sauvages qui ont les premiers habité le monde, ou ne connaissaient point ces choses-là, ou n'y avaient fait aucune attention. Ils n'expliquaient donc les effets de la Nature que par des choses plus grossières et plus palpables qu'ils connaissaient. Qu'avons-nous fait les uns et les autres? Nous nous sommes toujours représenté l'inconnu sous la figure de ce qui nous était connu; mais heureusement il y a tous les sujets du monde de croire que l'inconnu ne peut pas ne point ressembler à ce qui nous est connu présentement."[60]

Fontenelle just failed to reach the idea that religious beliefs and practices may be conditioned by national character and environment, the notion that is visible in Montesquieu's *Dissertation sur la Politique des Romains dans la Religion;* but nevertheless the establishment of a definite relationship between speculative belief and psychological factors was an important first step towards a sociological interpretation of religion. It was a belief in the immutability of human nature which prevented him taking his analysis further; this led him to suggest that all history could be deduced from basic human characteristics,[61] and in spite of a belief in the possibility of material progress, his view of the moral state of mankind was fundamentally pessimistic:

"Sur ce nombre prodigieux d'hommes, assez déraisonnables, qui naissent en cent ans, la nature en a peut-être fait deux ou trois douzaines de raisonnables, qu'il faut qu'elle répande par toute la Terre, et vous jugez bien qu'ils ne se trouvent jamais nulle part en assez grande quantité pour y faire un monde de vertu et de droiture."[62]

Considering the nature of man to be brutish and fixed, it was hardly surprising that he saw no religious spirit in him; thus his scientific explanation of religious phenomena depended on their reduction to

---

[60] *De l'Orgine des Fables, Oeuvres de Fontenelle*, Paris 1767, vol. III, pp. 274–275.
[61] *Sur l'Histoire:* "Quelqu'un qui aurait bien de l'esprit, en considérant simplement la nature humaine, devinerait toute l'histoire . . . . Il dirait: la nature humaine est composée d'ignorance, de crédulité, de vanité, d'ambition, de méchanceté, d'un peu de bon sens et de probité par-dessus tout cela . . . . Donc ces gens-là feront une infinité d'établissements ridicules." *Oeuvres*, Paris, Bastien, 1790, vol. V, pp. 432–434.
[62] *Dialogues des Morts*, Socrate-Montaigne.

natural, non-religious causes: to the primitive instincts of an irrational creature:

"dans toutes les divinités que les payens ont imaginées, ils y ont fait dominer l'idée du pouvoir, et n'ont eu presque aucun égard ni à la sagesse ni à la justice, ni à tous les autres attributs qui suivent la nature divine. Rien ne prouve mieux que ces divinités sont fort anciennes, et ne marque mieux le chemin que l'imagination a tenu en les formant. Les premiers hommes ne connaissaient point de plus belle qualité que la force du corps; la sagesse et la justice n'avaient pas seulement de nom dans les langues anciennes: ... d'ailleurs la première idée que les hommes prirent de quelque être supérieur, ils la prirent sur des effets extraordinaires, et nullement sur l'ordre réglé de l'univers qu'ils n'étaient point capables de reconnaître ni d'admirer. Ainsi ils imaginèrent les dieux dans un temps où ils n'avaient rien de plus beau à leur donner que du pouvoir, et ils les imaginèrent sur ce qui portait des marques de pouvoir, et non sur ce qui en portait de sagesse." [63]

Thus in spite of his retention of the traditional idea of an unchanging human nature, Fontenelle did not subscribe to the rational-idealist notion that it was basically reasonable; in his attitude to pagan religions he shared nothing with the supporters of natural religion, who were prepared to grant them at least a respect for the universal ideas of truth and justice. It is here that his real differences with Montesquieu lie, and that the full significance of the influence of Cicero and of the Oratory on the President's thought becomes apparent.

For if we turn now to the account of Montesquieu's discussion with Fontenelle on the origin of ideas of purity and impurity in religious thought, we certainly find a readiness to look for a natural cause within the sphere of basic human reactions: "L'origine de la pureté et de l'impureté des choses vient de ce qu'il est naturel d'avoir eu de l'aversion pour les choses désagréables à nos sens." [64] This explanation easily fits into the context of a sensationalist theory of the origin of ideas; but Montesquieu obviously sees in sense perception the natural mechanism through which the primitive religious imagination worked. For him sensationalism in no way undermines the validity of human religious inspiration; the operation of the religious imagination through the medium of the senses is clearly understood as a cause which is historically and generically adequate to the material nature of the facts it is held to explain.[65] The principle at stake in Montesquieu's

[63] *De l'Origine des Fables, Oeuvres*, 1767, vol. III, pp. 276–277.
[64] *Pensée* 1677 (Bkn. 2147); Nagel II, p. 499; Pléiade I, p. 1556.
[65] It is useful to remember that Malebranche, while maintaining the fallibility of the senses, accepted their validity and their necessity in so far as man was a corporal being: "L'esprit de l'homme ... est uni à un corps, qui non seulement le remplit de fausses idées,

mind is thus that a religious solution must account for religious facts, that their scientific explanation should not lead to the disintegration of their religious sense.[66] This is borne out by the suggestion made in the text that intellectual progress has brought a change or a modification of ideas of purity and impurity:

"Or, dans des temps ou l'on n'avait guère d'idée de la nature de l'âme et de sa distinction réelle avec le corps, distinction qui n'a été guère bien établie que depuis Descartes, on pouvait naturellement croire que ce qui souillait le corps souillait aussi l'âme et mettait l'être qui était touché, à une espèce d'état de péché et le rendait désagréable à Dieu, comme la souillure nous rendait désagréables les uns aux autres. Mais, quand l'âme a été bien distinguée du corps, on a bien vu qu'il n'y avait que le corps qui était souillé."[67]

There is still the same equivalence between the cause given: a deeper insight into the nature of the soul, and its effect: the dissociation of bodily uncleanliness from the idea of sin. In this way Montesquieu reconciled scientific relativism with his religious and moral convictions.

Further proof of Montesquieu's attitude is provided by his rejection of Fontenelle's explanation as ingenious but basically unsound. Now Fontenelle argues that ideas of impurity originated in the association of blood-stains with murder, and that in this way crime and uncleanliness came to be linked together. As there is undoubtedly an attempt here to provide a natural explanation, Montesquieu's objection must stem from the fact that the suggested cause is unrelated to the nature and mechanisms of religious imagination, and therefore inadequate to the phenomenon it pretends to explain.

Montesquieu develops his thesis in the refutation of Bayle's claims for the superiority of atheism to paganism. Starting from the same general principle that the senses determined man's first ideas of God, he argues that pagan notions of a plurality of gods in human form, and endowed with both rational faculties and physical appetites, were the natural, anthropomorphic products of the imagination, "les véritables fruits de l'enfance." Their beliefs were the logical if erroneous consequences of the original idea that God like man must possess physical

mais qui excite encore dans son coeur mille mouvements déréglés. Et comme il veut invinciblement être heureux, ce qui ne peut être actuellement que par quelque plaisir actuel, il n'est pas possible que ce corps ne le trouble et ne le dérègle, s'il ne trouve dans la recherche de la vérité et dans l'exercice de la vertu quelque douceur actuelle, qui fasse qu'il contemple et qu'il agisse avec plaisir," *Méditations Chrétiennes et Métaphysiques*, Plaignard, Lyon, 1707, XIV, section xiv, p. 310.

[66] This interpretation of Montesquieu's attitude to religion is also put forward by C. J. Beyer in "Montesquieu et l'Esprit Cartésien," *Actes du Congrès Montesquieu*, Bordeaux, 1956.

[67] *Pensée* 1677 (Bkn. 2147); Nagel II, p. 499; Pléiade I, p. 1557.

being. On the other hand, if paganism was misguided, atheism is inexcusable; for it was natural and inevitable for man to come to a knowledge of God's existence, and to refuse to acknowledge it is to deny reason and the evidence of the senses:

"Quant aux athées de M. Bayle, la moindre réflexion suffit à l'homme pour se guérir de l'athéisme. Il n'a qu'à considérer les Cieux, et il y trouvera une preuve invincible de l'existence de Dieu. Il n'est point excusable lorsqu'il ne voit point la Divinité peinte dans tout ce qui l'entoure: car, dès qu'il voit des effets, il faut bien qu'il admette une cause. Il n'en est pas de même de l'idolâtre: car l'homme peut bien voir et considérer l'ordre des Cieux et rester opiniâtrement dans l'idolâtrie. Cette disposition ne répugne point à la multiplicité des Dieux, ou, si elle y est contraire, ce ne peut être que par une suite de raisonnements métaphysiques, souvent trop faibles sans le recours de la foi, qu'ils le peuvent découvrir. Je dis plus: peut-être que la seule chose que la raison nous apprenne de Dieu, c'est qu'il y a un être intelligent qui produit cet ordre que nous voyons dans le monde. Mais, si l'on demande quelle est la nature de cet être, on demande une chose qui passe la raison humaine. Tout ce qu'on sait de certain, c'est que l'hypothèse d'Épicure est insoutenable, parce qu'elle attaque l'existence d'un être dont le nom est écrit partout." [68]

Here Montesquieu sets himself apart from both Bayle and Fontenelle, for one only has to recall the passage from the *De l'Origine des Fables*:

"la première idée que les hommes prirent de quelque être supérieur, ils la prirent sur des effets extraordinaires, et nullement sur l'ordre réglé de l'univers",

to realise the contrast in their attitudes towards paganism and religion in general. In his adherence to a sensationalist theory of the origin of ideas, Montesquieu may be regarded as a rationalist of the positivist school, but at the same time he salvaged something of the metaphysical outlook of orthodox Cartesianism, and this combined with a deep sympathy and admiration for Stoicism, formed the basis of his religious philosophy and of his moral thought.

Both these sources of inspiration were first opened to him by his teachers at Juilly, just as they also introduced him to the endlessly fascinating enigma of history. Indeed, the spectacle of the history of the nations, and the cause of natural religion were not entirely unrelated in Oratorian thought. Le Père Thomassin's vast, almost encyclopedic manual, *La Méthode d'étudier et d'enseigner chrétiennement et solidement les Lettres Humaines par rapport aux Lettres Divines et aux Écritures*, which was commissioned by the Congregation for teaching in the

[68] *Pensée* 1946 (Bkn. 673), Nagel II, p. 588; Pléiade I, p. 1176.

colleges, was designed to reinforce the truth of Christian revelation by relating Classical Literature, general history, and the history of philosophy to Scripture. Thomassin aimed to demonstrate the continuous revelation of God in time, by selecting on the basis of a rational eclecticism, scattered fragments of "truth" from the whole field of human knowledge, and reassembling them into one monumental and irrefutable proof. All diversities of belief and practice were to be drawn into the fold of natural religion. Significantly the inspiration of Thomassin's rationalism, and the basis for the *rapprochement* between men of reason which the work was designed to effect, was Cicero's moral philosophy, understood as a manifestation of that *pia philosophia*, belief in which formed the central core of the Platonic tradition of the Oratory, and which was strengthened by the idealism of Cartesian metaphysics. In the Preface,[69] Cicero is presented as an exponent of natural religion, and the treatise *De la Nature des Dieux* is singled out for special praise as a weapon against superstition and idolatry. Later in the fourth part of the work, devoted to philosophy, the exposition of Cicero's moral thought, supported by ample quotations from the *De Legibus* and the *De Officiis*, occupies a prominent position. Thomassin declares that the object of the exposition is to prove that:

"l'homme est un animal naturellement religieux, lié de commerce et en société avec Dieu, comme avec la Loi éternelle de justice; et cela est aussi évident et aussi nécessaire, qu'il est évident et nécessaire que la raison agisse raisonnablement selon la loi de la vérité et de la justice. Les autres lois sont émanées de notre raison, mais notre raison, pour faire de sages lois, et pour ne pas se laisser aller aux égarements dont elle est capable doit être réglée elle-même par une loi supérieure, éternelle et immuable de sagesse et de justice, qui domine sur toutes les intelligences créées, parce qu'elles sont aussi toutes naturellement sujettes au changement, aussi bien que celle de l'homme."[70]

The Malebranchian undertones of this passage, and their resemblance to the doctrines put forward by Montesquieu in Letter 83 of the *Lettres Persanes*, and in the First Book of the *Lois* are unmistakable. The notion of an eternal and immutable law of justice accessible to all

---

[69] *La Méthode d'étudier et d'enseigner ... les Lettres Humaines* etc., part I, vol. 1, Muguet, Paris, 1681; preface, section xix, "Les oeuvres philosophiques de Cicéron, et principalement les trois livres de la nature des Dieux font voir les efforts de plusieurs grands génies, qui combattaient la superstition et l'idolâtrie, par les lumières de la raison, par les restes de l'image de la loi divine, que le péché n'a pu entièrement effacer de nos coeurs, et par les secours généraux de la céleste lumière, qui se fait voir à tous les hommes qui viennent au monde."

[70] *La Méthode d'étudier et d'enseigner ... la philosophie par rapport à la religion chrétienne*, Muguet, Paris, 1685; part III, ch. 7, xviii, p. 639.

intelligent creatures must have dominated the teaching of moral philosophy in the Oratory, linking it with a wider movement in favour of rational idealism and natural religion throughout Europe. But besides its idealism, Thomassin's work is notable for its erudition, for the vast span of fact, legend, and opinion it comprises.[71] Its initial condemnation of an education designed only to teach

"L'élégance des expressions, ou les beaux tours d'esprit, ou les antiquités du Paganisme",[72]

is reinforced by a massive demonstration of painstaking research, and thorough scholarship. Thus in spite of its avowed object, it becomes in a way, an early monument to comparative science; and Thomassin may be said to have achieved the odd combination of a treatise devoted to natural religion, but relying for the demonstration of its *a priori* propositions on largely comparative methods. In works such as Thomassin's *Méthode*, the tension between scientific relativism and moral idealism, which was to some extent characteristic of European thought in general at the beginning of the 18th century, and which became acute in Montesquieu's work, although perhaps unconscious, was already present.

The case for maintaining that Montesquieu's attitude to religion, one of his earliest interests, and one in which this tension began to emerge, was particularly influenced by his Oratorian education, rests largely upon the features it shared with approaches like Thomassin's: a common conviction that man is naturally religious, coupled with a critical interest in diversities of belief and practice, both of which were associated with a predilection for Cicero. But there are other general details of Oratorian interests and activities which further strengthen the case.

The Congregation's open-mindedness with regard to contemporary scientific and philosophical questions is for example demonstrated by their association with some of the pioneers of the Enlightenment. Richard Simon, author of the *Histoire Critique du Vieux Testament* (1678), where for the first time in France the techniques of philology divorced from any philosophical or religious bias, were applied to biblical exegesis, was a priest of the Oratory, and taught philosophy and

---

[71] Thomassin, himself educated by the Oratorians of Marseilles, was something of a polymath; he was professor of mathematics at Juilly, but also taught heraldry, geography, history, Italian and Spanish. See Perraud, *L'Oratoire de France au XVIIIe et au XIXe siècle*, part II, ch. 5.

[72] *Méthode d'étudier et d'enseigner ... les Lettres Humaines*, Préface, vol. I, section xviii.

rhetoric at Juilly from 1664–1673. Nicolas Fréret, the authority on ancient chronology and oriental religions, was connected with the Paris Oratory; and le père Desmolets, librarian of the Congregation's house in the Rue Saint-Honoré, who probably introduced him to Montesquieu, was himself a literary figure of some importance. Desmolets was responsible for the publication of two unedited works of Pascal, *De l'esprit géométrique*, and the *Entretien avec M. de Sacy*, and also edited the *Continuation des Mémoires de Littérature*, a journal which brought to light rare and important documents. One of Fréret's close associates, and a pupil of Juilly, was the brilliantly individualistic Boulainviller, the author of a life of Mahomet, of a "refutation" of Spinoza, which was rather an exposition of his doctrines in thin disguise, and of a history of the feudal origins of the French monarchy.[73]

Besides these eminent associates, the Oratory counted among its members humbler scholars, whose contribution to the history of ideas was nevertheless of some significance. Besides the historians Lelong and Lecointe,[74] there was le Père Le Brun, who contributed to the comparative study of religion, by following up Fontenelle's *Histoire des Oracles*, with a critical study of alchemy, the *Histoire critique des pratiques superstitieuses*.[75] Henri Lelevel's *Conférences sur l'ordre naturel et sur l'histoire universelle*, also throw light on ideas current in the Oratory at the turn of the century.[76] Lelevel was basically sympathethic to the cause of the "Modernes," but while criticizing the confusion of Classical philosophies, an attitude which set him apart from Platonists like Thomassin, he produced the interesting theory that Paganism was inspired by the imagination, and in inventiveness far surpassed the religion of later ages.

"C'est par cette raison, qu'autant que les Modernes surpassent les Anciens dans tout ce qu'on appelle philosophie, autant leur sont-ils inférieurs dans tout ce qu'on appelle brillant de l'imagination. Il ne se pouvait que des hommes nourris uniquement d'idées profanes, et qui ne connaissent que le sensible, n'excellassent dans tout ce qui peut remuer les passions et présenter à l'esprit des fantômes agréables. La spiritualité de la religion dans laquelle nous sommes élevés, change tout."[77]

As we have seen, the notion that the senses determined pagan beliefs

---

[73] See R. Simon, *Henry de Boulainviller*, Paris, 1940.
[74] See above p. 117.
[75] Paris, 1702.
[76] Musier, Paris, 1698. His treatise on education, *Entretiens sur ce qui forme l'honnête homme et le vrai savant*, Couterot, Paris, 1690, also reflects much of the practice of Oratorian schools.
[77] *Op. cit.* Conférence VI, p. 298.

and customs is central to Montesquieu's refutation of Bayle;[78] and although there is no evidence to show that Montesquieu was in any way directly acquainted with Lelevel's work, the fact that the idea of an association between primitive religion and fertile imagination was also used by the President in his discussion of the poetic poverty of contemporary theology,[79] is at least a further demonstration of the community of ideas which existed between his early works and those of Oratorian writers.

Passing from religion to law, it is equally interesting to find in another of Lelevel's works, *La Philosophie Moderne par Demandes et par Réponses*,[80] a combination of idealism and relativism, which again suggests the later development of Montesquieu's thought. Lelevel proclaimed on the one hand the unity of the human race, and the universality of the law of reason and justice; but turning to civil law, he insisted that its primary aim was to procure men the benefits of life in society, and that it should therefore be designed to suit the character of the community it governed:

"Comme le bon effet des lois dépend de la proportion que'elles ont avec le génie de ceux à qui on les impose, il faut consulter ce génie dans toutes celles qu'on fait; et même en certains cas, il faut, comme si l'on n'avait point de raison à consulter, n'avoir égard qu'à la faiblesse des hommes."[81]

Nothing here approaches the complexity of Montesquieu's theory of the "esprit général d'une nation", yet the inspiration of the passage is clearly in harmony with the sociological insight which produced Book XIX of the *Lois*.

It would no doubt be possible find in a great variety of works totally unconnected with the Oratorians, examples of ideas that Montesquieu later made use of. The crux of our argument is simply that the intellectual life of the Oratory reflected to a greater extent than that of many other religious bodies, the climate of ideas in Europe at the end of the 17th century; and the relevance of this lies in the fact that it was to their care that the young Montesquieu was trusted. The ideas of his Oratorian masters provided his first intellectual stimulus: significantly, it was from Desmolets that he borrowed the notebook which constitutes the first half of the *Spicilège*. Therefore it is not unreasonable to suggest that their preoccupations, and the conflict latent in their

---

[78] See above, p. 132.
[79] In an early entry in the *Pensées*, 112 (Bkn. 446); Nagel II, p. 37; Pléiade I, p. 1018.
[80] Toulouse, 1698.
[81] *Op. cit.*, vol. III, ch. 14, p. 176.

attitude to contemporary debates can help us to situate Montesquieu's early thought in the climate of the day.

There is another respect in which Oratorian influence was important for Montesquieu's later development, and this is in the field of method. For several of its teachers, the reconciliation of scientific inquiry with idealism in moral philosophy, no longer depended on a deliberate subordination, in the manner of orthodox Cartesianism, of experimental and critical methods to the procedure of logical deduction from *a priori* propositions. The introduction of new, non-mathematical subjects into the curriculum, such as history and geography, demanded a new approach to method.

The results of their reflections in this field are best recorded in Lamy's *Entretiens sur les Sciences*, and the possibility of this work's influence on the methods used by Montesquieu in the composition of the *Lois* has already been investigated by H. Roddier in his article, *De la composition de "l'Esprit des Lois": Montesquieu et les Oratoriens de l'Académie de Juilly*.[82] There were of course other works on education which embodied Oratorian theories: Lelevel's *Entretiens sur ce qui forme l'honnête homme et le vrai savant* (1690), and the Abbé Fleury's *Traité du Choix et de la Méthode des Études* (1686),[83] for example; but they are more concerned with the aims and methods of education itself, than with the actual techniques at the disposal of the scholar engaged in academic work. Thus the importance of Claude Fleury's *Treatise*, a valuable and original contribution to the literature of education, lay in its advocacy of a universal right to education independent of social considerations, and in its emphasis on the necessity of vocational training for those occupying responsible positions.[84] His attitude to Plato does perhaps reveal a realisation that each subject demands its own particular techniques, for he dismisses the philosopher's scientific method on the grounds that

[82] *Revue d'histoire littéraire de la France*, 1952, pp. 440–450.

[83] Fleury was himself a Benedictine, and was educated by the Jesuits at Clermont; his treatise is however an indirect attack on the educational practices of that order, and clearly draws some of its inspiration from the methods and programmes of the Oratory and Port-Royal. See G. Dartigues, *Le Traité des Études de l'abbé Claude Fleury*, Paris and Auch, 1921, pp. 68–69; and F. Gaquère, *La Vie et les Oeuvres de l'abbé Claude Fleury*, Paris, 1925, p. 188.

[84] Fleury's outline of the kind of education suitable for a magistrate curiously anticipates some of the tasks which Montesquieu set himself: "Il est bon qu'ils sachent aussi l'histoire, par rapport à la jurisprudence. C'est-à-dire, qu'ils observent les lois et les maximes diverses qui ont régné dans leur pays, en divers temps. Ils doivent encore aller plus loin .... Il leur sied bien de remonter aux sources des loix: et d'en examiner les raisons, par les principes de la véritable morale, et de la véritable politique. En un mot, quoi qu'ils ne soient chargés que de l'exécution des lois, il est bon qu'ils soient capables d'être législateurs." *Op. cit.*, Paris, 1686, ch. XXXIX, pp. 288–289.

"étant accoutumé à raisonner moralement en morale, il a raisonné de même en physique et a voulu expliquer toute la nature par des convenances."[85]

Nevertheless, it is in the preface to his enormous *Histoire Ecclésiastique* (1691–1720) and not in the *Traité du Choix et de la Méthode des Études*, that he sets out the principles of his own comparative and critical historical method.

We must therefore return to Lamy's *Entretiens sur les Sciences* as our main source of information on the methods of work used and taught by the Oratorian scholars. Like most of the Oratorian teachers, Lamy was a man of considerable ability: he taught literature at Juilly from 1663 to 1671, philosophy at Saumur and then at Angers, where his Cartesian leanings earned him the bitter opposition of the Scholastics, and resulted in his transfer to the chair of theology at the Oratorian seminary in Grenoble, from whence he later moved to Paris and Rouen.[86] In the *Entretiens sur les Sciences* he does insist on the utility of mathematics in the development of good judgment and a sense of method – "c'est par une bonne logique qu'il faut commencer d'étudier" – but it is nevertheless clear that his own methods are not basically Cartesian, and that the study of history and philology occupy first place in his interests.[87] Logic must then combine with empirical and comparative methods, as it appears in the sixth *Entretien*, in order that an effective approach may be made to such subjects.

The first requirement of such a procedure is that the best editions of the best printed books should be consulted, together with sound summaries and abridgements. As a guide to these Lamy indicates the catalogues of the Oratorian library, the *Journal des Savants*, the *Nouvelles de la République des Lettres* and the *Bibliothèque Universelle* of Jean Leclerc. Dictionaries, glossaries, commentaries and criticisms are also indispensible tools, and in historical research, the independent evidence afforded by medals and inscriptions. Indeed, Lamy insists on the necessity of comparing and contrasting source materials:

"Ce n'est point dans un seul auteur qu'il en faut chercher le bout, il faut fouiller dans toutes les pièces, et en les confrontant démêler le noeud de la difficulté."[88]

After mastering the resources of the library, the student is advised

[85] *Op. cit.*, "Discours sur Platon," p. 316.
[86] A. Perraud, *L'Oratoire de France au XVIIe, et au XIXe siècle*, part II, ch. 3.
[87] Roddier points out in his article cited above p. 138, that Lamy's own *Introduction à l'Écriture Sainte* is in its examination of law, civil government, customs and institutions an anticipation of the comparative studies contained in the *Esprit des Lois*.
[88] *Op. cit.*, Bruxelles, 1684, VI, p. 207.

to follow a certain pattern and to apply certain techniques in his reading; he should fix a goal and work towards it in stages, arranging material obtained according to books, chapters and articles, and leaving spaces below his headings to be filled in when new evidence comes to light:

"Il faut digérer soi-même la matière sur laquelle on veut travailler, la disposer par livres, par chapitres, par articles, ou se servir de la disposition de la même matière faite par quelque habile homme. On laisse entre chaque titre beaucoup de vide qu'on remplit à mesure qu'on étudie, ou que l'on médite .... Cette manière de disposer ces recueils est la meilleure, et contribue davantage à faire un homme savant. On peut avoir un livre particulier pour les mélanges, c'est-à-dire pour les diverses choses et les différentes pensées qui se présentent à l'esprit, et pour lesquelles on ne trouve point de lieu propre."[89]

With large works, Lamy recommends the composition of paraphrases in the form of marginal notes, which can then be transferred into notebooks at will:

"Après quand je veux travailler sur quelque sujet en consultant mes marges, je tire en un moment tout ce qui est dans mes écrits sur ce sujet, et le transporte dans mes grands recueils, qui sont proprement des plans et des desseins d'Ouvrages, où après de longues méditations, et avoir trouvé l'ordre naturel, j'ai rangé sous des titres les principales parties de l'Ouvrage, dont j'ai tiré les premiers traits."[90]

Thus, Lamy claims, it is possible for a determined and able man to amass over a period of twenty years or so, enough material to compose a very rich work.

This as Roddier points out in his article on Montesquieu's methods in the *Lois*, is precisely what the President did over a similar period of time, and employing methods very close to those advocated by Lamy. Learned journals and the catalogues of the Oratorian library were in fact some of the sources of Montesquieu's erudition; while the list of Montesquieu's notebooks in the *Catalogue des Manuscrits envoyés à mon cousin en Angleterre*,[91] the surviving collections of annotated extracts such as the *Geographica*,[92] not to mention the *Spicilège* and the *Pensées*, are sufficient evidence of the way in which he set about his documentation, collecting extracts and paraphrases in separate books under specific headings,

---

[89] *Entretiens sur les Sciences*, VI, pp. 193–194.
[90] *Ibid.*, p. 195.
[91] Nagel III, Appendice V, pp. 1575–1582.
[92] Nagel II, p. 923; other fragments of annotated extracts published in vol. III, pp. 703–719.

leaving spaces for later additions, and jotting down his personal
reflections in yet another volume. Lamy's methods were designed
according to Roddier to effect a renewal of philosophical and historical
criticism which would produce works with an organic unity, rather
than a formal deductive order. Now what pattern Montesquieu
intended to follow when he began writing the *Lois* is still something of open question, and, at least according to the Preface, it was
for a time a cause of some bewilderment to the author himself:

"J'ai bien des fois commencé, et bien des fois abandonné cet ouvrage; j'ai
mille fois envoyé aux vents les feuilles que j'avais écrites; je sentais tous les
jours les mains paternelles tomber; je suivais mon objet sans former de dessein; je ne connaissais ni les règles ni les exceptions; je ne trouvais la vérité
que pour la perdre. Mais quand j'ai découvert mes principes, tout ce que je
cherchais est venu à moi; et dans le cours de vingt années, j'ai vu mon
ouvrage commencer, croître, s'avancer et finir." [93]

His concern to find the principles governing his subject make it at
least possible that he had some intention of proceeding in a logical
fashion; on the other hand his confusion could have been that of the
pioneer of any new science struggling to extract some meaning from a
formless mass of data. But if we take Montesquieu's advice to the reader
in the Preface at its face value:

"Si l'on veut chercher le dessein de l'auteur, on ne le peut bien découvrir que
dans le dessein de l'ouvrage",

then we are forced to admit that the only kind of pattern that the
theoretical, the scientific, and the historical parts of the work fall into,
is indeed organic.

Moreover, it can hardly be denied that although his approach to his
source materials, both in the *Lois*, the *Considérations sur les Romains*, and
elsewhere, was never as rigorous as Lamy might have desired, he did
indeed succeed in renewing historical and political thought, to the
extent of founding a new science in which both combine to discover
those conditions of life in society which determine the happiness of men.
But it was to be a social and not a natural science: a discipline in
which material and moral factors were equally involved. And the
methods employed in its creation were determined by the ambition
which Montesquieu inherited from his Oratorian masters, and which
can be found at the root of most of his works: a desire to reconcile the

[93] Nagel I, p. lxii; Pléiade II, p. 231.

moral values of an idealist tradition inspired by Plato and Cicero, and renewed by Descartes and Malebranche, with a growing mass of empirical data relative to the human condition and with the deeper understanding of causation which the scientific apparatus of Cartesianism had produced.

CHAPTER TWO

TOWARDS A METAPHYSICAL FRAMEWORK

I

"Admirable idée des Chinois, qui comparent la justice de
Dieu à un filet si grand que les poissons qui se promènent
croient être en liberté; mais réellement ils sont pris. Les
pécheurs croient de même, qu'ils ne seront pas punis de Dieu;
mais ils sont dans le filet."

Pensée 434 (Bkn. 2124).

It is of the greatest significance for the appreciation of Montesquieu's
moral idealism that the earliest indication of the notion of "esprit
général," that combination of moral, social and physical factors determining the life and destiny of nations, should occur in the *Traité des
Devoirs*. This idea, of seminal importance for sociology, seems to have
been the direct outcome of Montesquieu's meditations on justice and of
his consequent desire to rebut the principles and practices of that
"realpolitik" whose evil results were manifest in the economic and moral
decay of contemporary France, and to which the political thought of
Machiavelli, of Hobbes and even of the righteous Bossuet, had lent
powerful but illconceived support.[1] In the *Lettres Persanes*, using, as
Roger Caillois has demonstrated,[2] a relativistic sociological method of
profoundly disturbing implications, Montesquieu had already achieved
a caustic though not wholly negative satirical portrait of contemporary

---

[1] Although hostility to the policies of Louis XIV is necessarily implied in the *Lettres
Persanes*, it is more overt in the *Réflexions sur la Monarchie universelle* (1734) where Montesquieu
dealt specifically with the politics of aggrandizement, probably as a preliminary or compan-
ion study to the *Considérations sur les Romains* published at the same time. An unusual if brief
confirmation of his attitude is to be found in his annotations to a *Recueil des harangues prononcées
par Messieurs de l'Académie française* (Paris, 1798), published by L. Desgraves in the *Revue
historique de Bordeaux et du Département de la Gironde*, April-June 1952, pp. 149–151. The passage
is from a *Panégyrique du roi par l'abbé Tallement le jeune:* "C'est ici, messieurs, que j'aurais un
beau champ pour m'étendre sur la valeur de ce grand monarque, si j'osais m'y abandonner;
mais j'aurais peur d'être désavoué de tous ses sujets." Montesquieu simply comments, "Il
a raison."

[2] See "Montesquieu et la Révolution sociologique," *Cahiers de la Pléiade*, Automne 1949.

society; not wholly negative, since the notions of absolute justice, of republican virtue and of moderate government were weighed against the description of corruption and folly. The *Traité des Devoirs* inspired by Cicero and Marcus Aurelius, was conceived as a more systematic and comprehensive exposition of the theoretical grounds of this optimistic idealism;[3] however, when he reached the point of demonstrating in antithesis the injustice of "la politique," Montesquieu went beyond *a priori* argument, attempting to base his refutation on historical evidence.

"Il est inutile d'attaquer directement la politique en faisant voir combien elle répugne à la morale, à la raison, à la justice. Ces sortes de discours persuadent tout le monde et ne touchent personne. La politique subsistera toujours pendant qu'il y aura des passions indépendantes du joug des lois.

Je crois qu'il vaut mieux prendre une voie détournée et chercher à en dégoûter un peu les grands par la considération du peu d'utilité qu'ils en retirent. Je la discréditerai encore en faisant voir que ceux qui ont acquis le plus de réputation par elle, ont abusé de l'esprit du peuple d'une manière grossière."[4]

Intimately associated with this historical demonstration was the hypothesis of the "esprit general" and a related non-providentialist view of historical causation. The destinies of nations are controlled neither by God, nor by the intrigues of a handful of wily statesmen; historical events are rather the outcome of a constantly changing combination of causes operating over long periods of time, and having their origins in the moral and political character of a people:

Dans toutes les sociétés, qui ne sont qu'une union d'esprit, il se forme un caractère commun. Cette âme universelle prend une manière de penser qui est l'effet d'une chaîne de causes infinies, qui se multiplient et se combinent de siècle en siècle. Dès que le ton est donné et reçu, c'est lui seul qui gouverne, et tout ce que les souverains, les magistrats, les peuples peuvent faire ou imaginer, soit qu'ils paraissent choquer ce ton, ou le suivre, s'y rapporte toujours et il domine jusques à la totale destruction ... Si un ton donné se perd et se détruit, c'est toujours par des voies singulières et qu'on ne peut pas prévoir. Elles dépendent de causes si éloignées que toute autre semblerait devoir être aussi capable d'agir qu'elles, ou bien c'est un petit effet,

---

[3] Shackleton suggests that the subject of the work was actually put to Montesquieu by Madame de Lambert whose works include a *Traité de l'Amitié*, and a *Traité de la Vieillesse*, imitated from Cicero. See *op. cit.*, p. 70. But the problems of happiness and virtue also appear to have preoccupied the Académie de Bordeaux to whom Montesquieu first read parts of his *Traité*, during the same period; see P. Barrière, "Éléments personnels et éléments bordelais dans les *Lettres Persanes*," *Revue d'histoire littéraire de la France*, Jan. 1951, p. 32.

[4] *De la Politique*, opuscule originally constituting Chapters XIII and XIV of the *Traité des Devoirs; Nagel* III, p. 165; *Pléiade* I, p. 112.

caché sous une grande cause, qui produit d'autres grands effets, qui frappent tout le monde, pendant qu'elle garde celui-ci pour le faire fermenter quelques trois siècles après.''[5]

The *compte rendu* of Montesquieu's readings from the *Traité des Devoirs* to the Academy of Bordeaux clearly shows how these scientific and deterministic notions were introduced into the discussion on justice:

"Comme rien ne choque plus la Justice que ce que l'on appelle ordinairement la Politique, cette science de ruse et d'artifice, l'auteur, dans le chapitre XIII, la décrit d'une façon plus utile que s'il en prouvait l'injustice; il en montre l'inutilité par la raison. La plupart des effets, selon lui, arrivent par des voies si singulières, et dépendent de causes si imperceptibles ou si éloignées qu'on ne peut les prévoir. La politique, par conséquent, n'a pas lieu à l'égard de cette espèce d'événements. Elle est inutile encore sur les événements prévus, parce que toute révolution prévue n'arrive presque jamais.''[6]

Sadly, the *Traité* remained unfinished, and perhaps for this reason Montesquieu never directly confronted the problem of reconciling his theory of historical causation where individual action is shown to have only marginal significance, with the notion of justice as transcendent ideal, a notion that implies the autonomy of the human mind and will.[7] If the effort to control events is futile, then the desire to realise in them the ordered pattern of justice is equally so. How curious then that so impersonal and mechanistic a view of history should be introduced to add weight to the cause of common humanity and of civic virtue. Although, as the extraction from the treatise of those sections devoted to politics and the theory of history under the separate title of *De la Politique* shows, as does also of course the writing of the *Considérations sur les Romains*,[8] Montesquieu's attention became concentrated upon the notion of the "esprit général," eventually to such a degree that

[5] *Ibid., Nagel* III, pp. 168–169; *Pléiade* I, pp. 114–5.
[6] *Compte rendu* published in the *Bibliothèque française*, Amsterdam, mars 1726, pp. 238–243; see Nagel III, p. 161; Pléiade I, p. 110.
[7] Montesquieu gave his reasons for abandoning the *Traité* in a letter to Mgr de Fitz-James of October 8th., 1750.
[8] Some of the key passages in the *Considérations* are plainly an elaboration of the notions found in *De la Politique*, eg.: "Ce n'est pas la fortune qui domine le monde – on peut le demander aux Romains qui eurent une suite continuelle de prospérités quand ils se gouvernèrent sur un certain plan, et une suite non interrompue de revers lorsqu'ils se conduisirent sur un autre. Il y a des causes générales, soit morales, soit physiques, qui agissent dans chaque monarchie, l'élèvent, la maintiennent, ou la précipitent; tous les accidents sont soumis à ces causes; et, si le hazard d'une bataille, c'est-à-dire une cause particulière a ruiné un État, il y avait une cause générale qui faisait que cet État devait périr par une seule bataille: en un mot, l'allure principale entraîne avec elle tous les accidents particuliers." Ch. XVIII; Nagel I, p. 482; Pléiade II, p. 173.

from about 1734 he undertook the Herculean labour of gathering together all the materials necessary for a comprehensive analysis of each separate factor influencing the corporate character of a nation expressed in and through its laws, the account of the *Traité* itself does not suggest that he was simply using it as a vehicle for revolutionary notions on history and society. It was acclaimed as a work on morals, and at the time of its composition it was undoubtedly there that Montesquieu's interest lay:

"il y a environ trente ans que je formai le projet de faire un ouvrage sur les devoirs. Le *Traité des Offices* de Cicéron m'avait enchanté et je le prenais pour mon modèle."[9]

Thus while the subsidiary notion of the "âme universelle," otherwise "esprit général," subsequently proved to be the most fertile of Montesquieu's career as a thinker, it is nonetheless clear that the initial inspiration for his investigation of law and society stemmed from his belief in the paramount importance of the pursuit of justice. Reviewing the whole of his work, it seems almost as if the discovery of the idea of the "esprit général" provided him with the essential key to the description and analysis of those varying social and physical conditions within which the lawgiver or statesman must operate if his policies are to give effective expression to the joint ideals of universal justice and the good of the people. In the *Lois*, Montesquieu aimed to provide him with a surer, sounder, more honest science than Machiavelli's *Prince*:

"Si je pouvais faire en sorte que tout le monde eût de nouvelles raisons pour aimer ses devoirs, son prince, sa patrie, ses lois; qu'on pût mieux sentir son bonheur dans chaque pays, dans chaque gouvernement, dans chaque poste où l'on se trouve, je me croirais le plus heureux des mortels.
Si je pouvais faire en sorte que ceux qui commandent augmentassent leurs connaissances sur ce qu'ils doivent prescrire, et que ceux qui obéissent trouvassent un nouveau plaisir à obéir, je me croirais le plus heureux des mortels.
Je me croirais le plus heureux des mortels, si je pouvais faire que les hommes pussent se guérir de leurs préjugés. J'appelle ici préjugés, non pas ce qui fait qu'on ignore de certaines choses, mais ce qui fait qu'on s'ignore soi-même."[10]

The relativism that characterizes Montesquieu's treatment of political institutions in the *Lois* necessarily implies that environment largely determines social responses, yet he never conceded that the influence of *milieu*, instrumental though it was in producing the

[9] Letter to Fitz-James, Nagel III, p. 1327.
[10] *De l'Esprit des Lois*, Préface; Nagel I, p. lxi; Pléiade, II, p. 230.

astonishing range of laws and customs that he recorded, was entirely responsible for shaping human character. He retained the classical notion of an unchanging human nature; thus in the *Considérations*, side by side with the idea of the "esprit général" varying according to a multitude of factors from nation to nation, one finds the following statement:

"comme les hommes ont eu dans tous les temps les mêmes passions, les occasions qui produisent les grands changements sont différentes, mais les causes sont toujours les mêmes. [11]

Human nature, and presumably human reason are universal and immutable; and for this reason Montesquieu found it possible to repeat in the first chapter of the *Lois* his conviction that justice is absolute and unchanging:

"Les êtres particuliers intelligents peuvent avoir des lois qu'ils ont faites; mais ils en ont aussi qu'ils n'ont pas faites .... Dire qu'il n'y a rien de juste ni d'injuste que ce qu'ordonnent ou défendent les lois positives, c'est dire qu'avant qu'on eût tracé de cercle, tous les rayons n'étaient pas égaux." [12]

As long as society existed in a recognizable form, placing the individual in circumstances where he could not but acknowledge the idea of reciprocity fundamental to any definition of justice, then Montesquieu could rightly insist on his notion of justice as either the "rapport général" of the *Traité des Devoirs*, or the "rapport de convenance" of the *Lettres Persanes*. The precise significance of the qualification "de convenance" raises many questions it is true; Letter LXXXIII gives little indication of what is meant by a proper relationship actually existing between two things, a relationship said to be immutable and visible to all orders of intelligent beings. Are we to infer that such relationships are immanent in the natural order, or that they belong to an ideal transcendent order; do they exist between beings of different orders, or only between beings of the same order? In the absence of any specific textual information, the answers to such questions remain largely conjectural. Yet whatever conclusion one reaches as to the metaphysical nature of the relationship, or to the criterion that governs its "convenance," the most elementary moral interpretation of Montesquieu's definition remains unaffected, given the conception of man associated with it. As an intelligent being, once a member of society, he will determine his conduct according to a consideration of

11 *Op. cit.*, Ch. I; Nagel I, p. 354; Pléiade II, p. 71.
12 Nagel I, pp. 2–3; Pléiade II, p. 233.

his relationships with other members. Interpersonal relationships are likewise the main concern of the lawgiver or magistrate. Thus, although many other variable factors conditioning this relationship will have to be taken into account, and here obviously environmental forces are involved, recognition of the social bond is the essential basis of just conduct or of just government.

Neither the ideal, nor necessarily Montesquieu's definition of justice is incompatible with the sociological insights embodied in his work. Indeed, as the short essay *De la Politique* and the account of the parent work, the *Traité des Devoirs*, demonstrate, the elaboration of the most important of these insights, the theory of the "esprit général," appears to have been conditional upon a powerful conviction of the primacy of justice. Although with the beginning of the preparation of the *Considérations sur les Romains* in 1731, a marked change of emphasis from moral theorizing to historical reconstruction and scientific observation is evident in Montesquieu's researches, the change is not altogether unprepared as the remarkable and very early *Dissertation sur la politique des Romains dans la religion* shows;[13] and on the other hand it is inconclusive evidence that the moral idealism central to the early essays and fragments was completely abandoned in favour of scientific materialism as some scholars have maintained.[14] Analysis of the *Dissertation sur la politique des Romains* and related texts reveals an attempt on Montesquieu's part to provide a scientific explanation of religion considered as a social phenomenon without undermining the validity of religious belief in itself as the expression of the religious imagi-

[13] See above, Part II, ch. 1.

[14] The opinions of Davy, Martino and Althusser on this issue have already been mentioned, see above p. 113, note 2. As many scholars have been at pains however to demonstrate that moral idealism remained an imaginative force in Montesquieu's thought, and to reconcile the metaphysical theories supporting his definition of justice with the determinism implicit in many parts of the *Lois*. See for instance, P. Janet, *Histoire de la Science Politique*, Paris, 1872; part IV, ch. 5; G. Lanson, "Le Déterminisme historique et l'idéalisme social dans *l'Esprit des Lois*," *Revue de Métaphysique et de Morale*, année 23, janvier 1916, pp. 177–202; for Lanson, the *Lois* is "le véritable Antimachiavel du XVIIIe siècle"; Montesquieu distinguishes himself from other theorists in that he "fonde la correction du présent sur la connaissance exacte du passé"; E. Cassirer, *The Philosophy of the Enlightenment*, tr. F. C. A. Koelln and J. P. Pettegrove, Princeton, 1951, ch. 6; C. J. Beyer, "Le problème du déterminisme social dans *l'Esprit des Lois*," *Romanic Review*, vol. XXXIX, 1948, pp. 102–106; S. Cotta. "Il problema dell' ordine umano e la necessità nel pensiero di Montesquieu," *Rivista di Filosofia*, vol. XXXIX, 3e série, Oct.–Dec. 1948, pp. 368–380; J. Wróblewski, "La Théorie du Droit de Montesquieu," *Monteskuisz i jego dzieło*, Département des sciences sociales de l'Académie polonaise des Sciences, 1956; W. Stark, *Montesquieu, pioneer of the sociology of knowledge*, London, 1960; Stark defines the position of Montesquieu's idealism very succinctly, "the eternal principle of justice belongs to the noumenal world of lasting reality rather than the phenomenal world of shifting appearances." Ch. V, p. 182.

nation of humanity.[15] Similarly it is possible to see the *Lois* as a scientific and comparative study of human societies considered as phenomena, but a study which, far from invalidating the ideal of justice as the expression and aspiration of the rational moral conscience of a social creature, serves rather as has already been suggested, to provide an understanding of the laws governing the life and growth of societies, without which such an ideal is indeed no more than idle speculation. A short sentence from one of Montesquieu's less well known oriental stories *Arsace et Isménie* seems a sincere if naïve reflection of his own attitude to moral idealism: among the principles that govern Arsace's conduct as king is the conviction:

"Que le désir général de rendre les hommes heureux était naturel aux princes; mais que ce désir n'aboutissait à rien, s'ils ne se procuraient continuellement des connaissances particulières pour y parvenir."[16]

Two related points emerge then from those sections of *De la Politique* which we have considered; namely, the central importance of the ideal of justice in the genesis of Montesquieu's work as a whole and as its unifying principle; and secondly the lack of any clear demarcation in the presentation of his ideas, between the postulates of idealism and the hypotheses of inductive reasoning. But although these points immediately suggest something about Montesquieu's philosophical standpoint, for instance that he may have had some conception of an immanent reason, it is necessary to return to the *Lettres Persanes* in order to place his idea of justice in its full moral and metaphysical context.

Montesquieu gives his famous definition of justice in Letter LXXXIII:

"La Justice est un rapport de convenance, qui se trouve réellement entre deux choses."

Although this is one of the best known phrases in the work, and the letter containing it certainly one of the most outstanding, it is surprising how few of the others are in fact devoted to the straightforward exposition of moral or philosophical ideas. Or perhaps it is equally surprising that such an essay should find a place in a work remarkable for having accomplished what Roger Caillois calls "la révolution sociologique" through the use of the device of the foreign observer, a device which seriously handled implies a relativistic outlook with

15 See above pp. 131–133.
16 Nagel III, p. 513; Pléiade I, p. 495. Shackleton dates the novel at 1742, *op. cit.*, p. 226; Caillois is of the opinion that it could be the continuation of the *Histoire Véritable* dating from about 1731, Pléiade I, p. 1611.

regard to moral and social values.[17] Yet the definition itself has both
scientific and normative associations; the first element, *rapport*, recalls
the ordered structure of things which will yield to rational analysis,
the idea of a necessary correspondence between terms fundamental to
all theories of causal determinism; the second, *convenance*, implies the
existence of a transcendent criterion governing that structure, invokes
a metaphysical order, a teleological design. In fact, the definition
exemplifies the basic tension we have discerned in Montesquieu's
thought between the real and the ideal. Moreover, if we go on to
examine its presentation in Letter LXXXIII, we find surprisingly little
of the stock-in-trade of rational idealism and in its place unusual
argumentation incorporating elements of empirical psychology and
sensationalist epistemology.

Montesquieu opens the letter with what could pass as a variation of
Descartes's ontological proof: if God exists, then he is of necessity just,
for were he not so then he would be the most imperfect of all beings.
This is followed by the most important passage, the definition of
justice and the statement of its immutability. In terms reminiscent of
Malebranche's conception of truth as an invariable relationship,
Montesquieu defines justice as an actual and unchanging relationship
between things, a relationship visible to all beings. Such a notion raises
an obvious question: why injustice? In contrast to God, who is necessarily just, man's limited nature is such that he is sometimes blind to
justice, and indeed sometimes deliberately ignores it. The voice of
justice is strong, but not strong enough to overcome the influence of
the passions or of self-interest. Men are capable of injustice because it
serves their own interests, and because they prefer their own satisfaction to that of others. Interest is a determining factor in human
nature, and for this reason it is impossible to maintain that evil is
gratuitous. God on the other hand is self-sufficient, and needing
nothing, were he to act unjustly, he would be the wickedest of all
beings. From this, Montesquieu draws the conclusion that we should
continue to love justice even if God does not exist; we should direct all
our efforts to modelling our own behaviour on the fine idea we have of
a divinity of necessary and absolute justice. Free of the yoke of religion,
we should not cast aside that of justice. These are the reasons which
he considers will justify his contention that justice is eternal and
independent of human conventions; if the contrary were true, then
man would have to hide such knowledge from himself.

[17] See Pléiade I, pp. v–vi.

Montesquieu then approaches his subject from a slightly different angle. Metaphysical speculation apart, the actual situation in which most men find themselves is that of weakness. They are surrounded by others capable of harming them in a thousand different ways, most of the time with impunity. Were it not for the existence of a "principe intérieur," a principle of justice in the hearts of men capable of moving them to disregard their own interests, then, he declares, we would live our lives in continual terror, fearing men as we fear wild beasts, never for an instant assured of our life, our property or our honour. For such reasons also, Montesquieu finds it impossible to agree with those who, for fear of offending God's majesty, present him as a being of tyrannical power acting in a manner repugnant to our own ideals of behaviour; who thereby endow him with those very imperfections that he punishes in us, and, in their confusion create conflicting images, sometimes of an evil being, sometimes of a being who hates and punishes wickedness. The letter concludes with an evocation of the profound if sober sense of satisfaction enjoyed by the just man:

"Ce plaisir, tout sévère qu'il est, doit le ravir: il voit son être autant au-dessus de ceux qui ne l'ont pas, qu'il se voit au-dessus des tigres et des ours."

From this summary it can be seen that the argument of the letter is sketched very rapidly and consists basically of a comparison between the human nature and predicament and the divine nature. A series of concise statements is made in the antithetical style characteristic of Montesquieu, and although the effect is of dialectic, in fact very little logical proof is supplied to support the bald propositions. The striking definition of justice stands alone without further explanation – a fact which may lend support to the much repeated judgement that Montesquieu was no metaphysician, although it must be borne in mind that the *Lettres* are a work of satire and fiction and not a lengthy treatise. But Montesquieu does not even have recourse to a direct parallel with mathematical truth in order to demonstrate the immutability of justice, a method for which he would have found ample precedent in his reading of Malebranche, and which he himself later employed to considerable effect in the first chapter of the *Lois*. Instead of elaborating his abstract definition, he devotes more space to examining the differing responses of God and man to the eternal "rapport de convenance." He stresses the imperfect and indeterminate nature of human behaviour in contrast to divine perfection and fixity, accepting self-interest as a natural characteristic, an inevitable concomitant of the human condition. Furthermore it emerges from the discussion that he regards the description of the divine nature as a hypothesis: in fact, the actual definition of justice apart, both the metaphysical and the moral doctrine of the letter are presented not as the gift of revelation, nor as the discoveries of intuitive reason, but as ideas that would recommend themselves to a civilized intelligence adopting the scientific standpoint that all concepts are anthropomorphic.

What Montesquieu has to say about the nature of God hinges on the human notion of the perfection of a supreme being. If we conceive of a God, then that being must be perfect and we must include justice among his attributes; similarly, if God is perfect, then he is self-sufficient and can have no interest in unjust action. In making his point Montesquieu always uses the conditional mode:

"s'il y a un Dieu, il faut nécessairement qu'il soit juste, ... s'il existait, il serait nécessairement juste";

while this does not necessarily reveal an equivocal attitude on his part to the existence of God, it does indicate how he regards the source and nature of the moral imperative. God is of necessity perfect, self-sufficient and therefore just; but he is not presented as the author of justice, which subsists as an independent metaphysical entity, God contemplating it from eternity as man may do in his temporality. Hence we are not enjoined to exercise justice because God is its author or because we are presumed to love God.[18] The crux of the argument is to be found in the paragraph:

"Ainsi, quand il n'y aurait pas de Dieu, nous devrions toujours aimer la Justice."

While the transcendence and immutability of justice seems implicitly guaranteed by its quasi mathematical nature, the incentive to pursue it derives from the moral and indeed aesthetic satisfaction of emulating a concept of perfection:

"nous devrions ... faire nos efforts pour ressembler à cet être dont nous avons une si belle idée, et qui, s'il existait, serait nécessairement juste."

It is sanctioned not by the will or power of God, but by a human ideal. Indeed, God is here even reduced to a position of secondary importance,

[18] cf. *Pensée* 1080 (Bkn. 2071), "ceux qui disputent sur l'amour de Dieu n'entendent pas ce qu'ils disent, s'ils distinguent cet amour du sentiment de soumission et de celui de re-connaissance pour un être tout-puissant et bienfaiteur. Mais, pour de l'amour, je ne puis pas plus aimer un être spirituel que je puis aimer cette proposition: deux et trois font cinq." Nagel II, p. 294; Pléiade I, p. 1541.

for we can strip our "belle idée" of the concept of a supreme being:

"quand il n'y aurait pas de Dieu, nous devrions toujours aimer la Justice ....
Libres que nous serions du joug de la religion, nous ne devrions pas l'être
de celui de l'équité."

That Montesquieu is primarily concerned to establish the idea of
justice as a moral imperative, and that to do so he adopts a position
which appears to be a compromise between idealism and materialism
is further borne out by the paragraph closing the first half of Letter
LXXXIII:

"Voilà, Rhédi, ce qui m'a fait penser que la Justice est éternelle et ne dépend point des conventions humaines; et, quand elle en dépendrait, ce serait
une vérité terrible, qu'il faudrait se dérober à soi-même."

The implication of his argument is of course in part that justice must
be transcendent and invariable because human reason is capable of
perceiving it, but its real burden is that because man is capable of
conceiving of justice, therefore he is also capable of acting justly. The
idea of justice like the idea of God may be the artefact of the human
mind, yet neither its universal relevance nor its moral utility are thereby undermined.

Confirmation of the scientific epistemological foundation of the
moral doctrine of the letter is provided by a later passage where
Montesquieu sets up in opposition against those thinkers who have tried
to make justice dependent upon the arbitrary will of the Creator. Here
he clearly has orthodox theologians in mind. Montesquieu continues:

"Toutes ces pensées m'animent contre ces docteurs qui représentent Dieu
comme un être qui fait un exercice tyrannique de sa puissance; qui le font
agir d'une manière dont nous ne voudrions pas agir nous-mêmes, de peur de
l'offenser; qui le chargent de toutes les imperfections qu'il punit en nous, et,
dans leurs opinions contradictoires, le représentent tantôt comme un être
mauvais, tantôt comme un être qui hait le mal et le punit."

The arguments of those who declare the irrational, arbitrary nature of
the divine will are proscribed because they diminish the original and
superior concept of an all-perfect being, the concept which is alone
commensurable to the rational and social nature of the mind conceiving
it, thus –

"ils le font agir d'une manière dont nous ne voudrions pas agir nous-mêmes,
... ils le chargent de toutes les imperfections qu'il punit en nous."

Montesquieu is evidently deriving metaphysical and moral conclusions from the scientific notion that there must be a constant relationship of equivalence between the machine and its products; more specifically, from the theory that all ideas are anthropomorphic, that they reflect as sensationalist psychology supposed, the nature, character and experience of the individual. However, equally clearly, Montesquieu is far from accepting the thoroughgoing relativism that such a theory implies; he firmly believes that human nature is basically rational and moral.

In the previous chapter we saw how he used his insight into the anthropomorphic nature of religious perception and its development in order to explain certain pagan beliefs.[19] The discussion with Fontenelle reported in the *Pensées*[20] on the origin of ideas of purity and impurity in pagan religions shows that his explanation, the influence of the senses on the primitive imagination, while remaining generically adequate to the phenomena which it purported to explain, did not destroy their religious significance. Now in Letter LXXXIII Montesquieu is not seeking a natural explanation of historical beliefs, but his argument depends similarly on the supposition of an equivalence between the stage of development attained by moral perception – its capacity to formulate the concept of an all-perfect being or of an immutable order of justice for example – and the concepts which it produces. The mind must be adequate to its ideas, and by extension, the concepts must be worthy of their creator. Thus Montesquieu is here using this scientific notion of equivalence in the business of working out a moral code, and it can be seen that certain of his analytical techniques are common to both his scientific and his ethical thought.

Clearly, the letter is little more than a fragment and several crucial links in the argument are missing. For example it is not enough to demonstrate that man is capable of formulating this "belle idée" which is justice, without explaining at the same time the grounds for supposing that men will in fact act upon their ideal. It is true that Montesquieu indicates certain motives: moral and aesthetic satisfaction, psychological comfort and security;[21] such basically materialist and

---

[19] See above pp. 131–132.

[20] *Pensée* 1677 (Bkn. 2147).

[21] The description of justice as a "belle idée" and the mention of the "plaisir sévère" experienced by the just man, recalls Diderot's moral argument in the *Neveu de Rameau. Moi* attempts to prove to Rameau that virtue and happiness belong together: "Quelquefois avec mes amis une partie de débauche, même un peu tumultueuse, ne me déplaît pas; mais, je ne vous le dissimulerai pas, il m'est infiniment plus doux encore d'avoir secouru le malheureux, d'avoir terminé une affaire épineuse, donné un conseil salutaire, fait une lecture agréable, une promenade avec un homme ou une femme chère à mon coeur, passé quelques

utilitarian principles are not necessarily incompatible with the scientific hypothesis fundamental to his argument, but the most important factor, in that it links the conceptual argument to the definition of justice and the related metaphysical apparatus, the principle of human rationality, is not explicitly mentioned. We must simply assume that it is at the back of his mind, for on the other hand we are given a very clear indication of the reasons for unjust behaviour, of the selfish passions that hinder man in his pursuit of justice. Futhermore, reason and sociability are qualities that must be taken as given, if the possession by human creatures of an invariable notion of justice is to be accepted as a fact.

Once this point is understood however, then the moral doctrine of the letter places itself in the context of the Ciceronian humanism which was so marked an influence on Montesquieu's earliest essays[22] and at the same time anticipates its reappearance in the *Traité des Devoirs*, where according to a surviving fragment Montesquieu declared quite unambiguously:

"Les actions humaines sont le sujet des devoirs. C'est la raison qui en est le principe, et qui nous rend propres à nous en acquitter.[23]

Indeed the premisses of the argument in Letter LXXXIII tend to confirm rather than to contradict the view of reason that emerges from the *De Officiis*, in spite of the Malebranchian undertones of the definition of justice itself. The scientific hypothesis underlying the moral doctrine suggests a reason which is discursive rather than intuitive, which combines speculative and moral functions, which constitutes intelligence and will, personal and social discipline. Moreover, in this respect it is surely significant that Montesquieu shows considerable awareness of the importance of such auxiliary factors as sentiment and habit in determining the moral disposition. In Letter XI we find:

"il y a certaines vérités qu'il ne suffit pas de persuader, mais qu'il faut encore faire sentir. Telles sont les vérités de morale."

In the fragment of the *Devoirs* where he declares reason the principle of duty, Montesquieu nevertheless continues with a passage on the

heures instructives avec mes enfants, écrit une bonne page, rempli les devoirs de mon état ...." He simply demonstrates, however, that pleasure is his main motive, and that his moral principles are as materialistic as those of the dissolute Rameau. It seems likely that the aesthetic element in the thought of both Diderot and Montesquieu was derived from Shaftesbury's neoplatonism; his *Inquiry concerning Virtue or Merit* was a common source.

[22] See above pp. 122–124.
[23] *Pensée* 220 (Bkn. 597); Nagel II, p. 93; Pléiade I, p. 1126.

importance of habit:

"Le moyen d'acquérir la justice parfaite, c'est de s'en faire une telle habitude qu'on l'observe dans les plus petites choses, et qu'on y plie jusqu'à sa
manière de penser."

Similarly justice is characterized in Letter LXXXIII as a principle of the
heart not as an innate idea:

"Quel repos pour nous de savoir qu'il y a dans le coeur de tous ces hommes
un principe intérieur qui combat en notre faveur et nous met à couvert de
leurs entreprises."

Were justice conceived as an innate idea intimately associated with
intuitive reason, then feeling and habit might be considered more as
obstacles to its pursuit.

Montesquieu's attitude to human nature as well as to morals seems
well summarized in an early passage of the *Pensées* addressed to his
son:

"(C'est un grand ouvrier que celui qui a fait notre être et qui a donné à
nos âmes de certaines tendances et de certains penchants.)
   Comme le monde physique ne subsiste que parce que chaque partie de la
matière tend à s'éloigner du centre, aussi le monde politique se soutient-il
par ce désir intérieur et inquiet que chacun a de sortir du lieu où il est placé.
C'est en vain qu'une morale austère veut effacer les traits que le plus grand
de tous les ouvriers a imprimés dans nos âmes. C'est à la morale, qui veut
travailler sur le coeur de l'homme, à régler ses sentiments, et non pas à les
détruire."[24]

The nature of things and the general laws governing them cannot be
transformed; and indeed as numerous chapters in the *Lois* dealing
with obscure or bizarre customs and beliefs were to demonstrate, it is
far from being the case that apparently irrational tendencies or amoral
characteristics are without political or social utility. On the other hand,
human reason and the moral science at its disposal is a powerful means
of controlling and directing nature, of schooling the passions according
to the tenets of idealism. Throughout his writings Montesquieu's
lesson is that we should work within existing circumstances using the
material and all the means at our disposal towards the realisation of
our moral aims. As the nature of things is determined by a complex of
external causes, so scientific knowledge cannot be ignored, if the
pursuit of moral ideals is to be effective. In the fragment on reason and
duty which has already been quoted it is significant that Montesquieu

---

[24] *Pensée* 5 (Bkn. 69); Nagel II, p. 2; Pléiade I, p. 993.

suggests a way in which mechanistic psychological theory can be utilized in the study of morals:

"Nous avons tous des machines qui nous soumettent éternellement aux lois de l'habitude. Notre machine accoutume notre âme à penser d'une certaine façon. Elle l'accoutume à penser d'une autre. C'est ici que la physique pourrait trouver place dans la morale, en nous faisant voir combien les dispositions pour les vices et les vertus humaines dépendent du mécanisme."[25]

Thus, as in Letter LXXXIII, the principles of an empirical approach to psychology and epistemology, even the very basic assumptions of a belief in causal determinism, are given moral significance, and utilized in the cause of justice. Together, the method and content of Montesquieu's moral argument represent a viable if incomplete reconciliation of the postulates of scientific rationalism and Classical idealism. It is at least arguable in fact, that his approach to morals, while being a great deal more subtle, is as scientific as the naturalism of the materialists.

II

In spite of the great play made in Letter LXXXIII with the idea of the perfection of God, there is little in the way of coherent metaphysical theory linking the moral and the theological elements of the argument together, and placing the definition of justice with its geometric structural undertones in the context of a unified cosmological theory. We are left in doubt as to whether the "rapport de convenance, qui se trouve réellement entre deux choses," is a real relationship in the sense that it is immanent in the material world and therefore accessible to both scientific and speculative reason and also indicative that the general physical laws of the universe constitute its moral laws at the same time; or whether Montesquieu conceived of it as a real relationship in the sense of a transcendent truth akin to mathematical truths, subsisting in the divine intelligence, and constituting part of that "sagesse éternelle," that eternal and immutable order of essences, which Malebranche had seen as the universal law, but which he had maintained was quite distinct from the substance of the universe and was only linked to it by the operation of the divine will acting through separate natural laws.[26] We must acknowledge Montesquieu's debt to

---

[25] *Pensée* 220 (Bkn. 597); Nagel II, pp. 93–94; Pléiade I, pp. 1126–1127.
[26] See above, part I, ch. 2, pp. 11–15.

Malebranche, but nevertheless, the precise ontological significance of his definition of justice remains unclear. The immutability of the relationship and its accessibility to all intelligences are alone stressed.

Similarly, as the analysis of the moral argument of the letter demonstrated,[27] the discussion of the logical perfection and justice of the divine nature finally bears only a tenuous relation to the human moral predicament, and its introduction is hardly indispensable on the grounds of guaranteeing either the necessity or even the transcendence of justice. It does however serve another purpose by pointing a contrast with human nature and the human condition, a contrast which is clearly emphasized by the structure of the letter and its division into brief paragraphs dealing alternately with God and with man.

The perfection of God's nature demanding that absolute justice be included among his attributes, and capriciousness excluded, (the very harmony which Montesquieu requires among these attributes might itself be said to reveal again the search for a "rapport de convenance"), it follows that all his actions are of necessity just. Human nature is in contrast imperfect, for passion and self-interest together obscure man's vision of the relationships of justice. Thus though both God and man contemplate the same relationships, God is self-determining and of necessity just, while man may be determined by attributes and motives which conflict with justice. Here Montesquieu seems to be contrasting two determinisms: the internal, logical determinism of divine perfection, and the natural determinism governing the human condition, which paradoxically accounts for the indeterminate nature of human behaviour.

However, Montesquieu's analysis of the causes of human injustice does not stop short at the indictment of those natural passions that may be seen to constitute imperfection in metaphysical terms, and which stand in the way of the rational pursuit of justice. For the distinguishing feature of the human condition is indeed its insufficiency. Man is born into a complex of limiting relationships, whereas God is unique, self-causing and self-sufficient:[28]

"Mais il n'est pas possible que Dieu fasse jamais rien d'injuste; dès qu'on suppose qu'il voit la Justice, il faut nécessairement qu'il la suive, car, comme

---

[27] See above, pp. 150–53.
[28] The natural grounds which Montesquieu puts forward for injustice recall his natural explanation of the origin of society: "Si les hommes n'en formaient point, s'ils se quittaient et se fuyaient les uns les autres, il faudrait en demander la raison et chercher pourquoi ils se tiennent séparés. Mais ils naissent tous liés les uns aux autres; un fils est né auprès de son père, et il s'y tient: voila la société et la cause de la société." *Lettres Persanes*, XCIV.

il n'a besoin de rien, et qu'il se suffit à lui-même, il serait le plus méchant de tous les êtres, puisqu'il le serait sans intérêt." [29]

The fact of human interdependence is the explanation for human self-interest:

"C'est toujours par un retour sur eux-mêmes qu'ils agissent: nul n'est mauvais gratuitement."

Thus the whole problem of justice is seen to stem from the fact of relationship; the bonds which link us to others are balanced and sometimes cancelled by that which binds us to ourselves:

"Les hommes peuvent faire des injustices, parce qu'ils préfèrent leur propre satisfaction à celle des autres."

Significantly, Montesquieu's definition of justice itself reflects his analysis of the human condition. Once removed from the metaphysical plane where it may be understood as a structure of immutable archetypal relationships, justice becomes in real terms the regulation of dealings between men according to a given and constant ideal. It always implies reciprocity. Thus it is as if the perfection of the Divinity can only be parallelled in creation at a corporate level, by the realisation in society of the ideals of justice. The limitations imposed by human relationships do not become a source of evil, unless individuals deny their natural sociability by acting selfishly. Again paradoxically, the nature of things, human interdependence, is either the source of equity or the cause of wickedness.

The arguments of Letter LXXXIII indicate a deep awareness in Montesquieu of the complexity of the natural causes influencing human behaviour, but at the same time suggest that he was far from accepting a philosophical standpoint that could be described as deterministic either in the providentialist or the materialist sense. While he seems unwilling to burden man with that absolute freedom which carries with it the absolute responsibility for evil, and accordingly stresses the determining force of self-interest –

"nul n'est mauvais gratuitement. Il faut qu'il y ait une raison qui détermine, et cette raison est toujours une raison d'intérêt" –

he nevertheless implies that natural conditions themselves endow man

---

[29] In his articles "Parallels to ideas in the *Lettres Persanes*," A. S. Crisafulli points out the probable origin of this unusual argument in Shaftesbury's *Letter on Enthusiasm* (*Works* ed. Robertson, 1900, vol. I, p. 28): "There can be no malice but where interests are opposed. A universal being can have no interest opposite, and therefore can have no malice"; P.M.L.A., sept. 1937, p. 777.

with a sort of liberty, a liberty which translated into metaphysical terms is really imperfection or insufficiency contrasting with the necessary perfection of God. From this it is possible to infer that Montesquieu could hardly have considered the "rapports de convenance" representing justice and associated with the perfection of the Divinity, to be immanent in the natural order. For man they constitute only a potential order, in so far as he is a rational creature, and his rational insights may be given expression through the will. Taking Montesquieu's premisses in the *Lettres Persanes* alone into account, it would only be possible to affirm that his philosophy amounted to a doctrine of immanent reason, if he had clearly equated the "proper relationships actually existing between things" with the Divinity itself, or had maintained unequivocally that God was not simply of necessity just, but also that the relationships of justice were really consubstantial with him.

However, Montesquieu does emphasize in Letter LXXXIII the necessity to which God himself is subject: he explicitly rejects the idea that the divine will is arbitrary. In this his attitude may be compared with that of Samuel Clarke in his *Discourse concerning the Being and Attributes of God*; the English theologian, while discerning a certain necessity in the universe deriving from the principle of fitness,[30] but distinct from absolute necessity, nevertheless asserted that God was subject to the determinism of his own perfection:

"Quelque grande que soit la liberté d'un être, qui est tout ensemble infiniment intelligent, infiniment puissant et infiniment bon, il ne se déterminera jamais à agir d'une manière, qui soit contraire à ses perfections. De sorte que le libre arbitre, dans un être revêtu de ces perfections, est un principe d'action aussi certain et aussi immuable que la nécessité même des fatalistes."[31]

Whatever reservations are made, such a standpoint inevitably raises the question of Divine omnipotence, and ultimately brings one full circle to the problem of whether the natural order is governed by the same transcendent necessity as determines God's will, raising in due

[30] Montesquieu possessed the *Discourse* in the English edition of 1728, (see above, part I, ch. 4, p. 70); Ricotier's French translation of 1717 brings out terminological similarities more forcibly however. The passage in question is as follows: "J'y trouve, à la vérité, une nécessité de convenance, c'est-à-dire, que je reconnais, qu'afin que l'univers fût bien, il fallait que ses parties fussent dans l'ordre, où nous les voyons aujourd'hui. Mais je ne vois pas la moindre apparence à cette nécessité de nature et d'essence, pour laquelle les athées combattent." *De l'Existence et des Attributs de Dieu*, Amsterdam, 1717, ch. IV, 3e proposition, pp. 33–34.
[31] *Op. Cit.*, ch. XIII, 12e prop. p. 182.

course the related subject of human freedom, since, if the created order is no more than the emanation of transcendent perfection and justice, then in fulfilling their own natures, as they are so determined, all creatures may be deemed to be acting justly.

Montesquieu never claimed the authority of a philosopher or a theologian; in the *Lois* for example, he is at pains on several occasions to explain that his ideas should not be taken in their traditional moral or philosophical context.[32] But, his interests lying as much in the field of morals as of politics or law, he was bound to trespass on these traditional disciplines; and indeed, here and there, more particularly in his early works and in his personal notebooks, he attempted to grapple with the same philosophical problems as excited his contemporaries.

Before attempting to construct a coherent philosophical outlook from various scattered passages however, or to decide what light they throw on his definition of justice, it is perhaps advisable to outline the context in which Montesquieu himself habitually presented his philosophical and theological theorizing.

Certain characteristics of this presentation have already come to light. In discussing the moral doctrine of Letter LXXXIII, we noticed how the notion of divine perfection was presented as an hypothesis, as the artefact of the human intellect. This was moreover far from being an isolated instance, and represented rather a consistant historico-sociological approach to the phenomenon of speculative belief, which could be traced from the earliest *Discours sur la Politique des Romains dans la Religion* to the books on religion in the *Lois*. This attitude is best expressed in one of the *Pensées*[33] which Montesquieu entitled significantly: *Quelques Réflexions qui peuvent servir contre le Paradoxe de M. Bayle, qu'il vaut mieux être athée qu'idolâtre, avec quelques autres fragments de quelques écrits faits dans ma jeunesse, que j'ai déchirés.* Here Montesquieu worked out his theory of the development of religious perception, a theory on which he based his contention that religious belief is always morally valuable, the position he maintained in books 24 and 25 of the

---

[32] See for example the *Avertissement de l'Auteur* at the beginning of *De l'Esprit des Lois*, where Montesquieu carefully if somewhat ingenuously explains that for him *la vertu* is a political and not a moral or religious attribute. He uses a similar stratagem in the introductory chapter of the first of the books devoted to religion in the state, "Comme dans cet ouvrage je ne suis point théologien, mais écrivain politique, il pourrait y avoir des choses qui ne seraient entièrement vraies que dans une façon de penser humaine, n'ayant point été considérées dans le rapport avec des vérités plus sublimes."

[33] *Pensée* 1946 (Bkn. 673), Nagel II, p. 584; Pléiade I, p. 1173 ff. This entry can be dated using the system invented by Shackleton in his article *Les Secrétaires de Montesquieu* (reproduced in the Introduction to Nagel II) at some time after 1748; although, as the title indicates, it is simply a recopying of fragments from certain early works.

Lois.[34] The sensationalist basis of the theory is also to be found in his discussion with Fontenelle reported in the *Pensées*, on the origin of ideas of purity and impurity in pagan religions.[35]

Montesquieu begins his refutation of Bayle by explaining how, by the medium of the senses alone, primitive man came to possess the idea of God, of a Creator and First Cause, but of a God who was a material and not a spiritual being, and whom he imagined in the image of himself. Thus he emphasizes the anthropomorphic nature of pagan beliefs, demonstrating how the primitive imagination inevitably conceived of a plurality of gods, and pointing to the fact that even advanced religions cannot rid themselves of a human picture of God. His conclusion is that the pagans were in error only because of their mistaken supposition that God was a material being; the evidence of their senses as to the existence of a first cause was just, and the same evidence remains to disconcert Bayle's atheists:

"Quant aux athées de M. Bayle, la moindre réflexion suffit à l'Homme pour se guérir de l'athéisme. Il n'a qu'à considérer les Cieux, et il y trouvera une preuve invincible de l'existence de Dieu. Il n'est point excusable lorsqu'il ne voit point la Divinité peinte dans tout ce qui l'entoure: car, dès qu'il voit des effets, il faut bien qu'il admette une cause. Il n'en est pas de même de l'idolâtrie: car l'Homme peut bien voir et considérer l'ordre des Cieux et rester opiniâtrement dans l'idolâtrie. Cette disposition ne répugne point à la multiplicité des Dieux, ou, si elle y est contraire, ce ne peut être que par une suite de raisonnements métaphysiques, souvent trop faibles sans le secours de la foi, qu'ils le peuvent découvrir."

But, he goes on to imply, very little more can be learnt about God than that he is the first cause:

"Je dis plus: peut-être que la seule chose que la raison nous apprenne de Dieu, c'est qu'il y a un être intelligent qui produit cet ordre que nous voyons dans le Monde. Mais, si l'on demande quelle est la nature de cet être, on demande une chose qui passe la raison humaine. Tout ce qu'on sait de certain, c'est que l'hypothèse d'Épicure est insoutenable, parce qu'elle attaque l'existence d'un être dont le nom est écrit partout."

Modern speculation on the nature of the infinite as exemplified in Malebranche's "palais magnifique, qui se dérobe aux yeux, et qui se perd dans les nues," adds nothing to our knowledge, since in reality, it

---

[34] E.g. "la religion, même fausse, est le meilleur garant que les hommes puissent avoir de la probité des hommes," (*Lois* XXIV, 8). It is surprising in view of an anticlericalism even more virulent than Montesquieu's to find a similar opinion in Voltaire: "Il est nécessaire que chacun soit juste, et la plus sûre manière d'inspirer la justice à tous les hommes, c'est de leur inspirer la religion sans superstition." *Dictionnaire Philosophique*, article *Fraude*.

[35] See above p. 128, and pp. 131–32.

is impossible to imagine the infinite, and we can therefore have no true idea of eternity or of boundlessness.

God for Montesquieu is then the "Deus Absconditus" of Scripture; and faith and submission are more important in religion than knowledge. Thus paradoxically, although for different reasons, Montesquieu reaches the same fideistic position as Bayle adopted in the face of doctrinal illogicality.[36] They differ however, in that Montesquieu does not acquiesce in absurdity in spite of rational evidence; on the contrary, his reasoning confirms his belief in God's omnipotence and spirituality, his conviction that human reason is limited, and surprisingly his recognition of the necessity of rewards and punishments:

"On ne manquera pas de me dire qu'il s'ensuit de mon raisonnement que Dieu est trompeur, et qu'il jette les hommes dans l'erreur, sans toujours voir la vérité. Je réponds qu'il n'est point nécessaire que Dieu nous donne assez de lumières pour conserver notre être.[37] Cela doit nous suffire. Il nous a faits aussi parfaits et aussi imparfaits qu'il a voulu; il a pu nous rendre plus ou moins intelligents. Quand il nous découvre quelque chose, il nous fait une grâce; mais il pouvait nous la cacher sans injustice. Dieu nous trompe-t-il parce que les sens, ces infidèles témoins, nous déçoivent à chaque instant? Non, sans doute! Peut-être que Dieu n'a pas voulu que nous eussions plus de certitude des choses, afin que nous connaissions mieux notre faiblesse."

and:

"Dieu, qui est un pur esprit, ne pouvait se faire connaître aux hommes par idée ou par image représentative de lui-même. Il ne pouvait non plus se faire connaître que par sentiment, que de la même manière qu'il se fait sentir aux Anges et aux Bienheureux dans le Ciel. Mais, comme un si grand bonheur, qui est la félicité suprême, était une grâce que l'Homme devait mériter avant que de l'obtenir, et qu'il ne pouvait même acquérir que par la voie des peines et des souffrances, Dieu choisit un troisième moyen pour se faire connaître, qui est celui de la foi; et, par là, s'il ne lui donna pas des connaissances claires, il l'empêcha, du moins, de tomber dans l'erreur."

Clearly then, Montesquieu's attitudes towards religion in general,

[36] Illustrated by such passages as the following from the Article *Pauliciens* in the *Dictionnaire Historique et Critique*: "Il vaut mieux croire et se taire . . . . Il faut captiver son entendement sous l'obéissance de la foi et ne disputer jamais sur certaines choses . . . . Il faut humblement reconnaître que toute la philosophie est ici à bout." Whether Bayle's fideism was as profound and sincerely held as some critics have maintained, (notably R. H. Popkin in "Pierre Bayle's place in 17th. century Scepticism," published in *Pierre Bayle, le Philosophe de Rotterdam*, ed. Dibon, Paris, 1959; and E. D. James in "Scepticism and Fideism in Bayle's *Dictionnaire*," in *French Studies* XVI, 1962) is however open to question. The articles *Pyrrhon* and *Manichéens*, to name but two of his best known demolitions of Christian dogma, provide striking evidence that he was far from bridling his reason and submitting humbly to the authority of revelation.
[37] Here as Roger Caillois suggests in the Pléiade edition of the *Pensées*, vol. I, p. 1644, n. 106, the context of the argument would imply an alternative reading: "Je réponds qu'il est seulement nécessaire . . . ."

towards theology, and towards revealed dogma were of considerable complexity. First of all there is the initial reservation, suggestive of a sustained scepticism based on a scientific approach to religious psychology, that beliefs are relative to the degree of enlightenment attained by human reason. Such a stance fits in quite naturally with his relativistic sociological attitude towards religion as a social institution, as later exemplified in the *Lois*. It also helps to explain the coexistence in the *Pensées* of the refutation of Bayle's atheists with a passage like the following, where Montesquieu conceeds that even the most elementary postulates of religious belief may be completely alien to peoples of a different culture:

"Les théologiens soutiennent qu'il n'y a point d'athées de sentiment. Mais peut-on juger de ce qui se passe dans le coeur de tous les hommes? L'existence de Dieu n'est pas une vérité plus claire que celles-ci : l'homme est composé de deux substances; l'âme est spirituelle. Cependant, il y a des nations entières qui doutent de ces deux vérités. C'est que notre sentiment intérieur n'est pas le leur, et que l'éducation l'a détruit. Il est vrai que ce sont des vérités claires; mais il y a des aveugles. Ce sont des sentiments naturels; mais il y a des gens qui ne sentent point." [38]

Related to this apparent scepticism are likewise a marked antipathy towards the excesses of metaphysical speculation, visible in his reflecttions on Bayle as in several other fragments,[39] and a complementary belief that the proper function of human reason is the practical business of living, its application to the real and pressing issues of morals and politics:

"Je vois ici des gens qui disputent sans fin sur la religion; mais il me semble qu'ils combattent en même temps à qui l'observera le moins.

Non seulement ils ne sont pas meilleurs chrétiens, mais même meilleurs citoyens, et c'est ce qui me touche: car, dans quelque religion qu'on vive, l'observation des lois, l'amour pour les hommes, la piété envers les parents, sont toujours les premiers actes de religion." [40]

---

[38] *Pensée* 64 (Bkn. 2077); Nagel II, p. 22; Pléiade I, p. 1542.
[39] One rather humorously disparaging estimation of the attraction of metaphysics has typically a serious twist at the end, revealing Montesquieu's awareness of the deep human need for speculative beliefs of some kind:
"La métaphysique a deux choses bien séduisantes.
Elle s'accorde avec la paresse: on l'étudie partout, dans son lit, à la promenade, etc.
D'ailleurs, la métaphysique ne traite que de grandes choses: on y négocie toujours pour de grands intérêts. Le physicien, le logicien, l'orateur, ne s'occupent que de petits objets; mais le métaphysicien s'empare de toute la nature, la gouverne à son gré, fait et défait les Dieux, donne et ôte l'intelligence, met l'Homme dans la condition des bêtes ou l'en ôte. Toutes les notions qu'elle donne sont intéressantes, parce qu'il s'agit de la tranquillité présente et future." *Pensée* 202 (Bkn. 2060); Nagel II, p. 74; Pléiade I, p. 1536. Other *Pensées* criticize in particular the essentialism of the Platonists and Malebranche, e.g.: 156 (Bkn. 2061), 410 (Bkn. 2062), 799 (Bkn. 2093).
[40] *Lettres Persanes*, XLVI; Nagel I, p. 88; Pléiade I, p. 194.

To compound these reservations into a thoroughgoing relativistic materialism complete with atheistic undertones, one needs only to quote other passages on the organization of the universe, and the relative insignificance in this context of the entire human species. Here we have Montesquieu implying that all forms of life comprising the physical order, and all the associated processes of development and reproduction, including the acquisition of the sophisticated faculties of thought and feeling, are simply the product of the general movement of matter:

"On peut dire que tout est animé, tout organisé. Le moindre brin d'herbe fait voir des millions de cerveaux. Tout meurt et renaît sans cesse. Tant d'animaux qui n'ont été reconnus que par hasard doivent bien en faire soupçonner d'autres. La matière qui a eu un mouvement général, par lequel s'est formé l'ordre des cieux, doit avoir des mouvements particuliers qui la portent à l'organisation ... (Laissant la pensée à l'homme, il est difficile de refuser le sentiment à tout ce qui existe.)" [41]

Side by side with this scientific materialism very much in the Fontenellian mould, is a characteristic understanding of the vastness and complexity of the universe, into which humankind and its destiny disappear almost without trace. When discussing the legal prohibition of suicide, Usbek in the *Lettres Persanes* argues its absurd injustice on the grounds that the taking of ones own life does nothing to upset the order of the universe: the general laws governing the organization of matter continue unimpeded by any human interference with nature:

"Lorsque mon âme sera séparée de mon corps, y aura-t-il moins d'ordre et moins d'arrangement dans l'Univers? Croyez vous que cette nouvelle combinaison soit moins parfaite et moins dépendante des lois générales? ... Pensez-vous que mon corps, devenu un épi de blé, un ver, un gazon, soit changé en un ouvrage de la Nature moins digne d'elle? et que mon âme, dégagée de tout ce qu'elle avait de terrestre, soit devenue moins sublime?

Toutes ces idées, mon cher Ibben, n'ont d'autre source que notre orgueil: nous ne sentons point notre petitesse, et, malgré qu'on en ait, nous voulons être comptés dans l'Univers, y figurer et y être un objet important. Nous nous imaginons que l'anéantissement d'un être aussi parfait que nous dégraderait toute la nature, et nous ne convenons pas qu'un homme de plus ou de

[41] *Pensée* 76 (Bkn. 690); Nagel II, p. 23; Pléiade I, p. 1187; cf. *Pensées* 1187 (Bkn. 2064) and 1341 (Bkn. 2065) where Montesquieu expounds a sensationalist theory of knowledge. The first of these begins conventionally: "Les bouts des fibres de notre cerveau reçoivent un petit ébranlement, qui produit un chatouillement ou sentiment en nous. Cela suffit pour expliquer tout. Par exemple, nous voyons pour la première fois un carré. Il suffit que nous sentions que nous le voyons, pour en avoir une idée: car, sans cela, l'on ne verrait point le carré ... etc.", but again ends with a question suggesting that sensationalism is far from solving all the problems, "Mais, si ce que je viens de dire est bien vrai, pourquoi les bêtes ne raisonnent-elles pas comme les hommes?" Nagel II, p. 316; Pléiade I, p. 1537.

moins dans le monde – que dis-je? – tous les hommes ensemble, cent millions de têtes comme la nôtre, ne sont qu'un atome subtil et délié, que Dieu
n'aperçoit qu'à cause de l'immensité de ses connaissances." [42]

This conviction that the human creature is no more than a drop in the
cosmic ocean, seems indeed to draw Montesquieu very close to the
same hylozoism as, later in the *Traité des Devoirs*, he attributed to
Spinoza and condemned. [43] It appears again in the *Lettres Persanes* in a
passage arguing the relativity of judgements and beliefs:

"Il me semble, Usbek, que nous ne jugeons jamais des choses que par un retour secret que nous faisons sur nous-mêmes. Je ne suis pas surpris que les
Nègres peignent le diable d'une blancheur éblouissante et leurs dieux noirs
comme du charbon; ... On a dit fort bien que, si les triangles faisaient un
dieu, ils lui donneraient trois côtés.
    Mon cher Usbek, quand je vois des hommes qui rampent sur un atome,
c'est-à-dire la Terre, qui n'est qu'un point de l'Univers, se proposer directement pour modèles de la Providence, je ne sais comment accorder tant d'extravagance avec tant de petitesse." [44]

a combination of ideas which would indeed tend to confirm a strong
leaning in Montesquieu at this stage towards a relativistic materialism.
    Paradoxically however, his very conviction of the weakness of human
reason, either as a speculative or as a moral faculty, and this same
understanding of the insignificance and powerlessness of man seen
against the immensity of the universe, and the awful simplicity and
regularity of its laws, appear in fact to have drawn him in just the
opposite direction. Just as his deterministic theory of historical causation formed the scientific basis of his justification of moral idealism in
the *Traité des Devoirs*, so here also his critical attitude towards speculative belief coupled with the scientific rationalism of his physics,
however suggestive of scepticism they seem, constitute the essential
groundwork for a rehabilitation of religious faith, and even for a renewed
confidence in revelation. If Montesquieu had simply asserted that

---

[42] *Lettres Persanes* LXXVI; Nagel I, pp. 157–158; Pléiade I, p. 247; cf. *Pensées* 22 (Bkn.
2191), 54 (Bkn. 2193).
[43] See *Pensée* 1266 (Bkn. 615); Nagel II, pp. 342–343; Pléiade I, p. 1138: "Cependant,
un grand génie m'a promis que je mourrai comme un insecte. Il cherche à me flatter de
l'idée que je ne suis qu'une modification de la matière. Il emploie un ordre géométrique et
des raisonnements qu'on dit être très forts, et que j'ai trouvés très obscurs, pour élever mon
âme à la dignité de mon corps, et, au lieu de cet espace immense que mon esprit embrasse,
il me donne à ma propre matière et à une espace de quatre ou cinq pieds dans l'univers."
[44] Letter LIX; Nagel I, p. 119; Pléiade I, pp. 217–218. In his note to this passage,
(Garnier ed., Paris, 1960, p. 124), Paul Vernière attributes its attack on anthropomorphic
beliefs to a source in the *Tractatus theologico-politicus*, so accentuating the ambivalence of
Montesquieu's attitude towards Spinoza. He also mentions the equally probable influence
of Fontenelle.

some kind of religious feeling was natural and necessary in man, and if, affirming that the ordered pattern of the universe was evidence of the existence of an intelligent and all-powerful first cause, and only that, he had inclined to a view of God remote and indifferent to his creation, it would have sufficed to describe him as an advocate of natural religion, a Deist. But he goes much further than that, for in *Pensée* 1946 revelation and heavenly rewards are presented as marks of divine grace, solace for the ignorance and limitations of man.[45]

Moreover, it is difficult to dimiss this orthodoxy as a defensive stratagem, an easy fideism cynically displayed to pull the wool over the eyes of censorious schoolmen. First of all, Montesquieu had no real motive to disguise his thoughts as he recorded them in the *Pensées* and the *Spicilège*, since for most of his life he considered these as private notebooks. And although it is true that certain entries there demonstrate a laudable tolerance:

"Dieu est comme ce monarque qui a plusieurs nations sous son empire: elles viennent toutes lui porter le tribut, et chacune lui parle sa langue."[46]

while others reveal a thoroughly rationalist caution towards revelation:

"Quand je crois ce que je pense, je cours risque de me tromper. Mais, quand je crois ce qu'on me dit, j'ai deux craintes: l'une, que celui qui me parle se trompe; l'autre, qu'il ne veuille me tromper."[47]

nevertheless others are clearly intended to give it support with a pessimism that is almost Pascalian:

"Ce qui me prouve la nécessité d'une révélation, c'est l'insuffisance de la Religion naturelle, vu la crainte et la superstition des hommes: car, si vous aviez mis aujourd'hui les hommes dans le pur état de la Religion naturelle, demain ils tomberaient dans quelque superstition grossière."[48]

Although his outlook on life is hardly as joyless as Pascal's, the appeal to sentiment on which he founds his defence of religious belief in one of the fragments from the *Devoirs* is strongly reminiscent of the spirit of the *Pensées*. How, Montesquieu asks, once we have freed ourselves of the burden of error and prejudice represented by belief in God, can we face with equanimity the miseries of illness, old age, and worse, the terror of death? Perhaps there is nothing but annihilation to follow,

---

[45] See above p. 163.
[46] *Pensée* 1454 (Bkn. 2117); Nagel II, pp. 420–421; Pléiade I, p. 1551.
[47] *Spicilège* 632, MS (598–599); Nagel II, p. 868; Pléiade II, pp. 1388–1389.
[48] *Pensée* 825 (Bkn. 2110); Nagel II, p. 243; Pléiade I, p. 1550.

but what if the soul survives, isolated and helpless, deprived of the pleasures of physical existence, and yet irritated by an impossible desire for happiness; mean, empty and frustrated by its own inadequacy?

"Accablante immortalité! S'il n'est pas bien sûr qu'il n'y ait point de Dieu, si notre philosophie a pu nous laisser là-dessus quelque doute, il faut bien espérer qu'il y en a un." [49]

Moreover, he argues, our very existence is strong proof of the benevolence of God, for he has given us life which we value above all else, and conciousness of our individual being. In return for his beneficence, we should love God; that is to say, we should show our gratitude through contented service. [50] It is impossible to imagine so perfect a being simply creating the universe, and then abandoning it to its own fate; and indeed, if the organization of the universe as we see it, must have required infinite power, one cannot conceive of God either losing this power, or suspending his providence as far as the human part of creation is concerned. And again, if we have known happiness during life, why should we fear that God would suddenly deprive us of it? His power is proof of his will; and since our happiness costs him nothing, he would be more imperfect than men, were he to deprive us for no reason.

Although the substance of Montesquieu's defence could doubtless be compiled from the innumerable volumes of rationalist apologetic that followed in the wake of the critical exegesis of Spinoza and Richard Simon, not to mention the remorseless logic of Bayle, [51] its tone and presentation are far from being rationalistic in the Cartesian sense. Perhaps Montesquieu would have agreed with the "rationaux" that faith and reason are complementary and not contradictory, but he does not invoke geometric proofs or the stock-in-trade of idealist metaphysics. Hardly a mystic, his appeal is nevertheless directed to "sentiment intérieur" rather than to reason; indeed, as we have seen, he is far from conceding that all the principles of natural religion, let alone those of Christian theology, are accompanied by that "évidence"

[49] Pensée 1266 (Bkn. 615); Nagel II, p. 342; Pléiade I, p. 1137.
[50] Montesquieu accepts a personal bond with God, but hesitates to see this as love, cf. Pensée 1080 (Bkn. 2071), "... mais je dis bien que ceux qui disputent sur l'amour de Dieu n'entendent pas ce qu'ils disent, s'ils distinguent cet amour du sentiment de soumission et de celui de reconnaissance pour un être tout-puissant et bienfaiteur. Mais, pour de l'amour, je ne puis pas plus aimer un être spirituel que je puis aimer cette proposition: deux et trois font cinq." Nagel II, p. 294; Pléiade I, p. 1541.
[51] See A. Monod, De Pascal à Chateaubriand, 1916, chs. IV–VI.

that so recommended itself to enlightened believers; on the contrary, rational perception is a limited faculty, and the way to religious knowledge, if indeed there is a way, is through faith.

Nevertheless, Montesquieu's acceptance of revealed religion, hedged about as it was by scientific theory and utilitarian considerations[52] which one imagines were largely unacceptable to his orthodox contemporaries, did not deter him from indulging on his own account in a little theological speculation.

"Tu ne te serais jamais imaginé que je fusse devenu plus métaphysicien que je ne l'étais: cela est pourtant, et tu en seras convaincu quand tu auras essuyé ce débordement de ma philosophie."

declares Usbek at the beginning of a letter on divine prescience,[53] where Montesquieu does indeed show himself ready to use those concepts which were in his estimation acceptable to reason, that is to say those based on empirical evidence such as the organization of the universe, as premises in a purely deductive argument whereby further attributes of the Divinity are defined. We have in fact already seen this characteristic procedure employed in Letter LXXXIII, where in spite of his assertion in *Pensée* 1946 that human reason is incapable of fathoming God's nature, Montesquieu founds his argument on its hypothetical perfection and also rejects the assumption that the divine will is purely arbitrary. In Letter LXIX, using the same method, he goes on to tackle the related problems of cosmic determinism, divine omniscience, and human freedom.

Here he begins by examining once again the notion of divine perfection; as in Letter LXXXIII, his contention is that most philosophers have encumbered the Divinity with all kinds of attributes, which, though men may regard them as the sum of perfection, are in fact contradictory. Apparently oblivious of the fact that the logic of perfection as he envisages it, is open to an idential criticism, Montesquieu continues by reiterating his persuasion that God is bound by his own nature to act in a particular way:

"Ainsi, quoique Dieu soit tout-puissant, il ne peut pas violer ses promesses, ni tromper les hommes. Souvent même l'impuissance n'est pas dans lui, mais dans les choses relatives; et c'est la raison pourquoi il ne peut pas changer l'essence des choses."

[52] Such considerations are subsequently well illustrated in Books 24 and 25 of the *Lois*: religion is a safeguard of morality; certain dogmas such as the existence of heavenly rewards and punishments may supplement or replace civil sanctions; a single, established religion is preferable for the tranquillity of the state, etc..

[53] *Lettres Persanes*, LXIX; Nagel I, p. 145; Pléiade I, p. 238.

Montesquieu thus makes two points: the first is that in spite of his omnipotence, the justice essential to God's perfection prevents him from subjecting his creatures to conditions which he knows they cannot fulfil, just as in Letter LXXXIII he had argued that it prevented arbitrary action. The example of Adam, which Montesquieu cites at the end of the letter reveals that he has the problem of sin in mind:

"Dieu met Adam dans le Paradis terrestre, à condition qu'il ne mangera point d'un certain fruit: précepte absurde dans un être qui connaîtrait les déterminations futures des âmes; car enfin un tel être peut-il mettre des conditions à ses grâces sans les rendre dérisoires? C'est comme si un homme qui aurait su la prise de Bagdat disait à un autre: 'Je vous donne cent to-mans si Bagdat n'est pas pris.' Ne ferait-il pas là une bien mauvaise plai-santerie?"

Thus, while presumably accepting the omniscience which is the logical accompaniment of divine omnipotence, Montesquieu infers that man must be assumed to enjoy freedom. The second related point refers to the theory of the natural laws governing creation as Montesquieu might have found it in Malebranche or in Leibniz, a theory designed to resolve the problem of evil.

Malebranche had maintained that the natural laws governing the universe were immutable; that it was wholly in accordance with God's wisdom and perfection that they should be so; and that the physical and moral evils incidental to their operation were countered in the overall scheme of things by the establishment of occasional causes, governed by divine grace.[54] Similarly, and perhaps more significantly as far as Montesquieu's metaphysical ideas are concerned, Leibniz, while freeing the divine will from the determinism of metaphysical reason by the invention of a second principle, "la raison suffisante" or the moral principle of "convenance," according to which he supposed, God was pleased to order creation,[55] averred that the natural order was the best of all possible orders, and that evil was a purely human notion, for the phenomenon itself disappeared in the universal scheme of things:

"l'existence de certains inconvénients particuliers qui nous frappent, est une marque certaine que le meilleur plan ne permettait pas qu'on les évitât, et qu'ils servent à l'accomplissement du bien total."[56]

Now when Montesquieu writes of God in Letter LXIX,

[54] See above Part I, ch. 2, p. 15.
[55] See above Part I, ch. 2, pp. 24–25.
[56] *Théodicée*, art. 359.

"Souvent même l'impuissance n'est pas dans lui, mais dans les choses relatives; et c'est la raison pourquoi il ne peut pas changer l'essence des choses,"

although his terminology is misleading, he seems in fact to be sub-
scribing to a similar theory.[57] God's will is inevitably determined by
considerations of perfection, therefore, if creation exhibits certain
shortcomings, it must be concluded that these are an inevitable result
of the grand scheme, and that God would be belying his own perfection
and constancy in altering it.

But Montesquieu does not pursue this point directly; he moves
instead to the very reasonable objections made by "quelques-uns de
nos docteurs"[58] to the theory of divine omniscience. How, they had
asked, could omniscience and justice together be predicated of a
being who has created a world where evil and sin appear the inevitable
consequences of its organization? Either God must be assumed to have
set certain general forces in action, and left them free to combine at
random, in which case human will is as free as it could wish to be, and
divine foreknowledge is reduced to mere conjecture; or, God's
prescience is real in that all phenomena and events are the necessary
effects of certain predetermined causes; in which case, human actions
are no freer than the movements of one billiard ball in collision with
another.

Montesquieu, evidently reluctant in the early stages of the letter
to sacrifice either omnipotence or justice in God, nevertheless argues
the case of the opposition with considerable force. The tone of personal
conviction colours his affirmation of the freedom of the will:

"L'âme est l'ouvrière de sa détermination; mais il y a des occasions où elle
est tellement indéterminée qu'elle ne sait pas même de quel côté se déterminer. Souvent même elle ne le fait que pour faire usage de sa liberté; de
manière que Dieu ne peut voir cette détermination par avance, ni dans
l'action de l'âme, ni dans l'action que les objets font sur elle."

Indeed his solution to the problem, rather unsatisfactory in rigorous
philosophical terms, turns out to be a compromise designed to salvage
the advantages of metaphysical determinism and the Socinian doctrine
of freedom. Montesquieu happily suggests that although God is all-
powerful and all-seeing –

[57] In his edition of the *Lettres Persanes* (Belles Lettres, 1929), Élie Carcassone indicates the
influence of Leibniz on Letter LXIX. Montesquieu possessed the 1714 edition of the *Théodicée*, cf. L. Desgraves, *op. cit.*, p. 32, No. 405. This influence is most important in view of the
probable source in the *Théodicée* of Montesquieu's definition of justice.
[58] As Vernière suggests (ed. cit., p. 150, n. 5), "nos docteurs," may well signify the
Socinian theologians attacked by Leibniz in the *Théodicée*.

"il fait agir les créatures à sa fantaisie, il connaît tout ce qu'il veut connaître" –

he is usually simply content to allow his creatures the freedom to earn rewards or punishments.[59] When he wishes to know the future pattern of events, he has only to will that they should happen:

"Mais, quand il veut savoir quelque chose, il le sait toujours, parce qu'il n'a qu'à vouloir qu'elle arrive comme il la voit, et déterminer les créatures conformément à sa volonté. C'est ainsi qu'il tire ce qui doit arriver du nombre des choses purement possibles, en fixant par ses décrets les déterminations futures des esprits, et les privant de la puissance qu'il leur a donnée, d'agir ou de ne pas agir."

This tactic, so facile as to seem almost an evasion of the whole issue of cosmic determinism and free will, whether envisaged from a theological or a scientific angle, nevertheless throws some light on the apparently contradictory philosophical notions scattered throughout Montesquieu's early work. The doctrine of what might aptly be termed the benevolent indifference of the Divinity, renders for instance the reiterated notion that men, to plagiarize Voltaire, are no more than

"des insectes se dévorant les uns les autres sur un petit atome de boue"[60]

much more compatible with the idea of God as a being of infinite justice, and of man as a creature of moral dignity.

In Montesquieu's view the moral and physical world is determined by an intricate pattern of causation controlled in turn by transcendent laws which God as Creator, in the necessity of perfect wisdom, has chosen to follow. Whether these laws were conceived on the Malebranchian pattern as the eternal and immutable laws of reason hardly distinct from the Godhead itself; or whether Montesquieu followed Leibniz in relating them to a principle of sufficient reason subject to the divine will and distinct from immutable, mathematical reason, is not immediately clear. One must weigh the implications of the idea found in Letter LXXXIII that the relationships of justice (or of reason) are immutable, eternal, visible to, but distinct from God, against the incorporation in the definition of justice itself of the notion of *convenance*, bearing in mind that the principle of "convenance" or of sufficient reason was presented by Leibniz as the source of moral and physical necessity.[61]

---

[59] A similar doctrine also emerges from one of the *Pensées* dealing with the notion of predestination (1945 (Bkn. 674)); see below p. 176.

[60] *Zadig* (1747), "La Femme Battue."

[61] See *Discours de la Conformité de la Foi avec la Raison*, II; and above p. 24.

Within this structure of causation, Montesquieu assumes that man enjoys free will on two grounds. The first of these depends as we have seen, on the theological argument that a just God will leave his creatures free to earn their salvation. The second, implicit in the reasoning of Letter LXXXIII,[62] and confirmed by certain passages in the *Pensées* is the argument of human imperfection, of the limitations of human reason, and the obstacles imposed by the human condition.[63] This second argument is, we shall see, closely connected with Montesquieu's definition of justice as a "rapport de convenance."

Other evidence exists to show that he considered that the laws of the moral and indeed the physical universe determined in only the most general way. In the earlier letter on suicide he expressed the view that the order of Providence was not greatly disturbed by human interference with the natural laws of creation:

"Troublé-je l'ordre de la Providence, lorsque je change les modifications de la matière et que je rends carrée une boule que les premières lois du mouvement, c'est-à-dire les lois de la création et de la conservation, avaient faite ronde? Non, sans doute: je ne fais qu'user du droit qui m'a été donné, et, en ce sens, je puis troubler à ma fantaisie toute la nature, sans que l'on puisse dire que je m'oppose à la Providence."[64]

Within the general physical structure of the world man is free to act as he wishes. Montesquieu follows a similar line of argument with regard to the moral world. In an early entry in the *Pensées* where the lawfulness of incestuous marriage and the prohibition of this institution since primitive patriarchal societies is under discussion, he puts forward the view that it is not in fact contrary to Natural Law: its prohibition is simply a custom derived from filial respect, a custom which God has incorporated into Divine Law, since it happened to fit in with his general moral purpose:

---

[62] See above p. 160.

[63] This theory of causation and human freedom is reproduced exactly in the first chapter of the *Lois*: "Ainsi la création, qui paraît être un acte arbitraire, suppose des règles aussi invariables que la fatalité des athées. Il serait absurde de dire que le Créateur, sans ces règles, pourrait gouverner le monde, puisque le monde ne subsiterait pas sans elles.

. . . .

Mais il s'en faut bien que le monde intelligent soit aussi bien gouverné que le monde physique. Car, quoique celui-là ait aussi des lois qui, par leur nature, sont invariables, il ne les suit pas constamment comme le monde physique suit les siennes. La raison en est que les êtres particuliers intelligents sont bornés par leur nature, et par conséquent sujets à l'erreur; et, d'un autre côté, il est de leur nature qu'ils agissent par eux-mêmes." Nagel I, pp. 2-3; Pléiade II, p. 233.

[64] *Lettres Persanes* LXXVI, Nagel I, p. 157; Pléiade I, pp. 246-247.

"Ceci étant une fois gravé dans l'esprit des hommes, Dieu a voulu s'y conformer; et il en a fait un point fondamental de sa loi: car, lorsque Dieu a donné des lois aux hommes il n'a eu qu'une vue générale, qui était d'avoir un peuple fidèle, source naturelle de tous les préceptes."[65]

Thus again, within the limits of certain transcendent moral purposes, God is assumed to have left men and societies to their own devices.[66]

Enlarging for a moment on this theological attitude, and without wishing to suggest that Montesquieu subscribed to a doctrine of economy of means in creation of the type later advanced by Maupertuis,[67] it often seems however that behind much of his theorizing there lies a certain notion of a universal economy. This may be in reality simply an impression fostered by his scientific approach to social phenomena, his readiness to seek out and in some cases invent a rational explanation for beliefs and customs. On the other hand, the passage quoted above seems to denote a conviction, perhaps not consciously formulated, that the nature of things, besides being explicable in scientific terms, actually contributes to the realization of certain divinely appointed moral ends, the ultimate significance of which transcends human understanding. One recalls for instance the passage in *Pensée* 1946, where Montesquieu touches on the very limitations of human reason:

"Il nous a faits aussi parfaits et aussi imparfaits qu'il a voulu; il a pu nous rendre plus ou moins intelligents ... Dieu nous trompe-t-il parce que les sens, ces infidèles témoins, nous déçoivent à chaque instant? Non, sans doute! Peut-être que Dieu n'a pas voulu que nous eussions plus de certitude des choses, afin que nous connaissions mieux notre faiblesse."

Human limitations possess a transcendent significance; similarly, as we have seen in Letter LXIX, human liberty serves the purpose of sorting the sheep from the goats in preparation for heavenly rewards. Again in Letter LXXVII, the reply to Usbek's defence of suicide,[68] Montesquieu seems to be arguing that in spite of the insignificance of individual death seen in the context of cosmic harmony, the prohibition of suicide may well serve some moral purpose:

[65] *Pensée* 205 (Bkn. 1928); Nagel II, p. 76; Pléiade I, p. 1464.

[66] It is noticeable here how easily Montesquieu's theological outlook could be reconciled with a relativistic, sociological understanding of institutions and customs.

[67] See above Part I, ch. 2, pp. 30–31. In the *Spicilège* 511, (MS 470–471), Montesquieu does actually refer to the refutation of atheism from the argument of the perfection and economy of the universe, although a subsequent allusion makes it clear that he has Leibniz in mind once again.

[68] This letter first appeared in the supplement to the 1754 edition of the *Lettres Persanes;* Vernière suggests (ed. cit. p. 162 n. 1) that it was intended to counter criticisms of irreligion, but this would not necessarily undermine the sincerity of the opinions expressed in it.

"Si un être est composé de deux êtres, et que la nécessité de conserver l'union marque plus la soumission aux ordres du Créateur, on en a pu faire une loi religieuse. Si cette nécessité de conserver l'union est un meilleur garant des actions des hommes, on en a pu faire une loi civile."

Returning to the limitations of human nature, these according to one of the *Pensées* are the explanation for and justification of Revelation, for men unaided are incapable of persevering in Natural Religion.[69] Finally, if Montesquieu did indeed hold to some notion of a universal economy, then the fideistic tone adopted at the end of Letter LXIX for example:

"Mon cher Rhédi, pourquoi tant de philosophie? Dieu est si haut que nous n'apercevons pas même ses nuages. Nous ne la connaissons bien que dans ses préceptes. Il est immense, spirituel, infini. Que sa grandeur nous ramène à notre faiblesse. S'humilier toujours, c'est l'adorer toujours."

would certainly indicate a faith inspired more by a Leibnizian teleological optimism, than by a Baylian scepticism.[70] Elsewhere after all, Montesquieu did proclaim his confidence in some metaphysical ideas:

"Quand l'immortalité de l'âme serait une erreur, je serais très fâché de ne pas la croire. Je ne sais comment pensent les athées. (J'avoue que je ne suis point si humble que les athées.) Mais, pour moi, je ne veux point troquer (et je n'irai point troquer) l'idée de mon immortalité contre celle de la béatitude d'un jour. Je suis charmé de me croire immortel comme Dieu même. Indépendamment des vérités révélées, des idées métaphysiques me donnent une très forte espérance de mon bonheur éternel, à laquelle je ne voudrais pas renoncer."[71]

A general rather than particular determinism is also indicated in a late and rather different passage in the *Pensées* where Montesquieu returns to the question of divine prescience, this time in connection with the doctrine of predestination. After pointing out that this must be a rare occurrence, "car il n'arrive que rarement que Dieu nous ôte la liberté," he maintains that when God does predestine, then it can only be to salvation; for how could a just God punish by damnation a creature whom he has deliberately deprived of this special grace. Those that are not predestined must surely have the chance to earn their own salvation; the words of the apostle can only signify that God knew in a general way, because of the laws governing his creation, that some would succumb to temptation:

[69] *Op. cit.*, 825 (Bkn. 2110); Nagel II, p. 243; Pléiade I, p. 1550.
[70] Vernière suggests a source in Bayle's *Dictionnaire*, article "Pauliciens," for this passage; see ed. cit., p. 152, n. 3.
[71] *Pensée* 57 (Bkn. 2083); Nagel II, pp. 20–21; Pléiade I, p. 1543.

"Quand saint Paul dit que Dieu a prédestiné l'un pour être le fils de la colère, l'autre pour être le fils de la miséricorde, il veut dire que Dieu a vu généralement qu'il y aurait des damnés et des sauvés, sans sacrifier tel ou tel: car il voyait bien, par l'arrangement des causes secondes, qu'il y en avait qui seraient bien plus susceptibles des objets que les autres." [72]

Thus as creatures we enjoy the freedom to err, but we are still trapped in the net of universal justice, for ultimate retribution is inescapable:

"Admirable idée des Chinois, qui comparent la justice de Dieu à un filet si grand que les poissons qui s'y promènent croient être en liberté; mais réellement ils sont pris. Les pécheurs croient de même, qu'ils ne seront pas punis de Dieu; mais ils sont dans le filet." [73]

Our liberty, even the freedom to ignore the laws of justice, is only a human condition, the tempoary result of our imperfection and our ignorance, as much as the dispensation of a just God. And to God, it goes without saying, all the laws of justice are visible:

"La liberté est en nous une imperfection: nous sommes libres et incertains, parce que nous ne savons pas certainement ce qui nous est le plus convenable. Il n'en est pas de même de Dieu: comme il est souverainement parfait, il ne peut jamais agir que de la manière la plus parfaite." [74]

That Montesquieu equates perfect knowledge with perfect justice becomes clear at this point; in contrast to God, the human moral dilemma stems from imperfect reason, as was implied in Letter LXXXIII. In a sense then, injustice is latent in the order of things, although in so far as doubt is only cast upon the speculative powers of reason, and not upon its discursive function, the door is left open to a moral optimism as much foreshadowing positivist doctrines as reminiscent of the Cartesian idea of scientific progress, and based essentially upon confidence in the relevance of scientific knowledge to the solution of moral problems. It seems as if rational perception of various orders of truth, be they the invariable relationships of justice, the precepts of revelation, or positive fact, and even though this insight may be limited, does constitute in Montesquieu's estimation a sufficient motive for moral action,[75] without however cancelling the uncertainty inseparable from the human condition:

[72] *Pensée* 1945 (Bkn. 674); Nagel II, p. 584; Pléiade I, p. 1180.
[73] *Pensée* 434 (Bkn. 2124); Nagel II, p. 164; Pléiade I, p. 1552.
[74] *Spicilège* 391 (336); Nagel II, p. 787; Pléiade II, p. 1310.
[75] Although reason is considered an effective motive force, it is by no means the only factor involved in virtuous action. As the Troglodytes cycle in the *Lettres Persanes* demonstra-

"Dans les actions ordinaires de ma vie, lorsque j'agis, j'agis toujours par un motif qui est efficace, parce que j'agis; qui ne m'ôte point la liberté, parce que je pouvais ne pas agir. Il en est de même des oeuvres qui ont besoin de la grâce. J'agis de la même manière, j'agis librement, j'agis efficacement, mais par une grâce, c'est-à-dire par un motif qui me vient de l'autre monde: car, si je n'avais eu aucune connaissance des vérités révélées, je ne me serais point déterminé à faire le bien."[76]

Knowledge of the ultimate and transcendent harmony of the cosmos is what surpasses human understanding, and what, as *Pensée* 1946 indicates, is moreover superfluous to human existence. Just as the influence of Leibniz is visible in Letter LXIX on divine prescience, so also it is possible to discern traces in Montesquieu's thought of such passages as the following:

"Une vérité est au-dessus de la raison quand notre esprit ne la saurait comprendre: et telle est, à mon avis, la Sainte Trinité; tels sont les miracles réservés à Dieu seul, comme par exemple la création; tel est le choix de l'ordre de l'Univers, qui dépend de l'harmonie universelle, et de la connaissance distincte d'une infinité de choses à la fois."[77]

one recalls Usbek's last words in Letter LXXVII:

tes, habit and education are equally important in predisposing towards just behaviour; and as this would suggest, emotional forces are also involved. Montesquieu does not draw these into a systematic moral theory, but such passages as the following clearly indicate an awareness of them: "C'est l'envie de plaire qui donne de la liaison à la Société, et tel a été le bonheur du Genre humain que cet amour-propre, qui devait dissoudre la Société, la fortifie, au contraire, et la rend inébranlable." (*Pensée* 464 (Bkn. 1042)), Nagel II, p. 168; Pléiade I, p. 1274. In this he is at least a forerunner of the "philosophes" and the theorists of "sensibilité," and much less of a disciple of the "rationaux" of the early part of the century. His idea of the function of "amour-propre" can be compared to the attitude to self interest revealed for instance by Voltaire in his *Remarques premières sur les Pensées de Pascal* (1732-3): "Il est aussi impossible qu'une société puisse se former et subsister sans amour-propre, qu'il serait impossible de faire des enfants sans concupiscence, de songer à se nourrir sans appétit. C'est l'amour de nous-mêmes qui assiste l'amour des autres; c'est par nos besoins mutuels que nous sommes utiles au genre humain; c'est le fondement de tout commerce; c'est l'éternel lien des hommes." (*Lettres Philosophiques*, Garnier, Paris, 1956, p. 152); and to Rousseau's specific isolation of "amour de soi" as the real source of justice: "Le précepte même d'agir avec autrui comme nous voulons qu'on agisse avec nous n'a de vrai fondement que la conscience et le sentiment; car où est la raison précise d'agir, étant moi, comme si j'étais un autre, surtout quand je suis moralement sûr de ne jamais me trouver dans le même cas? et qui me répondra qu'en suivant bien fidèlement cette maxime, j'obtiendrai qu'on la suive de même avec moi? Le méchant tire avantage de la probité du juste et de sa propre injustice; il est bien aise que tout le monde soit juste, exepté lui. Cet accord-là, quoi qu'on en dise, n'est pas fort avantageux aux gens de bien. Mais quand la force d'une âme expansive m'identifie avec mon semblable, et que je me sens pour ainsi dire en lui, c'est pour ne pas souffrir que je ne veux pas qu'il souffre; je m'intéresse à lui pour l'amour de moi, et la raison du précepte est dans la nature elle-même qui m'inspire le désir de mon bien-être en quelque lieu que je me sente exister. D'où je conclus qu'il n'est pas vrai que les préceptes de la loi naturelle soient fondés sur la raison seule, ils ont une base plus solide et plus sûre. L'amour des hommes dérivé de l'amour de soi est le principe de la justice humaine. *Émile*, Bk. IV. (Garnier, Paris, 1961, pp. 278-279.)

[76] *Pensée* 435 (Bkn. 2081); Nagel II, p. 164; Pléiade I, p. 1542.
[77] *Discours de la Conformité de la Foi avec la Raison*, XXIII.

"tous les hommes ensemble, cent millions de têtes comme la nôtre, ne sont qu'un atome subtil et délié, que Dieu n'aperçoit qu'à cause de l'immensité de ses connaissances."

The vastness of the universe which dwarfs man physically could only be accessible to a boundless intelligence.

Indeed Montesquieu's theory of the necessary perfection and justice of the Divinity, exhibited in the complete intelligence of universal harmony, that is to say, of those "rapports de convenance" which inform its structure, together with the associated theory of human liberty coupled to human imperfection, shows striking affinity to some of the major doctrines of the *Théodicée*.[78] For instance, the burden of the short passage from the *Spicilège* quoted above,[79] is that human imperfection results from ignorance of the principle of "convenance" which should govern man's actions as it governs those of God, the sum of moral perfection. Now we have seen in the analysis of Letter LXXXIII that Montesquieu defines justice as an immutable "rapport de convenance," and how in *Pensée* 434 he considers supernatural justice to be inescapable in its totality. Thus it seems that for Montesquieu as for Leibniz, the moral order of the universe was determined by the principle of fitness. God's will is not arbitrary in so far as his absolute wisdom and perfection, his absolute justice, lead him to establish that order of reality which is most "convenable," which in its perfection most fully represents his nature.

Bearing in mind this common notion of "convenance' as the principle of cosmic harmony, or equally the notion of a moral order consisting of "rapports de convenance," an examination of the actual passage from the *Théodicée* which was the probable source of Montesquieu's definition of justice[80] tends to confirm the philosophical similarities between the two thinkers. Significantly, Leibniz is here arguing against Hobbes, in defence of the necessity of justice, a task to which Montesquieu also applied himself in the *Lettres Persanes* and the *Traité des Devoirs*, and which may have originally drawn his attention to the passage:

"Il y a pourtant une espèce de justice et une certaine sorte de récompenses et de punitions, qui ne paraît pas si applicable à ceux qui agiraient

---

[78] Significantly, most of the material drawn from the *Pensées* and the *Spicilège* dates from the period before 1738, and a large proportion of this from before 1731, that is from the time when the theory of justice was still a major preoccupation for Montesquieu.

[79] P. 176.

[80] Indicated by A. S. Crisafulli in "Parallels to ideas in the *Lettres Persanes*," P.M.L.A., vol. LII, 1937, p. 773 sq.

par une nécessité absolue, s'il y en avait. C'est cette espèce de justice qui n'a point pour but l'amendement, ni l'exemple, ni même la réparation du mal. Cette justice n'est fondée que dans la convenance, qui demande une certaine satisfaction pour l'expiation d'une mauvaise action. Les Sociniens, Hobbes et quelques autres, n'admettent point cette justice primitive, qui est proprement vindicative, et que Dieu s'est réservée en bien des rencontres: mais qu'il ne laisse pas de communiquer à ceux qui ont droit de gouverner les autres, et qu'il exerce par leur moyen, pourvu qu'ils agissent par raison, et non par passion. Les Sociniens la croient être sans fondement; mais elle est toujours fondée dans un rapport de convenance, qui contente non seulement l'offensé, mais encore les sages qui la voient, comme une belle musique ou bien une bonne architecture contente les esprits bien faits. Et le sage législateur ayant menacé, et ayant, pour ainsi dire, promis un châtiment, il est de sa constance de ne pas laisser l'action entièrement impunie, quand même la peine ne servirait plus à corriger personne. Mais quand il n'aurait rien promis, c'est assez qu'il y a une convenance qui l'aurait pu porter à faire cette promesse; puisqu'aussi bien le sage ne promet que ce qui est convenable. Et on peut même dire qu'il y a ici un certain dédommagement de l'esprit, que le désordre offenserait, si le châtiment ne contribuait à rétablir l'ordre."[81]

Leibniz clearly had in mind the kind of cosmic justice evoked by Montesquieu in his metaphor of the fishing net; it is this transcendent justice that is satisfied by the administration of rewards and punishments; such recompense serves to restore cosmic harmony, producing aesthetic as well as moral satisfaction in those that contemplate it. And the principle on which it depends is plainly that "convenance" or sufficient reason, which Leibniz had seen as the source of moral and natural order, a principle that is eternal and immutable in that it proceeds from the perfection of the Divinity:

"Mais quand il n'aurait rien promis, c'est assez qu'il y a une convenance qui l'aurait pu porter à faire cette promesse; puisqu'aussi bien le sage ne promet que ce qui est convenable."[82]

It is interesting that Leibniz goes on in the following section to link the existence of heavenly rewards and punishments with the operation of the principle of "convenance":

"C'est ainsi que les peines des damnés continuent, lors même qu'elles ne servent plus à détourner du mal; et que de même les récompenses des bienheureux continuent, lors même qu'elles ne servent plus à confirmer dans le bien."

Now we have already seen how in Letter LXIX and *Pensée* 434 Montes-

---

[81] *Op. cit.*, I, sec. 73; *Oeuvres*, ed. Janet, 1866, vol. II, pp. 147–148.
[82] For a more detailed discussion of Leibniz's idea of justice, see above pp. 26–29.

quieu found a place for rewards and punishments in his theory of human freedom and divine justice, and in this his thought again seems to follow that of Leibniz closely. But although he appears to accept the doctrine in a philosophical framework,[83] other passages reveal a certain doubt as regards its acceptability in the context of revealed religion. Rewards and punishments are admissable where they express the demands of metaphysical justice, but can we credit them when they cease to redress evil, and are distributed according to belief or unbelief:

"Ceux qui disent qu'il n'y a point de peines ni récompenses dans l'autre vie ne le disent pas en faveur des bons: car ils les privent des récompenses. Ils établissent donc leur système en faveur des méchants qu'ils soulagent de la peine. – Cet argument, que le cardinal de Polignac a mis dans son *Lucrèce*, serait plus fort dans la Loi de Nature ou une religion qui n'admettrait que l'équité, que dans une loi, qui, admettant une révélation, damne ceux qui ne croient pas, et où l'Enfer est et le Paradis est distribué entre les croyants et les non-croyants."[84]

One is again confronted by the incredible breadth of vision, and corresponding lack of dogmatism, which enabled Montesquieu to examine an idea from all its angles with a disturbing and sometimes misleading objectivity. Thus, yet another passage, an incidental remark in Letter CXXIX dealing with the wisdom of legislators who seek to strengthen paternal authority, seems to indicate a sound appreciation of the doctrine in religious psychology:

"les pères sont l'image du Créateur de l'Univers, qui, quoiqu'il puisse conduire les hommes par son amour, ne laisse pas de se les attacher encore par les motifs de l'espérance et de la crainte,"[85]

while elsewhere Montesquieu even seems to align himself unreservedly with the universalist cause, questioning the reasonableness of the doctrine of hell on grounds characteristic of the enlightened magistrate, who regards punishment primarily as a reformative deterrent:

"Il est difficile de comprendre par la raison seule l'éternité des peines des damnés: car les peines et les récompenses ne peuvent être établies que par rapport à l'avenir. On punit aujourd'hui un homme, afin qu'il ne faille pas demain; afin que les autres ne faillent pas aussi. Mais, lorsque les bienheu-

[83] In the *Lois* (XXIV, 14) he also brings out its important effect on the morals of particular societies.

[84] *Pensée* 422 (Bkn. 2087); Nagel II, p. 161; Pléiade I, p. 1544.

[85] Nagel I, p. 258; Pléiade I, p. 323; cf. *Lois* XXV, 2, "Les hommes sont extrêmement portés à espérer et à craindre; et une religion qui n'aurait ni enfer ni paradis, ne saurait guère leur plaire." Nagel I, p. 108; Pléiade II, p. 737.

reux ne seront pas libres de pécher, ni les damnés de bien faire, à quoi bon des peines et des récompenses?"[86]

Thus it is at least conceivable that Montesquieu would have hesitated to concur with Leibniz on the question of eternal damnation; although the general pattern of his metaphysical thought is remarkably similar. A comprehensive summary suggests then that Montesquieu understood his definition of justice as "un rapport de convenance" in the context of a theory of the universe where fitness constituted, as it did for Leibniz, the transcendent and immutable principle governing its moral and physical structure through the agency of the natural law.[87] Whether this principle equalled in his mind that of sufficient as opposed to necessary reason; that is to say, whether, again like Leibniz, he considered it dependent upon the divine will, "le choix du Sage," and distinct from necessary or mathematical reason, is not fully certain. In view of the asserted perfection of the Divinity it must in a sense be considered as a necessary principle: God is bound by his perfection to choose that order of things which is most "convenable". Yet as we have seen in the theological letters and fragments, Montesquieu supports the idea of an omnipotent and omniscient God, and repeatedly affirms that men are incapable of penetrating his ultimate designs. Such a persuasion would seem to set him apart from Malebranche, who, although he put forward the idea, akin to Montesquieu's, that justice like truth consisted in real and immutable relationships,[88] nevertheless affirmed that such relationships belonged to an eternal, necessary and all embracing metaphysical order, consubstantial with the divine intelligence, and predetermining the divine will. Malebranche saw no real distinction between necessary reason and sufficient reason, between metaphysical truth, scientific truth and moral truth:

"Ainsi Dieu a deux sortes de lois qui le règlent dans sa conduite. L'une est éternelle et nécessaire, et c'est l'ordre: les autres sont arbitraires, et ce sont les lois générales de la Nature et de la Grâce. Mais Dieu n'a établi ces der-

---

[86] *Pensée* 82 (Bkn. 2088); Nagel II, p. 27; Pléiade I, p. 1544. cf. *Lettres Persanes* CXXV, on the difficulty of conceiving the nature of heavenly rewards.

[87] The complete definition, as it stands in Letter LXXXIII, "La justice est un rapport de convenance, qui se trouve réellement entre deux choses," does, it is true, retain a strong geometrical element. The "qui se trouve réellement entre deux choses" may have been added to drive home the absolute universality and necessity of the principle of "convenance"; or it may be a reflection of the notion of reciprocity characteristic of orthodox juristic definitions of justice; cf. the juristic significance of his definition of law, below pp. 228–229; or of his essentially mathematical conception of knowledge, see below pp. 229–230.

[88] Malebranche did use the phrase "rapport de convenance" in the *Recherche de la Vérité*, Book III, Conclusion (1678 ed. p. 228); but in a context with no significance for the topic of justice.

nières que parce que l'ordre demande qu'il agisse ainsi. De sorte que c'est l'ordre éternel, immuable, nécessaire ... qui est la loi que mon père consulte toujours, qu'il aime invinciblement, qu'il suit inviolablement, et par laquelle il a fait et conserve toutes choses." [89]

In fact his ontological theories were such that he found it difficult to persuade his contemporaries of any convincing distinction in his system between the divine substance, metaphysical reason, and the extended universe; that the eternal, immutable and necessary order of archetypal relationships was not an immanent rather than a transcendent order. [90]

Montesquieu however, at least during the period represented by the material we have covered, [91] is far from positing an immanent conception of order. The "rapports de convenance" which constitute justice belong to a transcendent order of perfection, to which man as a rational but imperfect creature may aspire, and in part fulfil in the context of his social existence. As far as the totality of cosmic harmony is concerned, man is unable to fathom its reason, and partakes in it by virtue of his immortality, through the operation of eternal rewards and punishments. [92] In his early works, "convenance" is for Montesquieu a teleological principle in both a metaphysical and a moral sense. For we infer from his discussion of divine foreknowledge and the arrangement of secondary causes, that fitness governs the ultimate design of the created order, although within this structure man is endowed with an apparent freedom. Thus with the notion of "convenance" as the final cause, Montesquieu can be placed, at least until the writing of De l'Esprit des Lois adds a new and disturbing dimension to his thought, in the august company not only of Malebranche, but perhaps even more important of Leibniz and indeed of Clarke, [93] as an upholder of rational idealism, against those other thinkers of more materialist outlook like Fréret and Saint-Hyacinthe, [94] who considered that relationships of conformity belonged not to a transcendent order of justice, but were no more than symptomatic of the spontaneous organization of matter; who used them to elaborate a relativistic and hedonistic ethic, rather than a constant ideal of virtue proclaiming the ultimate goodness and perfection of the universe.

---

[89] *Méditations Chrétiennes*, VII, para 18.
[90] See above Part I, ch. 2, pp. 12–14.
[91] This would extend from the date of the *Lettres Persanes*, 1721, to approximately 1738, basing the second limit on the system of dating developed by Shackleton in *Les Secrétaires de Montesquieu* (Nagel II, Introduction II), and applied to the *Pensées* by L. Desgraves (Nagel II, Introduction III).
[92] Thus Spinoza's idea that man may attain moral perfection through the fulfilment of his rational nature and in the context of a finite existence is equally far from Montesquieu's mind.
[93] See above, Part I, ch. 4, pp. 84–87.
[94] See above, Part I, ch. 3, pp. 59–66.

JUSTICE AND LAW
THE SIGNIFICANCE OF
"DE L'ESPRIT DES LOIS" BK. I

I

"Les bêtes, qui ont toutes des intérêts séparés, s'entrenuisent toujours. Les hommes seuls, faits pour vivre en société, ne perdent rien de ce qu'ils partagent.
J'ai mille avantages à vivre, non pas dans un grand état, mais dans une grande société."

Pensée 1747 (Bkn. 366).

In spite of its shortness in relation to the rest of the work and its somewhat eclectic philosophy, the first book of *De l'Esprit des Lois* has remained from the time of its publication in 1748 to the present day the centre of disproportionately heated debate. It achieves that rare distinction, usually reserved for the sacred books of great religions, of being all things to all men. Indeed after reviewing its fortunes and taking stock of innumerable commentaries, interpretations, denunciations and dismissals, one hardly needs more convincing evidence of the truth of Montesquieu's own remark in the *Essai sur les Causes qui peuvent affecter les Esprits* that opinions are formed in the heart and not in the mind.

The bewildered reactions of some of the author's contemporaries to this first book, and especially to the unusual definition of law at the very beginning, are partly accounted for by Shackleton in his critical biography of Montesquieu.[1] They were expecting the theories and definitions of a jurist: to see law set down in the style of Grotius as

"a rule of moral actions, obliging as to that which is just and reasonable,"[2]

or alternatively of Pufendorf, as

"the will of a superior by which he obliges those dependent upon him to act in the particular way he prescribes";[3]

---

[1] *Op. cit.*, above (p. 9 n. 3), ch. XI, section II.
[2] *De Jure belli ac pacis*, I, i, 9.
[3] *De Jure naturae et gentium*, I, vi, 4.

or they looked at the very least for an echo of the generalities of lexico-graphers, exemplified by the definition of *loi* in the dictionary of the French Academy, as "constitution écrite qui ordonne ce qu'il faut faire et qui défend ce qu'il ne faut pas faire."[4]

Small wonder then that the invective of the *Nouvelles ecclésiastiques*[5] whose virulence provoked Montesquieu's *Défense*, was directed first of all against this new definition of law:

"Les lois, dans la signification la plus étendue, sont les rapports néces-saires qui dérivent de la nature des choses,"

evidence in the eyes of the Jansenist reviewer of his adherence to the pernicious doctrines of Spinozism:

"Les lois, des rapports! Cela se conçoit-il? . . . Cependant l'auteur n'a pas changé la définition ordinaire des lois sans dessein. Quel est donc son but? le voici . . ."[6]

Even David Hume, an enlightened and enthusiastic admirer of the *Lois* as a political work, took exception to the theories of the first book:

"This illustrious writer sets out with a different theory, and supposes all right to be founded on certain *rapports* or relations; which is a system that, in my view, will never reconcile with true philosophy."[7]

Similarly the equally enthusiastic Charles Bonnet, who wrote flat-teringly though rather more perceptively:

"Newton a découvert les lois du monde matériel: vous avez découvert, Monsieur, les lois du monde intellectuel."[8]

later insisted in his *Essai analytique sur les facultés de l'âme*, that the definition of law as a relationship as it stood in the *Lois* needed further elaboration.[9]

It seems indeed in spite of the title of the work and Montesquieu's references in the Preface to its purpose:

"J'ai d'abord examiné les hommes, et j'ai cru que, dans cette infinie di-versité de lois et de moeurs, ils n'étaient pas uniquement conduits par leurs fantaisies.
J'ai posé les principes, et j'ai vu les cas particuliers s'y plier comme d'eux-

---

[4] *Grand Dictionnaire de l'Académie française*, 2nd. ed., Amsterdam, 1696.
[5] Of the 9th. and 16th. October 1749.
[6] *Défense de l'Esprit des Lois*, première objection; Nagel I, p. 435; Pléiade II, p. 1122.
[7] *An Enquiry concerning the principles of morals*, London, 1751, p. 54.
[8] Letter to Montesquieu, 14th. November 1753.
[9] *Op. cit.*, (Copenhagen, 1760), 2nd. ed., Copenhagen and Geneva 1769, ch. XXVII, para. 856, p. 310.

mêmes; les histoires de toutes les nations n'en être que les suites; et chaque loi particulière liée avec une autre loi, ou dépendre d'une autre plus générale."[10]

that hardly any of the *savants* of the day, not to mention the jurists and theologians, grasped the compound significance of the term *loi* as it appeared in the first book. While objecting in the *Essai analytique* that laws were not properly defined as *rapports*, but rather as the effects of relationships between the qualities of objects as determined by primitive reason,[11] Bonnet on the one hand perceived, it is true, that Montesquieu's most fundamental objective in the *Lois* was scientific: the isolation and description of the causal relationships or laws which govern the infinitely varied institutions of human society; as he expressed it in his letter to Montesquieu, the discovery of the "lois du monde intellectuel." On the other hand, Hume's comment reveals an acuter awareness of the possible juristic and philosophical significance of Montesquieu's use of *loi* in book I. Thus as he sees it, Montesquieu has wrongly attempted to found all *right* on certain *rapports*.

Similarly, although criticism in the wake of Comte's analysis of the *Lois* as a straightforward explanation of positive laws in terms of the influence of environment,[12] has in general acknowledged the scientific conception of law to be found there, individual commentators have still tended to favour dogmatic interpretations in which the scientific is emphasized at the expense of the moral and juristic or vice-versa. Thus the kind of description of Montesquieu's purpose to be found for example in Cassirer's *Philosophy of the Enlightenment*[13] is unexceptionable and fairly commonplace:

"As a jurist he asks the same question that Newton the physicist had raised. He is not content with the empirically known laws of the political world. He attempts to trace the variety of these laws back to a few definite principles. The existence of such an order, of such a systematic interdependence among the various normative legal forms constitutes the 'spirit of the laws.' He is thus enabled to begin his work with an explanation of the concept of law which formulates this concept in its most comprehensive and universal sense, not limiting it to any special field of factual data."[14]

But representative of the more dogmatic extremes of interpretation are Barthélemy Saint-Hilaire, who in an article comparing Plato, Aristotle

[10] Nagel I, p. lix; Pléiade II, p. 229.
[11] *Op. cit.*, para. 856, pp. 310–311.
[12] *Cours de Philosophie positive*, 47e leçon.
[13] *Die Philosophie der Aufklärung* (Tübingen, 1932), translated by F.C.A. Koelln and J.P. Pettegrove, Princeton, 1951.
[14] *Op. cit.*, Beacon Press, Boston, 1961; pp. 242–243.

and Montesquieu, fiercely rebuked the latter for his definition of law, on the grounds that the exclusive concern of a political writer should be positive law understood as the expression of free will, firmly rooted as to its contents in human nature:

"Ainsi Montesquieu débute par un défaut de méthode, et tout son premier livre, qui traite des lois en général, est 'd'une métaphysique faible et obscure' comme le lui reprochent Voltaire ... et Helvétius,"[15]

and, in contrast, the modern writer L. Althusser, who, in his enthusiasm for the work as a cornerstone of sociology, declares of the opening definition of law:

"cette loi ne sera plus un ordre idéal, mais un rapport immanent aux phénomènes,"

excluding any possibility of reference to moral principles on Montesquieu's part; and who sees actual mentions of justice in the text as nothing more than convenient exploitation of "une tradition la plus fade," included for the sole purpose of attacking Hobbes.[16]

The business of interpretation would certainly have been less bewildering had Montesquieu departed from his normal stylistic practice of aiming for the most economical expression of his thoughts, and instead allowed some of the passages intended for the Preface to remain in place, rather than relegating them to the *Pensées*. His readers might then have understood where he stood in relation to orthodox political theory, and also why. They would have known for instance that he had no intention of emulating recent eminent practitioners in this field:

'Je rends grâces à MM. Grotius et Pufendorf d'avoir exécuté ce qu'une grande partie de cet ouvrage demandait de moi, avec cette hauteur de génie à laquelle je n'aurais pu atteindre."[17]

Equally they would have gained some inkling of the interdependence of scientific attitudes and moral awareness in the conception of the work:

"On a, dans notre siècle, donné un tel degré d'estime aux connaissances physiques que l'on (n)'a conservé que de l'indifférence pour les morales. Depuis les Grecs et les Romains, le bien et le mal moral sont devenus un sentiment plutôt qu'un objet de connaissance."[18]

---

[15] "Mémoire sur la science politique, et particulièrement sur la politique de Platon, d'Aristote et de Montesquieu," *Séances et Travaux de l'Académie des Sciences morales et politiques*, 2e série, vol. 4, 1848; p. 151.
[16] *Montesquieu, la Politique et l'Histoire*, P.U.F., Paris, 1959, ch. II.
[17] *Pensée* 1863 (Bkn. 191), Nagel II, p. 556; Pléiade II, p. 1038.
[18] *Pensée* 1871 (Bkn. 199); Nagel II, p. 557; Pléiade II, p. 1040.

These and several similar *rejets* testify to an attempt by Montesquieu to explain the nature and purpose of his work more clearly than he does in the existing Preface. Perhaps his confidence was such that he subsequently decided that this was unnecessary:

"Si tout le monde ne sent pas ce que je dis, j'ai tort." [19]

or perhaps he was already practising the principle which he expounds at the end of book XI: the reader must be stimulated, not sated: "Il ne s'agit pas de faire lire, mais de faire penser." [20] Whatever the case, concision to the point of elision was its outcome in the Preface as in book I, where, regrettably, he never distinguishes between the various senses in which he employs the term *loi*, senses of which three can be isolated immediately: *law* with the scientific meaning of causal relationship; *law* with the juristic force of commandment; and *law* in the moral and philosophical sense of a principle of reason. Misunderstanding and confusion of these senses is all too easy, when both the scientist and the moralist, though working within philosophical frameworks which are poles apart, may start out from the supposition that the mind inhabits a rational world, with the result that the dividing line between logical and causal relationships begins to blur.

II

The first chapter of book I of the *Lois*, entitled somewhat ambiguously *Of laws in general*, deals with laws in their relationship to various beings, giving the immediate, though as it proves, unfounded impression that Montesquieu is flying in the face of the Aristotelian dictum that man alone is a social animal. His argument develops from the opening definition of law in its *broadest* sense as the necessary relationships which derive from the nature of things; in this sense Montesquieu claims, all beings may be considered to possess their own laws: God, the material world, creatures of superior intelligence to man, brute creation, and man. Its next stage is the association of the nature of things with the existence of a primitive reason, which he proves by citing the existence of intelligent creatures in the world. To claim

[19] *Pensée* 1863 (Bkn. 191); Nagel II, p. 556; Pléiade II, p. 1038.
[20] cf. Montesquieu's formula for good style: "Pour bien écrire il faut sauter les idées intermédiares, assez pour n'être pas ennuyeux; pas trop, de peur de n'être pas entendu. Ce sont ces suppressions heureuses qui ont fait dire à M. Nicole que tous les bons livres étaient doubles." *Pensée* 1970 (Bkn. 802); Nagel II, pp. 604–605; Pléiade I, p. 1220.

as some have done, meaning of course the so-called Spinozists, that blind fatality is the principle governing the organization of matter, is according to Montesquieu patently absurd. Thus laws orginate in reason, and comprise both the relationships between this primitive reason and various orders of beings, and the relationships between beings themselves. They correspond to the twofold relationship, as both creator and conserver, of God with the universe; the laws of creation and of conservation are identical, and God created and sustains his creation in accordance with them because ultimately they derive from his wisdom and power:

"Il agit selon ces règles parce qu'il les connaît; il les connaît parce qu'il les a faites; il les a faites, parce qu'elles ont du rapport avec sa sagesse et sa puissance." [21]

Montesquieu then goes on to describe the precise nature of these laws. Their most important characteristic is the invariability which belies the apparently arbitrary nature of the act of creation. It is demonstrated by the inanimate universe, which, although the simple product of the movement of matter, and obviously devoid of intelligence, nevertheless continues to exist. This would be impossible if its motion was not governed by invariable laws; indeed these are so much the condition of all organization and all existence that without them God would be powerless to govern the universe. In the terms of Montesquieu's original definition, they are "constantly established relationships," and are exemplified by the uniform and constant law of movement, consisting invariably in the relationship of speed and mass of the objects concerned.

But the sphere of these general laws of primitive reason is not confined to the organization of matter. It extends to include the world of intelligent creatures also, for the potential order of relationships linking such beings together would remain the same whether they actually existed or not:

"Avant qu'il y eût des êtres intelligents, ils étaient possibles; ils avaient donc des rapports possibles, et par conséquent des lois possibles. [22]

Hence Montesquieu argues, intelligent beings are not governed solely by positive laws of their own making, but are subject to the rule of primitive justice:

[21] Nagel I, p. 2; Pléiade II, p. 232.
[22] Nagel I, pp. 2–3; Pléiade II, p. 233.

"Dire qu'il n'y a rien de juste ni d'injuste que ce qu'ordonnent ou défendent les lois positives, c'est dire qu'avant qu'on eût tracé de cercle, tous les rayons n'étaient pas égaux." [23]

Just as a circle is not a circle unless its radii are equal, so intelligent beings stand in a relationship of justice towards each other, prior to or in the absence of positive laws giving expression to it. Montesquieu then gives several instances of this relationship of justice: the social bond, which sanctions obedience to the laws of any community; the relationship of indebtedness which compels gratitude, and so on.

However Montesquieu has an important restriction to make concerning the operation of these laws of justice to which intelligent creation is subject. Having already observed that the purely inanimate world by its very nature can only subsist through the operation of invariable laws, he points in contrast to the two distinctive characteristics of intelligent beings, which, while they do not invalidate the invariable laws of justice, nevertheless radically affect the relationship of the individual to them. The intelligent creature is distinguished on the one hand by his limitations and on the other by his freedom; and as a result, he does not conform invariably to his own laws.

Other orders of being form a chain linking the inconsistency of the intelligent world to the invariability of the physical. Animals for example, while possessing no closer links with God than the rest of material creation, nevertheless enjoy inter-personal relationships as human beings do, with the essential difference that theirs is a community of feeling rather than intelligence. These purely affective relationships constitute the natural laws to which they are peculiarly subject, positive laws being precluded by their lack of intelligence. Thus the way in which their various appetites relate to themselves and to their fellows governs the conservation of both the individual and the species. But they are in general less successful than the plant world in observing their own laws, for the latter, devoid of both feeling and understanding, is much nearer to inanimate invariability.

Man, while belonging to intelligent creation, is equally subject by virtue of his emotions to the government of natural laws, though here again, as a result of the complexity of his nature, is inclined to observe them irregularly; for example, his hopes make him a prey to fear, and his passions the victim of intemperance.

Finally, as a preparation for his true subject, the laws peculiar to mankind, Montesquieu recapitulates the various attributes of human

[23] *Ibid.*

nature which he has isolated in the course of his discussion, and correlates them with the particular order of law which they sustain, indicating the degree to which they may be said to determine man's conduct. Thus it is only as a purely physical body, that he is subject to invariable laws in the same way as the rest of the material universe. As a sentient being subject to natural law, his conduct is swayed by a thousand passions; while as an intelligent but imperfect creature, and consequently a free agent, he violates not only the laws of his own making, but also the law of reason.

Yet even if imperfection and instability are inseparable from the human condition, Montesquieu implies that the very laws men neglect still provide them with the means of approaching the invariable perfection of absolute wisdom:

"Un tel être pouvait, à tous les instants, oublier son créateur; Dieu l'a rappelé à lui par les lois de la religion. Un tel être pouvait, à tous les instants, s'oublier lui-même; les philosophes l'ont averti par les lois de la morale. Fait pour vivre dans la société, il y pouvait oublier les autres; les législateurs l'ont rendu à ses devoirs par les lois politiques et civiles." [24]

In chapter II, *Of the laws of nature*, Montesquieu passes from the essence of laws considered in relation to the structure of the universe and the nature of created beings, to an examination of the evolution of laws in time. The context of the discussion changes in effect from the metaphysical to the historical, at least in so far as the framework he adopts is the same hypothesis of a state of nature preceding the inception of organized society as was commonly used by the philosophers of the School of Natural Law.[25] But at the same time chapter II remains a clearly consistent development of certain integral assumptions of chapter I.

He opens his argument however with a statement which appears largely contradictory to the central notion of this chapter, namely

---

[24] Nagel I, p. 4; Pléiade II, p. 234.

[25] This is not to say that Montesquieu had the same conception of the state of nature as Grotius, Pufendorf and their disciples. They were not in fact concerned with historical explanations of social evolution, but used the idea as a brilliant fiction with which to oust theological explanations of the origin of political power. If the theory of divine right was to be replaced by that of the origin of sovereignty in human conventions, then it was necessary to posit the existence of a state of nature prior to the inception of the political state, in which men were free, equal, and subject only to the law of reason. (For natural law theory of the priority of the individual to the community, see O. Gierke, *Natural Law and the Theory of Society*, (E. Barker's translation of part of the fourth volume of *Das deutsche Genossenschaftsrecht*), C.U.P., 1934, ch. II, section I, part 16, ii.) It is clear from the beginning of the *Lois*, that for Montesquieu the battle against theology was already won, and in *Lettres Persanes* XCIV, he attacks the individualism in natural law theories; but he was far from dispensing entirely with the idea of a state of nature; see below pp. 210–225.

that the structure of the universe and its laws are grounded in primitive reason:

"Avant toutes ces lois, sont celles de la nature, ainsi nommées, parce qu'elles dérivent uniquement de la constitution de notre être. Pour les connaître bien, il faut considérer un homme avant l'établissement des sociétés. Les lois de la nature seront celles qu'il recevrait dans un état pareil." [26]

Unless one is to assume that Montesquieu has carelessly lumped together two alternative accounts of the origin of laws in order to dispatch the tiresome chore of introducing his work with the minimum of intellectual effort, one must of course read this as a further comment upon those "lois de la religion," "lois de la morale," and "lois politiques et civiles," which he introduced at the end of chapter I. It serves first of all to confirm that these three categories are intended to represent varieties of positive laws or written precepts, as opposed to the invariable laws governing the structure of the universe upon which he concentrated most of his attention. The laws of nature which he now intends to examine precede the establishment of such varieties of positive law, and are to be discovered by considering the nature of pre-social man. Not that Montesquieu thereby concedes the actual existence of such a creature, although he does go on to cite the behaviour of certain "hommes sauvages" found in the forests of Hanover as empirical evidence of his portrait. He simply implies in this first paragraph that primitive man and his laws would of necessity more vividly reflect particular aspects of the essential human nature described in chapter I, since the conditions of his existence would be such that the "constitution de notre être" alone would govern his relationships.

Thus the idea that emerges is of a stage of human development, pre-social but not necessarily anarchic, where individual behaviour would be determined by the less sophisticated elements of human nature, by feelings rather than reason. At this stage in fact, men would more closely resemble the beasts described in chapter I, in that emotional relationships would define their laws to the exclusion of the more complex elements present in the social intercourse of fully rational creatures; hence the emphasis of Montesquieu's opening words,

"ainsi nommées, parce qu'elles *dérivent uniquement* de la constitution de notre être."

[26] Nagel I, p. 5; Pléiade II, p. 235.

Accordingly when he constructs the psychology of this pre-social being in order to indicate the laws which would arise from it, he admits only those faculties and emotions which would be proper to such a primitive creature existing before the establishment of organized institutions. He rejects the theological notion that the first law of nature is that which establishes and governs man's relationship to God, on the grounds that while it may be the most important, it cannot be the first in the chronological order of these laws, since it originates in a concept entirely beyond the reach of the primitive mind:

"L'homme, dans l'état de nature, aurait plutôt la faculté de connaître, qu'il n'aurait des connaissances. Il est clair que ses premières idées ne seraient point des idées spéculatives: il songerait à la conservation de son être, avant de chercher l'origine de son être." [27]

In a state of nature the individual's first relationships would be determined by subjective emotions; overwhelmed by his own weakness, his behaviour would reveal only timidity; his ideas and consequently his intentions would extend no further than self-preservation, and he would exist in a condition of comparative isolation. Inter-personal relationships would be governed by mutual feelings of inferiority. Consequently the first law of nature would be peace:

"Dans cet état, chacun se sent inférieur; à peine chacun se sent-il égal. On ne chercherait donc point à s'attaquer, et la paix serait la première loi naturelle." [28]

In addition however, each would feel certain basic needs, and so a second law of nature would be the impulse to nourish oneself.

Yet conditions in the state of nature would be far from static, for in time these simple emotions would give rise to more complex relationships and further laws. Thus consciousness of mutual fear would bring about the transformation of conditions of isolation, and in combination with the pleasures of communal living and the power of sexual attraction, would produce a third law, that of sexual union. More complex relationships would also lead to the perfecting of the mental faculties and gradually men would acquire ideas as well as feelings. In this way they would enter the world of rational intercourse, and a new and generically different order of relationships would arise marking the transition to true social existence, and constituting the basis of positive laws. This transition would be governed by the fourth and final natural law: the desire to live in society.

[27] Nagel I, p. 5; Pléiade II, p. 235.
[28] *Ibid.*

For Montesquieu then, the laws of nature form a distinct category of laws originating in and proper to a particular stage in the development of human faculties, and therefore characteristic of a particular type and level of communal existence. The laws themselves consist in those simple relationships of feeling of which a potentially intelligent yet unsophisticated creature would be capable. Furthermore, although, providing the state of nature is accepted as a historical possibility rather than a mere hypothesis, they may be said to govern the later evolution of society and its laws, and although, presumably, they remain valid in so far as man continues to be a feeling as well as a thinking creature, there is no evidence in chapter II that Montesquieu conceives of their possessing anything more than a limited descriptive and causal significance. Given a state of nature and a particular kind of creature, he is arguing, these are the laws of behaviour which would obtain; but nowhere does he suggest that such *primitive* patterns will exclusively sanction the far more complex relationships of the intelligent being.

The historical method which Montesquieu adopts in chapter II leads to an important digression concerning Hobbes's conception of the state of nature. The English philosopher's proverbial view of the natural condition of mankind as

"solitary, poor, nasty, brutish, and short ... a war of every man against every man,"[29]

was already notorious; Montesquieu, like him, links the idea of a state of nature to a particular analysis of human nature, but counters his description of the former by disputing his version of the latter. Hobbes's psychology, he objects, is anachronistic; he blunders by attributing to an unsophisticated creature, feelings and desires which are properly speaking attributes of the fully fledged social being. Where Montesquieu sees fear, timidity and diffidence, Hobbes sees aggression, and the more complex motives of conquest and dominion, but:

"L'idée de l'empire et de la domination est si composée, et dépend de tant d'autres idées, que ce ne serait pas celle qu'il aurait d'abord."[30]

The proof of Hobbes's error lies in the evidence he cites to support his portrait of human nature:

[29] *Leviathan*, Part I, ch. 13.
[30] Nagel I, pp. 5–6; Pléiade II, p. 235.

"Hobbes demande 'pourquoi, si les hommes ne sont pas naturellement en état de guerre, ils vont toujours armés? et pourquoi ils ont des clefs pour fermer leurs maisons?' Mais on ne sent pas que l'on attribue aux hommes, avant l'établissement des sociétés, ce qui ne peut leur arriver qu'après cet établissement, qui leur fait trouver des motifs pour s'attaquer et pour se défendre." [31]

The conditions which arise following the establishment of organized society and the developments which they induce in the emotional and intellectual constitution of the human being, are indeed the historical causes which Montesquieu himself then puts forward in chapter III, to account for the creation of positive laws. Once men are in society, they exchange their comparative independence and weakness for a sense of security; fear becomes aggression, equality gives way before acquisitiveness, and the state of war begins. Exactly the same process is witnessed among the society of nations, where as each begins to feel its strength, expansionism and war ensue. As a result of such conflict, the various kinds of positive laws come into being.

Montesquieu goes on to apply the same method as he used in the foregoing chapter to identify and describe the classes of this law; he proceeds by examining the nature of the individuals concerned, whether citizens or societies, and then induces from his analysis the nature and purpose of the relationships which arise from it. Particular laws are not however identified as each law of nature was, since obviously the number and complexity of the relationships to be considered is infinitely greater, and their analysis will in any case form the body of the work. At this stage Montesquieu is content to isolate the general principles which will govern the nature and purpose of each class of law.

Three main classes are isolated: the law of nations, political law, and civil law. The first of these comprises the relationships between peoples, whose necessity Montesquieu establishes rather naïvely by referring to the vast size of the globe. The purpose he ascribes to international law is logically identical with that attributed to the laws of nature in chapter II, and in the first chapter, to all general laws governing the structure of the universe, namely conservation. It is his view that all beings and entities, considered in relation to themselves, will, assuming reality to be grounded in reason, have this as their natural end. Thus international law will so regulate the conditions of peace and war that each nation enjoys the maximum opportunity of conserving itself:

[31] *Ibid.*

"Le droit des gens est naturellement fondé sur ce principe: que les diverses nations doivent se faire, dans la paix, le plus de bien, et, dans la guerre, le moins de mal qu'il est possible, sans nuire à leurs véritables intérêts."[32]

From it a second principle arises, namely that the proper object of war is the conservation of the conquered people.

The second class of positive law, political law, consists of the relationships arising from the distribution of power between the members of any given society, which in turn derives from the society's nature as a political entity, formed by "la réunion de toutes les forces particulières," and needing government to maintain its existence. Montesquieu distinguishes two possible ways in which collective power may be distributed within the state: it may be entrusted to one person, or to several. Such consequences of the natural structure of the state constitute the general principles governing the political law of any society; but Montesquieu declines to elaborate any further details, since, if the object of conservation is to be fulfilled, each particular state will require the government best suited to its own character and conditions.

For this reason he disputes the arguments of the patriarchal theorists,[33] who drawing a false analogy between the structure of the state and the nature of the family, maintained that monarchic government, on the pattern of paternal authority, best answered the needs of every society. The vice of their method is proved, Montesquieu claims, by the fact that it can be used to justify not only monarchic government, but also the very democratic forms it is designed to exclude, for on the death of the father, paternal authority gives way to the power of brothers and uncles, and so on. Indeed there can be no analogy between the structure of the family and the state, since the latter is by definition, a union of several families.

The third class of positive law, civil law, comprises all other relationships between the members of a society, and derives from its nature as a civil entity constituted by "la réunion de toutes les volontés." Once again its object is conservation, and in all respects it is closely linked to political law.

As regards the innumerable individual laws which fall into each class, and which are to occupy the centre of his study, Montesquieu simply confirms the conclusion of chapter II, that social existence is the proper state of rational creatures, for he sees them all as particular

[32] Nagel I, p. 7; Pléiade II, pp. 236–237.
[33] Best represented by Bossuet's *Politique tirée des propres paroles de l'Écriture Sainte*, Paris, 1709; and Filmer's *Patriarcha*, London, 1680.

applications of human reason. But although grounded in reason, they do not simply express those invariable and universally applicable precepts which Cartesian idealism would have attributed to rational intuition. On the contrary they are here conceived to be the product of rational insight into, and reflexion upon the manifold factors governing the life of each society. Montesquieu insists that they should be:

"tellement propres au peuple pour lequel elles sont faites, que c'est un très grand hasard si celles d'une nation peuvent convenir à une autre."[34]

Ideally they will be related to both the nature and the principle of the established or proposed form of government. They will take into account the physical conditions of each society's existence, for example, climate, geographical situation, territorial extent, and nature of the terrain; also such related factors as pastoral or agricultural economies. They will have equal regard to moral factors: to the degree of liberty consistent with the established constitution, to religion, to customs and national characteristics, to commercial and demographic circumstances. Finally, they will be relative to each other, to their origin, to the intentions of the legislator, and to their particular field of jurisdiction.

The study of all these related aspects of law, forms, Montesquieu declares, the task which he has set himself. He intends to examine not just positive laws in themselves, but their relationship to the nature of things; in other words, he intends to discover the laws governing positive law:

"J'examinerai tous ces rapports: ils forment tous ensemble ce que l'on appelle l'ESPRIT DES LOIS."[35]

III

The feature of this opening book which must first be underlined is its closely knit argument. Whatever strictures may be made on the logic of its parts – for instance, the deduction of the existence of an intelligent first cause from the existence of intelligent creatures – Montesquieu's determination to forge strong links between his analysis of positive laws and his first, essentially *a priori* principles becomes obvious as soon as the oddly dislocated effect produced by his elliptical style is removed by elaboration of each point and stage in the argument.

[34] Nagel I, pp. 8–9; Pléiade II, p. 237.
[35] Nagel I, p. 9; Pléiade II, p. 238.

We may deplore or applaud his efforts, but it is no longer easy to acquiesce in the superficial jibes at scholastic pastiche paraded by the abbé Bonnaire:

'J'entre dans le premier livre et je suis étonné d'y voir prendre les allures du *sottisier* des scolastiques. C'est une discussion hors-d'oeuvre des divers sens du mot loi." [36]

or with more wit, by Voltaire:

"Ne discutons point la foule de ces propositions qu'on peut attaquer et défendre longtemps sans convenir de rien. Ce sont des sources intarissables de dispute. Les deux contendants tournent sans avancer, comme s'ils dansaient un menuet; ils se retrouvent à la fin tous deux au même endroit dont ils étaient partis. Je ne chercherai point si Dieu a ses lois ou si sa pensée, sa volonté sont sa seule loi; si les bêtes ont leur loi, comme dit l'auteur; ni s'il y avait des rapports de justice avant qu'il y eût des hommes, ce qui est l'ancienne querelle des réaux et des nominaux . . . . Ne nous jouons pas dans les subtilités de cette métaphysique, gardons-nous d'entrer dans ce labyrinthe!" [37]

Although it is certainly not possible to judge on a simple reading of book I, the actual methods which Montesquieu employed in arriving at each proposition, for in at least one case, the evidence of collateral texts points to the probable application of inductive methods,[38] while this is belied by the deductive presentation of the argument, nevertheless they are all ably brought together to suggest the outline of a coherent, if derivative philosophy, designed to illuminate the origin and significance, as well as the structure of human societies and their laws. He assigns to man and society their place in the order of nature, thereby linking their positive laws to a universal principle, which not only accounts for them in metaphysical terms, and furnishes criteria by which they may be judged, but at the same time, serves to guarantee the validity of his own scientific analysis.

Indeed, once the stylistic obstacles to comprehension have been removed, it is the very confrontation with an analysis that in several respects fully merits the qualification scientific, even in the restricted modern sense of the word, rather than the dubious parentage of Montesquieu's metaphysics, which gives rise to the question of the pertinency of book I. And this is the question which has lain at the heart of so much subsequent debate as to the real significance of Montesquieu's various references to law and laws.

[36] *L'Esprit des lois quintessencié par une suite de lettres analytiques*, 1751, vol. I, p. 26.
[37] *Commentaire sur quelques maximes de l'Esprit des Lois*, I.
[38] See below pp. 218–220.

The structure of the work does indeed suggest as Lanson ruefully remarked when retracting his original theory that both the form and the content of the *Lois* were typical expressions of a rigidly systematic Cartesianism,[39] that the sole method of research employed by Montesquieu was deduction from *a priori* principles; but Lanson's amended conclusion, namely that the reason at work there may have recognized transcendent ideals, yet still proceeded from the facts, seems in the light of other consideration, much more acceptable.[40] Some such considerations, largely based on related texts, particularly the legacy of Montesquieu's Oratorian masters, of a highly eclectic methodology combining logic, experiment and historical comparison, have been set out by H. Roddier in an article which endorses Lanson's conclusion.[41] But without engaging here and now in a thoroughgoing investigation of such obvious test cases as the empirically based theory of climate in book XIV, which is in striking contrast to the ruthlessly logical idealism of the demolition of the "droit d'esclavage" in the following book, it is possible on the sole basis of book I to argue the probable implementation of empirical methods by Montesquieu. The notion that positive law is relative to many external forces, both physical and moral, is fundamental to his description of its nature in chapter III; consequently it is automatically implied by his declared intention of discovering the constant pattern of these influences, that they – the physical and moral phenomena – will be his starting point.

The comment which Montesquieu himself makes at the end of chapter III on the way he has approached his task would also be difficult to reconcile with a work exclusively dominated by methods of definition and deduction:

"... comme je ne traite point des lois, mais de l'esprit des lois, et que cet esprit consiste dans les divers rapports que les lois peuvent avoir avec diverses choses, j'ai dû moins suivre l'ordre naturel des lois, que celui de ces rapports et de ces choses."[42]

Even the apparent confession of Cartesian orthodoxy which occurs in the Preface:

"J'ai posé les principes, et j'ai vu les cas particuliers s'y plier comme d'eux-mêmes; les histoires de toutes les nations n'en être que les suites; et chaque

---

[39] See "L'influence de la philosophie cartésienne sur la littérature," *Revue de métaphysique et de morale*, 1896.

[40] See "Le rôle de l'expérience dans la formation de la philosophie du 18e siècle en France," *Revue du mois*, Jan.-June, 1910; part I.

[41] *Op. cit.*, above part II, ch. 1, p. 121, n. 32.

[42] Nagel I, p. 9; Pléiade II, p. 238.

loi particulière liée avec une autre loi, ou dépendre d'une autre plus générale."[43]

has been taken by at least one eminent historian of sociology as a declaration of Montesquieu's intention to proceed by the isolation of types, which, in constituting an intermediate stage between meaningless diversity and absolute ideals, will serve to render this diversity intelligible, and thereby complement the function of causal analysis.[44] Similarly, it is the application of a strikingly original sociological method, the method of "ideal types," that Cassirer discerns in books II and III, where Montesquieu, in contradiction to his declared intentions, appears to revert in his analysis of governments to a method of definition and logical deduction.[45]

One may find it difficult in the light of certain cogent and well documented articles demonstrating the persistence in Montesquieu's early essays and in the *Lettres Persanes* of typically Cartesian solutions to the problems of physics and psychology, and even in later works, to those of metaphysics, to differentiate in any significant way between the simple extension of a method recognizably related to Cartesian procedures to the field of politics and social organization, and the introduction of an original and distinctively sociological method.[46] Yet for all that, the relativism and determinism inseparable from his conception of positive law, in theory undoubtedly demand the implementation of inductive methods in the ensuing analysis. The fact that, when he subsequently confronts the phenomenon of government, Montesquieu ostensibly reverts to the old procedure of deduction from general assumptions, working towards particular instances and not from them, can be accounted for not only in terms of recourse to the new method of "ideal types," but also in very simple terms of an overall empirical approach which nevertheless finds room for other methods as and when necessary. Thus Montesquieu is prepared to take a Cartesian

[43] Nagel I, p. lix; Pléiade II, p. 229.

[44] Raymond Aron, *Les étapes de la pensée sociologique*, (N.R.F.: Bibliothèque des Sciences Humaines), 1967, part I, p. 29.

[45] *Op. cit.*, above (p. 148, n. 14), ch. V, pp. 210–212. It is not difficult to put a Cartesian construction on such passages as the following: "Il y a trois espèces de gouvernements: le RÉPUBLICAIN, le MONARCHIQUE et le DESPOTIQUE. Pour en découvrir la nature, il suffit de l'idée qu'en ont les hommes les moins instruits. Je suppose trois définitions, ou plutôt trois faits .... Il faut voir quelles sont les lois qui suivent directement de cette nature, et qui par conséquent sont les premières lois fondamentales." (II, 1), Nagel I, p. 10; Pléiade II, p. 239.

[46] See for instance, E. Buss, "Montesquieu und Cartesius," *Philosophische Monatshefte*, 1869–70, Band IV, pp. 1–37; and C. J. Beyer, "Montesquieu et l'esprit cartésien," *Actes du Congrès Montesquieu*, Bordeaux, 1956.

short cut to isolate the respective natures of the republic, the monarchy and the despotism:

"Pour en découvrir la nature il suffit de l'idée qu'en ont les hommes les moins instruits";

but when their principles are in question, he invokes the empirical evidence of history as well as "la nature des choses," whether by the latter he is alluding to the inner logic of type, or alternatively to the necessity of a rationally ordered universe:

"Ce que je dis est confirmé par le corps entier de l'histoire, et est très conforme à la nature des choses."

The semblance of a grand Cartesian design in the exposition of the complete analysis of positive laws, which is created by Montesquieu's initial concentration on the political forms of social structure, as if its every detail were implicity contained in their laws, arises of course from his evaluation of the relative importance of the factors which make up the spirit of the laws. From the very beginning in chapter III, he underlines the particular significance of political forces:

"J'examinerai d'abord les rapports que les lois ont avec la nature et avec le principe de chaque gouvernement: et, comme ce principe a sur les lois une suprême influence, je m'attacherai à le bien connaître; et si je puis une fois l'établir, on en verra couler les lois comme de leur source. Je passerai ensuite aux autres rapports, qui semblent être plus particuliers,"[47]

and the dominance which he accords them is obvious throughout the work. It is well illustrated by a remark from the book dealing with the central unifying notion of the whole thesis, that of the "esprit général":

"C'est au législateur à suivre l'esprit de la nation, lorsqu'il n'est pas contraire aux principes du gouvernement."[48]

If we accept then that the logical implication as well as the actual result of Montesquieu's remarks concerning positive law in book I, is the adoption in the body of the work of a method which is at least in part empirical, and likewise, bearing in mind the didactic purpose expressed in the Preface:

"Si je pouvais faire en sorte que ceux qui commandent augmentassent leurs connaissances sur ce qu'ils doivent prescrire ... je me croirais le plus heureux des mortels,"[49]

[47] Nagel I, p. 9; Pléiade II, p. 238.
[48] Nagel I, p. 413; Pléiade II, p. 559. (Book XIX, ch. 5).
[49] Nagel I, p. lxi; Pléiade II, p. 230.

that he is consequently urging legislators themselves to base their craft upon scientific foundations, what are we to make of the postulates of chapter I, for all that they are so skilfully dovetailed into the main scientific thesis?

The writing of *De l'Esprit des Lois* may reasonably be judged and applauded, as has already been suggested,[50] as the completion of a task which Montesquieu set himself years before in the inconspicuous fragment of the *Traité des Devoirs*, subsequently entitled *De la Politique*, where he contrived to vindicate his own ideal of justice by drawing on historical evidence which demonstrated the futility of statecraft. The art of politics legitimized injustice in the mistaken belief that events could be manipulated to foster selfish ends, but against it Montesquieu argued that their real causes lay outside human control. Now the *Lois* forestalled the counsel of indifference which too superficial a reading of his theory of historical causation might have prompted. Human reason might be relatively powerless to manipulate history, but it was by no means incapable of analysing its pattern. Consequently there were sound grounds for the muted optimism voiced in Montesquieu's Preface: knowledge will be the key to statesmanship and the safeguard of human happiness. Yet what relation does the original ideal of justice retain to all this, the ideal which, in harness with the notion of virtuous citizenship, presupposed the active pursuit of moral ends? For if the statesman can aspire only to imitate a necessary pattern of events, then it follows logically if disturbingly, that the pursuit of justice exactly equals the practice of injustice in its futility. As G. Davy clearly reveals in an article on Montesquieu's method,[51] once all arbitrary elements are excluded from an analysis of causation in the moral and political spheres, as they must be if its laws are assumed to be necessary and constant on the model of physical laws, then the legislator who applies the principles of this science may reorganize, but can never transcend a given determinism.

Yet although the practical expression of Montesquieu's sociological thesis seems inevitably restricted to an empirical conservatism, and this approach certainly colours his attitude not only to the active role of the legislator, but also to the related theoretical problem of historical evolution,[52] being discernible as much in the caution of the *Préface:*

---

[50] See above Part II, ch. 2, pp. 145–146.
[51] "Sur la méthode de Montesquieu," *Revue de métaphysique et de morale*, année 46, 1939.
[52] See R. Hubert's article "Le devenir historique chez Montesquieu," *op. cit.*, above n. 51.

"Je n'écris point pour censurer ce qui est établi dans quelque pays que ce soit. Chaque nation trouvera ici les raisons de ses maximes; et, on en tirera naturellement cette conséquence, qu'il n'appartient de proposer des changements qu'à ceux qui sont assez heureusement nés pour pénétrer d'un coup de génie toute la constitution d'un État." [53]

as in the sudden disquieting pessimism which shatters the vision of a liberal constitution in book XI, chapter 6:

"Comme toutes les choses humaines ont une fin, l'État dont nous parlons perdra sa liberté, il périra. Rome, Lacédémone et Carthage ont bien péri. Il périra lorsque la puissance législative sera plus corrompue que l'exécutrice." [54]

nevertheless we find him boldy reaffirming in his introductory chapters both the transcendent reality of justice and its validity as a moral ideal:

"Avant qu'il y eût des lois faites, il y avait des rapports de justice possibles. Dire qu'il n'y a rien de juste ni d'injuste que ce qu'ordonnent ou défendent des lois positives, c'est dire qu'avant qu'on eût tracé de cercle, tous les rayons n'étaient pas égaux." [55]

Thus one is forced to conclude that in the conception of the *Lois*, whatever the logical philosophical and moral implications of his approach to positive law, some of which are indeed quite plainly expressed in the work, the desire to vindicate the idealism of the *Traité des Devoirs* remained a recognizably active force.

Such a conclusion is inescapable that is, and one must accordingly accept book I on what appear to be Montesquieu's terms, as an integral part of the whole work, attempting by detailed analysis to illuminate its precise significance and thereby demonstrate its philosophical relevance to his central thesis, unless one credits certain fairly commonplace hypotheses issuing from a rigid psychological determinism coupled to an oversimplified and somewhat anachronistic view of the 18th century as an age when scientific materialism came into its own, which together create a Montesquieu whose narrow mental horizons scarcely correspond to the fertile and flexible intelligence which emerges from such records of research and speculation as the *Pensées*.[56] Such hypo-

---

[53] Nagel I, p. lx; Pléiade II, p. 230.
[54] Nagel I, p. 221; Pléiade II, p. 407.
[55] Book I, ch. 1; Nagel I, p. 3; Pléiade II, p. 233.
[56] A German scholar, V. Klemperer, expounding the not entirely convincing thesis that Montesquieu was really a poet in an unpoetical age, produced many years ago a stimulating reappraisal of the entire corpus of his works as then known. In spite of a disregard, curiously reminiscent of the interpretations which he seeks to discredit, for the part that creative

theses range between G. Davy's comparatively mild reduction of Montesquieu's preliminary philosophical discourse to an insipid expression of his

"intention de fonder sur une sorte d'instinct foncier vers le bien la recherche tâtonnante des lois les mieux adaptées aux conditions diverses dont elles doivent dépendre,"[57]

and its outspoken dismissal by P. Martino as a satirically conceived hotchpotch of scholastic definition, designed simply to pull the wool over the eyes of hostile and suspicious theologians.[58]

If however, while conceding that Montesquieu may in elaborating the theories of book I have anticipated and attempted to forestall the kind of criticism which he was later obliged to answer in the *Défense de l'Esprit des Lois*, one rejects on historical, biographical and critical grounds such hypotheses, then perhaps the most immediately acceptable interpretation which leaves Montesquieu's scholarly integrity and his sincerity in book I unscathed, and contrives to do justice to its ostensibly philosophical purpose, at the same time drawing solely on textual evidence, is that offered by Shackleton in his critical biography.[59]

Shackleton concludes that Montesquieu does not in fact present us in book I with a personal philosophy of law, which, while largely derivative, nevertheless achieves logical consistency, but rather with a demolition of the deductive philosophical framework traditionally utilized by jurists, in whose place he introduces empirically derived first principles better fitted to the sociological thesis of the *Lois*. Book I records his movement away from the Cartesian habits of mind characteristic of 17th century political thought towards scientific materialism. Thus:

"The framework of his legal system, with its stress on the eternity of justice, has close terminological resemblances with the deductive systems of Grotius and Domat, and can legitimately be regarded as having Cartesian affinities. Within this framework are found, as his starting point, natural laws reminiscent of Descartes's descriptive and scientific laws of nature. They are ascertained by the method of animal analogy, which (since beasts are machines) involves an exclusion of any rational element.

imagination plays in scientific work, which leads him to overstate his case, it remains a useful antidote to such limited appreciations of his genius. See *Montesquieu*, 2 vols., Heidelberg 1914–15 (Band VI in the series *Beiträge zur neueren Literaturgeschichte*).

[57] Art. cit. above (p. 201 n. 51), p. 575.

[58] "De quelques résidus métaphysiques dans *l'Esprit des Lois*," *Revue d'histoire de la philosophie d'histoire générale de la civilisation*, Fasc. 43, (July–Sept. 1946), pp. 235–243.

[59] *Op. cit.*, above (p. 9 n. 3); ch. XI.

To this point Montesquieu remains, though not without inconsistencies, under the banner of Descartes.

But he proceeds to base his moral and political system on these rigid *données* of the physical world, and herein his departure, silent and unadmitted, from Cartesianism is signalized. He has become more of an anti-Cartesian than a Cartesian, and so he must finally be defined."[60]

This summary is based on the enquiry which Shackleton conducts in the foregoing sections of his chapter on Montesquieu's conception of law, into the probable sources of key notions in the first two chapters of book I. Here he brings out Montesquieu's reliance upon philosopher-theologians like Malebranche and Clarke for his opening definition of law, rather than upon legal writers, and he contrasts such sources with the more conventional origin of his assertion of the transcendence of justice in the conceptions of the Natural Law school of jurists. This assertion is then characterized as the idealistic framework within which Montesquieu proceeds in chapter II to enclose, not the *a priori*, God-given precepts posited by this school, but purely descriptive laws, isolated by a method for which he was indebted once again to sources largely unacceptable to the standard juristic authorities of his day. The method concerned is the same "animal analogy" referred to in the above quotation, and this he traces back through the concept of *lex promiscua* found in the *Origines iuris civilis* of the Italian jurist Gravina, to Ulpian's definition of natural law in the *Institutes* as that which nature has taught all animals.[61]

His case for claiming that Montesquieu proceeded to identify basic natural impulses in human beings by analysing the instincts common to all animal creation, and that he then erected these impulses into a fixed natural foundation for positive law, in apparent ignorance of the illogicality of using descriptive laws as normative principles, rests on the restoration to book I chapter 2, *Des lois de la nature*, of three paragraphs found in the manuscript which never appeared in the published text:

"Les animaux (et c'est surtout chez eux qu'il faut aller chercher le droit naturel) ne font pas la guerre à ceux de leur espèce, parce que, se sentant égaux, ils n'ont point le désir de s'attaquer. La paix est donc la première loi naturelle.

[60] *Op. cit.*, above (p. 9 n. 3), p. 260.
[61] Reproduced in the *Digest* I, 1, i: "Ius naturale est, quod natura omnia animalia docuit: nam ius istud non humani generis proprium, sed omnium animalium, quae in terra, quae in mari nascunter, avium quoque commune est. Hinc descendit maris atque feminae coniuncto, quam nos matrimonium appellamus, hinc liberorum procreatio, hinc educatio.'

Je sais bien qu'en disant ceci je contredis de très grands hommes mais je les prie de faire réflexion sur ce sentiment de plaisir que chaque animal trouve à l'approche d'un animal de même espèce que lui. Ils ne sont donc pas en état de guerre et vouloir les mettre dans cet état, c'est vouloir leur faire faire ce que les lions ne font pas.

Que si nous voyons des animaux faire la guerre à ceux de leur espèce, ce n'est que dans des cas particuliers et parce que nous les y instruisons pour notre commodité propre."[62]

The sentence in parenthesis: "et c'est surtout chez eux qu'il faut aller chercher le droit naturel" is obviously the most important clue to his sources, and Shackleton cites the argumentation to be found in a fragment dating from 1725, *Pensée* 1266 (Bkn. 615), as evidence that Montesquieu would in any case already have been sympathetic towards the adoption of this particular method even before he came across Gravina's work.

In judging the merits of Shackleton's interpretation one must first pay tribute to its cogency and to the highly interesting nature of the source material upon which he draws. But it is none the less open to serious objections, which, while they do not necessarily undermine the relevance of this material to certain features of Montesquieu's theory of natural law, would seem on the other hand to invalidate the conclusions to which allegedly it lends so much weight. These objections fall into two categories according to whether they stem from those aspects of Montesquieu's theories in chapters I and II that Shackleton neglects, or from alternative interpretations of some of his supporting evidence.

The most general criticism that can be levelled against his interpretation is its implication that Montesquieu's right hand was scarcely aware of what his left hand was doing. Thus the assertion in chapter I of the transcendence and anteriority of justice is ultimately left unaccounted for; why, if Montesquieu's real object was to elaborate a close parallel between the laws of the physical universe and those of human behaviour, was it then included at all? Similarly, it is difficult to understand, if we accept Shackleton's version of his philosophical purpose, why his most important points appear only in parenthesis, or were even omitted from the published work. It is almost impossible to credit the explanation which he offers for the deletion of those crucial paragraphs of chapter II where Montesquieu allegedly reveals his methodological device for the investigation of natural law.[63] The

---

[62] Nagel III, p. 579; Pléiade II, p. 996 (in part only).
[63] Given in a footnote, *op. cit.* above, (p. 9 n. 3), p. 259, n. 1.

reason Shackleton suggests is that Montesquieu *subsequently* added reasonableness and the attainment of intellectual maturity to his list of natural laws, and then, realizing that the analogy with animal creation no longer held good decided to excise the whole passage. But his explanation, besides insinuating that the author of so vast and complex a work made little attempt to sort out his ideas before putting pen to paper, overlooks the important and extensive comparison, occupying at least a third of chapter I, between the nature and laws of various orders of beings. Here already, Montesquieu emphasizes that man's distinguishing feature is his intelligence, and indeed also implies that while, as a sentient creature, he may be subject with the beasts to a certain order of law just as he shares the invariable laws of motion with inanimate matter, an entirely different set of principles, relative only to his intelligence, will govern his social existence.

Needless to say, Montesquieu was hardly likely to have forgotten this comparison when he embarked on chapter II. It is much more likely, since, from its context, the manuscript passage in question could as well have served to introduce an attack on Hobbes's conception of the state of nature, that Montesquieu omitted it because he decided it was more effective to argue from the same basis as his adversary, namely, from an analysis of *human* nature. This he does, citing Hobbes by name, and pointing out how anachronistic the characteristics he attributed to his pre-social man really were.

Moreover, almost the whole of chapter II, with the exception of the short preamble situating the laws of nature in relation to other classes of law:

"Avant toutes ces lois, sont celles de la nature, ainsi nommées, parce qu'elles dérivent uniquement de la constitution de notre être."

and the formal homage paid to belief in God as the most important of natural laws, consists of a systematized elaboration of ideas first propounded in *Pensée* 1266, which Shackleton does indeed draw into his discussion, if only marginally,[64] as evidence that Montesquieu had previously "toyed with the notion of animal analogy in relation to natural law."

This fragment was originally part of the unfinished *Traité des Devoirs*, though Montesquieu clearly indicates in a note that he later drew on it for the *Lois*. Every feature of the theory of chapter II is to be found there in embryo, the main difference being that after mentioning Hobbes's

---

[64] *Op. cit.*, above (p. 9 n. 3), p. 258, n. 1.

linking of natural right to the principle of self preservation, Montesquieu does not proceed to formulate his objections in terms of an alternative set of natural laws, but simply concentrates on demonstrating the falseness of Hobbes's notions concerning the natural state and primitive disposition of men. As in chapter II, the main plank of his attack is the absurd anachronism of the motives and feelings with which Hobbes endows humans in their pre-social condition:

"il ne faut pas, comme il fait, supposer les hommes comme tombés du ciel ou sortis tout armés de la terre, à peu près comme les soldats de Cadmus, pour s'entre-détruire: ce n'est point là l'état des hommes."[65]

In relation to this criticism, Montesquieu goes on to present the key notion of chapter 2, the idea of a gradual and natural transition from the natural to the social state:

"Le premier et le seul ne craint personne. Cet homme seul, qui trouverait une femme seule aussi, ne lui ferait point la guerre. Tous les autres naîtraient dans une famille, et bientôt dans une société. Il n'y a point là de guerre; au contraire, l'amour, l'éducation, le respect, la reconnaissance: tout respire la paix."[66]

But this is developed no further; instead, to drive home his objections to Hobbes he imagines an extreme situation: "deux hommes tombés des nues dans un pays désert," and attempts, by reconstructing their emotional reactions, to predict its outcome. The progress he sketches here, from mutual fear and flight, through loneliness, to mutual attraction and the pleasure of companionship, corresponds to the stages set out in chapter II of the evolution of natural man and his laws, and it is only in passing that he makes a brief comparison with the behaviour of other animal species:

'Premièrement, la crainte les porterait, non pas à attaquer, mais à fuir. Les marques de crainte respective les feraient bientôt approcher. L'ennui d'être seul et le plaisir que tout animal sent à l'approche d'un animal de même espèce, les porteraient à s'unir, et plus ils seraient misérables, plus ils y seraient déterminés. Jusque-là on ne voit point d'antioccupation. Il en serait comme des autres animaux, qui ne font la guerre à ceux de leur espèce que dans des cas particuliers, quoiqu'ils se trouvent tous les jours dans les forêts, à peu près comme les hommes de Hobbes. Les premiers sentiments seraient pour les vrais besoins que l'on aurait (prières naturelles), et non pas pour les commodités de la domination .... Hobbes veut faire faire aux hommes, ce que les lions ne font pas eux-mêmes. Ce n'est que par l'établissement des so-

---

[65] Nagel II, p. 344; Pléiade I, p. 1139.
[66] Nagel II, p. 344; Pléiade I, p. 1139.

ciétés qu'ils abusent les uns des autres et deviennent les plus forts; avant cela, ils sont tous égaux."[67]

Thus, while Montesquieu clearly regards mankind as being in various respects indistinguishable from other animal species, there is little evidence that he is here attempting, even tentatively, to use the instinctive behaviour of beasts as a special device for the discovery of man's primitive laws.[68] The mention of lions towards the end of the passage, probably for stylistic effect alone, echoes the attack on Hobbes in *Lettres Persanes* LXXXIII, where Montesquieu imagines the terrible insecurity that would burden men, were they not assured of the justice of their fellow creatures:

"Sans cela nous devrions être dans une frayeur continuelle; nous passerions devant les hommes comme devant les lions, et nous ne serions jamais assurés un moment de notre bien, de notre honneur et de notre vie."[69]

and sure enough, the whole attack on Hobbes in *Pensée* 1266 forms part of a much wider discussion where Montesquieu defends the existence of God and of Providence, and not only hits out at the English philosopher for his voluntarist conception of law, but also decries Spinoza for his alleged hylozoism, and the moral indifference to which this leads.

In the light of his attitude to such wider issues it seems at least doubtful that Montesquieu was consciously concerned, either here or in related passages of the *Lois*, with the "analogy of animals" as a device for determining specifically human laws of nature. Conse-

---

[67] Nagel II, pp. 344–345; Pléiade I, pp. 1139–1140.

[68] His case against Hobbes rests here as it does in the published version of chapter 2, primarily on the need to apply a degree of psychological and historical insight if one sets out to base first principles on the effects of certain circumstances on human nature. In any case, there exists a fragment of the early *Pensées morales*, subsequently incorporated into the *Devoirs* and into chapter 1 of the *Lois*, which constitutes almost a formal rejection of the case for arguing that Montesquieu ever entertained the notion that animal behaviour could provide the measure of human law:

"Les actions humaines sont le sujet des devoirs. C'est la raison qui en est le principe, et qui nous rend propres à nous en acquitter, ce serait abaisser cette raison que de dire qu'elle ne nous a été donnée que pour la conservation de notre être: car les bêtes conservent le leur, tout comme nous. Souvent même, elles le conservent mieux: l'instinct, qui leur laisse toutes les passions nécessaires pour la conservation de leur vie, leur privant presque toujours de celles qui pourraient la détruire. Au lieu que notre raison ne nous donne pas seulement des passions destructives, mais même nous fait faire souvent un très mauvais usage des conservatrices." (*Pensée* 220 (Bkn. 597), Nagel II, p. 93; Pléiade I, p. 1126.)

The careful distinction between men and beasts made here must also be compared with later entries in the *Pensées*, e.g. 938 (Bkn. 1097), 1747 (Bkn. 366):

"... Les bêtes, qui ont toutes des intérêts séparés, s'entrenuisent toujours. Les hommes seuls, faits pour vivre en société, ne perdent rien de ce qu'ils partagent.", (Nagel II, p. 523; Pléiade II, p. 1094.)

[69] Nagel I, p. 170; Pléiade I, p. 257.

quently, the whole interpretation of Montesquieu's philosophical purpose which Shackleton rests upon its adoption is laid open to question; for obviously it no longer follows that he was thereby signalling his rejection of a rationally based moral system, and proclaiming his espousal in its place of the tenets of scientific materialism.

Indeed, even if Shackleton's thesis were valid, it would still be impossible to claim as he does,[70] that Montesquieu then proceeds even tacitly, to base his moral and political system on the descriptive laws established in chapter II. A single quotation from book X illustrates more than adequately the multiplicity of criteria, moral and scientific, that Montesquieu could invoke in any one instance:

"Lorsqu'un peuple est conquis, le droit que le conquérant a sur lui, suit quatre sortes de lois: la loi de la nature, qui fait que tout tend à la conservation des espèces; la loi de la lumière naturelle, qui veut que nous fassions à autrui ce que nous voudrions qu'on nous fît; la loi qui forme les sociétés politiques, qui sont telles que la nature n'en a point borné la durée; enfin la loi tirée de la chose même. La conquête est une acquisition; l'esprit d'acquisition porte avec lui l'esprit de conservation et d'usage, et non pas celui de destruction."[71]

Yet clearly, providing one accepts that Montesquieu is in effect expressing the conviction in book I chapter 3, that the great diversity of positive laws can be traced back to a small number of principles which will contain them as individual phenomena and completely describe them, then the incentive, or dare one say obligation, to search for evidence of a consistently scientific approach in the rest of book I, particularly for evidence of a method, explicable in terms of contemporary currents of thought, adequate to the isolation of descriptive principles, remains strong. Shackleton discerned the application of procedures deriving from Cartesian physics, though the evidence for this is at least debatable; yet it is possible to suggest an alternative interpretation of book I, which likewise contrives to credit Montesquieu with a degree of methodological consistency in his approach to the phenomenon of law.

[70] *Op. cit.*, above (p. 9 n. 3), p. 252; 260.
[71] Chapter 3; Nagel I, p. 184; Pléiade II, p. 378.

CHAPTER FOUR

JUSTICE AND LAW:
AN ALLIANCE OF SCIENCE AND MORALS

I

> "... l'injustice est mauvaise ménagère, ... elle ne remplit pas même ses vues."
> *Considérations sur les Causes de la Grandeur des Romains*, chapter IV.

Once prudence, deviousness, a kind of pedantic frivolity, or the rhetorical sleight of hand at which Voltaire was so adept have been dismissed as credible explanations of the philosophical complexities of book I, and the entire seriousness of his enterprise from start to finish has been conceded, then it is not really the contents of chapter 1 which hold the greatest surprise for the reader familiar with an image of Montesquieu as the founder of a science of legislations, but the inclusion and development of the ideas of chapter 2, *Des lois de la nature*. For as Montesquieu himself exclaimed in the *Défense*, the subject of his work is unmistakable:

"Ceux qui auront quelques lumières verront du premier coup d'oeil que cet ouvrage a pour objet les lois, les coutumes et les divers usages de tous les peuples de la terre," [1]

and if, as a self-proclaimed idealist, he wished nevertheless to clear himself in the introduction to his study of any taint of materialism, of the faintest suspicion that the relativism and causal determinism implicit in his theory of positive law had necessarily transformed him into a campfollower of Spinoza, or worse, into a disciple of the infamous Hobbes, and did so by confirming his belief in the anteriority of justice and in human freedom, while at the same time endeavouring to base his work, as a serious contribution to scientific knowledge, on a conception of the universe as a structure regular and ordered even in its smallest details, subject to invariable laws and therefore accessible

---

[1] Part II; Nagel I, p. 456; Pléiade II, p. 1137.

to reason, then he fulfilled both these objects more than adequately in chapter 1. In that case, what more was to be gained from dabbling even desultorily in the peculiar concepts of the apparently distinct and specialized discipline of jurists and political theorists, whose business it was to expound a philosophy of right,[2] to lay bare the abstract foundations of authority rather than to winkle out the uniform principles hidden beneath the endless diversity of statute law and unwritten custom; and from whom moreover, as we know from a *rejet* from the Preface, Montesquieu had been at one stage eager to dissociate himself formally?[3] As long as his scientific axioms and the universally valid criteria upon which he intended to found his value judgments were clear for all to understand, then there was surely no need to resurrect the odd hypothesis of a patently unhistorical state where the individual, "tombé des nues," exists in complete isolation, in order to establish another, superfluous set of principles; unless we assume of course that Montesquieu was as much in thrall to tradition in the matter of content as Lanson would have us believe he was as regards the presentation of his work.[4]

Thus since its main purpose appears to be the provision of a platform from which an attack directed specifically against Hobbes could be launched, chapter 2 would seem to possess all the qualities of a classic digression, but nothing more. Even this attack on Hobbes seems strangely misdirected, for whereas one might reasonably suppose that Montesquieu's opposition to absolutism would have prompted him to select as his special target the other's use or abuse of the theory of contract to justify tyranny, he actually makes no mention of it at all.[5] His primary concern is obviously the rehabilitation after Hobbes of the original benevolence of mankind, and the direct bearing of the hypothesis of the state of nature on the theoretical mode and political consequences of the establishment of society carried no interest for him. One may object at this point that once Montesquieu has set out to

[2] See below p. 223.
[3] See above p. 186.
[4] See above p. 198.
[5] A fragment of the *Pensées morales* shows that this feature of Hobbes's doctrine had at one time preoccupied him: "C'est un principe bien faux que celui de Hobbes: que, le peuple ayant autorisé le prince, les actions du prince sont les actions du peuple, et, par conséquent, le peuple ne peut pas se plaindre du prince, ni lui demander aucun compte de ses actions: parce que le peuple ne peut pas se plaindre du peuple. Ainsi Hobbes a oublié son principe du droit naturel: *Pacta esse servanda*. Le peuple a autorisé le prince sous condition; il l'a établi sous une convention. Il faut qu'il l'observe, et le prince ne représente le peuple que comme le peuple a voulu ou est censé avoir voulu qu'il le représentât." (*Pensée* 224 (Bkn. 601); Nagel II, p. 94; Pléiade I, p. 1127).

explain scientifically the diversity of positive laws, then it was naturally incumbent upon him to account also for their origin; and that the solving of this problem would, given the intellectual climate of the age, almost automatically involve him in some discussion, however brief, of the origin of society and the idea of natural law. This may just possibly have been the case, though it hardly serves to transform chapter 2 from a digression into an essential element of book I. For Montesquieu's main theories would still be just as valid, and his work surely better planned, if he had passed immediately from the concluding sentence of chapter 1, which, by implying that man is naturally a social creature, apparently obviates the necessity of drawing on the hypothesis of the state of nature:

"Fait pour vivre dans la société, il y pouvait oublier les autres; les législateurs l'ont rendu à ses devoirs par les lois politiques et civiles,"

to the general definition of positive law which he gives in the middle of chapter 3:

"La loi, en général, est la raison humaine, en tant qu'elle gouverne tous les peuples de la terre; et les lois politiques et civiles de chaque nation ne doivent être que les cas particuliers où s'applique cette raison humaine,"

having delayed the preceding analysis of the basic political structure common to all societies until the beginning of book II, where it would have constituted the logical preamble to his classification of governments.

Yet although logic and economy would appear to favour such a reorganization of the material of book I, this is in turn open to objections which contrive to re-establish the complete seriousness of Montesquieu's intentions, and the validity in scientific terms of the inclusion of chapter 2.

The first of these arises from the *Défense de l'Esprit des Lois*, where Montesquieu, explaining his dismissal of the natural law linking mankind to God, confirms that his use of the hypothesis of the state of nature in chapter 2 was a deliberate choice:

"Il ne lui a pas été défendu, pas plus qu'aux philosophes et aux écrivains du droit naturel, de considérer l'homme sous divers égards: il lui a été permis de supposer un homme comme tombé des nues, laissé à lui-même et sans éducation, avant l'établissement des sociétés." [6]

Now this confirmation, considered in the light of certain other re-

---

[6] I, "Réponse à la sixième objection"; Nagel I, p. 446; Pléiade II, p. 1131.

flexions bearing on the usefulness of the hypothesis of the state of nature in political science, rather than vindicating Montesquieu's philosophical integrity, appears to undermine it. For, as general appreciations of his contribution to political thought almost invariably stress, the basic tendency of his social theory was anti-contractualist, being exemplified in *Lettres Persanes* XCIV where the notion of the state of nature is dismissed outright as irrelevant to all discussion of the origins of society:

> "Je n'ai jamais ouï parler du droit public, qu'on n'ait commencé par rechercher soigneusement quelle est l'origine des sociétés; ce qui me paraît ridicule. Si les hommes n'en formaient point, s'ils se quittaient et se fuyaient les uns les autres, il faudrait en demander la raison, et chercher pourquoi ils se tiennent séparés: mais ils naissent tous liés les uns aux autres; un fils est né auprès de son père, et il s'y tient: voilà la société, et la cause de la société." [7]

On the basis of this evidence, and the implications of the myth of the Troglodytes,[8] at least one critic has argued strongly that Montesquieu had, as early as the composition of the *Lettres Persanes*, already abandoned the hypothesis of the state of nature in favour of a properly scientific approach to the beginnings of social organization.[9] If this was indeed the case, then the open acknowledgement of its readoption in the *Lois* cannot fail to mystify, even though it is clearly no part of Montesquieu's intention to combine it with a contractualist view of the origin of society, this being presented here on the contrary as the inevitable outcome of the sociability characteristic of intelligent creatures. Fortunately however, Montesquieu left other material bearing on his conception of the beginning of social organization, which, while it leaves intact the conclusion based on the *Lettres Persanes* that his attitude there reveals a nascent sociological approach to the problem, nevertheless provides valuable clues to the reasons for his perplexing retreat in the *Lois* to the doctrine of Grotius and Pufendorf.

In Letter XCIV we encounter the substitution of the notion of a natural organic origin for society, the family group, for the idea

---

[7] Nagel I, p. 187; Pléiade I, p. 269.

[8] *Lettres Persanes* XI–XIV.

[9] S. Cotta in *Montesquieu e la scienza della società*, Torino, 1953. Cotta maintains that the myth of the Troglodytes does not comprise two contrasted views of the state of nature, but a study of the possible evolution of society according to whether it is governed by the principle of egoism or by that of virtue (ch. 3, p. 152). The hypothesis of the state of nature is then implicitly rejected, and "l'abbandono di questa ipotesi a favore di uno studio limitato all'orrizonte della realtà effettuale, segna il punto di passaggio da una impostazione filosofica del problema dello Stato et della società ad una impostazione scientifica. E questa una preziosa indicazione offertaci dalle *Lettres*, forse la più preziosa sul piano metodologico." (Ch. 3, p. 165).

entrenched in the thinking of most Natural Law School jurists that individual isolation necessarily precedes social cohesion. But significantly, although this central principle of natural law theory is rejected, no *direct* reference is made to the closely related hypothesis of the state of nature. When we turn then to the fragments of the *Devoirs* refuting Hobbes's theory of natural aggression and the patriarchalist arguments in favour of despotism, both of which were extensively exploited for book I of the *Lois*,[10] we find Montesquieu alluding quite happily to "l'état naturel des hommes," and to "les hommes avant l'établissement des sociétés." However, while he is prepared for the purposes of argument to accept Hobbes's case on its own terms:

"Il n'est pas même vrai que deux hommes tombés des nues dans un pays désert, cherchassent, par la peur, à s'attaquer et à se subjuguer ...,"[11]

he objects beforehand that the whole hypothesis of isolated individuals coming together solely for the purposes of mutual destruction is unacceptable in itself:

"il ne faut pas, comme il fait, supposer les hommes comme tombés du ciel ou sortis tout armés de la terre, à peu près comme les soldats de Cadmus, pour s'entredétruire: ce n'est point là l'état des hommes."[12]

Taking up the theme of Letter xciv, he maintains instead that a state of complete individual isolation would be of short duration, rapidly giving way before natural sociability in its instinctive form and the emergence of the family group:

"Le premier et le seul ne craint personne. Cet homme seul, qui trouverait une femme seule aussi, ne lui ferait point la guerre. Tous les autres naîtront dans une famille, et bientôt dans une société. Il n'y a point de guerre; au contraire, l'amour, l'éducation, le respect, la reconnaissance: tout respire la paix."[13]

Two important and permanent features of Montesquieu's thinking about the origin of society are illuminated by this counter-argument. The first is that he retains the hypothesis of a state of nature, but gives it a content not only radically different from that of Hobbes's notion, but also largely at variance with that generally favoured by Natural Law theoreticians. In Montesquieu's hands, as the idea of a natural state characterized by the existence of primitive social groups, it ceases

---

[10] *Pensées* 1266 (Bkn. 615), and 1267 (Bkn. 616); see above pp. 206–208.
[11] Nagel II, p. 344; Pléiade I, p. 1139.
[12] *Ibid.*
[13] *Ibid.*

to be a hypothesis whose sole validity lies in its purely logical necessity, and which was often openly acknowledged by its most enthusiastic exponents to be quite unrelated to historical probability.[14] Instead it acquires some of the qualities of a genuine scientific thesis. For empirical evidence would indeed suggest that the complex institutional structure of a mature community could be traced back ultimately to the most basic form of social organization – the family group. In consequence of this changed conception, the transition, in Montesquieu's theory, from a state of nature to a properly social state is no longer abrupt, nor artificially contrived. As we have mentioned, he shows no interest whatsoever in incorporating the notion of a social contract into his work. The old antithesis between a hypothetical world of isolated sovereign individuals and organized sovereign states made up of subject citizens thus disappears; and although it is quite clear from his outline of the complex factors which govern positive law in book I of the *Lois* for instance, that the inception of society properly speaking, marks the transition to a completely new level of social existence, this development nevertheless represents the fulfilment of all the latent potentialities of the state of nature, and of the individual in that state. Thus in the counter-argument to Hobbes, the implied evolution from family to society is linked with "l'amour, l'éducation, le respect, la reconnaissance," fostered in the state of nature; and again at the end of the debate, Montesquieu indicates a natural continuity of development from one condition to the next:

"S'ils établissent les sociétés, c'est par un principe de justice. Ils l'avaient donc."

For him then the contrast between the state of nature and organized society is really the contrast between the primitive and the mature form of the same phenomenon, not that between one phenomenon and another completely different.

The modifications which he imposes on the hypothesis of the state of nature are reflected in the fragment of the *Devoirs* incorporating the refutation of the patriarchalist justification of despotism that later found its way into *Lois* I, 3.[15] Here again his introduction to their argument makes it clear that he disputes not their recourse to the hypothesis of the state of nature as such, but the inferences that they draw from it.

[14] E.g. Hobbes, *Leviathan*, part I, ch. 13.
[15] *Pensée* 1267 (Bkn. 616).

"En considérant les hommes avant l'établissement des sociétés, on trouve qu'ils étaient soumis à une puissance que la nature avait établie: car l'enfance étant l'état de la plus grande faiblesse qui se puisse concevoir, il a fallu que les enfants fussent dans la dépendance de leurs pères, qui leur avaient donné la vie, et qui leur donnaient encore les moyens de la conserver.

Ce que l'on dit n'est pas juste, sur le pouvoir sans bornes des pères: il ne l'est pas, et il n'y en a pas de tel. Les pères ont la conservation pour objet, comme les autres puissances, et encore plus que les autres puissances."[16]

The patriarchalist theoreticians erred not by faulty intuition of the probable nature of primitive existence – they traced society back to the family group, not to the individual – but by the inadequacy of the procedures used in the further elaboration of their theories. They drew an analogy between the structure of the original social group, the family with its paternal head and dependent children, and the state with its monarchic ruler and dependent subjects. Now although, as with Hobbes, Montesquieu's real target is their justification of absolutism, the manner in which he discredits their argument is most significant for what it reveals about his own concepts and methods. Thus the use of analogy as a device for investigating the field of morals and politics is rejected because it is here unhistorical, and, by inference, time is a dimension that cannot be ignored in the truly scientific examination of social phenomena. Such an analogy is invalid because it assumes that the family is a static group, ignoring its inevitable and natural growth and fragmentation.

"La nature elle-même a borné la puissance paternelle en augmentant, d'un côté, la raison des enfants, et, de l'autre, la faiblesse des pères; en diminuant, d'un côté, les besoins des enfants, et augmentant, de l'autre, les besoins des pères.

Les familles se sont divisées; les pères étant morts ont laissé les collatéraux indépendants. Il a fallu s'unir par des conventions et faire par le moyen des lois civiles, ce que le droit naturel avait fait d'abord.

Le hasard et le tour d'esprit de ceux qui ont convenu ont établi autant de différentes formes de gouvernements qu'il y a eu de peuples: toutes bonnes, puisqu'elles étaient la volonté des parties contractantes.

Ce qui était arbitraire est devenu nécessité; il n'a plus été permis qu'à la tyrannie et à la violence de changer une forme de gouvernement, même pour une meilleure: car, comme tous les associés ne pouvaient point changer de manière de penser en même temps, il y aurait eu un temps entre l'établissement des nouvelles lois et l'abolition des anciennes, fatal à la cause commune.

Il a fallu que tous les changements arrivés dans les lois établies fussent un effet de ces lois établies: celui qui a aboli d'anciennes lois ne l'a pu faire que

---

[16] Nagel II, p. 345; Pléiade I, pp. 1140–1141.

par la force des lois; et le peuple même n'a pu reprendre son autorité que lorsque cela lui a été permis par la loi civile ou naturelle.

Ce qui n'était que convention est devenu aussi fort que la loi naturelle; il a fallu aimer sa patrie comme on aimait sa famille; il a fallu chérir les lois comme on chérissait la volonté de ses pères.

Mais comme l'amour de la famille n'entraînait pas la haine des autres, aussi l'amour de sa Patrie ne devait point inspirer la haine des autres sociétés."[17]

The final paragraph of Montesquieu's counter-argument makes it clear that he himself did not reject outright the use of analogical methods in ethics; but equally obviously, its content is tailored to meet the requirements of the principle invoked by his original objections, namely that an analogy is only valid when a real basis for comparison exists between the terms involved. The analogy drawn by the Patriarchalists was false because it left out of account the transcience of paternal authority; as Montesquieu later paraphrases himself in *Lois* I, 3:

"Mais l'exemple du pouvoir paternel ne prouve rien. Car, si le pouvoir du père a du rapport au gouvernement d'un seul, après la mort du père, le pouvoir des frères ou, après la mort des frères, celui des cousins germains ont du rapport au gouvernement de plusieurs."[18]

Now this condemnation of the abuse of the analogical method has a certain significance, if of a largely negative kind, for such interpretations of book I, as seek to demonstrate its employment there for the isolation of normative principles.[19] In view of Montesquieu's insistence on a proper basis for comparison between the factors involved it is most unlikely that he himself would have accepted the instinctive behaviour of animals as a valid criterion for judging the conduct of intelligent creatures. Apart from this indirect methodological relevance, the outline of the transition from family to society which he opposes to the patriarchalist case clearly proceeds from his own special conception of the state of nature, its basic assumption being that an embryonic form of society exists prior to the establishment of society in its true sense. Similarly, the causes which occasion the latter event are shown to originate in the very nature of the primitive community.

In passing, it is perhaps also worth pointing to other important features of Montesquieu's political and social doctrine anticipated in this fragment. For example, again in relation to book I of the *Lois*,

[17] Nagel II, p. 346; Pléiade I, pp. 1141–1142.
[18] Nagel I, p. 8; Pléiade II, p. 237.
[19] See above pp. 203–205.

the idea behind much of what he has to say about positive law in chapter 3, indeed the idea that lies at the root of the work as a whole, namely that the political state of man constitutes an entirely new order of existence governed by its own very complex laws, is already present here:

"Ce qui n'était que convention est devenu aussi fort que la loi naturelle; il a fallu aimer sa patrie comme on aimait sa famille; il a fallu chérir les lois comme on chérissait la volonté des pères."

And already allied to this, as one might expect, one discerns the notion of the overriding significance for the description and analysis of the political order of the "esprit général" behind the explanation he advances, anticipating the cautious conservatism of the *Lois*, of the dangers attendant upon reform of political institutions:

"car, comme tous les associés ne pouvaient point changer de manière de penser en même temps, il y aurait eu un temps, entre l'établissement des nouvelles lois et l'abolition des anciennes, fatal à la cause commune."

Although details of the actual mechanics of the transition from the natural to the social state are largely missing from the *Lois*, perhaps because Montesquieu wished to avoid associating his account with the conventional theory of a social contract, nevertheless chapter 3 reflects the idea expressed here that governments are established by a voluntary convention, for he there defines the civil state as "la réunion des volontés," and makes political organization conditional upon it.

These fragments from the *Devoirs* do indeed provide important evidence of a high degree of consistency in Montesquieu's ideas concerning the origin and structure of political society, and also of a coherence in his social and moral theory in general which is easily overlooked. But concerning the particular concept of the state of nature, it is rather the *Essai sur les causes qui peuvent affecter les esprits et les caractères* which provides the most important if also most unusual clues to the transformation which it undergoes in his work.[20]

The second part of the *Essai*, which as a whole is of major significance for the genesis of the theory of causation embodied in the *Lois*, is devoted to a study of moral influences on the formation of individual and national character. Of these the first and most extensive is education, of crucial significance Montesquieu explains, for perfecting the union of mind and body, and for developing the faculty of reason.

[20] Shackleton dates the composition of the *Essai* between 1736 and 1743, and that of books I-III of the *Lois* between 1741 and 1743 (*op. cit.*, above, p. 9 n. 3; pp. 238-239; 314).

Education however is virtually the exclusive property of civilized societies:

"nous la trouvons chez les nations policées. Là comme j'ai dit, nous en recevons une particulière dans notre famille, et une générale dans la société,"[21]

and to prove his point, Montesquieu examines the mental equipment of barbarian nations. The ideas of such peoples, he asserts, are restricted to those concerning self-preservation; and the intellectual poverty and crudeness universal among them is demonstrated by the sterility of their languages:

"Ceux qui naissent chez un peuple barbare n'ont proprement que les idées qui ont du rapport à la conservation de leur être; ils vivent dans une nuit éternelle à l'égard de tout le reste. Là, les différences d'homme à homme, d'esprit à esprit, soint mons grandes: la grossièreté et la disette d'idées les égalisent en quelque manière.

Une preuve qu'ils manquent d'idées, c'est que les langues dont ils se servent sont toutes très stériles: non seulement ils ont peu de mots, parce qu'ils ont peu de chose à exprimer, mais aussi ils ont peu de manières de concevoir et de sentir."[23]

The American natives are singled out as an example; experience shows these tribes to be incapable of discipline or correction, quite closed in fact to any kind of instruction. To all intents and purposes, such peoples are practically indistinguishable from wild beasts, so great is their mental stupor:

"La grossièreté peut aller à un tel point chez ces nations que les hommes y seront peu différents des bêtes: témoin ces esclaves que les Turcs tirent de Circassie et de Mingrélie, qui passent toute la journée la tête penchée sur leur estomac, sans parole et sans action, et ne s'intéressent à rien de ce qui se passe autour d'eux.

Des cerveaux ainsi abandonnés perdent leurs fonctions: ils ne jouissent presque pas de leur âme, ni elle de son union avec le corps."[23]

Two points which Montesquieu makes in this description of the mental capacities of primitive nations link it with his accounts of the condition of men in the state of nature. These are that primitive people are very limited, and that such ideas as they do possess are restricted to the business of self-preservation. In addition, the comparison between savages and beasts anticipated the notion implicit in *Lois* I, 1, and understood as regards I, 2, that man shares with other animals the

[21] Nagel III, p. 415; Pléiade II, p. 54.
[22] Nagel III, p. 414; Pléiade II, p. 53.
[23] Nagel III, p. 414; Pléiade II, pp. 53–54.

characteristics and behaviour which arise from the purely sensuous part of his nature. Now these points of contact again suggest that the essential features of Montesquieu's account of the state of nature, at least as it appears in chapter 2 of the *Lois*, if not in the earlier fragments (although the intimate connection between these two is beyond question), rested on a scientific foundation. Once one conceeds the significance of this part of the *Essai sur les causes*, not perhaps as the primary stage in the gestation of his ideas about the primitive condition of mankind, but certainly as representing more directly, in view of the straightforward scientific design of the whole, the empirical origins of his thinking, then one can reasonably maintain that the conclusions provided by the analysis of more theoretical materials are confirmed. The psychological grounds for the distinction he draws in the *Essai* between primitive and civilized peoples coincide exactly with those characteristics which he attributes to man in the natural state in the fragments of the *Devoirs* and in the *Lois*. Moreover, not only is there evidence in the theoretical passages of the *Devoirs* that the state of nature is seen not as a condition of complete individual isolation, but as a time when the most basic forms of communal life are already in being, but there also exists a short fragment devoted to the inestimable value of scholarship, where the contrast drawn between barbaric and civilized peoples seems to anticipate the very theories later developed in the *Essai*, as well as the way in which they are reflected in the account of the origin of political society given in the *Lois*:

"La seule différence qu'il y a entre les peuples policés et les peuples barbares, c'est que les uns se sont appliqués aux sciences; les autres les ont absolument négligées.

C'est peut-être à ces connaissances que nous avons, et que les peuples sauvages ignorent, que la plupart des nations doivent leur existence." [24]

It therefore seems justifiable to conclude that Montesquieu derived his conception of the state of nature from a picture, pieced together at an early date from the accounts of travellers and missionaries, of the condition and mentality of barbarian peoples.

Further evidence of such an origin is to be found in a variety of other fragments, noted down in the *Pensées* over quite a lengthy period, where barbarian peoples are consistently presented as devoid of any political attributes. Time and again Montesquieu describes them as destitute of laws and civil institutions, ignorant of any duties, in short, "hommes

[24] *Pensée* 1263 (Bkn. 613); Nagel II, p. 338; Pléiade I, p. 1134.

et non pas citoyens"; and here also his observations appear to have been inspired by documentary accounts of primitive tribes.[25]

Yet if it is indeed true that Montesquieu anticipated social anthropology in the way he envisaged the state of nature, intentionally transforming it from a dialectically convenient conjecture into an empirically demonstrable phase of man's existence as a social animal, as likely with some tribes to have continued into the present as, with civilized nations, to be unimaginably remote in time, then one may well wonder why his presentation of it in the *Lois* is so styled as to almost completely obscure such crucial modifications of meaning. For example, its denotation of a primitive, a-political, but essentially social or communal condition is only faintly discernible in the turns given to one or two apparently insignificant phrases. Thus eventually one may perceive that the initial association of natural law with the condition of "un homme avant l'établissement des sociétés." and not with that of "l'homme avant l'établissement de la société," together with the closing reference to intelligence as a link between men which, unlike feeling, is not shared with other animals and which consequently constitutes "un nouveau motif de s'unir," can only point to the presence of the idea that human beings in the natural state already display certain forms of sociability, and that this state anticipates, not the establishment of community where previously nothing even remotely like it had existed, but the transition to distinct and separate *societies*, each endowed with its peculiar political institutions. More obviously of course, the factors which Montesquieu links with the institution of the third natural law: mutual apprehension, natural gregariousness, and so on, also presuppose some kind of community between individuals. But as regards the empirical foundation of his theories, one notices only the passing reference to the timidity of "les hommes sauvages," coupled with a brief footnote explaining that a typical "wild" man had been

[25] Two of the fragments in question, *Pensée* 498 (Bkn. 567) and *Pensée* 1555 originated in the lost *Histoire de la Jalousie*, written some time before 1732. *Pensée* 498 comprises material roughly paraphrased from Herodotus's *Histories* Bk. IV, dealing with the customs of Libyan tribes. Montesquieu's comment upon them: "Pour les peuples de l'intérieur, ils étaient si barbares qu'ils n'avaient point de lois. Hommes et non pas citoyens, ils respiraient l'air et ne vivaient pas. La plupart ne connaissaient point le mariage et ne trouvaient les enfants qu'à la ressemblance," (Nagel II, p. 175; Pléiade I, p. 1070), was renoté at *Pensée* 1555 in vol. II soon after 1741 when the composition of the first books of the *Lois* was underway; cf. *Pensée* 1379 (Bkn. 1754) which also appears in vol. II: "Par l'éducation, on apprend aux hommes leurs devoirs, à mesure qu'ils sont en état de les connaître; on leur apprend, en quelques années, ce que le Genre humain n'a pu savoir qu'après un très grand nombre de siècles, et ce que les peuples sauvages ignorent encore aujourd'hui." (Nagel II, p. 408; Pléiade I, p. 1419).

found in the forests of Hanover and brought to England during the reign of George I.

Apart from Montesquieu's natural and almost self-defeating terseness, the evident explanation for the singular presentation of the chapter on natural laws is that it is dominated by the need to rebut Hobbes's theory of internecine war. Although the passage attacking Hobbes by name has every appearance of a digression, Montesquieu prepares for it at considerable length in so short a chapter, setting out the psychological basis of his counter argument from the assertion,

"L'homme, dans l'état de nature, aurait plutôt la faculté de connaître, qu'il n'aurait des connaissances,"

onwards. Moreover, the style of his refutation, with its repeated references to man in a state of nature as if he were an isolated individual, culminating in the not entirely accurate recapitulation,

"J'ai dit que la crainte porterait les hommes à se fuir,"

is obviously reminiscent of its original presentation in *Pensée* 1266 within an overtly hypothetical framework, the fantasy of two men popping up from nowhere in a desert. Montesquieu's preoccupation with Hobbes is also demonstrated in chapter 3 by the emphasis placed on the idea that the outbreak of war subsequent to the establishment of societies occasions the creation of positive laws, a notion again transferred from *Pensée* 1266. As we have already seen,[26] a related fragment contains an alternative explanation of their origin, namely the natural division and extension of the family group. Now, while this second theory is admittedly more closely linked to the subject of the actual mechanics of transition from a pre-social to a fully social state, a subject peripheral to Montesquieu's main theme, and while, in any case, the two explanations are by no means mutually exclusive, it would still have remained a perfectly viable alternative, even given Montesquieu's purpose of accounting in chapter 3 for international as well as civil and political laws. As it is, this valuable idea is merely acknowledged summarily at the end of the digression on patriarchalist theories: "La puissance politique comprend nécessairement l'union de plusieurs familles."

The consequence of this anti-Hobbesian bias is thus a chapter on natural laws which whether incidentally or by design, retains something of the flavour of more orthodox prototypes to be found in the

[26] See above pp. 216–217.

works of Grotius, Pufendorf and their numerous disciples. And quite apart from such distortions as are attributable to polemical asides, it seems more than likely in view of his marked tendency to strive after a synthesis of traditional and modern concepts,[27] that at some stage Montesquieu consciously realized the possibility of reconciling certain elements of the conventional idea of the state of nature with his historical conception of social evolution. For he shares such features of his thesis as the belief that the natural state, if not yet a fully social state, is at any rate one of sociability, not only with Grotius and Pufendorf, but with Thomasius, Boehmer and several other contemporary jurists.[28] It is true that they simply recognized the illogicality of asserting the existence of a body of natural laws, unless it was conceded at the same time that natural legal obligation presupposed the existence of some kind of community; whereas for Montesquieu, the proposition was based at least in part on the empirical evidence of family and tribal life. But again, the most distinctive doctrine of all natural law theory, the idea that civil society could only be the artefact of intelligent individuals, also anticipates Montesquieu's psycho-sociological analysis of the development of primitive society, since the decisive factor in the transition from natural to political society remained for him the ability to acquire and transmit knowledge.

These similarities in no way undermine, however, the essentially scientific nature of Montesquieu's thesis, even in the version of it that appears in the *Lois*. He envisages the state of nature not as a logical hypothesis, but as the simplest phenomenon to which complex societies may be reduced. Although it is difficult to estimate the extent of his acquaintance with the new empiricism, which after Locke and Newton,[29] gained more and more ground in the natural sciences, we know

[27] See above part II, chs. 1, 2.
[28] See O. Gierke, *Natural law and the theory of society, 1500–1800*, tr. E. Barker, Beacon Press, Boston, 1960; ch. II, section I, p. 100 and p. 290 n. 16.
[29] E. Buss in her article "Montesquieu und Cartesius," (see above p. 199 n. 46) made great play with the fact that Montesquieu's early scientific essays contain no reference to Locke and practically none to Newton either. The allusion in the *Discours sur la cause de la transparence des corps* (August 1720), repeated in the *Observations sur l'histoire naturelle* (November 1721), to Newton's experiments to determine the relative opacity of bodies, does not in her opinion outweigh the absence of any mention of his theory of gravity in the *Discours sur la cause de la pesanteur des corps* (May 1720). But even if his knowledge of Newton was for a time restricted to the *Optics*, (he possessed Coste's translation, Amsterdam, 1720; *Catalogue*, No. 1509 (p. 111)), this could still have been of some importance for his philosophical formation since the conclusion of the work comprises a summary of the principles of the empirical method.
  Montesquieu also possessed Coste's translation of Locke's *Essay concerning human understanding* in the 1700 edition, (see above p. 70).

that he adapted its inductive methods and utilized them at least in part for his analysis of the incredible diversity of laws and institutions to be found in the civilized world. But as he was at pains to point out at the very beginning of the work, social phenomena are far from possessing the same stability and uniformity as the physical universe; their analysis must be conducted in two dimensions at once, both the geopolitical and the historical. The dimension of time is not neglected in the *Lois*; for instance, there emerges from Montesquieu's analysis of positive laws an unmistakable distinction between the political forms characteristic of the ancient world and those of the modern. But ancient or modern, Asian or European, the admittedly scant and primitive documentation available suggested a common original form to which all societies at least in their historical aspect could be reduced. The state of nature was for Montesquieu, as far as could be established, a final phenomenon in something of the same way that gravity for the physicist, was, at least provisionally, an irreducible element of nature.

However, at a certain point, the analogy with the physical sciences ceases to be fruitful. For as was implied most forcibly, for instance, in the exposition of historical causation in the *Considérations*, the processes of evolution revealed by historical analysis were essentially irreversible. The state of nature was to all intents and purposes a unique stage, a process within a continuing process, whereas gravity on the other hand, was a phenomenon as general and universal as the matter to which it was indissolubly linked. Consequently, although the natural laws which Montesquieu inferred from the simple psychological resources and primitive social behaviour of men in this condition completely describe it, their scope is strictly limited, extending beyond this level of social evolution only in so far as certain human attributes may be seen to remain constant.

Thus, considered in relation to the conception of *De l'Esprit des Lois* as a whole, book I chapter 2 may be regarded as a minor but integral part of Montesquieu's sociological thesis. The descriptive principles isolated there properly belong to his scientific analysis of social phenomena, and to establish this beyond reasonable doubt is to make a valuable step forward in the search for the moral framework of his thinking. For, temporarily disregarding the ideas contained in chapter 1, and conversely, in the absence of substantial evidence in the body of the work that Montesquieu consistently, if tacitly, subscribes to the basic assumption of ethical naturalism, namely that men ought to do what they habitually or instinctively perform, as soon as it is clear in chapter 2 that his concern for natural laws is in inspiration scientific rather than moral, then one may reasonably conclude that the naturalistic fallacy is not built into his philosophy.

II

But apart from this negative evidence, the imputation to him of a scientific materialist creed is of course ruled out paradoxically by the very findings arising from the application of his own empirical procedures. No matter how rudimentary his methods and debatable his conclusions by our standards, the evidence of such materials as the *Essai sur les Causes* is that he considered as simple facts of nature, first that two distinct phases exist in the evolution of the human intellect; secondly, that in its mature condition, the mind inhabits a conceptual world radically different from the narrow sphere of crude sensation to which in its infancy it is confined, namely a world informed by the intangible principles of morals and aesthetics.[30]

Apart from being reflected in Montesquieu's conception of the laws of nature, these findings were plainly also involved in the genesis or confirmation of the allied notion recurrent in chapter 1 of a hierarchy of beings and a corresponding hierarchy of laws:

"Les lois, dans la signification la plus étendue, sont les rapports nécessaires qui dérivent de la nature des choses: et, dans ce sens, tous les êtres ont leurs lois; la Divinité a ses lois; le monde matériel a ses lois; les intelligences supérieures à l'homme ont leurs lois; les bêtes ont leurs lois; l'homme a ses lois."[31]

[30] That the sensationalist core of the *Essai* does not prevent Montesquieu from acknowledging the validity of such principles is demonstrated at two crucial points: his description of the function of education in its individual aspect as, "1° à nous procurer des idées; 2° à les proportionner à la juste valeur des choses." (Nagel III, p. 415; Pléiade II, p. 54); and his portrait of the *homme d'esprit*, "Un homme d'esprit connaît et agit de la manière momentanée dont il faut qu'il connaisse et qu'il agisse; il se crée, pour ainsi dire, à chaque instant, sur le besoin actuel; il sait et il sent le juste rapport qui est entre les choses et lui." (Nagel III, p. 418; Pléiade II, p. 57.)

[31] Nagel I, p. 1; Pléiade II, p. 232. A late and rather curious entry in the *Pensées* may confirm the empirical basis of this theory:

"Je disais qu'il était très naturel de croire qu'il y avait des intelligences supérieures à nous: car, en supposant la chaîne des créatures que nous connaissons, et les différents degrés d'intelligence, depuis l'huître jusqu'à nous, si nous faisions le dernier chaînon, cela serait la chose la plus extraordinaire, et il y aurait toujours à parier 2, 3, 400 mille ou millions contre un, que cela ne serait pas, et que, parmi les créatures, ce fût nous qui eussions la première place, et que nous fussions la fin du chaînon, et qu'il n'y a point d'être intermédiaire entre nous et l'huître, qui ne pût raisonner comme nous.

Il est vrai que nous sommes les premiers parmi les êtres que nous connaissons. Mais, quand nous en concluons que nous sommes les premiers des êtres, nous triomphons de notre ignorance, et de ce que nous ne connaissons pas la communication de notre globe à un autre,

As it emerges from this chapter, he conceives of a chain of created beings ascending from inanimate matter, through plant life, to animals, man and the higher intelligences, with the nature of each group in the hierarchy overlapping to a certain extent that of the group below. Thus plant life shares to a degree the attributes of inanimate creation, being in motion and devoid of intelligence; and man shares with beasts the faculty of feeling, although his limited intelligence links him on the other hand with superior beings. The laws of organization and conservation related to the given nature of each group form a corresponding hierarchy. Simple matter is governed by necessary and invariable laws, and in so far as they are all physical bodies, plants, animals and men, are governed by the same laws; but in so far as beasts and men are also sentient creatures, they share additional laws, which Montesquieu calls natural laws; and man alone, as a creature endowed with both mind and senses, is subject to a further complex made up of the transcendent laws of reason and various classes of positive law. But in Montesquieu's view, it also follows from human nature, more specifically from the limitations of human intelligence, that this last group of laws differs radically from the first. Whereas the laws of the physical universe constitute the invariable and necessary principles of its organization, the universal law of reason, the positive laws of man's own making, and to a certain extent, natural laws as well, while continuing to operate as causal principles, loose the quality of necessity. Thus, though the nexus in which they combine, the institutional structure of societies, may be subjected to scientific and historical analysis, considered in relation to the actions of individuals they remain simple imperatives. Rational precepts, legal conventions or instinctive drives, man can and does ignore or contravene them. It is implicit in what Montesquieu says in chapter 1 of God and man and their laws, that given the freedom inseparable from intelligence, the necessity and invariability characteristic of the physical universe could only reproduce themselves in the moral world if human reason imitated in every way the perfection of the divine. Invariable principles of conduct exist, but their recognition and implementation are conditional upon men's intelligence and will, both imperfect. Of God alone can it be declared:

ni même tout ce qui existe dans notre globe." 1676 (Bkn. 2204), Nagel II, p. 498; Pléiade I, p. 1574. Raymond Aron's *Les Étapes de la Pensée sociologique* (see above p. 199, n. 44) contains in the chapter devoted to Montesquieu, a lucid and convincing demonstration to which I am much indebted, of how he utilizes the idea of hierarchy in order to salvage the relevance and authority of value judgements in face of the deterministic implications of his sociological thesis; Part I, pp. 57–60.

"Il agit selon ces règles, parce qu'il les connaît; il les connaît parce qu'il les a faites, parce qu'elles ont du rapport avec sa sagesse et sa puissance."[32]

Thus no matter how sterile the notion of a hierarchy of beings remains in itself as regards its relevance to jurisprudence proper, it obviously constitutes the centrepiece of the philosophical foundation on which Montesquieu deliberately erected his study of laws. It enabled him to bring the relationship of his scientific and moral principles into clear perspective; for through it the function and sphere of each kind of law is delimited, while at the same time they are all drawn back to his central concern with the human social predicament. If the evidence of the *Essai sur les Causes* for the empirical basis of the real burden of the theory of hierarchy, namely the idea of an autonomous intellectual world incorporating knowledge of transcendent principles, is accepted as valid, then the real measure of his only partially explicit determination in book I to meet and counter the exponents of ethical naturalism and legal positivism on their own ground can be gauged.[33] At the same time, the conception of human intelligence embodied in the theory lends weight to his own scientific aims, and illuminates the limitation he imposes on them.[34] While on the one hand it enables him to vindicate the law of reason and the freedom of the individual as a moral agent, on the other, it prepares the way for the virtual apotheosis of the various kinds of positive law and precepts that he isolates. For they are presented as the means of salvation at the disposal of a creature of *limited* intelligence:

"Un tel être pouvait, à tous les instants, oublier son créateur; Dieu l'a rappelé à lui par les lois de la religion. Un tel être pouvait à tous les instants, s'oublier lui-même; les philosophes l'ont averti par les lois de la morale. Fait pour vivre dans la société, il y pouvait oublier les autres; les législateurs l'ont rendu à ses devoirs par les lois politiques et civiles."[35]

and these claims naturally enhance the value and significance of his own scientific analysis of the laws of society. Conversely, the very same postulate of a limited intelligence adds force to the cautious conservatism of the Preface:

---

[32] Nagel I, p. 2; Pléiade II, p. 232.

[33] One may profitably compare the logic behind the empirical groundwork of Montesquieu's counter-argument with that which inspired the procedure adopted by Thomas Reid in his refutation of Hume in the *Esaays on the Active Powers*, V, 7. Reid perceived that Hume's critique of rational idealism in the *Treatise of Human Nature*, III, 1, i, could be countered by affirming the self evidence, self sufficiency, and non-deductive nature of first moral principles.

[34] See above pp. 201–202.

[35] Nagel I, p. 4; Pléiade II, p. 234.

"Chaque nation trouvera ici les raisons de ses maximes; et on en tirera naturellement cette conséquence, qu'il n'appartient de proposer des changements qu'à ceux qui sont assez heureusement nés pour pénétrer d'un coup de
génie toute la constitution d'un État." [36]

The close link which Montesquieu establishes between the faculty
of reason and moral and positive laws also illuminates in retrospect
the versatility of his general definition of law. As various scholars have
been eager to point out,[37] Montesquieu broke new ground by incorporating in the definition set at the head of a political treatise, the idea
that all knowledge is a knowledge of relations. Now the idea that justice and law were theoretically bound up with interpersonal relationships was a commonplace of jurisprudence which could be traced back
to Aristotle and beyond;[38] it thus seems that Montesquieu, in accordance with the aims avowed in the Preface, contrived to amalgamate
the basic tenets of his creed both as scientist and as jurist. At some
point the conceptual affinities between certain characteristic epistemological assumptions associated with current methodological procedures, whether inductive or deductive, and this traditional axiom of
his chosen discipline must have impressed itself on his mind, and in
consequence, his striking definition fits any and all of the categories of
law to which he alludes in this first book.[39] First and foremost of course,
the scientific laws governing the nature and evolution of societies may
be envisaged in terms of the manifold relationships between the environ-

---

[36] Nagel I, p. LX; Pléiade II, p. 230.
[37] E.g. Ernst Cassirer, *op. cit.* above (p. 148 n. 14), ch. VI, part 1; pp. 242–243; C. E.
Vaughan, *Studies in the History of Political Philosophy before and after Rousseau*, Manchester
U.P., 1925, vol. I, ch. 5, p. 260.
[38] The notion is frequently present in Aristotle's references to justice and law, e.g., *Ethics*,
Bk. V, ch. 6: "Political justice means justice as between free and (actually or proportionate-
ly) equal persons, living a common life for the purpose of satisfying their needs... For justice
can only exist between those whose mutual relations are regulated by law, and law exists
among those between whom there is a possibility of injustice."
G. del Vecchio in his historical study of the idea of justice traces its juridical formulation
back to the Pythagoreans who added the idea of correspondence between opposite terms,
and, by extension, of proportion in society, to the primitive Greek notion of order and harmony; see, *Justice, an Historical and Philosophical Essay*, trans. Guthrie, Edinburgh, 1952, ch. V.
[39] *Lettres Persanes* XCVII suggests that Montesquieu may already have glimpsed some
kind of analogy between the concepts of scientific and of positive law: "Il y a ici des philosophes qui, à la vérité, n'ont point atteint jusqu'au faîte de la sagesse orientale ... mais,
laissés à eux-mêmes, ils suivent, dans le silence, les traces de la raison humaine.
Tu ne saurais croire jusqu'où ce guide les a conduits. Ils ont débrouillé le cahos; et ont
expliqué, par une mécanique simple, l'ordre de l'architecture divine ... Que les législateurs
ordinaires nous proposent des lois pour régler les sociétés des hommes; des lois aussi sujettes
au changement, que l'esprit de ceux qui les proposent, et des peuples qui les observent:
ceux-ci ne nous parlent que des lois générales, immuables, éternelles, qui s'observent sans
aucune exception, avec un ordre, une régularité, et une promptitude infinie, dans l'immensité
des espaces." (Nagel I, pp. 193–194; Pléiade I, pp. 274–275.)

mental factors upon which positive laws are conditional; but it is equally possible to apply his definition of law as a necessary relationship to positive laws themselves, seen as symptoms of the life of men in mutual interrelation, or to the laws of the physical universe understood as the invariable mathematical formulae which express the structural and dynamic relationships of its parts; and indeed this is exactly what he invites us to do:

"les lois ... sont les rapports nécessaires qui dérivent de la nature des choses: et dans ce sens tous les êtres ont leurs lois ..."

Finally Montesquieu's definition anticipates his conception of positive law as the special property of the intelligent creature. For, if it proceeds from the assumption that relationship is an irreducible element of intelligence, then it follows that positive law, considered as an artefact of the human mind, will reflect those relationships, metaphysical, moral and physical, which it can encompass.

These remarks point to one inescapable conclusion with regard to the ontological basis of the argument in chapter 1. Every kind of law reflects indirectly or directly the way in which the nature of things is ordered. This conclusion Montesquieu himself puts into words when he writes,

"il y a donc une raison primitive; et les lois sont les rapports qui se trouvent entre elle et les différents êtres, et les rapports de ces divers êtres entre eux."

The nature of things, even if not identical with rational thought as the Cartesians would have it, in that the clear and distinct idea epitomizes reality, is nonetheless constructed in such a regular way as to correspond exactly to it. In this Montesquieu undoubtedly aligned himself with classical rationalism. The peculiar logic embodied in his opening volley against materialism:

"Ceux qui ont dit qu'une fatalité aveugle a produit tous les effets que nous voyons dans le monde, ont dit une grande absurdité; car quelle plus grande absurdité qu'une fatalité aveugle qui aurait produit des êtres intelligents?"[40]

is not so very far removed from that of the *cogito*, for both imply that the evidence of coherent thought is the sign and guarantee of the nature of existence. For Montesquieu, undoubtedly, as would befit a thinker acquainted with the theories of sensationalist epistemology, it is the mode as well as the fact of intellection which, rather than simple experience of lucid consciousness, carries most metaphysical significance.

[40] Nagel I, p. 2; Pléiade II, p. 232.

The orderly sequence of our ideas is proof of the regular and invariable structure of external nature from which they are formed. On the basis of this reasoning he thus suggests that existence without harmony and uniformity is inconceivable:

"si l'on pouvait imaginer un autre monde que celui-ci, il aurait des règles constantes, ou il serait détruit";

similarly, he defines these rules as

"un rapport constamment établi",

adding the rider,

"chaque diversité est *uniformité*, chaque changement est *constance*."

Here perhaps it would be even more apt to draw a comparison between Montesquieu's thinking and the primitive Cartesian intuition of a fundamental correspondence between the laws of nature and the laws of mathematics embodied in the *Regulae ad Directionem Ingenii*,[41] which antedates the *cogito* though its repercussions on the progress of science were more profound and enduring. This postulate was indeed carried over into Newtonian physics, in so far as Newton and his disciples, though eager to reject the inference that the real structure of the physical world could be produced by mathematical deduction operating in a void, still recognized no divorce between the world of fact and the world of ideas. Newton presupposed the existence of universal law, and indeed set out to put empirical procedures to work in demonstrating it.[42] To a certain extent therefore, the speculation which Montesquieu allows himself in chapter 1 is explicable and acceptable in terms of the most fundamental philosophical assumptions of the two scientific traditions with which he was in contact, and hence also, it goes almost without saying, compatible with his own scientific aims and methods.

Further to this, however, it is worth elaborating the point that in spite of the Cartesian affinities of Montesquieu's thinking in chapter 1, it can have been no part of his design to exploit the full resources of Cartesian epistemology for the purpose of establishing the invariability of the moral law. This he achieves by positing a structural analogy between the physical and the moral world: logically, the uniformity and invariability exhibited by the one will be equally characteristic of the other, and presumably, the intelligibility of the nature of things

---

[41] See above pp. XII–XIII.
[42] See Cassirer, *op. cit.*, above (p. 148 n. 14), ch. 1.

which supports the postulate of a primitive reason, will guarantee both. Thus he writes:

"Dire qu'il n'y a rien de juste ni d'injuste que ce qu'ordonnent ou défendent les lois positives, c'est dire qu'avant qu'on eût tracé de cercle, tous les rayons n'étaient pas égaux." [43]

Just as the invariable laws of mathematics express the structure of the universe, so also the invariable relationships between intelligent creatures express the archetypal structure of the moral world, for it is as impossible to conceive of the existence of society without laws, as of that of the material world:

"Avant qu'il y eût des êtres intelligents, ils étaient possibles; ils avaient donc des rapports possibles, et par conséquent des lois possibles. Avant qu'il y eût des lois faites, il y avait des rapports de justice possibles." [44]

Now Montesquieu identifies these invariable laws of the moral world, it is true, by a deductive process; working from the premiss of essentially intelligent, and therefore essentially equal beings, he infers for example that they will be bound together in society by relationships of mutual respect and gratitude, which in their various forms will constitute its necessary laws:

"supposé qu'il y eût des sociétés d'hommes, il serait juste de se conformer à leurs lois; que s'il y avait des êtres intelligents qui eussent reçu quelque bienfait d'un autre être, ils devraient en avoir de la reconnaissance; que si un être intelligent avait créé un être intelligent, le créé devrait rester dans la dépendance qu'il a eue dès son origine; qu'un être intelligent, qui a fait du mal à un être intelligent, mérite de recevoir le même mal, et ainsi du reste." [45]

It is difficult to describe such a procedure as anything but Cartesian, in that Montesquieu is apparently convinced that knowledge of the particular nature of the moral world can be derived from general concepts. But it is essentially a Cartesian excursion in an argument which in Montesquieu's estimation may well have possessed a solid empirical groundwork. For his notion of human intelligence takes into account the paradoxical experience of human error and human inconsistency, against which he checks his own conjectures. Thus in the text, hypothesis gives way to description:

[43] Nagel I, p. 3; Pléiade II, p. 233.
[44] *Ibid.*
[45] *Ibid.*

"Mais il s'en faut bien que le monde intelligent soit aussi bien gouverné que le monde physique. Car, quoique celui-là ait aussi des lois qui, par leur nature, sont invariables, il ne les suit pas constamment comme le monde physique suit les siennes. La raison en est que les êtres particuliers intelligents sont bornés par leur nature, et par conséquent sujets à l'erreur; et, d'un autre côté, il est de leur nature qu'ils agissent par eux-mêmes. Ils ne suivent donc pas constamment leurs lois primitives; et celles même qu'ils se donnent, ils ne les suivent pas toujours." [46]

The laws of the moral world, though invariable, are demonstrably not necessary.

And entirely in keeping with his acknowledgement of human limitations, Montesquieu himself never claims that the validity of these laws resides in their self-evidence, or in their universality as innate principles. In book I he implies consistently that knowledge is but a secondary and precarious possession of the human animal; and, indeed, perhaps most significant of all is his preference, when referring to man's rational capacities, for such terms as *connaissances* and *la faculté de connaître* over *raison* or *lumière naturelle*.[47] On this point his epistemology is completely compatible with the sensationalist psychological theories of the *Essai sur les Causes*, and one infers therefore that he remained in full agreement with his master, Locke, in regarding knowledge of the law of reason as something essentially acquired and not necessarily universally distributed.[48] As his drily humorous allusion to the law of the Iroquois in chapter 3 demonstrates, he could not have endorsed that kind of unqualified idealism most strikingly illustrated at the turn of the century in the writings of the mainstream apologists of natural religion:[49]

"Toutes les nations ont un droit des gens; et les Iroquois même, qui mangent leurs prisonniers, en ont un. Ils envoient et recoivent des ambassades; ils connaissent des droits de la guerre et de la paix: le mal est que ce droit des gens n'est pas fondé sur les vrais principes." [50]

He would no doubt have confirmed the references to *ordo* and *con-*

---

[46] Nagel I, p. 3; Pléiade II, pp. 233–234.
[47] When in chapter 3 he refers for the first time to la *raison*, the context reveals plainly that he here regards it as a discursive faculty: "La loi, en général, est la raison humaine, en tant qu'elle gouverne tous les peuples de la terre; et les lois politiques et civiles de chaque nation ne doivent être que les cas particuliers où s'applique cette raison humaine."
[48] See above pp. 218–220 and pp. 72–73.
[49] For accounts of their works see among others A. Monod, *De Pascal à Chateaubriand*, Paris, 1916, chs. I–V; P. A. Sayous, *Histoire de la Littérature française à l'Étranger*, vol. I, bk. 1, chs. 5, 6; and C. L. Thijssen-Schoute, "Le Cartésianisme aux Pays-Bas", in *Descartes et le Cartésianisme hollondais*, Paris, 1950.
[50] Nagel I, pp. 7–8; Pléiade II, p. 237.

venientia in the definition of natural laws produced for example by the Genevan theologian J. A. Turrettini:

> "Nihil sunt igitur Leges Naturales, nisi Rationis ipsius dictamina, quae ex ipso rerum ordine et convenientia tamquam ex fonte deducuntur, suamque secum demonstrationem et confirmationem ferunt." [51]

but surely little else besides.

Thus, although there remains an obvious and important metaphysical element in Montesquieu's moral as in his natural philosophy, the speculative rôle of reason is severely limited. Indeed, bearing in mind the primary importance of an analogy between the structure of the world of human relationships and that of the material universe, not only in establishing the invariability of the moral law, but also in determining his approach to positive laws, one is hardly surprised when he imposes the major burden of redeeming human imperfection upon reason applied discursively in the art of the legislator. Moreover, the metaphysical premiss which underpins both his scientific and moral vision, namely that the structure of things is dependent on primitive reason and is therefore constant and intelligible, was, as we have already noted, as much an axiom of natural science for Newton as it had been for Descartes, or, indeed, for Kepler and Galileo. This very presupposition seems to have inspired the conviction expressed in the closing paragraphs of the *Optics* that the perfecting of natural philosophy would in turn extend the boundaries of moral science:

> "For so far as we can know by natural philosophy what is the first Cause, what power he has over us, and what Benefits we receive from him, so far our duty towards him, as well as that towards one another, will appear to us by the Light of Nature." [52]

Montesquieu infringes the Newtonian canon only in so far as he refuses to abandon his moral hypotheses when they fail the test of experience; but in his defence it must be said that to have done so would have been to sabotage at the same time, by a denial of primitive reason, the very foundations of his science of law. The only solutions open to him, apart from introducing as he does the notion of the imperfection of the moral world, would have been to adopt an essentially Spinozist standpoint, positing the identity of the ideal and the natural, however imperfect the latter according to conventional standards.

However, it is virtually impossible to accept that such a retreat into

---

[51] *Cogitationes et Dissertationes theologicae*, Geneva, 1737; VIII, "De Theologia naturali."
[52] *Optics*, London, 1719, trans. S. Clarke; Bk. III, quest. 31, p. 381.

rigorous determinism could ever have been contemplated by Montesquieu as a deliberate and conscious development of his premises, at least as long as one credits his sincerity when condemning Spinoza's alleged immorality in the *Traité des Devoirs*, and declaring in the *Défense de l'Esprit des Lois* his intention of refuting such nefarious doctrines.[53]

When Charles Bonnet a decade after the *Lois* objected in his *Essai analytique sur les Facultés de l'Âme* to Montesquieu's definition of laws as "des rapports," on the grounds that he was in fact really concerned with the results of relationships between the essences and qualities of objects as fixed by a "raison primitive,"[54] his objection originated in the awareness of a similarly deterministic development. Bonnet's idea is that the laws governing intellectual behaviour can be isolated in exactly the same way as the laws governing the organization of matter, human psychology being sufficiently uniform and human experience sufficiently homogeneous:

"Le monde intelligent est donc gouverné par des lois invariables; car il n'est point d'être intelligent qui n'agisse d'une manière conforme à son Essence intellectuelle, ou aux idées qu'il se fait des choses."[55]

But this is precisely to overlook the crucial distinction which Montesquieu draws between the way men do behave and the way they should; for although Bonnet's criticism admittedly proceeds from a more faithful application of empirical principles in the field of ethics, Montesquieu, while, forced to conceed that the moral law cannot be considered necessary in the same way as physical laws, does succeed by conserving the traditional notion of human imperfection, essentially theological maybe, but in itself only too frequently confirmed by experience, in salvaging the autonomy of reason and the transcendence of first principles.

Montesquieu's definition of laws as "les rapports nécessaires qui dérivent de la nature des choses" is rooted then in a particular vision of the structure of the universe, originating in, and largely guaranteed

---

[53] cf. *Pensée* 1266 (Bkn. 615): "Il (Spinoza) m'ôte le motif de toutes mes actions et me soulage de toute la morale. Il m'honore jusqu'au point de vouloir que je sois un très grand scélérat sans crime et sans que personne ait le droit de le trouver mauvais." (Nagel II, p. 343; Pléiade I, pp. 1138–1139), and *Défense*, "Réponse à la première objection": "L'auteur a dit que les lois étaient un rapport nécessaire: voilà donc du spinosisme, parce que voilà du nécessaire. Et ce qu'il y a de surprenant, c'est que l'auteur, chez le critique, se trouve spinosiste à cause de cet article, quoique cet article combatte expressément les systèmes dangereux." (Nagel I, p. 436; Pléiade II, p. 1123.)

[54] *Op. cit.* (1760), 2nd. ed. 1769, Copenhagen and Geneva; ch. 27, art. 856.

[55] *Essai analytique sur les Facultés de l'Âme*, ch. 27, art. 857, p. 313.

by a profoundly mathematical conception of the processes of reason and the form of knowledge. This view of intelligence as the perception and reconstruction of the relationships linking things together in a regular and harmonious manner, in fact enables him to establish the inter-dependence of their ideal structure and their existence as phenomena, to posit the homogeneity of moral or metaphysical and scientific knowledge.

Just as the discovery and demonstration of the order of the material universe leads to the formulation of physical laws, so also, he aims to show, the infinitely more complex phenomena of that part of the intellectual world which comprises man's existence as a political creature may be reduced to regular patterns wherein we shall discern "l'esprit des lois." To this point nothing in fact stands between Montesquieu's thinking and that which lay behind Bonnet's criticism, except the terms in which Montesquieu chooses to formulate his definition of laws. But the very evidence of active intelligence provided by human capacity for ratiocination seems to have constituted decisive proof in Montesquieu's mind, of the age old assumption that, as regards the intellectual world, in traditional terms, as regards his historical destiny, man is engaged in a more creative rôle than that of a simple pawn. That is not to say that he is increate in the sense that omniscience equips him to shape himself with complete freedom; on the contrary, all evidence points to the fact he is involved in a process the dynamics and purpose of which are largely inaccessible to him; in the words of the remarks in the *Spicilège* which anticipate the des-cription of the human condition in chapter I of the *Lois*:

"La liberté est en nous une imperfection: nous sommes libres et incer-tains, parce que nous ne savons pas certainement ce qui nous est le plus con-venable. Il n'en est pas de même de Dieu: comme il est souverainement par-fait, il ne peut jamais agir que de la manière la plus parfaite."[56]

But on the other hand human beings are far removed from the complete passivity of inanimate matter; they are not, to borrow a metaphor from *Lettres Persanes* LXIX, simply billiard balls set on a collision course by some unseen hand. They are consciously involved in their destiny, and some if not all of its mechanisms are accessible to them. Thus the world of intelligence, or, seen from a different angle, the phenomenon of history, is not only a scientific object of the human mind, but the very element of its own existence and activity.

---

[56] *Op. cit.*, MS 336; Nagel II, p. 787; Pléiade I, p. 1542.

Furthermore, the nature and purpose of this activity will be determined by the nature and extent of the knowledge at its disposal. This
falls into two categories: intelligence of the individual predicament,
and knowledge of the historical, cultural and physical environment.
Given the classical notion of human nature as a stable entity, immutable in its essential elements, and the common acceptance of mathematics as the prototype of all knowledge, then the former in an ethical
context, emerges as a vision of the individual bound to his peers in
society by fundamental relationships of reciprocity. These are understood as invariable moral laws, precepts inseparable from the very
condition of humanity, and they must be distinguished from the causal
principles constituting the second category of knowledge, which, though
they also bear upon individual actions as part of the historical process,
govern a vaster, more intricate and fluctuating pattern of relationships,
linking the various phenomena of human organization with those of
the material universe, a pattern still in the making, and consequently
comprehensible only in part and in retrospect. These are the principles
and causes which necessarily determine the context of actions and the
forms of institutions, and knowledge of them is indeed an essential
prerequisite of just behaviour; but in themselves they are amoral forces
operating upon human destiny, and even where they are discovered
and systematized, they cannot be erected into criteria of the justice or
injustice of our deeds. This can only be decided by reference to the
moral imperatives associated with human nature, which nevertheless
demand to be fulfilled within the actual circumstances imposed by
external causes.

Knowledge of the moral and scientific laws relative to the real
predicament of human agents boils down then to knowledge of a
variety of relationships either ideal or actual; and the transformation
of this knowledge into just action requires the perfect harmonizing of
the two. Justice may thus be said to consist in the realization or conservation within the causal nexus of the essential or ideal structure of
society; to borrow the terms of Montesquieu's definition in *Lettres
Persanes* LXXXIII, it does indeed consist in the perception of a "rapport
de convenance."

A further explanation beyond the perfectly natural appropriation
of a dominant feature of contemporary scientific epistemology, accordingly suggests itself for Montesquieu's controversial definition of
laws as relationships. It can clearly be related to the moral impetus
behind his scientific investigations, which induces him to eschew any

formula too closely identifying the ideal with the real order of things. As it stands, Montesquieu's definition: "les lois, dans la signification la plus étendue, sont les rapports nécessaires qui dérivent de la nature des choses," conveniently fits both moral and scientific categories of law. "La nature des choses" signifies not just order of being, but by extension also the horizon of man's knowledge of the structure of the ideal as of the real world; so that the statement as a whole becomes on reflection an introduction to the central discussion of the moral predicament of the human being as an intelligent agent.

For this reason the provocative interpretation of the definition presented by Roger Mercier in an article on the notion of moral law in Montesquieu's works is virtually impossible to accept.[57] Mercier's ingenious thesis is that Montesquieu combines in his definition two elements: necessity, and the notion of relationship, which provide the key to his philosophical attitudes at various stages of his development, as well as symbolizing the methods employed in his investigations. Necessity is the notion central to his early idealism as expounded in the *Traité des Devoirs*. There then followed a discernible transfer of emphasis to relativist conceptions, after his travels had broadened his intellectual horizons, a change reflected in a diminishing reliance on *a priori* methods, and an increased use of observation and experiment. This change is echoed in the definition by the presence of the notion of relationship, which anticipates the materialistic determinism and legal positivism implicit in the main sociological thesis of the *Lois*.

Clearly to ignore the presence of a partly scientific attitude to ethics in the *Lois* would amount to a preposterous denial of the work's originality; nevertheless the significance which Mercier attributes to the introduction of this idea of relationship seems basically misconceived. For not only does he overlook the fundamental importance of the notion of mathematical relationship in orthodox Cartesian thinking, and perhaps even more significant for Montesquieu, its ready association in Malebranche with the notion of necessary universal law; but also the possibility that defining law as a relationship was in fact one of the most important means which Montesquieu employed to avoid, by the exclusion of arbitrary or descriptive connotations, conveying the impression of a rigid determinism.[58]

[57] "La Notion de la Loi morale chez Montesquieu," published in *Literature and Science*, Blackwell, 1955, being the proceedings of the 6th. triennial congress of the International Federation for Modern Language and Literature, held in Oxford, 1955.
[58] Mercier's documentation is in part also open to question. For instance, it is doubtful whether *Pensée* 1946 which is made up of early fragments, constitutes valid proof that after

However such criticisms do not detract from the validity of Mercier's final verdict that Montesquieu's doctrine of liberty betrays an over-riding metaphysical optimism, an optimism which he describes in terms of faith in the power of knowledge to perfect the universal order:

"Le déterminisme qui règne dans le monde réel ne rend pas vain le désir de promouvoir un monde idéal, car celui-ci ne pourrait être qu'un monde où l'obéissance aux lois de la nature serait parfaite, et c'est la science qui, en définissant ces lois, rend possible le progrès." [59]

Now, while the logical consequence of Montesquieu's equation of liberty with imperfection is indeed that perfection and necessity, invariability and omniscience hang together – one recalls the description of the act of creation in *Lois* I, 1,

"Ainsi la création, qui paraît être un acte arbitraire, suppose des règles aussi invariables que la fatalité des athées" –

it is difficult in view of his contrasting emphasis on human imperfection, and of the historical pessimism which pervades his examination in the *Lois* of the fortunes of states, to envisage this optimism in terms of a belief in the perfecting of the natural order simply through scientific progress.[60] Montesquieu's optimism is much more traditional in mould,

---

1730 sensationalism dominated Montesquieu's philosophical outlook. Quite apart from the awkward presence there of a passage which contradicts basic sensationalist assumptions: "Dieu nous trompe-t-il parce que les sens, ces infidèles témoins nous décoivent à chaque instant? Non, sans doute ...", the fragments as a whole reflect the preoccupations of an earlier period, such as the controversy over the respective merits of paganism and atheism. Similarly, other evidence put forward to illustrate the trend towards empiricism – the *Observations sur l'Histoire naturelle*, for example, can be dated before 1725, and simply illustrate Montesquieu's interest in natural science and to a certain extent his application of Cartesian mechanist principles in this sphere. It is perhaps important when evaluating such material to bear in mind that the Cartesians were not averse to experimentation as such; they simply rejected its primary importance in science. The mathematician Pierre Varignon's *Nouvelles Conjectures sur la Pesanteur*, Paris, 1690, contains an amusing illustration of their prejudices; Mersenne, experimenting with a vertically aimed canon, and persistently losing the ball, refers the enigma to Descartes: "cependant, M. Descartes, qui était accoutumé aux choses extraordinaires, n'en fut point surpris; du moins, il le dit, et mande au Père Mersenne, que cette expérience s'accommode le mieux du monde avec sa manière d'expliquer la pesanteur." (p. 11.)

[59] "La Notion de la Loi morale chez Montesquieu", p. 192.

[60] In his article "Montesquieu et l'Esprit cartésien" (see above p. 132 n. 66) C. J. Beyer's account of the nature of Montesquieu's optimism and its relation to his analysis of the nature of things seems much closer to the truth: "... ce qui distingue la justice du mécanisme, c'est qu'elle est un ordre idéal, qui demande à se réaliser dans l'ordre temporel par l'activité libre des volontés humaines. Les 'rapports de convenance' qui la constituent ne s'expriment pas automatiquement; et, en passant par les limitations humaines, la perfection de la justice s'altère; les rayons des cercles tracés de main d'homme ne sont jamais parfaitement justes, ni entièrement injustes. Mais nos imperfections ne prouvent rien contre la géométrie, ni contre la morale; au contraire, c'est la perfection de ces dernières qui seule confère quelque valeur à nos réalisations." (p. 169.)

This opinion complements R. Hubert's conclusion in "Le Devenir historique chez

moral rather than scientific, in the sense that he persists in analysing the human condition partly in terms of individual decisions and actions. Thus it must be defined in terms of a belief in the capacity of the individual to emulate divine perfection by acting justly, though of course such achievement does indeed depend upon knowledge – knowledge of the moral as well as of the natural order. One may infer from this the possibility of a kind of personal scientific progress, but by no means the wholesale transformation, through the invention and application of techniques which imitate natural processes, of the destinies of nations.

A key passage from the *Essai sur les Causes* demonstrates the humanistic individualism of Montesquieu's approach to morals and also confirms the importance for him of that imponderable criterion proportion or harmony. He does not conceive of the intelligence which would characterize human perfection solely in terms of the possession of boundless erudition, but in terms of the rare capacity to impose a proper order upon acquired knowledge; "l'éducation," he says, "consiste à nous donner des idées, et la bonne éducation à les mettre en proportion." And he goes on to describe the singular attributes of the "homme d'esprit" :

"Un homme d'esprit connaît et agit de la manière momentanée dont il faut qu'il connaisse et qu'il agisse; il se crée, pour ainsi dire, à chaque instant, sur le besoin actuel; il sait et il sent le juste rapport qui est entre les choses et lui. Un homme d'esprit sent ce que les autres ne font que savoir. Tout ce qui est muet pour la plupart des gens lui parle et l'instruit. Il y en a qui voient jusqu'à l'âme. On peut dire qu'un sot ne vit qu'avec les corps; les gens d'esprit vivent avec les intelligences." [61]

This passage completes Montesquieu's moral theory by providing pointers to the way in which he would reconcile his vision of the ideal structure of things, epitomized in the definition of justice given in *Lettres Persanes* LXXXIII,

"la justice est un rapport de convenance qui se trouve réellement entre deux choses,"

with the determination implicit in his definition of laws as

"les rapports nécessaires qui dérivent de la nature des choses"

to discover and exploit the principles governing historical reality.

Montesquieu" (see above p. 115 n. 8), that Montesquieu's philosophy adds up to a theory of "devenir" but not of progress.

[61] Nagel III, p. 418; Pléiade II, p. 57.

Now and then the ideal is realized by the perfecting of human intelligence. Knowledge of the natural and moral laws, the "rapports nécessaires," is essential but not sufficient for this achievement, since it depends rather on a process of active synthesis. This consists in the brief glimpsing of the transcendent design of the universal order of things, of the totality of those "rapports de convenance" which forms the object of divine intelligence, the very ground and purpose of being, and which includes and completes the imperfections of the purely human order. Justice is then, not an imitation of the determinism apparent in the processes of nature, but of the necessity of perfect wisdom to which God himself is subject. Thus Montesquieu presents the "homme d'esprit" as one equipped to create himself within the grand scheme of things:

"Il se *crée*, pour ainsi dire, à chaque instant, sur le besoin actuel; il sait et il sent le *juste* rapport qui est entre les choses et lui."

The inspiration of Montesquieu's idealism is then basically metaphysical and little resembles the kind of faith in the powers of scientific knowledge, seen as a product of human intelligence, more characteristic of the convictions of his 19th century successors. However, his belief in a transcendent harmony at the very origin of all being need not be construed as a declaration of solidarity with orthodox theology; on the contrary, with its roots firmly planted in the pagan tradition of Platonic philosophy, the idea possessed a long and honourable history as a major stimulus of scientific endeavour often undertaken in defiance of the entrenched opposition of established authority.[62] As a presupposition, it hardly constituted an insuperable obstacle to the employment of empirical methods as Montesquieu understood them; moreover, aside from its relevance to his conception of science and his general theory of knowledge, it must be allowed that the system of ethics which it sustains provides a more satisfactory complement to his actual scientific achievement, his theories of political and historical causation, than the various scientific and naturalistic creeds often attributed to him, and more or less incompatible with the pessimism of his conclusions.[63] Perhaps his acute historical awareness itself persuaded

[62] See E. Cassirer, *Determinism and Indeterminism in Modern Physics*, Yale U. P., New Haven, 1956, ch. II.

[63] R. Aron remarks most pertinently in his monograph on Montesquieu (*op. cit.*, above p. 199 n. 44), that a placid acceptance of rigorous determinism is almost always compensated by faith in historical progress:

"'En fait, les uns dépassent la philosophie déterministe par l'appel à l'avenir, les autres grâce à des critères universels de caractère formel. Montesquieu a choisi la deuxième voie pour dépasser la particularité. Il ne me paraît nullement démontré qu'il ait eu tort." (p. 60.)

him that a rigorous empiricism would only transform reason from the source into the product of society, and moral rules into the results rather than the moderators of our instincts. What he wrote of the design of man-made laws would serve as well to justify and to explain the derivation of his moral principles from an abstract ideal:

"Parce que les hommes sont méchants, les lois sont obligées de les supposer meilleurs qu'ils ne sont."[64]

III

The reconciliation of a rationalistic moral idealism with the determinism implicit in the analysis of causation central to the *Lois*, which can be constructed from book I of this work, supported by the evidence of the equally scientifically orientated *Essai sur les Causes*, tends then to confirm those assumptions concerning the nature and structure of reality, which were isolated in the foregoing chapter from key passages in the *Lettres Persanes* and the *Traité des Devoirs*, together with allied fragments from elsewhere in the *Pensées*. There emerges from book I as a whole the same general rather than particular determinism, as can be inferred from Letter LXIX for example; the equation in Letter LXXXIII of human imperfection with human liberty in contrast to the omniscient perfection and fixity of the divinity is reproduced exactly in chapter I, as is also, at least by extension, the theory intimately related to this conception of the human condition, of an ideal and transcendent order of justice, which man as an intelligent creature may aspire to realize in the context of his moral and social existence. Furthermore, just as Montesquieu implies in Letter LXXXIII, by invoking the insufficiency arising from the interdependence with which men are burdened, that the perfection of the divinity may only be paralleled in the moral world at a corporate level, so also in chapter I of the *Lois*, he specifies the various categories of law which provide the means of realizing this ideal.

A certain continuity of philosophical method accompanies this consistency of ideas. As we have seen in chapter I, the metaphysical argument is underpinned by two or three major premises which have the weight of empirical evidence on their side: the existence of primitive reason is induced from the example of human intelligence; the invariability of the laws which originate in it from the spectacle of or-

[64] *Pensée* 824 (Bkn. 1943); Nagel II, p. 243; Pléiade I, pp. 1470-1471.

ganized matter; the status and rôle of man in creation from experience
of his limitations. The same careful selection of concepts acceptable
to scientific intelligence which are subsequently linked together in a
web of speculation, was the outstanding characteristic of Montesquieu's
procedures in *Lettres Persanes* LXXXIII and LXIX, procedures which could
be related to the scientific epistemological stance adopted for the
criticism of pagan religions in such early works as the *Essai sur la Politique des Romains dans la Religion*.[65] As in the early metaphysical texts also,
the use in the *Lois* of this bizarre philosophical method would seem to
connect with a conscientious avoidance in the doctrines which take
shape of any emphatic reference to reason, particularly considered as
a speculative faculty. In Letter LXXXIII the principle of reason as the
source of man's moral being is never explicitly mentioned, though
Montesquieu's doctrine is largely incomprehensible unless the fact of
human intelligence is taken for granted. Similarly, here in the *Lois*,
although the intimate connection between intelligence and the perception and creation of laws is stressed, Montesquieu eschews a facile reliance on the notion of direct intuition in order to prove the anteriority
and invariability of moral law; which again seems to confirm that he
envisaged reason as an essentially discursive faculty, combining scientific, philosophical and moral functions.[66] Indeed, while acquiring
knowledge of moral and positive laws remains the special business of
intelligence, in his theory, perception of the first or natural laws of
human behaviour becomes the distinctive property of feeling rather
than thinking creatures. Bearing in mind the origins of this theory in a
fragment of the *Traité des Devoirs* (*Pensée* 615), where the main issue
at stake is the demonstration of mutual tolerance and attraction, if
not of active benevolence in man, it is possible to link the rehabilitation
of the senses which is involved, not only with the formal sensationalist
epistemology revealed in the *Essai sur les Causes*, but with the appeal
to "sentiment intérieur" rather than "évidence" typical of Montesquieu's excursions into religious apologetics, and also with his awareness of the importance of habit and constitution to morality in general.[67]

Not surprisingly, associated with this continuity of philosophical

---

[65] See above pp. 153–154.
[66] See above pp. 230–233.
[67] See above pp. 155–157. Certain remarks addressed to Warburton (letter of May 1754,
Nagel III, p. 1509), on the subject of natural religion help to confirm this link:
  "Il n'est pas impossible d'attaquer une religion révélée, parce qu'elle existe par des faits particuliers, et que les faits, par leur nature, peuvent être une matière de dispute. Mais il n'en
est pas de même de la religion naturelle: elle est tirée de la nature de l'homme, dont on ne
peut pas disputer, et du sentiment intérieur de l'homme dont on ne peut pas disputer encore."

method and the interlocking of ideas which accompanies it, one discovers a continuity of probable sources and parallels. Shaftesbury,
whose likely influence on the *Lettres Persanes* and the *Devoirs* has already
been mentioned, again comes to mind when reading book I, particularly the second chapter.[68] In something of the same manner as
Montesquieu, he tended to allow the attributes of sense, sentiment,
judgement and perception of right and wrong to overlap each other.
More important, his opposition to Hobbes was founded on the conviction that some kind of natural sympathy bound men together prior
to the formal establishment of society, a sympathy without which no
contract, convention or law could be established.[69] Similar ideas under-
pin Montesquieu's attack on Hobbes and his account of the origin of
society and of natural laws.

Yet again, the idea carried over from *Lettres Persanes* LXXXIII to chapter 1 that divine actions are subject to a necessity as complete as "la
fatalité des athées" can be traced back to Samuel Clarke's *Discourse
concerning the Being and Attributes of God*, which may also have been the
source of Montesquieu's proof of the intelligence of the First Cause
from the existence of intelligent creatures.[70]

The ancestry of Montesquieu's idea of a hierarchy in creation, not
clearly formulated until the *Lois*, but crucial there for the differentia-
tion of physical, moral, natural and positive laws, is more difficult to
trace, though of course the antiquity of the traditional theological notion is beyond doubt. It may be that Montesquieu as P. Martino suggests, found the idea in certain contemporary philosophical treatises
which retained marked Scholastic traits, such as Edmé Pourchot's
Institutio Philosophica (1700), though Martino cites no textual evidence
to support this parentage.[71] Certainly, without specifying particular
works, one can justifiably assume in Montesquieu at least a working
knowledge of Scholastic philosophy, since the religious and philosophical instruction which he received at Juilly undoubtedly continued,
for all the liberal eclecticism of the Oratory, to be firmly based upon it.
The notion of a hierarchy of beings to be found in Aquinas or his
innumerable commentators was a not unpromising candidate for adoption. In spite of Orthodoxy's belief in divine goodness as the ultimate
reality and origin of the created order, and its deliberate avoidance of

[68] See above Part I, ch. 4, pp. 78–82.
[69] For a discussion of the bases of Shaftesbury's moral and political theory, see E. Cassirer,
The Platonic Renaissance in England, trans, J. P. Pettegrove, Nelson, 1953, ch. VI.
[70] See above Part I, ch. 4, p. 86; and Part II, ch. 2, p. 160.
[71] See article cited above p. 113, n. 2.

theories of primitive reason, the idea of natural law as the natural tendencies of non-rational creatures, by which they participated in the eternal law, was a central feature of its doctrine of creation. The Scholastic scale of being and value, beginning with inert matter, then climbing upwards through orders of life endowed with a vegetative soul, a sensitive soul, a human soul, until the pinnacles of supernatural existence were reached, obviously corresponded to an order of intelligence. Thus animals were esteemed capable of a certain degree of knowledge, although it was limited to material things and acquired exclusively through the functioning of material organs. Man emerged significantly as a creature still closely bound to the terrestrial order, though his proper role in creation was defined by his limited intelligence, which opened knowledge of the moral law, of the simple dictates of right reason to him.

An adaptation of Scholastic theory was to be found in the work of the Italian Cartesian Gravina, with which Shackleton reveals, Montesquieu was well acquainted.[72] In his *Origines Iuris Civilis* (1708), Gravina distinguishes two orders of law: the common law of nature, "lex promiscua," and the law of reason, "lex solius mentis"; the first order governs the whole creation, man included, at least as concerns his physical existence; on the other hand, as a partly intelligent being, man, unlike other animals, is equally subject to the "lex solius mentis." A similar distinction between man and beast is also sketched in the second part of S. Clarke's *Discourse concerning the Being and Attributes of God*.[73] Clarke maintains that the more perfect the creature, the more closely it follows the law of reason, recognition of which constitutes in nature the special characteristic of human beings.

Equally accessible to Montesquieu, and as we have already seen, of major importance for his definitions both of justice and of law, were the works of Malebranche. Although his chief legacy was, for Montesquieu as well as for posterity in general, the placing of the notion of a constant relationship between cause and effect at the very axis of metaphysics, he retained and utilized in his ontological as in his moral theory, the idea of a scale of value and being.[74] The general laws of reason were conceived as relationships, but fell into two categories: "les rapports de grandeur" and "les rapports de perfection"; the latter,

---

[72] *Op. cit.*, above, p. 9 n. 3; ch. XI, section 3.
[73] In Part II, *A Discourse concerning the Unchangeable Obligations of Natural Religion, etc.*
[74] See above Part I, ch. 2, pp. 11–12.

existing between the archetypal ideas of the divine intelligence, constituted the order governing creation:

"les rapports de perfection sont des vérités et en même temps des lois immuables et nécessaires: ce sont les règles invariables de tous les mouvements des esprits ... Ainsi ces vérités sont l'ordre que Dieu même consulte dans toutes ses opérations. Car aimant toujours toutes choses à proportion qu'elles sont aimables, les différents degrés de perfection règlent les différents degrés de son amour, et la subordination qu'il établit entre ses créatures." [75]

Now while certain features of any or all of these versions of the notion of a hierarchy in nature may have influenced the genesis of Montesquieu's own particular conception, none of them fully account for it. Thus the intimate association of the idea in Malebranche with the notion of transcendent reason, might seem, despite the completely abstract mathematical style of its formulation, to possess a special significance for Montesquieu in view of his desire to establish the invariability of the moral law, similarly defined in terms of relationships, by reference to primitive reason. But at the same time there is little trace in chapter I of the *Lois* of the essentialism characteristic of Malebranche's theory. On the other hand, the old Scholastic notion, once removed from its theological context, would seem with its obvious reliance on an attempted classification of the actual qualities and attributes of things, to have provided a more likely source of useful detail. Whatever weight one allots to potential influences however, all comparisons point to one general conclusion regarding Montesquieu's conception of a hierarchy in nature, namely, that it was designed to answer the requirements of a moralist and scientist, not those of a metaphysician. The main focus of interest for him is clearly *not* the relative importance of classes of creatures in a grand scheme of things, nor the varying degrees of perfection which separate them from the infinite majesty of their creator. He is only concerned to establish the imperfection of human intelligence relative, one infers, to that of superior creatures and God, in order to explain the problem confronting him as a scientist and perhaps to a lesser degree as a moralist, of human inconsistency. Indeed the scale which emerges from his account of the order of creation, rather than being one of increasing perfection and value, appears as one of ascending imperfection, a feature attributable without doubt to his scientific preoccupation with the invariability of physical laws. As regards conformity to the laws governing their organi-

---

[75] *Méditations chrétiennes et métaphysiques*, Lyon, 1707, IV, 8; pp. 57-58.

zation, inanimate matter and simple plant life are both shown to be considerably superior to mankind; but in reverse, one looks almost in vain for some compensatory indication of man's superior status or of the greater intrinsic worth of his laws. The cryptic:

"Les bêtes n'ont point les suprêmes avantages que nous avons: elles en ont que nous n'avons pas,"

is Montesquieu's only gesture in the direction of a theocentric interpretation of the order of things. In accordance with the overall design and purpose of the *Lois* he has already adopted an objective approach to each part of nature and its laws. Concerned primarily to describe and explain, and only secondly to evaluate, convinced of the usefulness of scientific knowledge, but aware of the limitations of its human inventors, he is content to establish that they are also equipped to discover certain absolute values, a transcendent moral order, in order that they may guard against or remedy their natural inconsistencies.

By far the most controversial candidate for inclusion in the ranks of thinkers to whom Montesquieu owed some if not all of the ideas welded together in book I is Spinoza. The *Défense* reveals the importance that Montesquieu himself attached to scuttling the allegations of "spinozisme" that his overzealous and none too scrupulous critics had levelled against him, though his impassioned rhetoric has failed on several subsequent occasions to convince his scholarly judges of an entire innocence of any conscious design to model certain features of his thinking on the notorious system.[76] Yet in Montesquieu's favour it must be allowed that nothing in the bare text, no singular and revealing twist to an idea, no incriminating formula, betrays the presence of any such intention. Since we are no longer victims of a hysterical fear of Spinozism, it is impossible, as R. Shackleton points out in his sober appraisal of those philosophical affinities between the two thinkers that can be established, to believe that Montesquieu was a deliberate disciple of Spinoza.[77] Whether or not he became one unintentionally, through unfamiliarity with his works or through incautious logic, is another question, and one whose final answer depends on a careful weighing of the premisses and implications of his philosophy of law.

---

[76] Charles Oudin's curious work *Le Spinozisme de Montesquieu*, Paris, 1911, sets out to prove Montesquieu a disciple, often at the price of unreliable textual interpretation.

P. Vernière's *Spinoza et la Pensée Française avant la Révolution*, (see above Part I, ch. 2, p. 8 n. 2) contains (Part II, ch. 3) a much sounder study of the doctrinal similarities in the *Lois* and of the significance of Montesquieu's allusions to Spinoza elsewhere.

[77] *Op. cit.*, above (p. 9 n. 3), ch. XI, section 4, p. 261.

First of all, although at the beginning of the 18th century Spinoza's ideas were still often misrepresented or abused rather than seriously debated, the suggestion that Montesquieu was likely to know them only by hearsay cannot be accepted without qualification. His personal acquaintance with the eminent mathematician and scientist Dortous de Mairan, the same Mairan who shocked Malebranche by declaring his system to be well nigh indistinguishable from Spinoza's, is well established.[78] Mairan became a convert to Spinozism, and remained so; his case is cited by P. Vernière as confirmation of Spinoza's gradual rehabilitation as an authority, and gradual assimilation into the mainstream of philosophical discussion.[79] Quite possibly, during his first stay in Paris from 1709–1713, Montesquieu also met through his friendship with Fréret the eccentric and mysterious Boulainviller, who as the author of a work purporting to be a refutation of Spinoza though in fact more of an exposition of his theories, was one of the few Frenchmen of the foregoing generation with any real understanding of the Dutch philosopher.[80] Any impressions which Montesquieu may have gained in discussion with these acquaintances could moreover have been consolidated by first hand study of selected works. For the post-mortem inventory of his library in Paris lists a copy of the *Tractatus Theologico-Politicus*, and the Academy of Bordeaux also possessed in addition to this, the *Opera Posthuma* and its French version *Traité des cérémonies superstitieuses des Juifs*.[81]

Such evidence actually proves nothing; it merely suggests a possible acquaintance with those works of Spinoza where criticism of religious belief accompanied by political theorizing outweighs metaphysics in importance, an order of preference which would have corresponded exactly to Montesquieu's own preoccupations. In his own works, however, references to Spinoza are invariably hostile in tone, and his criticisms never venture as far as detailed technical discussion. In the *Spicilège* he touches on the parallelism of motion and thought which is the weak point in Spinoza's system;[82] and in the *Pensées* he attacks him, on the one hand, for the arid abstraction of his metaphysics:

[78] See above p. 13
[79] See *op. cit.*, above (p. 8 n. 2), Part I, ch. 5, p. 287.
[80] See Shackleton, *op. cit.*, above (p. 9 n. 3), pp. 12–13. Vernière (*op. cit.*, p. 451) also mentions certain "amateurs du spinozisme" like the Comte de Plélo and the *parlementaire* Pérelle, whom Montesquieu may have known at the Club de l'Entresol, assuming that he did in fact belong to it.
[81] See *Catalogue de la Bibliothèque de Montesquieu*, p. 243; and Vernière, *op. cit.*, Part II, ch. 3, p. 463.
[82] Article 399, MS 346–347.

"Cette philosophie (Cartesianism) ... diminue le goût que l'on a naturelle-ment pour la poésie. Ce serait bien pis si quelque peuple allait s'infatuer du système de Spinoza: car, outre qu'il n'y aurait point de sublime dans l'agent, il n'y en aurait pas seulement dans les actions."[83]

and, on the other, for the materialism and amoral determinism implicit in his philosophy.[84] Such attacks do indeed reveal little more than a rudimentary knowledge, and, as we have already remarked, Montes-quieu seems never to have noticed any inconsistency between the stance adopted in them, and certain unorthodox speculations, with implications dangerously reminiscent of Spinoza's thinking, actually published in the *Lettres Persanes*.[85]

As far as those metaphysical theories in this work, the *Devoirs*, and associated fragments in the *Pensées*, which fall into a consistent and coherent pattern are concerned, however, no evidence is to be found of any unconscious adoption or indirect confirmation of a doctrine of immanent reason. The "rapports de convenance" of Letter LXXXIII constitute a transcendent order of justice, related to the perfection of God, and certainly not immanent in the created order, whose principal adornment, man, is pitifully ensnared by his own limitations.

Almost the same theories are brought together at the beginning of the *Lois* to form the philosophical groundwork for Montesquieu's study of positive laws, and they are fitted together we have argued, in such a way that the premisses of moral idealism are satisfactorily reconciled with the deterministic implications of the scientific analysis which ensues. Even the enigmatic definition of laws in general as necessary relationships which derive from the nature of things, has been shown to facilitate this reconciliation, as long as its epistemological as well as its metaphysical significance is taken into account.

The question is, did the very ingenuity displayed by Montesquieu in his metaphysical juggling inadvertently produce the partial outlines of a general philosophy whose implications were far more radical than he himself ever recognized? Does the juxtaposition of his conception of laws as necessary relationships deriving from the nature of things, and the assertion that there exists an immutable order of justice anterior to positive laws, not add up, as long as the nature of things is not clearly distinguished from the material universe, to a doctrine of immanent as opposed to transcendent reason? J. S. Spink argues that such a doctrine

[83] *Pensée* 112 (Bkn. 446), Nagel II, p. 38; Pléiade I, p. 1019.
[84] *Pensée* 1266 (Bkn. 615).
[85] See above Part II, ch. 2, pp. 165–166.

could be explained as the unforeseen result of a gradual interpenetration in Montesquieu's mind of the rational principles common to philosophical and political thought in the late 17th century, typically expressed in a widespread enthusiasm for the idea of natural law, and the assumptions underlying the methods of contemporary science.[86]

Spinoza had consciously and systematically preached the identity of reason and nature, the exact coincidence of *is* and *ought*, freedom and obligation, in an attempt to overcome certain difficulties arising out of orthodox Cartesian metaphysics. Rejecting, like Malebranche, the principle that order was dependent upon an arbitrary and transcendent divine will, he asserted instead the basic rationality and intelligibility of the universe. God, reason and the universe are one and the same self-caused, self-limited substance, containing all finite modes, or imperfect objects, in an immutable and necessary order.[87] Reason, *natura naturans* is the immanent generative principle of all finite things, *natura naturata*. Thus mechanical causation is replaced by immanent necessity and immanent teleology combined: reason equals the living purposes of the organism, and also equals freedom. This is the basic equation of Spinoza's thought.[88] All things are constantly present in their absolute totality, and every conceivable possibility is actualized in the universe, with the result that time and number must be regarded as fictions of a limited human imagination.[89] Similarly, the imperfect mode, or finite object is simply that which expresses more or less reality, and therefore moral judgements are equally constatations of deficiency, although our imaginative limitations cause us to make artificial comparisons, transforming them into notions of good and bad.[90] No moral law can accordingly exist distinct from natural law. The good for each thing is that which helps it to exist, and ability to secure this good is virtue; similarly, Divine Providence is nothing but the striving found in the whole of nature and in individual things to maintain and preserve their existence.[91]

But, although Spinoza in the *Tractatus* states plainly that natural right is co-extensive with the determinate power of the individual object to preserve itself without regard to anything else, it must be remembered that he saw reason as both the measure and the source

[86] *French Free Thought from Gassendi to Voltaire*, London, 1960, ch. XII, p. 251.
[87] *Ethica* I, 26–27.
[88] *Ibid.*, V, 35–36.
[89] *Ibid.*, Appendix I.
[90] *Politica*, 2, 8; *Tractatus* XVI, i, 4.
[91] *Ethica* IV, 20.

of this power. It is impossible to assert that his concept of *jus naturale* is divorced from the notion of universal reason in its fullest sense. Each finite mode uses its determinate power in accordance with its determinate nature, which varies according to the amount of reality it embodies; as we have seen, this was the reason why human judgements of good and bad had no general validity. But it is clear from the Preface of *Ethica* IV, that they have validity within their own bounds:

"by good, therefore, I understand in the following pages everything which we are certain is a means by which we may approach nearer and nearer to the model of human nature which we set before us."

Man's specific nature is rationality, and his moral dignity lies in his development as a thinker. Consequently, both freedom and virtue consist in the conscious realization of this nature. In political terms, it follows from this that the individual in society foregoes his right to follow his individual physical desires. Spinoza readily accepts for instance Hobbes's assertion of human imperfection; but he differs fundamentally in his conception of the state as a means to the realization of the rational life, not an alien force imposed from without. The sovereign is an objectivization of the intrinsic nature of man; accordingly, as soon as the state ceases to serve this end, the individual has the right to reform it.[92]

Natural law, political law, and scientific law all reflect the determinate nature of things, and are necessary expressions of an immanent and universal reason; moral law is at once descriptive and normative.

Now certain points of contact between the doctrines of *Lois* I, and important features of Spinoza's system can be established. For example, the description of natural laws in chapter 2 does seem to draw on the conception of them as those laws proper to the determinate nature of each part of the created order. Similarly, one can argue that Montesquieu like Spinoza sees intelligence or rationality as the specific nature of the human being, and considers that his moral dignity depends on his development as a thinker. Furthermore, both maintain that political organization is the natural outcome of this intelligence.

Nearer to the heart of the matter, Montesquieu's definition of law presupposes the fundamental intelligibility of the universe and the dependence of the material order upon necessary reason. But here we reach the nub of the question: it does not presuppose their identity. God himself may have his laws; he is equally subject to reason. He may

---

[92] *Tractatus Theologico-Politicus*, ch. XVI.

indeed be nothing more than primitive reason itself, yet Montesquieu still clings to the notion of creation, to a distinction between the source of order, and the order realized. The proof of this and the decisive evidence against the hypothesis that book I as it stands concedes the central principle of immanentist rationalism, is precisely, if paradoxically, that, as Montesquieu surveys reality, its order reveals itself in at least one crucial case as incomplete. Human nature is irregular and inconstant in both its sensitive and its intellectual aspects so that its perfection is always virtual not actual.

This point leads on to another fundamental difference between the two thinkers: Montesquieu's conception of reason remains essentially mathematical and scientific, whereas Spinoza's is organic. Reason for him was an immanent generative principle, and consequently, although he could talk of creatures embodying more or less reality, and define moral judgements as constations of deficiency, to posit, as Montesquieu does, a real antithesis between their behaviour and its laws was simply impossible in the terms of his thought.[93] The way in which Montesquieu insists as regards both law and justice on defining them as relationships is another more obvious sign of his consistently mathematical conceptions; and he maintains his style even with regard to natural and positive laws. Thus, the natural laws of chapter 2 are defined, not in terms of the human instincts of preservation from which they derive, but in terms of the personal relationships which these instincts promote. Such definitions are absent in Spinoza.

The principles of book I of the *Lois* constitute then as inadequate a defense of rigorous rationalistic determinism as of its materialist counterpart. This simple comparison does, however, leave out of account those critical passages from the *Spicilège* and the *Essai sur les Causes* which show how Montesquieu would probably have chosen to develop the positive aspect of his moral theory.[94] These passages, by implying that human imperfection is a relative rather than an absolute condition, and that if it is defined only in terms of limited knowledge, may in fact, at least in the case of exceptional individuals, be overcome, might support a modified conclusion. While they do not in any way alter Montesquieu's conception of reason, one could argue taking them into account, that by conceding that the gap between God and man

[93] cf. *Tractatus Theologico-Politicus*, ch. XVI: "Whatsoever, therefore, an individual (considered as under the sway of nature) thinks useful to himself, whether led by sound reason or impelled by the passions, that he has a sovereign right to seek and to take for himself as best he can, whether by force, cunning, entreaty, or any other means."
[94] See above pp. 239–240.

can be abolished, and the order of perfection made actual, so that the "rapports de convenance" become immanent rather than transcendent, he has indeed gone half way to admitting the central principle of Spinozism.

Nicolas Fréret, one of his earliest eminent acquaintances, and the likely author of the clandestine *Lettre de Thrasibule à Leucippe*, there sets out a neo-Spinozist conception of the nature of things, using the phrase "rapport de convenance" in his definition of necessary law:

"Cette loi nécessaire, qu'est-elle elle-même? . . . N'est-ce que la perception des rapports de convenance ou de disconvenance qui sont entre les choses, ou leurs idées?" [95]

This furnishes certain evidence that mechanist terminology could be fitted to Spinoza's organic concepts. Yet there is still precious little evidence to suggest that Montesquieu set out to compose his introductory chapters even faintly suspecting that the ideas he was setting down, could or would be constructed as an ill-disguised adaptation of the notorious system. Their natural development from earlier works and fragments, where thinkers like Shaftesbury, Clarke and Leibniz were the likeliest influences, is easily traced. The outstandingly different characteristic of the finished philosophy, which is captured immediately in the opening formula, is indeed Montesquieu's greatly increased emphasis on the ontological and scientific significance of the notion of necessary primitive reason. But this again could be, if not the direct outcome of his own scientific research, simply a belated legacy from Malebranche, whose dizzy metaphysics concealed a rationalism ruthless enough to provoke comment even from that archsceptic Bayle.[96] The assertion that science is impossible unless the laws of reason are assumed to be necessary and independent of God,[97] that understanding the rational order is more important for the attainment of virtue than faith,[98] and the other radically subversive pronouncements that, not without justification, brought down the wrath of Bossuet and Arnauld upon him, should not be overlooked.[99] Voltaire's judgement of him as usual goes straight to the point:

[95] See above Part I, ch. 3, p. 60.
[96] "A proprement parler, Malebranche suppose que la bonté et la puissance de Dieu sont renfermées dans des bornes assez étroites, qu'il n'y a aucune liberté en Dieu, qu'il est nécessité par sa sagesse à créer, et puis à créer précisément un tel ouvrage, et puis à la créer précisément par de telles voies. Ce sont trois servitudes qui forment un fatum plus que stoïcien.", *Réponse aux Questions d'un Provincial*, vol. III, ch. CLI.
[97] *Recherche de la Vérité*, 10e Éclaircissement.
[98] *Traité de Morale*, II, 11, 12.
[99] See above Part I, ch. 2, pp. 12-14.

"Pour réduire le système de Malebranche à quelque chose d'intelligible, on est obligé de le réduire au spinozisme." [100]

One need hardly add that what Spinozism there is in Montesquieu could as well be laid at his door.

[100] *Traité de Métaphysique*, ch. III.

CHAPTER FIVE

JUSTICE AS A "LEITMOTIF"

I

"Une chose n'est pas juste parce qu'elle est loi; mais elle doit
être loi parce qu'elle est juste."
Pensée 460 (Bkn. 1906).

Montesquieu's conception of justice manifests itself in his works in two distinct ways. First of all, certain theoretical and technical details of his political doctrines can be related to the metaphysical and epistemological apparatus which supports it; and, secondly, the moral idealism which through it is renewed and reconciled with historical and environmental determinism, reveals itself both directly in the form of a literature of ethics, and indirectly though no less distinctively, in the criteria which inform his judgement of laws and institutions.

The framework supporting Montesquieu's theory of justice may be reduced to a few elementary notions concerning the nature and organization of the universe, which for the most part coincide, fortuitously if unsurprisingly, with certain assumptions at the very origin of the Western tradition of speculative thinking. We rediscover for instance, the invaluable notion of the correspondence of the form of human thought to the order governing the nature of things; the same postulate, reached by an analogy with the idea of the harmoniously regular workings of nature, of the invariability of justice; the conviction that the theories of the intellect should be given reality within the life of the community. As we have already noted, even specific elements of Montesquieu's definition of justice can be traced back to Greek sources: thus the idea of *rapport*, even though actually adopted from Cartesian physics, may be compared to the peculiarly Pythagorean contribution to juridical theory.[1] Similarly, if one takes it that the

---

[1] See above Part I, Intro., p. x. For the nature and origins of the idea of justice in Greek philosophy see P. Guérin, *L'Idée de Justice dans la Conception de l'Univers chez les premiers Philo-*

familiar word which Claude Fleury selects in his *Traité des Études* to characterize the shortcomings of Plato's method in the *Timon*:

"étant accoutumé à raisonner moralement en morale, il a raisonné de même en physique et a voulu expliquer toute la nature par des *convenances*," [2]

was a common term in the discussion of Greek philosophy, then the philosophical heritage with which Montesquieu endowed himself simply by alluding to fitness in his definition, is seen to extend far beyond a mere handful of late 17th century scholars and theologians.

Now, despite the complex significance of the term *rapport*, Montesquieu's definition of justice was in a juristic context strictly speaking inadequate. For while it incorporated the essential notion of reciprocity, the equally fundamental concept of parity between subjects was ignored. It is true that both ideas are included in Montesquieu's account of primitive justice as it appears in *Lois* I, 1:

"Il faut donc avouer des rapports d'équité antérieurs à la loi positive qui les établit ...,"

but even so, the whole drift of his thinking on the subject of law runs counter to the traditional direction of juridical enquiry. The concrete problem for 18th century jurisprudence remained what it had been for the Romans, namely the delimitation of mutual claims between persons. As a trained magistrate Montesquieu could not have ignored the classic formula,

"justitia est constans et perpetua voluntas jus suum cuique tribuens," [3]

---

sophes grecs, Paris, 1934; and E. Cassirer, *Logos, Dike, Kosmos in der Entwicklung der griechischen Philosophie*, Göteborgs Högskolas Årsskrift XLVII, 1941.

The essence of the Greek tradition handed down to the West is summarized in two well known passages from Aristotle:

"He therefore who bids the law to rule seems to be bidding God and reason to rule alone; but he who bids a man rule adds a beast thereto." *Politics*, III, 16, and:

"In fact, there is a general idea of just and unjust in accordance with nature, as all men in a manner divine, even if there is neither communication nor agreement between them. This is what Antigone in Sophocles evidently means when she declares that it is just, though forbidden to bury Polynices, as being naturally just:

(Antigone 456) "For neither today nor yesterday, but from all eternity, these statutes live and no man knoweth whence they came.'" *Rhetorica* 1373, b.

[2] See above Part II, ch. 1, p. 138, and *op. cit.*, "Discours sur Platon", p. 316.

[3] The section *Morales* in the Catalogue of the library at La Brède is headed by a similar quotation from Justinian, "Honeste vivere alterum non laetere suum cuique tribuere." Montesquieu mentions the traditional definition of distributive justice in a discussion of Aristotle's defence of the right of personal vengeance (*Ethics* V, 5); typically, he considers action according to the principle of rendering to each his just deserts to be the exercise of a magistrature existing only in a state of nature; in civil society this magistrature belongs only to appointed tribunals and not to individuals. See *Pensée* 469 (Bkn. 1944).

which also provided most contemporary dictionaries with their definition of justice.[4] The importance of the Roman contribution to jurisprudence lay precisely in the positive developments, the idea of right,
and its corollary, the wilful pursuit of a claim, which it brought to the
Greek notion of justice as that which is fitting. In the essentials of his
theory of justice however, Montesquieu remained closer to this juris-
tically less sophisticated concept, for the obvious if paradoxical reason
that, in order to reconcile moral idealism with his scientific insights, he
relied upon metaphysical ideas very similar to those used by the
Ancients in its original elaboration.

The neglect of a theory of rights anticipated by his, on balance,
non-juristic concepts of justice and of law is revealed in his treatment
of the civil and political condition of the individual. This is not to
say that Montesquieu has to be interpreted as a Machiavelli in 18th
century clothes, since his political doctrine embodies nothing beyond
the time honoured equation of *salus populi* with *raison d'état*.[5] Far from
it, for the briefest glance at his exposure of the injustice of slavery and
his plea for religious toleration in the *Lois*, will amply demonstrate his
championship of basic *moral* rights against the advocates of expediency
and of the superior interest of the state.[6] But as B. Groethuysen concludes in the first of two articles devoted to defining the quality of
Montesquieu's liberalism, his conception of liberty is basically that of
a historian of laws and institutions; through his understanding of the
manifold forms of human organization he respects the collective
personality of peoples and the individual personality of the citizen.[7]
But he is not concerned, as is Rousseau for instance, or any other political thinker, who in elaborating his doctrines remained within the
traditional framework of enquiry, to define in the abstract the limits
of individuals' powers of voluntary action vis-à-vis each other and the
community at large. As Groethuysen writes:

"La liberté, telle que l'envisage Montesquieu, est une manière de sentir et
d'agir, de se comporter envers les autres et envers soi-même, plutôt qu'un

[4] E.g. *Le Dictionnaire Universel Français et Latin*, Trévoux, 1704: "Justice ... on la définit
en Droit, Volonté ferme et constante de rendre à chacun ce qui lui appartient."
[5] Henri Sée's *L'Évolution de la Pensée politique*, Paris 1925, contains in the introduction to
the 18th. century an interesting study of the relative evolution of the notion of popular sovereignty and the principle of individual rights. Montesquieu's conception of liberty he concludes, remains "nettement étatiste".
[6] See Bk. XV, chs. 2–5; Bk. XXV, ch. 13.
[7] "Montesquieu et l'Art de rendre les Hommes libres", *Fontaine* vol. 10, Nov. 1946, pp.
505–519; and "Le libéralisme de Montesquieu et la liberté telle que l'entendent les républicains", *Europe*, 27e année, No. 37, Jan. 1949, pp. 2–16.

droit bien acquis et bien défini. C'est souvent l'esprit de la liberté, plutôt que la liberté elle-même, un sentiment plutôt qu'une réalité." [8]

Already with regard to Montesquieu's conception of natural laws, we noted how in contrast to Spinoza, he does not go beyond isolating the laws which describe man's primitive relationships; there is no progression in I, 2 from the recognition of instinctive drives to the affirmation that natural right is co-extensive with the individual's power to satisfy them.[9] In this he may also be contrasted with Hobbes, who in chapter XIV of *Leviathan* for instance, carefully distinguishes between right and law:

"For though they that speak of this subject use to confound *jus* and *lex*, *right* and *law*: yet they ought to be distinguished; because RIGHT, consisteth in liberty to do, or to forbear; whereas LAW, determineth, and bindeth to one of them: so that law, and right, differ as much as obligation and liberty; which in one and the same matter are inconsistent."

For Hobbes as for Spinoza, the logical concomitant of unchecked freedom in the state of nature is unlimited rights.

Montesquieu does not conceive of the natural condition of man as one of anarchy, however; in his account of the state of nature it is already implied that liberty is in effect the security which the laws of his own nature guarantee him. His conception of political liberty is basically similar: liberty and obligation, right and duty, coincide exactly. The extent of the citizen's freedom depends on the moderation of the laws incorporated in each particular constitution, and it is maintained by his observation of them. Considered from the angle of what the individual actually enjoys, it does then consist simply of the common security gained through a common acceptance of duty. The one supreme right of Montesquieu's citizen is his right to be protected by and judged according to the law.

In contradistinction, the distribution of political *power*, the measure of the participation of the individual or class in the process of legislation does not in Montesquieu's opinion constitute the special yardstick of freedom. Thus introducing his theory of the separation of the powers in book XI, he dismisses the common misconception that liberty resides solely in the democracy:

"Enfin, comme dans les démocraties le peuple paraît à peu près faire ce qu'il veut, on a mis la liberté dans ces sortes de gouvernements: et on a confondu le pouvoir du peuple avec la liberté du peuple." [10]

[8] *Ibid.*, p. 514.
[9] See above Part II, ch. 4, p. 251.
[10] Chapter 2; Nagel I, p. 205; Pléiade II, p. 394.

He continues in chapter 4:

"La liberté politique ne se trouve que dans les gouvernements modérés. Mais elle n'est pas toujours dans les États modérés; elle n'y est que lorsqu'on n'abuse pas du pouvoir." [11]

and this holds the key to the real significance of his theory of the separation of the powers. The importance of his famous analysis of the English constitution is not that it provides a model of how the powers of government may be effectively or justly distributed between the various orders of the realm, still less that it is a first class example of mixed government, or constitutional monarchy, but rather that it demonstrates how constitutional laws may be so composed that authority is restrained from oppressing the individual. As Montesquieu puts it:

"Une constitution peut être telle que personne ne sera contraint de faire les choses auxquelles la loi ne l'oblige pas, et à ne point faire celles que la loi lui permet." [12]

His definition of political liberty does not make its first appearance in the *Lois*, but seems on the evidence of one of the earliest entries in the *Pensées*, to have been in his mind from the time of his early meditations on justice. Indeed it may owe its origin to the austere notions of civic duty derived from his reading of the Stoics, which inspired some of his earliest literary endeavours.[13] More important, while it is obviously compatible with the relativistic approach to political institutions adopted in the *Lois*, it also appears to answer the logical demands of Montesquieu's theory of justice. For with its starting point in the notion that perfect reason and perfect freedom together constitute perfect necessity, and its conclusion that justice consists in the imitation of this necessity in the context of social existence, this would seem to imply that the attainment of moral perfection depends to a certain extent on the freedom of each human being to fulfil his rôle as a citizen through observance of the law. His idea of liberty may therefore be taken as further evidence that the evolution of Montesquieu's scientific

[11] Nagel I, p. 206; Pléiade II, p. 395.
[12] Book XI, ch. 4; Nagel I, p. 206; Pléiade II, p. 395.
[13] A fragment of the *Pensées Morales* later incorporated into the *Devoirs* begins for example:
"Les actions humaines sont le sujet des devoirs. C'est la raison qui en est le principe et qui nous rend propres à nous en acquitter." (Pensée 220 (Bkn. 597).
In yet another fragment which probably belonged to the *Devoirs* (Pensée 1252 (Bkn. 603), one finds:
"Il n'y a pas de bon sens de vouloir que l'autorité du Prince soit sacrée, et que celle de la Loi ne le soit pas."

thought and that of his moral ideas were at every stage closely inter-connected.

The main definition given in *Lois* XI, 3:

"Dans un État, c'est-à-dire dans une société où il y a des lois, la liberté ne peut consister qu'à pouvoir faire ce que l'on doit vouloir, et à n'être point contraint de faire ce que l'on ne doit pas vouloir.

Il faut se mettre dans l'esprit ce que c'est que l'indépendance, et ce que c'est que la liberté. La liberté est le droit de faire tout ce que les lois permettent; et si un citoyen pouvait faire ce qu'elles défendent, il n'aurait plus de liberté, parce que les autres auraient tout de même ce pouvoir."[14]

can be traced back to a surviving fragment of a lost manuscript entitled *La Liberté Politique*:

"Un peuple libre n'est pas celui qui a une telle ou une telle forme de gouvernement, c'est celui qui jouit de la forme de gouvernement établie par la Loi .... De là, il faut conclure que la liberté politique concerne les monarchies modérées comme les républiques ... et tout homme est libre qui a un juste sujet de croire que la fureur d'un seul ou de plusieurs ne lui ôteront pas la vie ou la propriété de ses biens."[15]

This in turn develops the main theme of the early entry in the *Pensées* mentioned above:

"Le seul avantage qu'un peuple libre ait sur un autre, c'est la sécurité où chacun est que le caprice d'un seul ne lui ôtera point ses biens ou sa vie. Un peuple soumis, qui aurait cette sécurité-là, bien ou mal fondée, serait aussi heureux qu'un peuple libre ..."[16]

Elsewhere allied notions are expressed in more vivid terms. In the *Voyage en Italie* for example, Montesquieu dismissed the kind of liberty enjoyed by the citizens of Venice as repugnant to honest people, and continues:

"il faut être gêné: l'homme est comme un ressort qui va mieux, plus il est bandé."[17]

And in the *Pensées* again, a curious sequence of entries occurs where one can follow stage by stage, the gradual tailoring of a single image until it exactly expresses his conception of political liberty. The period of their composition, 1734–1738, corresponds roughly with the dates of the notebook *Geographica* II, which contains lengthy extracts of con-

---

14 Nagel I, pp. 205–206; Pléiade II, p. 395.
15 *Pensée* 884 (Bkn. 631); Nagel II, p. 256; Pléiade I, p. 1152; on the basis of this entry in the *Pensées* Shackleton suggests an approximate date of 1734 for the work.
16 *Pensée* 32 (Bkn. 1802); Nagel II, p. 12; Pléiade I, p. 1431.
17 Nagel II, p. 481.

temporary works on China, as well as a redraft of the original notes of Montesquieu's conversations with the Chinaman Hoange in 1712 or 13.[18] It was undoubtedly in one of these sources that Montesquieu found a proverb which expressed some of his own thoughts on the subject of justice and human freedom. It consisted of a striking comparison between justice and a fishing net:

"Admirable idée des Chinois, qui comparent la justice de Dieu à un filet si grand que les poissons qui s'y promènent croient être en liberté; mais réellement ils sont pris. Les pécheurs croient de même, qu'ils ne seront pas punis de Dieu; mais ils sont dans le filet." [19]

The image of the net fascinated Montesquieu, and he took it up again four times, each time altering it slightly. First the subjects of a well regulated monarchy are compared to the captive fish; then the simile is developed into a comparison between the state of men in a democracy seen as fish swimming freely in the sea, and that of men in a despotism where they resemble fish confined in a tight net; then the whole thing is reduced to a simple comparison between free government and despotism symbolized as fishnets large and small respectively; and finally, the complete theory of liberty emerges:

"La liberté pure est plutôt un état philosophique qu'un état civil. Ce qui n'empêche pas qu'il n'y ait de très mauvais gouvernements, et même qu'une constitution ne soit plus imparfaite à mesure qu'elle s'éloigne plus de cette idée philosophique que nous avons.

Un ancien a comparé les lois à ces toiles d'araignée qui n'ayant que la force d'arrêter les mouches, sont rompues par les oiseaux. Pour moi, je comparerais les bonnes lois à ces grands filets dans lesquels les poissons sont pris, mais se croient libres, et les mauvaises à ces filets dans lesquels ils sont si serrés que d'abord ils se sentent pris." [20]

The repercussions of the conception of reason revealed in the analysis of Montesquieu's idea of justice and subsequently confirmed by the account of the origin of society which he gives in the *Lois*, are, like those of his conception of law, visible in other aspects of his political and sociological doctrine.

Lettres Persanes LXXXIII and book I of the *Lois* point, as we have seen, to a conception of reason as an essentially discursive faculty which equips the individual to acquire both moral and scientific knowledge. Furthermore the evolution of society proper is presented as a direct result of the

---

[18] See Nagel II, F. Weil, "Introduction aux *Geographica*", p. lxxvii.

[19] *Pensée* 434 (Bkn. 2124); Nagel II, p. 164; Pléiade I, p. 1552.

[20] *Pensée* 943 (Bkn. 1798); Nagel II, pp. 267–268; Pléiade I, p. 1430. See also *Pensées* 597 (1800); 828 (1801); 874.

development of this latent faculty in primitive human creatures, of the acquisition of "connaissances." Thus there is no real psychological or moral divide between natural man or the savage, and the fully fledged citizen, the latter having merely progressed a stage further.

Since then the crucial factors in the process of advancement to political and moral maturity, as undergone not only by entire primitive communities but also by young people in established societies, are the awakening of the intellect and the furnishing of the mind with ideas, that Montesquieu is elsewhere at pains to emphasize the central importance of education in the life of a nation goes without saying.

"Ceux qui commencent à faire usage de leur raison se trouvent chez un peuple barbare, où l'on n'a aucune sorte d'éducation, ou bien chez un peuple policé, où l'on reçoit une éducation générale dans la société." [21]

Education plays a vital rôle not only as the means of progress beyond the state of nature, but equally, one assumes, as a mainstay of civilization, a bulwark against the forces of corruption. In the *Pensées* Montesquieu describes its function as safeguarding and transmitting the accumulated experience of centuries. Already in one of the earliest fragments he had declared reason to be the principle of duty, the means by which we acquit ourselves of it;[22] now he presents education as the means by which we first acquire a knowledge of the duties of a citizen:

"Par l'éducation, on apprend aux hommes leurs devoirs, à mesure qu'ils sont en état de les connaître; on leur apprend en quelques années ce que le Genre humain n'a pu savoir qu'après un très grand nombre de siècles, et ce que les peuples sauvages ignorent encore aujourd'hui." [23]

And if one goes back to the famous allegory of the Troglodytes in the *Lettres Persanes*, or dips almost at random into the *Lois*, one finds over and over again the paramount importance of education for the well-being of society and its members confirmed. The virtuous Troglodytes pay special attention to their paternal duty of education, illustrating their moral precepts with the sad example and pitiful fate of their unjust compatriots. The sequel to the four letters, excluded from the published work, drives home the lesson of the allegory even more clearly. The Troglodytes, having already instituted monarchic government under the pressure of increasingly complex social relationships, decide it is time also to introduce commerce and industry into the

[21] *Essai sur les Causes*, Part II; Nagel III, pp. 413-414; Pléiade II, p. 53.
[22] *Pensée* 220 (Bkn. 597).
[23] *Pensée* 1379 (Bkn. 1754); Nagel II, p. 408; Pléiade I, p. 1419.

state; in their assembly, the king voices his fears that the people are about to abandon virtue for wealth, but a citizen replies that the morals of the nation will depend now as never before on the example set by the king himself and on the force of education:

"Vous connaissez, Seigneur, la base sur quoi est fondée la vertu de votre peuple: c'est sur l'éducation. Changez cette éducation, et celui qui n'était pas assez hardi pour être criminel rougira bientôt d'être vertueux." [24]

The point at issue in the dispute with Hobbes which is dramatized in the myth is not the precise mechanisms by which society is established, or even Hobbes's justification of absolutism, but the nature of the psychological and moral resources of human beings, and the way in which these govern the destinies of a community.[25] Montesquieu believes that there is no innate justice in men, though it may be acquired along with other virtues and deliberately cultivated by example and education; its neglect or deliberate rejection in favour of the exclusive pursuit of self-interest, far from ushering in even the arbitrary justice of Leviathan as Hobbes would have it, will in fact only lead to chaos and eventual destruction;[26] furthermore, even if civic virtue has been a formative influence in the growth of a nation, the need for it and for the education which conserves and strengthens it, can only increase as the gradual sophistication of economic and political institutions gives rise to ever growing dangers of corruption.

Letter CXXIX on the characteristic shortcomings of legislators reasserts the fundamental interdependence of education and morality; a few of them, Montesquieu is happy to recall, have in the past shown proof of their wisdom by institutionalizing paternal authority:

"Rien ne soulage plus les magistrats; rien ne dégarnit plus les tribunaux; rien, enfin, ne répand plus de tranquillité dans un état, où les moeurs font toujours de meilleurs citoyens que les lois." [27]

The same theme obviously inspires book IV of the *Lois*, devoted to the laws of education and given a prominent position immediately

---

[24] *Pensée* 1616 (Bkn. 120); Nagel II, p. 464; Pléiade I, p. 378.

[25] Cf. S. Cotta's interpretation of the allegory in *Montesquieu e la scienza della società* (see above p. 213 n. 9) ch. 3. He sees in it not the contrasting of two contradictory ideas of the state of nature, but a study of the avenues of development open to societies according to the moral principles which flourish in them. By the weight this gives to the influence of external causes, it anticipates the sociological thesis of the *Lois*.

[26] In his article "Cicéron, Hobbes et Montesquieu", *Annales Universitatis Saraviensis*, Phil-Lettres, No. 1, 1952, pp. 19–47, P. Dimoff presents a detailed analysis of those facets of Hobbes's political theory which are dramatized in the allegory.

[27] Nagel I, p. 258; Pléiade I, p. 323.

following the book where Montesquieu sets out his theory of the moral principles which characterize each type of government. He begins by declaring roundly that the laws of education prepare men for citizenship, and must therefore accord with the moral force which upholds the state. They are naturally of outstanding importance in the particular type of government whose very principle is virtue, namely the republic. Here, where the passions are no longer conveniently harnessed to the principle of the government as in the monarchy, and where education has not been rendered superfluous by the combination of servility and ignorance indispensible for the conservation of the despotism, for the state to endure, it is essential that they teach men to conquer their selfish passions and to love the law above all things. In Montesquieu's mind education clearly constitutes a specific activity of the republic, considered as the historical embodiment of the ideal of justice; and the definition which he gives it, echoing that of the most important virtue of all, is hardly surprising:

"L'éducation ... consiste principalement à vivre avec les autres ..." [28]

The rôle which Montesquieu allots reason in the pursuit of justice by the individual corresponds in some respects to that with which he endows it with regard to the conservation of the state by the legislator. We know from the details of his theory of political liberty and from his definition of the republic, that he considers reverence for the law to be an essential prerequisite of just behaviour; furthermore, at the end of *Lois* I, 1, the legislator is presented as the moral saviour of the citizen:

"Fait pour vivre dans la société, il y pouvait oublier les autres; les législateurs l'ont rendu à ses devoirs par les lois politiques et civiles."

Such points suggest that Montesquieu conceived of the creation and preservation of a moral climate in which the citizen might fulfil his moral and political calling, as an essential part of the legislator's job of conserving the state. The notion of the purpose fulfilled by the law that he reveals in a *rejet* from the *Lois* would seem to confirm such a hypothesis:

"C'est une pensée admirable de Platon, que les lois sont faites pour annoncer les ordres de la raison à ceux qui ne peuvent la recevoir immédiatement d'elle." [29]

The laws must take into account the causal forces governing the life of

[28] Book IV ch. 3.
[29] *Pensée* 1859 (Bkn. 208); Nagel II, p. 555; Pléiade II, p. 1042.

the nation, they must be fashioned according to its history and geographical situation, but they must also aim to be just.

Thus, like the individual seeking to attain perfect justice through the comprehension of the sum of relationships linking his existence to the rest of his moral, historical and physical universe, the legislator must in his lawmaking endeavour to reconcile the demands of the moral law with the dictates of environment. This is surely the true significance of the deceptively platitudinous introduction of book XXIX on the science of legislation:

'Je le dis, et il me semble que je n'ai fait cet ouvrage que pour le prouver: l'esprit de modération doit être celui du législateur; le bien politique, comme le bien moral, se trouve toujours entre deux limites. En voici l'exemple.
Les formalités de la justice sont nécessaires à la liberté. Mais le nombre en pourrait être si grand qu'il choquerait le but des lois mêmes qui les auraient établies: les affaires n'auraient point de fin: la propriété des biens resterait incertaine; on donnerait à l'une des parties le bien de l'autre sans examen, ou on les ruinerait toutes les deux à force d'examiner.
Les citoyens perdraient leur liberté et leur sûreté, les accusateurs n'auraient plus les moyens de convaincre, ni les accusés le moyen de se justifier.
Cecilius, dans Aulu-Gelle, discourant sur la loi des Douze Tables, qui permettait au créancier de couper en morceaux le débiteur insolvable, la justifie par son atrocité même, qui empêchait qu'on empruntât au-delà de ses facultés. Les lois les plus cruelles seront donc les meilleures? Le bien sera l'excès, et tous les rapports des choses seront détruits?'[30]

Here Montesquieu's examples are not simply designed to illustrate the well worn dictum, *ne quid nimis*, as one might well infer from his allusion to "l'esprit de modération," but rather the idea that the legislator who ignores either material or practical considerations on the one hand, or the exigences of justice on the other, imperils the safety and happiness of his subjects. Justice is no less mocked by well-intentioned attempts to safeguard it by cumbersome legislation, than it is by brutally repressive laws. It is clear that the ideal which Montesquieu is proposing resembles a mean or even a compromise, but the more important point is that the limits between which it lies are again "les rapports des choses," the whole complex of moral and physical relationships which sustain the life and evolution of a society.

Yet another fragment from the *Pensées* throws light upon the immensely intricate and constantly changing materials of the legislator's trade:

[30] Chapters 1 and 2; Nagel I, pp. 269–270; Pléiade II, pp. 865–866.

"Il faut que chaque monarque ajoute à cet ouvrage car cet ouvrage (des lois) n'est jamais fini; parfait aujourd'hui, demain il est imparfait parce qu'il est soumis aux circonstances comme toutes les autres choses de l'univers, parce que chaque société d'hommes est une action, composée de l'action de tous les esprits. Le monde intellectuel, aussi en mouvement que le monde physique, change comme le monde physique."[31]

Alongside this notion that it is imperative for the legislator to discover the mainsprings of "le monde intellectuel," and adapt his laws to them, one can place various references in the *Lois* to his duty to recognize and uphold the moral law; from these one can deduce moreover, that in Montesquieu's eyes, this function if anything outweighs in importance the purely scientific aspect of the law-giver's work.

Seeking to define the nature and forms of climatic influence on laws, he describes the complete inertia to which extremes of heat reduce Indian peoples; but to explain is not to justify, rather to forewarn, and from his description a general principle of legislation emerges:

"Plus les causes physiques portent les hommes au repos, plus les causes morales les en doivent éloigner."[32]

In contrast to India, where legislation has simply confirmed the vices engendered by climate, Chinese legislators,

"considérant les hommes ... dans l'action propre à leur faire remplir les devoirs de la vie,"

have seen to it that all social and moral forces, religion, philosophy and the law issue in practical activity.[33] In the ensuing discussion of the institutions of domestic slavery, largely determined according to Montesquieu by climatic influence, he restates this golden rule of legislation in even plainer terms. Having decided that modesty in sexual relationships is the law of nature and of reason, he concludes:

"Quand donc la puissance physique de certains climats viole la loi naturelle des deux sexes et celle des êtres intelligents, c'est au législateur à faire des lois civiles qui forcent la nature du climat et rétablissent les lois primitives."[34]

---

[31] *Pensée* 2266; Nagel II, p. 677.
[32] Book XIV, ch. 5; Nagel I, p. 312; Pléiade II, p. 480.
[33] Book XIV, ch. 5.
[34] Book XVI, ch. 12; Nagel I, p. 361; Pléiade II, p. 518.

II

It is impossible to restrict a discussion of Montesquieu's ideas on the moral duties of the citizen to those works, essays of comparatively early date for the most part, whose titles announce an immediate concern with this subject. The *Éloge de la Sincérité* (1717), the *Discours sur l'Équité* (1725), *De la Considération et de la Réputation* (1725), or of course the most important of all, the *Traité des Devoirs* (1725) in its sadly fragmented state, besides standing in an almost contrapuntal relationship to each other, echo ideas sketched out in the *Lettres Persanes*, or in the *Pensées*, and anticipate themes which reappear, fully orchestrated, in the *Lois*.[35]

Taking as a starting point justice considered as the highest of moral duties, one finds the following definition in the *Analyse du Traité des Devoirs:*

"La plupart des vertus, ne sont que des rapports particuliers, mais la Justice est un rapport général; elle concerne l'homme en lui-même; elle le concerne par rapport à tous les hommes."[36]

From the terms he uses here, it is easy to guess that all other virtues will be presented as the offspring of justice, and so it proves. The passing reference to this idea in the *Analyse*[37] is confirmed by an entry in the *Pensées* apparently unconnected with the *Devoirs* itself:

"Presque toutes les vertus sont un rapport particulier d'un certain homme à un autre; par exemple: l'amitié, l'amour de la Patrie, la pitié, sont des rapports particuliers. Mais la justice est un rapport général. Or, toutes les vertus qui détruisent ce rapport général ne sont pas des vertus."[38]

As one would expect from the austere portraitist of republican democracy revealed in books III and IV of the *Lois*, who defines political virtue as voluntary self-renunciation for the sake of the

---

[35] The arguments put forward by X. Védère (Nagel III, pp. 175–178), and P. Dimoff ("La place dans l'oeuvre de Montesquieu de *l'Essai touchant les lois naturelles*," RHLF, 1957, 57e année, 4, pp. 481–493), for attributing the *Essai touchant les lois naturelles et la distinction du juste et de l'injuste*, published in Nagel III, pp. 175–199, to Montesquieu are, as R. Shackleton maintains, (*op. cit.*, above (p. 9 n.3) p. 249, n. 1), virtually impossible to accept. Apart from stylistic incompatibility, there is a marked contradiction between the main doctrines of the essay and Montesquieu's ideas on law and justice; it presents for instance a crudely voluntarist conception of law: "La loi suppose un supérieur qui commande et des inférieurs qui lui obéissent ... Le supérieur c'est Dieu, et les inférieurs sont les hommes." (p. 180); and morals are made to depend on the principle of self interest aided by "la religion de l'instinct."

[36] Nagel III, p. 157; Pléiade I, p. 110.

[37] Summary of ch. III of the original *Traité*; Nagel III, p. 159; Pléiade I, p. 109.

[38] *Pensée* 1008 (Bkn. 1214); Nagel II, p. 282; Pléiade I, p. 1304.

common good, Montesquieu rejects in his formal theory of morals all false divisions between public and private conduct; just as justice is envisaged elsewhere in the *Devoirs* as the moral foundation of political society in general,[39] so it is inevitably held at the same time to constitute the cornerstone of personal morality.

The definition proposed here, "un rapport général," distils the element of reciprocity central to any idea of justice, that was presented in a metaphysical framework in Lettres Persanes LXXXIII, and juxtaposed at the beginning of the *Lois* with the notions of structural and functional relationship implicit in the ideas of scientific and social laws. But here it is no longer a question of relationships within a supernatural design, still less of the laws of mechanical necessity; envisaging it in the context of morals pure and simple, Montesquieu strips his definition down to bare essentials: the single idea of undifferentiated reciprocity. For the proper limits of the sphere of justice are now set down, and they extend no further than inter-personal relationships:

"Le chapitre III traite de nos Devoirs envers les hommes. Ces devoirs sont de deux espèces, selon l'auteur. Ceux qui se rapportent plus aux autres hommes qu'à nous, et ceux qui se rapportent plus à nous qu'aux autres hommes. Il met parmi les devoirs de la première espèce tous ceux qui tirent leur origine de la justice." [40]

Thus although simple reciprocity logically constitutes an irreducible element of particular virtues and duties, like friendship and patriotism, it is entirely absent from the relationship which links men and God. According to the *compte rendu* of the *Devoirs* Montesquieu does not there place religious duties in the same category as those derived from justice, for the former are completely one-sided:

"nos devoirs envers Dieu sont d'autant plus indispensables qu'ils ne sont pas réciproques, comme ceux que les hommes se rendent, car nous devons tout à Dieu et Dieu ne nous doit rien." [41]

Similar ideas about justice considered from this more strictly moral or even juristic standpoint, are to be found as one would expect, in the *Discours sur l'équité qui doit régler les jugements et l'exécution des lois,* which Montesquieu probably wrote shortly after the *Devoirs* (read 12th November, 1725), for the edification of the members of the Parlement of Bordeaux at the beginning of a new session. The definition of the

[39] *Pensée* 1266 (Bkn. 615).
[40] *Analyse*, Nagel III, p. 159; Pléiade I, p. 109.
[41] *Ibid.*

Devoirs is echoed for example in the words he uses here to describe
equity:

"cette affection générale pour le genre humain, qui est la vertu de l'homme
considéré en lui-même." [42]

And, indeed, the idea implied in its definition as a general relationship,
of the universality of justice, of its virtual identity as the fount of all
virtues, with common humanity, receives particular emphasis in the
Discours:

"La justice doit être en nous une conduite générale. Soyons justes dans tous
les lieux, justes à tous égards, envers toutes personnes, en toutes occasions." [43]

The judge above all must eschew the example of Cato, just in the
tribunal but not in his family.

Such entreaties doubtless appear as platitudinous as they were in-
effectual, not that Montesquieu's sincerity is thereby in any way
impugned. They were clearly inspired, however, by the classical
humanism which was so marked an influence upon Montesquieu's
moral thought, and indeed in various disguises, upon that of his
generation as a whole, notwithstanding the relativist cross currents
to which he himself contributed. Descartes, Malebranche and Clarke
before him, to name but a significant handful, had all been moved by a
similar respect for the integrity of human nature and the dignity of
mankind as a whole, to express their conviction that the duties of man
took precedence over any particular allegiance.[44] The hierarchy of
values which Malebranche establishes in the *Traité de Morale* in order
to demonstrate the low priority of purely sectional interests:

"Il faut être homme, chrétien, français avant que d'être grammarien, poète,
historien, étranger."

anticipates by its universalist spirit, the personal credo confided by
Montesquieu in the *Pensées*:

"Si je savais quelque chose qui me fût utile, et qui fût préjudiciable à ma
famille, je la rejetterais de mon esprit. Si je savais quelque chose utile à ma
famille et qui ne le fût pas à ma patrie, je chercherais à l'oublier. Si je savais
quelque chose utile à ma patrie, et qui fût préjudiciable à l'Europe, ou bien
qui fût utile à l'Europe et préjudiciable au Genre humain, je la regarderais
comme un crime." [45]

[42] Nagel III, p. 213; Pléiade I, p. 47.
[43] Nagel III, p. 214; Pléiade I, p. 48.
[44] See Descartes, *Lettre à la Princesse Élisabeth*, 15th. Sept. 1645, in *Correspondance* IV, ed.
Adam and Tannery, Paris, 1901; Malebranche, *Traité de Morale*, Part II, ch. X, para. 14;
S. Clarke, *De l'Existence et des Attributs de Dieu*, 1717, II, ch. III, p. 55.
[45] *Pensée* 741 (Bkn. 11); Nagel II, pp. 221–222; Pléiade I, p. 981.

The cosmopolitanism sustaining this declaration again descends in a straight line from the *Devoirs*, where it is expressed in the form of a general maxim reminiscent of his definition of justice, and rounded off with an impeccably Ciceronian refrain:

"... tous les devoirs particuliers cessent lorsqu'on ne peut pas les remplir sans choquer les devoirs de l'homme ... le devoir du citoyen est un crime lorsqu'il fait oublier le devoir de l'homme. L'impossibilité de ranger l'univers sous une même société a rendu les hommes étrangers à des hommes, mais cet arrangement n'a point prescrit contre les premiers devoirs, et l'homme, partout raisonnable, n'est ni Romain ni Barbare." [46]

As all other virtues are to justice as a "rapport particulier" is to a "rapport général," so the idea of reciprocity, central to its definition seems to colour Montesquieu's treatment of all its ramifications. Society in the abstract is seen as a complex of inter-personal relationships established for the sake of mutual utility and comfort, and the assumption underlying such widely separated studies as the Fable of the Troglodytes and book I, chapters 2 and 3 of the *Lois* is explicitly confirmed in certain fragments of the *Devoirs*. When writing of friendship for example, he says:

"Nous passons une espèce de contrat pour notre utilité commune, qui n'est qu'un retranchement de celui que nous avons passé avec la société entière, et semble même, en un certain sens, lui être préjudiciable." [47]

and more directly, describing the spirit of citizenship, he speaks of the kind of magistrature which membership of the body politic confers on everyone:

"il n'y a personne qui ne participe au gouvernement, soit dans son emploi, soit dans sa famille, soit dans l'administration de ses biens." [48]

Since each individual is thus bound indissolubly to his fellows, patriotism will obviously occupy first place among those virtues derived from justice.

On this second most general virtue, Montesquieu has a great deal to say; indeed, taking all his works together, there is no doubt that it constitutes one of the major themes. In the *Lettres Persanes*, it is already given pride of place after justice, when Montesquieu develops the argument in Letter XLVI that respect for the laws, love of one's fellows and filial piety, are the first duties of religion. Gratitude to God

---

[46] *Analyse*, Nagel III, p. 160; Pléiade I, p. 110. Cf. Cicero, *De Officiis*, III, vi.
[47] *Pensée* 1253 (Bkn. 604); Nagel II, p. 333; Pléiade I, pp. 1129–1130.
[48] *Pensée* 1269 (Bkn. 618); Nagel II, p. 349; Pléiade I, p. 1144.

can best be shown by loving his creatures; and the most effective expression of this love

"est d'observer les règles de la société et les devoirs de l'humanité."

But in the *Devoirs*, inspired at least according to Montesquieu, by the writings of the neo-Stoics, nostalgia for the ancient republics colours his treatment even more markedly, as if his essay were the prelude to the great lament for the passing of republican virtue developed in the *Considérations* and the early books of the *Lois*.

After deploring the treachery, cruelty and bloodshed which characterized the Spanish conquest of the Empires of South America and witnessed only too eloquently to a crude colonialism masquerading as religious zeal, Montesquieu pleads the cause of true patriotism, the patriotism celebrated in the histories of Greece and Rome. While it is on the one hand true, he says, that the abuse of this virtue has engendered the greatest crimes, on the other, once properly controlled, it honours and sustains the whole nation. He finds overwhelming proof of this in the depressing spectacle presented by contemporary morals when they are set against the soaring spirit of Antiquity:

'Quand je pense à la petitesse de nos motifs, à la bassesse de nos moyens, à l'avarice avec laquelle nous recherchons de viles récompenses, à cette ambition si différente de l'amour de la gloire, on (sic) est étonné de la différence des spectacles, et il semble que, depuis que ces deux grands peuples ne sont plus, les hommes se sont raccourcis d'une coudée." [49]

Similarly, while he begins his description of the spirit of true citizenship with a stern warning against aggressive nationalism:

"L'esprit du citoyen n'est pas de voir sa patrie dévorer toutes les patries. Ce désir de voir sa ville engloutir toutes les richesses des nations, de nourrir sans cesse ses yeux des triomphes des capitaines et des haines des rois, tout cela ne fait point l'esprit du citoyen." [50]

its details confirm the supreme importance of true patriotism for the moral and political health of the nation. For the patriot will cherish its laws as custodians of the general good, even in such cases as might not favour his personal interests; and beyond this he will desire and rejoice in public order and tranquillity, the stringent administration of justice, the dignity and prosperity of magistrates and rulers, in short, the complete stability of the monarchy or republic.

[49] *Pensée* 1268 (Bkn. 598); Nagel II, p. 348, Pléiade I, p. 1127.
[50] *Pensée* 1269 (Bkn. 618); Nagel II, pp. 348–349, Pléiade I, p. 1143.

This ideal of patriotic virtue is strongly reflected in several minor essays related to the *Devoirs*. Montesquieu embodies it in particular in the character of Xanthippus, the Spartan hero of his *Dialogue de Xantippe et de Xénocrate* (1727), who puts duty to mankind before any purely national allegiance, and seeks happiness and honour only in exact obedience to the laws of his country. Taking a realistic look at a subject much nearer to the hearts of his contemporaries, *De la Considération et de la Réputation* (1725), he still insists, if in a somewhat wry tone, that virtue is the surest means to conserve a reputation, and will even compensate for its loss, and that love of our fellow citizens is the very best means of acquiring one.

Whether loving one's fellow citizens is actually feasible, however, or consists in anything more positive than the remote, paternalistic benevolence which emerges from the pages of this essay is another question. In the *Devoirs* he concedes that for practical purposes, friendship is the main and regrettably partial form which this love takes.[51]

If men were perfectly virtuous, they would indeed have no friends, for they would cherish a total stranger as their dearest friend, having no need of external tokens or emotional props, as long as they were sustained by their sense of community. But men are not made of such stuff, neither is it physically possible to know all one's fellow citizens; therefore, after the fulfilment of civic duty, which we know Montesquieu regarded as the special province of reason, friendship, defined as a kind of sub-contract with a select group of citizens, constitutes the second among particular virtues, and the highest affective form of the social bond:[52]

"... ces liens qui détachent l'homme de lui-même pour l'attacher à autrui faisaient faire les grandes actions. Sans cela tout est vulgaire, et il ne reste qu'un intérêt bas, qui n'est proprement que l'instinct animal de tous les hommes."[53]

Friendship was of course the great strength of the Romans, and Montesquieu does not overlook the opportunity to digress upon its central importance to the constitution of their government, which inevitably leads him back to the perennial subject of the decay of

---

[51] *Pensée* 1253 (Bkn. 604).

[52] On the evidence of a comment on Fénelon's *Explication des Maximes des Saints sur la Vie intérieure* (1697), it is perhaps surprising that Montesquieu did not also politicize love:

"Je disais: 'Le livre de M. de Cambrai détruit en trois mots: l'amour est un rapport.'" *Pensée* 1054 (Bkn. 902), Nagel II, p. 290; Pléiade I, p. 1247.

[53] *Pensée* 1253 (Bkn. 604); Nagel II, p. 334, Pléiade I, p. 1130.

contemporary morals, but presented this time with a significant political twist:

"Les citoyens tenaient aux citoyens par toutes sortes de chaînes: on était lié avec ses amis, ses affranchis, ses esclaves, ses enfants. Aujourd'hui, tout est aboli jusqu'à la puissance paternelle: chaque homme est isolé. Il semble que l'effet naturel de la puissance arbitraire soit de particulariser tous les intérêts."[54]

This analysis of political degeneracy in terms of the isolation of individuals within the community, of the breaking of all social bonds, anticipates the major features with which Montesquieu endows the despotism in the *Lois*.[55] Indeed, as the logic of his original definition of virtue would demand, he seems to have regarded the breakdown of social relationships on every level as the main symptom of decadence. Thus in a *rejet* from the *Lois* he notes that the word which characterizes the good republic where high moral standards prevail, is *nous*, as opposed to the *moi* typical of the monarchy.[56] Describing in his *Réflexions sur le Caractère de quelques Princes* (1731–3), the state of affairs leading to civil war which religious fanaticism often induces, he again has recourse to such terms:

"C'est pour lors que tous les esprits sont outrés; que les intérêts de l'État sont sacrifiés au succès de l'idée de chacun, qu'il ne reste plus de liens dans la société que ceux d'une haine et d'une fureur commune; que les gens les plus faibles s'emparent du pouvoir pour mettre à leur tête les plus fourbes qui se présentent; que toute extravagance est écoutée, et que l'hypocrisie prend la place des moeurs, des vertus et des lois."[57]

And in yet another *rejet* from the *Lois*, under the stern heading *Moeurs Corrompues* he sums up the lot of the honest man living in a corrupt society in the same vein:

"C'est pour lors qu'un honnête homme passe sa vie dans une espèce d'étonnement; qu'il est, pour ainsi dire, seul dans le monde; que tous les liens d'humanité l'effarouchent, parce qu'il ne trouve aucun homme dont il voulût être le protecteur, aucun homme sociable qu'il voulût avoir pour ami, aucune femme dont il voulût être le mari, aucun enfant dont il voulût être le père."[58]

But although Montesquieu's *honnête homme* would not feel out of place dressed in a tunic or toga, his austerity is moderated by his creator's

---

[54] *Pensée* 1253 (Bkn. 604); Nagel II, p. 334, Pléiade I, p. 1130.
[55] See especially Book IV, ch. 3.
[56] *Pensée* 1891 (Bkn. 233).
[57] Nagel III, p. 549; Pléiade I, pp. 529–530.
[58] *Pensée* 1921 (Bkn. 327); Nagel II, p. 576; Pléiade II, p. 1078.

sophisticated intelligence. His sociological insight into politics in general enables him to appreciate the manners which foster and facilitate the practice of virtue. Thus his emphasis on *bienséance* seems less a homage to Antiquity than an admission of the need to reconcile, if not to adapt, the inflexible ideal to the ever changing character of nations. As he concedes in the *Devoirs*:

"telle est la disposition des choses et des esprits dans une nation polie qu'un homme, quelque vertueux qu'il fût, s'il n'avait dans l'esprit que la rudesse, serait presque incapable de tout bien et ne pourrait qu'en très peu d'occasions mettre sa vertu en pratique."[59]

In the *Discours sur l'Équité, bienséance* is presented as an integral part of justice, but it is in the *Devoirs* that Montesquieu explains how and why. In addition to justice and honesty, men demand from their close associates deference, attention, affection and understanding:

"Il y a donc certains devoirs différents de ceux qui viennent directement de la justice et ces devoirs sont fondés sur la bienséance et ne dérivent de la justice qu'en ce sens qu'il est juste, en général que les hommes aient des égards les uns pour les autres, non seulement dans les choses qui peuvent leur rendre la société plus utile, mais aussi dans celles qui peuvent la leur rendre plus agréable."[60]

The kind of behaviour that we demand from our closest fellows should be the model for our manners towards all others, the only limit to the duties of politeness and civility being regard for our own probity. As a result of fulfilling them, social intercourse is greatly facilitated and general happiness and contentment consequently increased.

Manners always take the form of an external and rigid ceremonial,

"une espèce de code de lois non écrites que les hommes ont promis d'observer entre eux";

and as such, he explains elsewhere, they clearly derive from the communal rather than the individual conscience,[61] although they utilize to general advantage, the egotism which would otherwise undermine social stability.[62] The ceremonial varies however in form and complexity from nation to nation, ranging from the scant and rudimentary customs of barbarian peoples to the tyrannic rituals of the Chinese.[63]

---

[59] *Pensée* 1270 (Bkn. 619); Nagel II, p. 350; Pléiade I, p. 1145.
[60] *Op. cit.*, Nagel II, pp. 349–350; Pléiade I, pp. 1144–1145.
[61] *Pensée* 1904 (Bkn. 334).
[62] *Pensée* 464 (Bln. 1042).
[63] *Pensée* 1271 (Bkn. 620).

For Montesquieu happiness in general was linked in a most intimate way to the pursuit of virtue and the fulfilment of duty.[64] The idyllic condition of his virtuous Troglodytes is proof enough of this, and elsewhere one encounters scattered aphorisms on this subject which clearly reflect the idea of reciprocity at the heart of his definition of justice. In *Arsace et Isménie* for example, the hero describes the true happiness which reigned in his household in terms of the reverence for, and active enjoyment of natural equality:

"Nous descendions avec plaisir à l'égalité de la nature; nous étions heureux, et nous voulions vivre avec des gens qui le fussent. Le bonheur faux rend les hommes durs et superbes, et ce bonheur ne se communique point. Le vrai bonheur les rend doux et sensibles, et ce bonheur se partage toujours."[65]

Arsace's advice is echoed in the *Pensées*: neither the winged horse of Ariosto, nor yet the ring whose wearer may pass unseen would bring a man more happiness, unless he also possessed the shield which turns all other men to stone; "pour être heureux," in short, "il ne faut pas désirer de l'être plus que les autres."[66]

Truth, no less than the pursuit of justice and the safeguarding of communal prosperity and individual contentment, is, in Montesquieu's eyes, an important object of virtue. In the *Éloge de la Sincérité* (1717) he disputes the efficacy of the method of self-examination recommended by the Stoics for acquiring self-knowledge, on the grounds that self-esteem invariably constitutes an insurmountable obstacle to impartial self-appraisal. Consequently, in the discovery of truth, as in every aspect of moral life, men are interdependent; as members of society,

---

[64] For a full account of the relation between Montesquieu's conception of happiness and his moral idealism see M. W. Rombout, *La Conception stoïcienne du bonheur chez Montesquieu et chez quelques-uns de ses contemporains*, Leiden, 1958; Part III. In his *L'idée du bonheur dans la littérature et la pensée française au XVIIIe siècle*, Armand Colin, Paris, 1960, R. Mauzi studies Montesquieu's account of the experience of happiness rather than his ideas on the moral conditions which favour it. However, the conception of happiness summarized in the following comment upon Maupertuis's *Essai de Philosophie Morale* (1751), as the enjoyment of habitual wellbeing rather than transitory pleasure, accords well with his insistence on the fulfilment of duties as the necessary prerequisite for happiness:

"M. de Maupertuis ne fait entrer dans son calcul que les plaisirs et les peines, c'est-à-dire tout ce qui avertit l'âme de son bonheur ou de son malheur. Il ne fait point entrer le bonheur de l'existence et la félicité habituelle, qui n'avertit de rien, parce qu'elle est habituelle. Nous n'appelons *plaisir* que ce qui n'est pas habituel. Si nous avions continuellement le plaisir de manger avec appétit, nous n'appellerions pas cela un *plaisir*; ce serait *existence et nature*. Il ne faut pas dire que le bonheur est ce moment que nous ne voudrions pas changer pour un autre. Disons autrement: le bonheur est ce moment que nous ne voudrions pas changer pour le non-être." *Pensée* 2010 (Bkn. 994); Nagel II, pp. 620–621; Pléiade I, p. 1267.

[65] Nagel III, p. 488; Pléiade I, p. 471.

[66] *Pensée* 2046 (Bkn. 1004).

they have a duty to reveal all faults and shortcomings to each other, a duty of honest sincerity:

"Les hommes, vivant dans la société n'ont point eu cet avantage sur les bêtes pour se procurer les moyens de vivre plus délicieusement. Dieu a voulu qu'ils vécussent en commun pour se servir de guide les uns aux autres, pour qu'ils pussent voir par les yeux d'autrui ce que leur amour-propre leur cache, et qu'enfin, par un commerce sacré de confiance, ils pussent se dire et se rendre la vérité." [67]

The theme of sincerity reappears in the *Devoirs*, albeit in a slightly different form. Just as men have a duty to reveal the truth to each other, so they also bear an obligation to judge their forbears; with this in mind, Montesquieu sings the praises of historians, and recommends the reading of history, particularly national history. This he sees not so much after the Classical tradition as a study of morals in itself, than as a tribute to those heroes whose good example has encouraged virtue, and a punishment or condemnation of the wicked. Thus the publication of historical truth could be compared to the administration of justice, just as the virtue of sincerity was deemed indispensable for its practice:

"Le sentiment d'admiration que leurs belles actions excitent en nous est une espèce de justice que nous leur rendons, et l'horreur que nous avons pour les méchants en est une autre. Il n'est pas juste d'accorder aux méchants l'oubli de leur nom et de laisser les grands hommes dans ce même oubli que les méchants ont paru souhaiter." [68]

As regards the actual acquisition and propagation of virtue, Montesquieu naturally sets great store by example and education. The virtuous Troglodytes of the *Lettres Persanes* devote the whole of their attention to inculcating, through precept and the example of their wretched forebears, the notion of the absolute priority of justice into the heads of their children. [69] Example is a most powerful moral agent, whether for good or for evil, as Usbek's ominous portrayal in Letter CXLVI of the pestilential corruption with which John Law's financial manipulations infected France, eloquently demonstrates:

"J'y ai vu une nation, naturellement généreuse, pervertie en un instant, depuis le dernier des sujets jusqu'aux plus grands, par le mauvais exemple d'un ministre ... le mal se communiquer, et n'épargner pas même les membres les plus sains; les hommes les plus vertueux faire des choses indignes; et violer les premiers principes de la justice, sur ce vain prétexte qu'on la leur avait violée." [70]

---

[67] Nagel III, pp. 60–61; Pléiade I, p. 100.
[68] *Pensée* 1260 (Bkn .611); Nagel II, p. 337; Pléiade I, p. 1133.
[69] Letter XII.
[70] Nagel I, p. 307; Pléiade I, p. 361.

With characteristic psychological penetration, Montesquieu saw that reason alone, although equipping us to grasp first principles and supporting argumentation, was insufficiently strong to combat the pernicious influence of such bad examples:[71]

"il y a certaines vérités qu'il ne suffit pas de persuader, mais qu'il faut encore faire sentir. Telles sont les vérités de morale."[72]

Consequently he returns again and again to the important rôle not just of emotional response to moral ideas, but more especially of the development of this response into an ingrained habit. In the early *Pensées Morales* he explains that the best way to acquire a perfect sense of justice is to make a habit of observing it in the slightest things – "qu'on y plie jusqu'à sa manière de penser." The faculty of judgement can be excercised on subjects not necessarily connected with morals or society, since any kind of practice prepares it for more important decisions.[73] According to the *compte rendu*, this recommendation was later incorporated into the *Devoirs*, but for an account of the results of such therapy, one must go back to Rica's eulogy in *Lettres Persanes* L of those people,

"chez qui la vertu était si naturelle qu'elle ne se faisait pas même sentir: ils s'attachaient à leur devoir sans s'y plier et s'y portaient comme par instinct."[74]

The ideal of spontaneous perfection presented here, anticipating the special qualities which distinguish the "homme d'esprit" in the *Essai sur les Causes*:

"(il) connaît et agit de la manière momentanée dont il faut qu'il connaisse et qu'il agisse; il se crée pour ainsi dire, à chaque instant, sur le besoin actuel,"[75]

has a certain affinity with the peculiarly Stoic concept of *decorum*, the virtue in which the notions of propriety and grace are combined.[76] *Decorum* characterized the external aspect of human conduct in so far as it revealed its internal excellence; and when it is considered in conjunction with the theory of *persona*, of the special rôle which,

---

[71] See above pp. 155–157.
[72] *Lettres Persanes* XI; Nagel I, p. 26; Pléiade I, p. 145.
[73] *Pensée* 220 (Bkn. 597).
[74] Nagel I, p. 100; Pléiade I, p. 203.
[75] Nagel III, p. 418; Pléiade II, p. 57. See above p. 239.
[76] For the origins of this notion and its definition in Cicero's *De Officiis*, see E. Bréhier, *Études de Philosophie Antique*, P.U.F., Paris, 1955, XIV, "Sur une des origines de l'humanisme moderne: le *De Officiis* de Cicéron."

according to the Stoics, each individual played in the scheme of things by virtue of his particular attributes, the presence of a notion akin to Montesquieu's idea of perfect integrity effortlessly expressed in individual conduct is revealed.

This resemblance is hardly surprising in view of the many tributes to Stoicism which he contrived to include in his works,[77] and of his special enthusiasm for Cicero in particular.[78] It is true that in the case of the *Traité des Devoirs*, some doubt has been expressed as to the significance, if not the reliability, of Montesquieu's own account of his models in his letter of October 1750 to Monsignor de Fitz-James.[79] Shackleton suggests that analysis of the surviving fragments of the essay points to Pufendorf's short treatise, *De Officio Hominis*, in Barbeyrac's French translation, *Les Devoirs de l'Homme et du Citoyen*, rather than to Cicero's *De Officiis*, as his chief guide.[80] Nevertheless, even in the *Devoirs*, although there is no trace of the Ciceronian plan, Montesquieu refers specifically to his definition of *honestas*,[81] and touches on several of the moral attributes included in the *De Officiis*. While he naturally treats Cicero's abstractions in terms relevant to contemporary society, in essence, the nobility of mind, modesty in deportment and appointments, gravity of disposition and fidelity in formal relationships, which he recommends,[82] are the same *dignitas, frugalitas, gravitas* and *fides*, that grace the Stoic pantheon. Beyond this, the portrait of the republic, sustained by virtue, or by that kind of patriotism defined as love of the laws, of equality and of frugality, which emerges from the early books of the *Lois*,[83] constituting, in spite of the emphatic declaration in the *Avertissement* that conventional virtue has nothing to do with the "vertu politique" which he intends to treat, a great syn-

---

[77] See for example, *Analyse du Traité des Devoirs*, Nagel III, p. 160; Pléiade I, p. 109; and *Lois* XXIV, 10.

[78] See above pp. 122–124.

[79] See above p. 146.

[80] See *op. cit.*, above (p. 9 n. 3), pp. 71–72; and Shackleton, "La Genèse de l'*Esprit des Lois*," RHLF, 1952.

[81] *Pensée* 1263 (Bkn. 613).

[82] See *Pensées* 1256 (Bkn. 607); 1257 (Bkn. 608); 1262 (Bkn. 543); 1251 (Bkn. 602).

[83] See especially Books IV, ch. 5 and V, ch. 3. At various times Montesquieu expressed a strong attachment to the ideal of economic equality, although he maintains that its existence in a monarchy is contrary to the moral principle of this form of government. The theory of distributive justice hardly preoccupies him in his moral writings, but certain isolated references to equality stand out; e.g. *Lettres Persanes* CXXII:

"L'égalité même des citoyens, qui produit ordinairement de l'égalité dans les fortunes, porte l'abondance et la vie dans toutes parties du corps politique et la répand partout." (Nagel I, p. 244; Pléiade I, p. 313) and *Pensée* 2084 (Bkn. 1130):

"Les richesses sont un tort que l'on a à réparer, et l'on pourrait dire: 'Excusez-moi si je suis riche'." (Nagel II, p. 638; Pléiade I, p. 1290.)

thesis of the themes scattered through Montesquieu's moral writings, immortalizes the spirit of Antiquity of which Stoicism was the quintessential expression.

III

A nostalgic adaptation of the moral ideals of Antiquity was far from being the only form in which Montesquieu's love of justice found expression. Although his field of study in the *Lois* was positive law rather than theoretical jurisprudence, details of legislation and established institutions are sometimes judged as well as explained,[84] and judged with humanitarian as well as utilitarian considerations in mind. Indeed these two seem to overlap each other to a certain extent, though the overlap is not just attributable to the age-old assumption by which the virtuous Troglodytes set so much store: "la justice pour autrui est une charité pour nous," but rather to Montesquieu's profound conviction that the pursuit of justice is the natural end of rational beings, and its realization essential to the conservation of any society worthy of the name. Injustice survives, even becomes institutionalized in despotism, but the tranquillity of this state, he reminds us, is that of a city awaiting the sack of the enemy.[85] There are few exceptions indeed to the general rule tacked on to a reference in the *Considérations* to Carthaginian oppression in Spain:

"L'injustice est mauvaise ménagère . . . elle ne remplit pas même ses vues."[86]

One of the most striking examples of Montesquieu's refusal at all times to take refuge in a nice scientific impartiality, is his treatment of the related topics of the right of conquest and the institution of slavery.[87]

---

[84] In the *Défense de l'Esprit des Lois*, (2e partie), he declares openly that his purpose was to do both:
"On peut dire que le sujet en est immense, qu'il embrasse toutes les institutions qui sont reçues parmi les hommes; puisque l'auteur distingue ces institutions . . . qu'il en cherche l'origine; qu'il en découvre les causes physiques et morales; qu'il examine celles qui ont un degré de bonté par elles-mêmes, et celles qui n'en ont aucun . . ." Nagel I, p. 456; Pléiade II, p. 1137.
[85] *Lois* V, 14. Montesquieu's treatment of despotism is the subject of an exhaustive study by B. Kassem, *Décadence et Absolutisme dans l'Oeuvre de Montesquieu*, Études d'Histoire économique, politique et sociale, XXXIV, Droz, Geneva and Paris, 1960.
[86] Chapter 4; Nagel I, p. 374; Pléiade II, pp. 86–87.
[87] Montesquieu's treatment of slavery has been dealt with at some length by R. P. Jameson in his thesis entitled *Montesquieu et l'Esclavage, étude sur les origines de l'opinion anti-esclavagiste en France au XVIIIe siècle*, Paris, 1911. Though some points of his interpretation of Montesquieu's theories are debatable, the work is valuable for its review of traditional juridical sources,

On the evidence of the *Lettres Persanes* his hostility to both accepted theories and the practices they legitimized had early beginnings. In Letter xcv he sets out the principles which in his estimation should govern international law, supplanting the politics of prestige and aggrandizement commonly pursued. They issue from the premiss that the rules appropriate to this field of relationships are basically no different from those which apply to civil law. Thus parallel to the individual citizen's right of self-defence, nations may have recourse to war when they are threatened by an aggressor. The only just war is the defensive war, and Montesquieu is at pains to show that even this is an extreme resort:

"comme la déclaration de guerre doit être un acte de justice, dans laquelle il faut toujours que la peine soit proportionnée à la faute, il faut voir si celui à qui on déclare la guerre mérite la mort: car faire la guerre à quelqu'un, c'est vouloir le punir de mort."[88]

If, as in civil law, the punishment is to fit the crime, then offences which carry no threat to the very existence of a nation, merit reprisals on a lesser scale, such as the curtailment of concessions and agreements, or the severance of alliances.

Finally, Montesquieu declares that conquest in itself confers no rights, for it effectively dissolves the defeated society, and the victor himself can only establish tyranny in place of government. Peace treaties are just only when the reparations imposed are in proportion to the losses suffered; otherwise the party attached by their clauses is entitled to seek redress in further violence.[89]

Book X of the *Lois*, *Des lois dans le rapport qu'elles ont avec la force offensive* proceeds from exactly the same assumption as Letter xcv, namely that the principles governing the lives of states are analogous to those governing the lives of men; similarly, Montesquieu's target is yet again those great blood-letting pretexts,

"les principes arbitraires de gloire, de bienséance, d'utilité".

As before he isolates the defensive war as the sole legitimate form of violence, but brackets with it a sub-species, arising indirectly from the

---

and for its thorough examination of the economic and moral climate in which Montesquieu wrote.

[88] Nagel I, p. 189; Pléiade I, p. 271.

[89] In the 1721 editions. The supplement to the 1754 edition introduced a new conclusion, more closely related to the text of *Lois*, X, 3. It replaces the valid but inconsequential assertion of the earlier version, that conquest dissolves the vanquished society, with the much more powerful idea that the survival of the defeated nation is, in itself, a guarantee of redress.

right of self-defence, the preventive war, undertaken to pre-empt attack by a threatening neighbour.

Here however, unlike Letter xcv, Montesquieu identifies the origin of the right of war. Like the citizen's right of self-defence, it arises in the natural law of conservation. Now "natural law" is apparently used here as a generic term embracing all those fundamental unwritten laws originating in human attributes of thought and feeling, by which man regulates and therefore perpetuates his existence as a social being; for the specific origin of the right of war lies in the notion of parity between subjects, generally held to be an essential element of any valid conception of justice. Though strictly speaking absent from Montesquieu's own definition of justice, here it is precisely this element which constitutes his criterion.

"Dans le cas de la défense naturelle, j'ai droit de tuer, parce que ma vie est à moi, comme la vie de celui qui m'attaque est à lui : de même un État fait la guerre, parce que sa conservation est juste comme toute autre conservation."[90]

The logic of parity can be seen at work also in his restriction of the right of engaging in preventive war to small nations; since their size renders them naturally insecure, the possession of this right to some extent restores the balance between them and their more powerful neighbours.

Montesquieu concludes that the right of war, as he defines it, derives from necessity and rigid justice, and his arguments certainly recall the idea expressed in book I, chapter 1 of invariable rules of justice, describing the basic relationships of social beings, upon whose observance political and moral survival ultimately depend.

As far as the right of conquest is concerned, in book X chapter 3, after insisting that, as a direct consequence of the right of war, it must also follow its spirit, Montesquieu enumerates four kinds of law which govern it:

". . . la loi de la nature, qui fait que tout tend à la conservation des espèces; la loi de la lumière naturelle, qui veut que nous fassions à autrui ce que nous voudrions qu'on nous fît; la loi qui forme les sociétés politiques, qui sont telles que la nature n'en a point borné la durée; enfin la loi tirée de la chose même. La conquête est une acquisition; l'esprit d'acquisition porte avec lui l'esprit de conservation et d'usage, et non pas celui de destruction."[91]

---

[90] Book X, ch. 2; Nagel I, p. 182; Pléiade II, p. 377.
[91] Nagel I, p. 184; Pléiade II, p. 378.

Here Montesquieu confirms the distinction implicit in chapter 2 between the law of nature understood as the body of original or primitive laws, whose function viewed from the standpoint of a sociologist, is indeed "la conservation des espèces," and the law of reason, or indeed of justice,

"qui veut que nous fassions à autrui ce que nous voudrions qu'on nous fît,"

whose effects could be grouped, if that standpoint were maintained, among the natural laws, but which is now considered, not scientifically, but morally, as a precept, from the standpoint of the rational being actively involved in the social predicament. The third kind of law which he cites, the law governing the formation of political societies, seems but a particular version, historical perhaps, of the natural law of conservation isolated by the scientist; while in the fourth, the curious "loi tirée de la chose même," he seems to isolate yet another, still more specific instance, namely one of the basic psychological principles at work within the social consciousness. This is perhaps no more than a scientific version of what the moralist would doubtless see in terms of the application if the rational principle of fitness.

Of these four different kinds of law, which, one feels, really represent four different ways in which the subject may be approached, the one he relies on most heavily for his demolition of the traditional account of the right of conquest, is the "loi de la lumière naturelle," the law which harks back to the rigid law of justice upon which he founded the principles of the right of war in the foregoing chapter.

His argument against the jurisconsults:

"Ils ont donné dans l'arbitraire; ils ont supposé dans les conquérants un droit, je ne sais quel, de tuer: ce qui leur a fait tirer des conséquences terribles comme le principe, et établir des maximes que les conquérants eux-mêmes, lorsqu'ils ont eu le moindre sens, n'ont jamais prises," [92]

starts from the assertion that they generally confused the dissolution of a society with the annihilation of its members; but, Montesquieu objects:

"La société est l'union des hommes, et non pas les hommes; le citoyen peut périr et l'homme rester." [93]

The right to destroy the conquered nation has no foundation in any law, for quite clearly killing is only justified as long as the necessity of

[92] Nagel I, pp. 184–185; Pléiade II, p. 379.
[93] *Ibid.*

engaging in defensive war persists; the conqueror, as opposed to the combattant, is no longer fighting for his life and consequently on an equal footing with his antagonist.

With the right to kill, the right to reduce the vanquished to slavery, usually considered as a legitimate and humane alternative, falls also. Montesquieu is of the opinion, an opinion which reveals his sociological awareness of the effects of defeat on national character, as well as his humanitarian concern, that slavery is only ever legitimate as a means of facilitating the preservation of the defeated nation by allowing it a space of time to adapt to the victor's habits and culture. The onus, he believes, and here one notes a distinct change of emphasis from *Lettres Persanes* xcv, where the conqueror's right to reparation was tacitly conceded, lies always with the victor to emancipate his victims. In chapter 4, indeed, indulging his idealism, he elaborates on those advantages in the way of moral regeneration, political renewal, enlightenment and even freedom, which the right of conquest, properly used, can bring, concluding unequivocally:

"C'est à un conquérant à réparer une partie des maux qu'il a faits. Je définis ainsi le droit de conquête: un droit nécessaire, légitime et malheureux, qui laisse toujours à payer une dette immense, pour s'acquitter envers la nature humaine." [94]

In his later treatment in book XV of the institution of slavery itself, the rôle played by moral idealism and the logic of his idea of justice is if anything even more striking, though at the same time also more ambiguous.

The theoretical and polemical half of the book, is largely a reworking of materials drawn from the *Pensées* and the *Lettres Persanes*. The last of these is, of course, from beginning to end a wholehearted condemnation in allegorical form of domestic slavery, whose laws, as implemented in Usbek's harem, are overthrown by Roxane in the name of freedom and nature.[95] It also contains explicit attacks on the political and civil slavery resulting from conquest and maintained for the purposes of colonial exploitation, together with the associated trade in Negroes promoted by the need to replenish the stock of slave labour.[96] In them, the iniquities of the Spanish conquest of South America, ever at the front of his mind when examples of barbarism, religious

[94] Nagel I, p. 188; Pléiade II, p. 381.
[95] Letter CLXI.
[96] See Letters LXXV, CXVIII, CXXI.

bigotry, Christian hypocrisy, and economic madness were called for,[97] rather than the methods used in developing the West Indian sugar colonies, methods in which the merchants and shipowners of Bordeaux were deeply involved, are singled out:

"Il n'y a rien de si extravagant que de faire périr un nombre innombrable d'hommes pour tirer du fond de la terre l'or et l'argent: ces métaux d'eux-mêmes absolument inutiles, et qui ne sont des richesses que parce qu'on les a choisis pour en être les signes." [98]

In addition to the barbarous injustice of transportation and slave labour, Montesquieu objects to the sheer waste of human life involved, yet surprisingly, it is the theme of depopulation which occasions his one favourable comment on the institution. The Romans and their benevolence towards slaves are, less surprisingly, the subject of his enthusiasm. In Letter cxv he praises the laws which, he imagines, by assuring Roman slaves of a secure, even comfortable living, and a fair chance of rapid emancipation, provided the republic with an inexhaustible supply of citizens and wealth. However, the favourable impression left by the Romans was to prove shortlived; the *Considérations* brought a complete reversal of attitude:

"Les Romains, accoutumés à se jouer de la nature humaine, dans la personne de leurs enfants et de leurs esclaves, ne pouvaient guère connaître cette vertu que nous appelons humanité. D'où peut venir cette férocité que nous trouvons dans les habitants de nos colonies, que de cet usage continuel des châtiments sur une malheureuse partie du genre humain? Lorsqu'on est cruel dans l'état civil, que peut-on attendre de la douceur et de la justice naturelle?" [99]

A vivid and fiercely rhetorical fragment from the *Dossier* of this work reveals an even harsher judgement:

"Les Romains avaient une manière de penser qui distingait entièrement les esclaves des hommes.

Ils les faisaient combattre contre les bêtes farouches. Ils s'en servaient comme des gladiateurs et les obligeaient pour leurs plaisirs de s'entredétruire. Ils les mettaient la nuit dans des fosses, où ils les faisaient descendre, et, ensuite, retiraient l'échelle qui les avait descendus. Ils les mettaient à mort à leur fantaisie. Lorsque le maître avait été tué dans la maison, on menait au supplice tous les esclaves, coupables ou non, en quelque nombre qu'ils fussent. Lorsqu'ils étaient malades ou vieux, ils les abandonnaient et

[97] See also for example *Pensée* 1268 (Bkn. 617); *Considérations sur les Richesses de l'Espagne* (1726–27); *Lois* X, 4 and XXI, 22.
[98] Letter cxviii; Nagel I, p. 237; Pléiade I, p. 307.
[99] Chapter XV; Nagel I, p. 451; Pléiade II, p. 148.

les faisaient porter au temple d'Esculape. Ils les privaient de tous les sentiments naturels les plus chers: ils les privaient de la vertu de leurs femmes, de
la chasteté de leurs filles, de la propriété de leurs enfants.

Pourquoi dégrader une partie de la nature humaine? Pourquoi se faire
des ennemis naturels? Pourquoi diminuer le nombre de ses citoyens? Pourquoi en avoir qui ne seront retenus que par la crainte?

Guerre servile! La plus juste qui ait jamais été entreprise, parce qu'elle
voulait empêcher le plus violent abus que l'on ait jamais fait de la nature
humaine."[100]

The actual material of debate which in *Lois* XV gives substance to
this moral indignation is to be found in an early entry in the *Pensées*.[101]
Here, he is solely concerned to demonstrate the logical incompatibility
of traditional expositions of the right of slavery with his idea of natural
law, by which he declares, all men are born free and independent.[102]

In his view only two kinds of dependence are compatible with
natural law: that of infants, and that of citizens upon their magistrates.
His explanation of the latter confirms that once again the initial basis
of his reasoning is a conception of natural law as the summary of those
processes by which human beings conserve themselves. For he founds
the legitimacy of civic dependence on the notion that anarchy is
contrary to natural law, since anarchy conduces to the destruction
rather than preservation of mankind. This amounts more or less to a
restatement of the idea of the natural origins of society, and brings to
mind the fourth natural law of book I, chapter 2 of the *Lois*.

Slavery has nothing in common with the natural dependence of
citizens upon their magistrates; it is illegitimate, because it has no
legitimate cause. The first argument put forward by the Roman
jurisconsults in its defence, namely that a man might sell his own
freedom, falls down because such a civil contract obviously violates the
original laws of human freedom and rationality. In addition, the
transaction which it embodies is manifestly unjust, since by the cession
of his person and his goods to the master, the slave in effect loses any
theoretical payment he may have received. It also cancels itself
automatically, for a slave can neither make nor be bound by any form
of contract; thus, all in all, it is absurd to suppose that men who are

---

[100] *Pensée* 2194 (Bkn. 171); Nagel II, p. 659; Pléiade II, p. 220.

[101] *Pensée* 174 (Bkn. 1935); in volume I, probably entered before 1728.

[102] Here and in *Lois* XV, 2, Montesquieu singles out Roman jurisprudence for attack.
But, as Jameson points out, (*op. cit.*, (p. 278 n. 87) 1, 4) in the *Institutes* (Bk. I, tit. 3, para. ii)
slavery is described as an institution of conventional law, subjecting one man to the domination of another, but *against natural law*. Its justification lies in the right of conquest, (para. iii).

naturally citizens can enter into a contract whose self-invalidating conditions involve the loss of their citizenship.

Against the second of the traditional justifications, the argument from the right of conquest, Montesquieu presents the same reasons as were later incorporated into book X of the *Lois*, summed up here in a comparison between the act of reducing the vanquished to slavery and the murders in cold blood committed by looting soldiers. The third justification, the argument that children may be born into slavery, is, he maintains, as fallacious as the others, and falls for identical reasons; if a man cannot sell himself nor a prisoner of war loose his freedom, still less can their unborn children.

In short, the institution of slavery flies in the face of all the laws by which men organize and conserve their existence, either as simple human beings, or as citizens; and appropriately, Montesquieu sums up his demolition of the arguments in its favour by comparing its function with that of all other institutions of society. To represent them, he takes a law which superficially at least, embodies the harshest penalty that society can inflict, and which in spirit seems completely counter to the principle of conservation. But this law, the law that punishes a murderer with death, in fact favours its subject in a way which the law of slavery never favours the slave. The criminal's death is just because the same law that condemns him has previously protected and sustained him. The same cannot be said for the law of slavery, always disadvantageous for the slave, which, Montesquieu avers, perfectly justifies flight or any other means the oppressed may employ to regain their liberty. The slave is outside society, unprotected and, therefore, unconstrained by civil law.

The dialectic of *Pensée* 174 is incorporated almost down to its last detail in chapter 2 of book XV. Montesquieu even carefully transcribes such clever points as his *reductio ad absurdum* of the argument that the transaction between master and slave must be valid since the latter is fed and kept in return for renouncing his freedom. Logically, one should then restrict slavery to those incapable of earning their own living,

"mais on ne veut pas de ces esclaves-là".

In chapter 1 he makes the additional point, carried over from *Lettres Persanes* xxxiv and the passages from the *Considérations* denouncing the barbarous way in which the Romans abused their slaves, that the practice of slavery is morally corrupting. The master looses all his virtue, while the slave, deprived of his citizenship, and therefore, it is understood, of his liberty and humanity, is rendered incapable of acting virtuously. Chapters 3, 4 and 5 are devoted to an ironical treatment of the other "origins of the laws of slavery," which Montesquieu without much difficulty isolates as racialism, religious bigotry, greed and luxury, and colour prejudice. Chapter 5 in particular is a masterly parody of conventional apologies for white dominance:

"Si j'avais à soutenir le droit que nous avons eu de rendre les nègres esclaves, voici ce que je dirais: ...
Ceux dont il s'agit sont noirs depuis les pieds jusqu'à la tête; et ils ont le nez si écrasé qu'il est presque impossible de les plaindre.
On ne peut se mettre dans l'esprit que Dieu, qui est un être très sage, ait mis une âme, surtout une âme bonne, dans un corps tout noir ...
Il est impossible que nous supposions que ces gens-là soient des hommes; parce que, si nous les supposons des hommes, on commencerait à croire que nous ne sommes pas nous-mêmes des chrétiens..."[103]

But if half of this book is so obviously inspired by the conviction that:

"Les connaissances rendent les hommes doux; la raison porte à l'humanité: il n'y a que les préjugés qui y fassent renoncer,"[104]

what is one to make of the completely serious volte-face with which we are presented in chapter 6? Without a trace of irony Montesquieu concedes in his very first sentence that slavery does indeed possess a true origin, and adds that it must be founded on the nature of things which he intends to examine. The manuscript version continues ominously,

"et par là nous verrons s'il y a des cas où il n'était pas contraire au Droit civil, et s'il y en a où il n'était point opposé au Droit naturel."[105]

One wonders what has become of the categorical assertion of *Pensée* 174:

"Pour le droit des maîtres, il n'est point légitime, parce qu'il ne peut point avoir eu une cause légitime."[106]

If the nature of things serves to justify slavery, what becomes of the elaborate condemnation built on principles reached by a careful consideration of the nature of men as rational, social creatures, whose observance Montesquieu, acutely aware of the importance of morals in

[103] Nagel I, pp. 330–331; Pléiade II, p. 494.
[104] Chapter 3; Nagel I, p. 329; Pléiade II, p. 493.
[105] *De l'Esprit des Lois*, ed. J. Brethe de la Gressaye, vol. II, Paris, 1955, p. 415, note 29.
[106] Nagel II, p. 57; Pléiade I, p. 1467.

the life of a people, also saw as an essential prerequisite not only of individual fulfilment, but of national survival?

The nature of things in fact provides Montesquieu with only two causes which in his estimation would justify the institution of slavery. These "natural" causes are the state to which a despotism reduces its subjects, and the moral repercussions of the enervating physical effect of hot climates. In the despotism, political servitude to all intents and purposes automatically entails the destruction of civil liberty; for the subjects, deprived by the régime of the spiritual and material advantages, the freedom and security of true citizenship, are only too ready to sell themselves in the hope of thereby enjoying at least a semblance of the benefits denied them:

"Dans ces États, les hommes libres, trop faibles contre le gouvernement, cherchent à devenir les esclaves de ceux qui tyrannisent le gouvernement.

C'est là l'origine juste, et conforme à la raison, de ce droit d'esclavage très doux que l'on trouve dans quelques pays; et il doit être doux parce qu'il est fondé sur le choix libre qu'un homme, pour son utilité, se fait d'un maître; ce qui forme une convention réciproque entre les deux parties."[107]

In torrid climates, slavery is much more crudely, the only means of forcing the demoralized inhabitants to work.[108]

What is to be made of the apparent abdication of his moral stance for a position beyond even the studied impartiality of the true scientific observer?

First of all, the contradiction between one of the justifications which he slips into chapter 6 for the "esclavage très doux" of the despotism, namely that it is the free choice of a citizen, and the forthright assertion in chapter 2 that liberty is inalienable seems so clear cut and fundamental as to be inexcusable, as well as inexplicable in the midst of so much careful logic. Similarly, the notion that the prospective slave enters for his personal advantage into a reciprocal agreement with the master, surely makes nonsense of his previous attacks on those jurisconsults who had attempted to justify slavery by likening it to a commercial transaction.[109]

But these inconsistencies should not be allowed to obscure the genuine moral concern which really accounts for Montesquieu's

[107] Nagel I, pp. 331–332; Pléiade II, p. 495.
[108] Chapter 7.
[109] Probably represented here by Pufendorf. In the *Droit de la Nature et des Gens*, (trad. Barbeyrac, Amsterdam, 1706), III, ii, 8, he rejects the idea of natural slavery, but later (VI, III) goes on to locate its origin and justification in the contract between master and slave, by which in return for voluntary submission, the slave receives the basic necessities of life.

perplexing acceptance of slavery as justifiable in certain circumstances;
nor, indeed, are they wholly confirmed once certain features of the
text of the first seven chapters are taken into account.

Pensée 174 began:

"L'esclavage est contre le Droit naturel, par lequel tous les hommes
naissent libres et indépendants"[110]

and in chapter 7 of book XV, after setting out the relationship between
servitude and climate, Montesquieu still insists that in spite of its
natural causes, it remains in conflict with nature:

"Mais, comme tous les hommes naissent égaux, il faut dire que l'esclavage est contre la nature, quoique dans certains pays, il soit fondé sur une
raison naturelle; et il faut bien distinguer ces pays d'avec ceux où les raisons naturelles même les (sic) rejettent, comme les pays d'Europe, où il a
été si heureusement aboli."[111]

Significantly, the essential characteristic of the natural state which is
now emphasized is neither liberty nor independence, but equality. It
is also worth noting that from the very beginning of the book, the
despotism is treated as an exception, whereas no mention appears in
Pensée 174 of any variations in political conditions. Chapter 1 gives us a
foretaste of what is to come:

"Dans les pays despotiques, où l'on est déjà sous l'esclavage politique,
l'esclavage civil est plus tolérable qu'ailleurs. Chacun y doit être assez content d'y avoir sa subsistance et la vie. Ainsi la condition de l'esclave n'y est
guère plus à charge que la condition du sujet."[112]

Even where Montesquieu confounds the supporters of the contract
theory, the question of constitutional variations is not entirely absent
from his mind:

"La liberté de chaque citoyen est une partie de la liberté publique. Cette
qualité, *dans l'État populaire*, est même une partie de la souveraineté. Vendre
sa qualité de citoyen est un acte d'une telle extravagance, qu'on ne peut pas
la supposer dans un homme."[113]

Such passages surely indicate that consistent with the enlarged
scientific horizons of the *Lois* as a whole, Montesquieu had realized
since the composition of *Pensée* 174, that in certain cases liberty and
independence could cease in practice if not in theory to be the birth-

---

[110] Nagel II, p. 57; Pléiade I, p. 1467.
[111] Nagel I, p. 332; Pléiade II, p. 496.
[112] Nagel I, p. 325; Pléiade II, p. 490.
[113] Nagel I, p. 327; Pléiade II, pp. 491–492.

right of citizens. Where this was the case, and political laws deprived citizenship of its meaning, then a change in civil conditions, the institution of slavery, might redress the balance, better answering the demands of justice and in closer conformity with the overriding principle of conservation governing natural law as well as social organization.

Thus, as regards the despotism and tropical latitudes, it is clearly *not* the external environmental cause, political or climatic, which really serves to justify the institution. These causes are indeed important factors contributing to a scientific explanation of its establishment in certain regions and types of state, but in isolation they justify nothing. The importance of "raisons naturelles" is that they distort the moral conditions, and sap the resources necessary for the political and moral fulfilment of human beings: on the one hand,

"leur liberté ne vaut rien,"

and on the other,

"la chaleur ... affaiblit si fort le courage, que les hommes ne sont portés à un devoir pénible que par la crainte du châtiment."[114]

In such predicaments then, recourse to slavery paradoxically constitutes the only means by which men may imitate, albeit in a limited way, the full life of the true citizen. The contract by which it is instituted is valid because here the slave does receive real benefits in exchange for the surrender of his nominal freedom.[115]

Thus it is the dictates of the law of nature which in these instances justify the institution of slavery, rather than the climatic or historical causes that actually occasion it. And the opinion that the proper

[114] Commentators on both Montesquieu's moral ideas and on his economic ideas agree on his puritanical attitude to work. Labour was for him not only a virtue but an essential prerequisite of happiness. See P. Duprat, "Les idées économiques de Montesquieu," *Journal des Économistes*, 3e série, tome 18, no. 51, April 1870, pp. 18–37; and M. W. Rombout, *op. cit.*, above (p. 274 n. 64), part III, ch. 1. The suggestion in book XV, 8 that the use of machinery disposes of the need for slaves (see below p. 290), should be compared to the sentiments expressed in book XXIII, 15: "... si les moulins à eau n'étaient pas partout établis, je ne les croirais pas aussi utiles qu'on le dit, parce qu'ils ont fait reposer une infinité de bras, qu'ils ont privé bien des gens de l'usage des eaux, et ont fait perdre la fécondité à beaucoup de terres." Nagel I, p. 54; Pléiade II, p. 692.

[115] It could be objected that if this is the case, Montesquieu, a lover of paradox, is unusually reluctant to make his point with characteristic force. However, the uncertain juggling of key terms such as *nature, raison, raison naturelle* in chapters 6 and 7 surely betrays a struggle to find terminology adequate for expressing his idea. In the *Réponse à des observations de Grosley sur l'Esprit des Lois*, he apologizes for such obscurities:

"Ce qui rend certains articles du livre en question obscurs et ambigus, c'est qu'ils sont souvent éloignés d'autres qui les expliquent, et que les chaînons de la chaîne que vous avez remarquée sont très souvent éloignés les uns des autres." Pléiade II, p. 1197.

end of men is the fulfilment of this law, certainly owes more to the *a priori* assumption of a moralist than the objective constatations of the scientist. Hence Montesquieu's dogmatic reply to the suggestion made by a contemporary critic, Grosley, that in chapter 6 he was really justifying feudalism, not true slavery:

> "Je n'ai point cherché ... l'origine de l'esclavage qui a été, mais l'origine de l'esclavage qui peut ou qui doit être."[116]

need cause no surprise; for the origin that he indicates, somewhat obscurely, is indeed "juste, et conforme à la raison."

Another point to be made is that even in these two exceptional cases, Montesquieu's justification remains reluctant. Chapter 8, where he is at pains to emphasize the complete irrelevance of slavery in countries where no special environmental factors predispose towards it, brings in the example of European mineworkers to illustrate his conviction that even the harshest work can be performed by free labour. The provision of material incentives, and more important, human ingenuity applied to the production of mechanical aids, in harness with human reason applied to legislation, might in every case overcome natural obstacles:

> "Je ne sais si c'est l'esprit ou le coeur qui me dicte cet article-ci. Il n'y a peut-être pas de climat sur la terre où l'on ne pût engager au travail des hommes libres. Parce que les lois étaient mal faites on a trouvé les hommes paresseux: parce que ces hommes étaient paresseux, on les a mis dans l'esclavage."[117]

In his study of Montesquieu's treatment of slavery, R. P. Jameson found it impossible to exonerate him from a certain lack of rigour in the application of his principles, and concluded ruefully that he was a humanitarian perhaps, but not a reformer.[118] Part of his disappointment was undoubtedly due to a failure to recognize that as a sociologist and historian of positive law, Montesquieu deliberately devoted half of book XV to describing rather than criticizing the institution of slavery.[119] As we have seen, Montesquieu struggled to uphold his principles, but the Preface of the *Lois* bears witness from the outset to a practical wisdom which would certainly never have mistaken polemics for the sound knowledge on which effective legislation must be based. If the

---

[116] *Op. cit.*, above p. 289 n. 115; Pléiade II, pp. 1196–1197.
[117] Nagel I, p. 334; Pléiade II, p. 497.
[118] See *op. cit.*, above (p. 278 n. 87), Part II, ch. 4, pp. 318–319.
[119] He suggests for example, that Montesquieu's discussion of historical cases conceals a criticism of the slave trade.

last sentence of chapter 8, attributing ultimate responsibility for the existence of slavery, not to climatic determinism but to bad laws, is unconvincing evidence of Montesquieu's fidelity to a view of man as a conscious moral agent alive to absolute values, and able to incorporate them in his own laws, then the plain words of his final judgement in book XVI on polygamy when it occurs as a prominent feature of domestic slavery, must be left to speak for themselves:

"Toutes les nations se sont également accordées à attacher du mépris à l'incontinence des femmes : c'est que la nature a parlé à toutes les nations. Elle a établi la défense, elle a établi l'attaque; et, ayant mis des deux côtés des désirs, elle a placé dans l'un la témérité, et dans l'autre la honte. Elle a donné aux individus, pour se consoler, de longs espaces de temps, et ne leur a donné, pour se perpétuer, que des moments.

Il n'est donc pas vrai que l'incontinence suive les lois de la nature; elle les viole au contraire. C'est la modestie et la retenue qui suivent ces lois.

D'ailleurs il est de la nature des êtres intelligents de sentir leurs imperfections : la nature a donc mis en nous la pudeur, c'est-à-dire la honte de nos imperfections.

Quand donc la puissance physique de certains climats viole la loi naturelle des deux sexes et celle des êtres intelligents, c'est au législateur à faire des lois civiles qui forcent la nature du climat et rétablissent les lois primitives."[120]

---

[120] Chapter 12; Nagel I, pp. 360-361; Pléiade II, pp. 517-518.

CONCLUSION

In the first part of this work Montesquieu's definition of justice was presented against the background of a range of assumptions current during the last decades of the 17th century and the first of the 18th, concerning the structure of reality, the epistemological groundwork of scientific enquiry and metaphysical speculation, and such speculation on the purpose and meaning of existence itself, in the formulation of which the key phrase *rapport de convenance* or one or other of its elements, was commonly involved. We discovered that in spite of its being one of the most characteristically recurrent phrases in moral and philosophical debate, its connotations were by no means fixed; that in fact it was almost infinitely adaptable within the wide limits set by the Cartesian and Newtonian traditions, fitting as easily into a sensationalist-materialist as into an idealist-essentialist analysis of the nature of things.

In the second part our purpose has been twofold: to reconstitute (as far as existing texts allow) Montesquieu's personal philosophy and its methods, and thereby to situate him in the context of contemporary speculation; and also, using this reconstruction as a framework of reference, to demonstrate the central importance of his idea of justice in the genesis and elaboration of some of his most characteristic political and social doctrines. His definition of justice as

"un rapport de convenance, qui se trouve réellement entre deux choses,"

emerges from this study as the formula which, re-echoing through his works, facilitated, by virtue of the metaphysical and epistemological associations of its key elements, the integration of a body of moral theory, venerable in the antiquity of its sources and strongly idealistic in orientation, into an original and disconcertingly deterministic analysis of historical causation and the life and fortunes of societies.

Taking both parts of the work together, once the rôle of the idea of justice as catalyst and dynamic of Montesquieu's historical and social doctrines is established, one is able to appreciate its full significance in the wider context of contemporary moral and political debate. On the one hand justice, defined as a *constant and immutable* relationship of *fitness*, successfully harnessed some of the resources of rational idealism and metaphysical optimism in the campaign against the 17th century tandem of absolutism and *raison d'état*, without in so doing, ceding an inch of the ground that jurisprudence had painfully wrested from theology. *Convenance*, no matter how vague and indefinable a concept in itself, was nonetheless accepted as the mark and sign of reasoned order, and as such constituted a criterion of surpassing and universal authority. What was the mere will of kings in its shadow, when even the heavens were subjected to it?

On the other hand, the equally crucial presence in Montesquieu's definition of the notion of relationship, not only mediated by virtue of its epistemological associations, between the ancient neo-Platonic tradition of transcendent moral truths and a new scientifically based empiricism, but also, and in a sense, paradoxically, offered the same epistemological resources stemming from the tradition of Cartesian rationalism, to a later generation for use as a counter to the facile materialism in ethics fostered by sensationalism. Against the school of thought represented for instance by Quesnay in the article *Évidence* of the *Encyclopédie:*

"il y a une correspondance certaine entre les corps et les sensations qu'ils nous procurent ... d'où résulte une évidence et une certitude de connaissances à laquelle nous ne pouvons nous refuser, et par laquelle nous sommes continuellement instruits des sensations agréables que nous pouvons nous procurer, et des sensations désagréables que nous voulons éviter. C'est dans cette correspondance que consistent, dans l'ordre naturel, les règles de notre conduite, nos intérêts, notre science, notre bonheur, notre malheur, et les motifs qui forment et dirigent nos volontés," [1]

Rousseau was to argue in *Émile* that there existed a real structure of moral relationships between beings, and that the perception of these relationships constituted the substance of moral life:

"L'étude convenable à l'homme est celle de ses rapports. Tant qu'il ne se connaît que par son être physique, il doit s'étudier par ses rapports avec les choses: c'est l'emploi de son enfance; quand il commence à sentir son être

---

[1] *Op. cit.*, vol. VI, 1756, p. 149.

moral, il doit s'étudier par ses rapports avec les hommes : c'est l'emploi de sa vie entière, à commencer au point où nous voilà parvenus." [2]

It is not simply the corpus of his own political works, that, through the richness and complexity of its associations, Montesquieu's idea of justice illuminates, but the moral thought of a whole century.

[2] *Op. cit.*, Part IV; Paris, Garnier, 1961, p. 249.

MONTESQUIEU'S AESTHETIC THEORIES

We examined in Part I, chapter 5 some of the terms and ideas characteristic of aesthetic thought during the second half of the 17th century, and sketched in the main lines of their development during Montesquieu's lifetime. Montesquieu's own late contribution to this field, his *Essai sur le Goût*, is heavily marked by sensationalism, the idea developed at its centre being that of the relativity of aesthetic norms to the sensory equipment of human beings,[1] an idea to be found, however, as early as Nicole's *Traité de la vraie et de la fausse beauté* where he may have discovered it.[2] In this sphere he seems to have been fully aware of the necessary anthropomorphism upon which both judgement and creation are based: the good, the true and the beautiful, conceived as some compound metaphysical entity closely allied to reason, are promptly dismissed:

"Les sources du beau, du bon, de l'agréable, etc. sont donc dans nous-mêmes; et en chercher les raisons, c'est chercher les causes des plaisirs de notre âme."[3]

Taste, and the rules of composition are dependent upon the arbitrary constitution of the mind and its given relationship to the body:

"Notre manière d'être est entièrement arbitraire; nous pouvions avoir été faits comme nous sommes, ou autrement. Mais, si nous avions été faits autrement, nous aurions senti autrement; un organe de plus ou de moins dans notre machine aurait fait une autre éloquence, une autre poésie; ... par exemple, si la constitution de nos organes nous avait rendus capables d'une plus longue attention, toutes les règles qui proportionnent la disposi-

---

[1] In "Montesquieu et les Beaux Arts," *Atti del quinto Congresso internazionale di lingue e letterature moderne*, Florence, 1955, p. 249 seq. Shackleton develops the theory that the sensationalism of the first chapters of the *Essai* gives way to *a priori* arguments drawn from Crousaz and Hutcheson.

[2] See above p. 97.

[3] *Essai sur le Goût dans les Choses de la Nature et de l'Art*, Nagel I, p. 612; Pléiade II, p. 1240.

tion du sujet à la mesure de notre attention, ne seraient plus; si nous avions été rendus capables de plus de pénétration, toutes les règles qui sont fondées sur la mesure de notre pénétration, tomberaient de même; enfin toutes les lois établies sur ce que notre machine est d'une certaine façon, seraient différentes, si notre machine n'était pas de cette façon." [4]

If the object of the study was primarily to discuss the laws dependent on our actual constitution, then the question of the relationship of this constitution to the underlying structures of nature was largely irrelevant, and Montesquieu did not comment directly upon it. Among the fragments of the *Essai* which remained undiscovered until the end of the 18th century,[5] there are sections entitled *Des Règles* and *Plaisir fondé sur la raison*: but, as they stand, these reveal no substantial evidence of rational idealism. In the first, Montesquieu simply seems to set limits to the applicability of the rules of composition laid down by theorists:

"Tous les ouvrages de l'art ont des règles générales, qui sont des guides qu'il ne faut jamais perdre de vue. Mais comme les lois sont toujours justes dans leur être général, mais presque toujours injustes dans l'application, de même les règles, toujours vraies dans la théorie, peuvent devenir fausses dans l'hypothèse ....
    Quoique chaque effet dépende d'une cause générale, il s'y mêle tant d'autres causes particulières que chaque effet a, en quelque façon, une cause à part: ainsi l'art donne les règles, et le goût les exceptions; le goût nous découvre en quelles occasions l'art doit soumettre, et en quelles occasions il doit être soumis." [6]

This throws interesting light on Montesquieu's understanding of the conditions governing the execution of a work of art, while revealing little of his conception of beauty. In the second fragment, he simply states his opinion, "que ce qui nous fait plaisir doit être fondé sur la raison," "la raison" being used here as a mere synonym of "le bon sens." The rest is largely a development of the second half of his opening proposition that:

"ce qui ne l'est pas à certains égards, mais parvient à nous plaire par d'autres, doit s'en écarter le moins qu'il est possible." [7]

Montesquieu's work offers initially a surprisingly empirical approach to aesthetics, and, as we shall see, the basis of this empiricism was laid

---

[4] *Op. cit.*, "Des plaisirs de notre âme"; Nagel I, pp. 613–614; Pléiade II, pp. 1241–1242.
[5] The chapter, "Des Règles,'" was first published in the *Oeuvres Posthumes* of 1798; the other fragments in Baron Walckenaer's *Annales littéraires* 1804, vol. II, p. 301; for further details, see Nagel III, p. 530.
[6] Nagel III, p. 531; Pléiade, II, p. 1260.
[7] *Ibid.*

down very early. Here it is perhaps worth noting, in order to situate him in relation to contemporary tendencies, that Montesquieu never belonged to the ultra-rationalist party in literature, which counted Fontenelle, Terrasson and La Motte among its advocates. As regards the dispute between the Ancients and the Moderns, Montesquieu was a moderate:

"J'aime à voir les querelles des Anciens et des Modernes: cela me fait voir qu'il y a de bons ouvrages parmi les Anciens et les Modernes."[8]

After his return from England, he dismissed all the opinions put forward by the French protagonists concerning Homer's greatness, condemning Mme. Dacier for pedantry, La Motte for insensibility, pettiness and ignorance, and Terrasson for complete senselessness.[9] The fragments on literature and criticism found in the *Pensées* leave no doubt of his avowed liking for Classical literature;[10] but he was aware of the need to judge a work in its correct historical context:

"Mais pour juger des beautés d'Homère, il faut se mettre dans le camp des Grecs, non pas dans une armée française,"[11]

rather than superimposing upon it the features and merits of works produced by later ages. On the other hand, Montesquieu seems to have been very alive to the harmful effects which the philosophic tendencies of his own age might produce; while pagan literature breathed simplicity and grandeur, the modern world was destroying the sublime by its infatuation with arid abstraction and systematization:

"... ce qui achève de perdre le sublime parmi nous et nous empêche de frapper et d'être frappés, c'est cette nouvelle philosophie qui ne nous parle que de lois générales et nous ôte de l'esprit toutes les pensées particulières de la divinité."[12]

Pedantry, and all its attendant evils, in particular the tendency towards hypercritical judgements and malicious satire, was in the process of stifling talent, and the utilitarianism encouraged by scientific progress held an even greater threat to literary activity.[13]

---

[8] *Pensées* 111 (Bkn. 445); Nagel II, p. 37; Pléiade I, p. 1018.

[9] *Pensées*, 894 (Bkn. 848), 895 (Bkn. 849); Nagel II, p. 259; Pléiade I, pp. 1231–1232.

[10] "J'avoue mon goût pour les anciens. Cette antiquité m'enchante, et je suis toujours porté à dire avec Pline:
"C'est à Athènes que vous allez. Respectez leur Dieux." (110, Bkn. 444).

[11] *Pensées*, 126 (Bkn. 460); Nagel II, p. 42; Pléiade I, p. 1023.

[12] *Ibid.*, 112 (Bkn. 446); Nagel II, p. 37; Pléiade I, p. 1019.

[13] A fragment in Book II of the *Pensées* makes these points, 1006 (Bkn. 542): "Le savoir... a pris parmi nous un air aisé ... qui fait que tout le monde se juge savant ou bel-esprit, et

Many of these reflections are found in the first book of the *Pensées* written between 1722 and 1728, and in the same place we find a key to the empiricism of the *Essai sur le Goût*. The text of the *Essai* that appeared in the *Encyclopédie* contains the following passage:

"... lorsque nous trouvons du plaisir à voir une chose avec une utilité pour nous, nous disons qu'elle est bonne; lorsque nous trouvons du plaisir à la voir, sans que nous y démêlions une utilité présente, nous l'appelons belle.

Les anciens n'avaient pas bien démêlé ceci; ils regardaient comme des qualités positives toutes les qualités relatives de notre âme; ce qui fait que ces dialogues où Platon fait raisonner Socrate, ces dialogues si admirés des anciens, sont aujourd'hui insoutenables, parce qu'ils sont fondés sur une philosophie fausse: car tous ces raisonnements tirés sur le bon, le beau, le parfait, le sage, le fou, le dur, le mou, le sec, l'humide, traités comme des choses positives, ne signifient plus rien." [14]

The argument that attributes of things have meaning only in relation to perception, and not in themselves, is drawn from two entries in the *Pensées*. The textual similarity between the second of these and the passage from the *Essai* make this certain:

"Les termes de beau, de bon, de noble, de grand, de parfait, sont des attributs des objets, lesquels sont relatifs aux êtres qui les considèrent.

Il faut bien se mettre ce principe dans la tête: il est l'éponge de la plupart des préjugés. C'est le fléau de toute la philosophie ancienne, de la physique d'Aristote, de la métaphysique de Platon; et si on lit les dialogues de ce philosophe, on trouvera qu'ils ne sont qu'un tissu de sophismes faits par l'ignorance de ce principe. Le père Malebranche est tombé dans mille sophismes pour l'avoir ignoré." [15]

This in turn summarizes the first entry, where the particular fault of Malebranche is dealt with in some detail:

"Substance, accident, individu, genre, espèce, ne sont qu'une manière de concevoir les choses, selon le différent rapport qu'elles ont entre elles. Par exemple, la rondeur, qui est un accident du corps, devient l'essence d'un cercle, et la rougeur, qui sert de coloris à un cercle matériel, devient l'essence d'un cercle rouge. Idem, l'idée du genre, qui n'est rien en elle-même ...; l'idée de l'infini, à qui le père Malebranche trouve tant de réalité qu'il croit que les idées particulières viennent de celle-là, en faisant une espèce de soustraction arithmétique ...: au lieu que ce n'est qu'en ajoutant sans cesse au fini, sans trouver de bornes, que je fais l'idée de l'infini. C'est ainsi que je pense à une étendue où j'ajoute toujours, à un être dont je bor-

avoir acquis le droit de mépriser les autres. De là, cette négligence d'apprendre ce qu'on croit savoir. De là, cette sotte confiance dans ses propres forces ... De là, ce ton continuel qui consiste à tourner en ridicule les choses bonnes et même les vertueuses ... etc."

[14] *Essai sur le Goût*, Nagel I, p. 612.

[15] *Pensées* 410 (Bkn. 2062); Nagel II, p. 158; Pléiade I, p. 1537.

nerai si peu les perfections que je pourrai toujours, par ma pensée, en ajouter de nouvelles. Mais je n'ai l'idée d'une matière, ni d'un être, auxquels je ne puisse rien ajouter, non plus que d'un temps, ni d'un nombre. Il est bien vrai que Dieu a été de toute éternité: car aucune chose ne peut être faite de rien; de manière qu'il y a eu une durée infinie. Mais je n'ai pas pour cela d'idée de cette durée, et je ne la vois que par des conséquences que je tire de certains principes."[16]

This partial rejection of rational idealism, partial in so far as it stops short of a complete denial that ideas may possess any universal significance, was probably drawn from the Jesuit Claude Buffier's *Traité des Premières Vérités* (1724). Buffier was something of an eclectic, but the notes on contemporary philosophers which end this work disclose a strong preference for Locke, whose thought is described as being as superior in comparison with that of Descartes and Malebranche, as history is to romance. Buffier accepted the universality and truth of general ideas derived from observation, while emphasizing that the information provided by the senses is relative to men, and gives no precise indication of the qualities of objects;[17] on this basis, he accepted that one may arrive at a general idea of infinity in power, but advanced the same argument as Montesquieu to demolish the idea of infinity in number, as used by Malebranche to demonstrate the existence of God.[18] Here then is the possible source of the philosophical criticism upon which Montesquieu based his aesthetic theory in the *Essai sur le Goût;* yet strangely enough, Montesquieu makes no mention in this work of the definition of beauty elaborated by Buffier from the same basis, and reported at length in the *Pensées*:

"Le Père Buffier a défini la beauté: l'assemblage de ce qu'il y a de plus commun. Quand sa définition est expliquée, elle est excellente, parce qu'elle rend raison d'une chose très obscure parce que c'est une chose de goût.

Le Père Buffier dit que les beaux yeux sont ceux dont il y en a un plus grand nombre de la même façon; de même, la bouche, le nez, etc. Ce n'est pas qu'il n'y ait un beaucoup plus grand nombre de vilains nez que de beaux nez; mais c'est que les vilains sont de bien différentes espèces; mais chaque espèce de vilains est en beaucoup moindre nombre que l'espèce des beaux. C'est comme si, dans une foule de cent hommes, il y a dix hommes habillés de vert, et que les quatre-vingt-dix restants soient habillés chacun d'une couleur particulière: c'est le vert qui domine . . . .

Ce principe du Père Buffier est excellent pour expliquer comment une beauté française est horrible à la Chine, et une chinoise, horrible en France.

---

[16] *Pensées* 156 (Bkn. 2061); Nagel II, pp. 49–50; Pléiade I, pp. 1536–1537.
[17] *Op. cit.*, Part I, ch. xv, para. 115.
[18] *Ibid.*, Part II, ch. xii.

Enfin, il est excellent peut-être pour expliquer toutes les beautés de goût, même dans les ouvrages d'esprit. Mais il faudra penser là-dessus."[19]

The President's future reflections were to be strongly coloured by his travels in Italy; and Buffier's definition, too crudely scientific in its purely statistical foundation, was replaced by a conception of beauty which drew instead on a more subtle appreciation of the elements of Classical art. The Jesuit's definition is mentioned once more very briefly in the *Pensées*,[20] but it is clearly of little significance in comparison with the idea of a correspondence between the natural constitution of the mind and the simple, but varied proportion exemplified in Greek architecture and Italian music and painting. Montesquieu recounts how the determination to elaborate this idea arose out of a conversation on the merit of French architecture which took place during his visit to Milan:

"les Anciens ont découvert que le plaisir que l'on a lorsqu'on voit un bâtiment, est causé par de certaines proportions qu'ont entre eux les différents membres d'architecture qui le composent. Ils ont trouvé qu'il y avait cinq différentes sortes de proportions qui excitaient ce plaisir, et ils ont appelé cela *ordres* .... Quelques ornements que l'on mette à ces ordres, quelque déguisement que l'on y fasse, cela ne les change jamais .... Cela fait qu'il est impossible de changer les ordres, d'en augmenter le nombre ou le diminuer, parce que ce ne sont pas des beautés arbitraires qui puissent être suppléées par d'autres. Cela est pris dans la nature, et il me serait facile d'expliquer la raison physique de ceci, et je le ferai quelque jour."[21]

In this passage one becomes aware with the words, "ce ne sont pas des beautés arbitraires qui puissent être suppléées par d'autres. Cela est pris dans la nature . . ." of the intrusion of *a priori* assumptions concerning the nature of things. The proportions immortalized in Greek architecture are so perfect an expression of the hidden structure of reality, that they can neither change nor be changed. So exactly do they correspond to the aesthetic leanings of human sensitivity, that they are an unfailing source of pleasure. Montesquieu's conception of beauty here draws close to the idea of justice expressed in Book I of the *Lois* through the analogy of the immutable structure of the circle.

The material of this *Pensée* reappears in the *Essai sur le Goût*, but loses most of its metaphysical resonances in the process of adaptation to a more technical context.

---

[19] *Pensées*, 272 (Bkn. 956); Nagel II, pp. 112–113; Pléiade I, pp. 1256–1257.

[20] 1449 (Bkn. 957): "Ce qui fait la beauté, c'est la régularité des traits, ce qui fait une femme jolie, c'est l'expression du visage."

[21] *Op. cit.*, 882 (Bkn. 982), Nagel II, pp. 254–255; Pléiade I, p. 1264.

"L'architecture grecque, au contraire, paraît uniforme; mais comme elle a les divisions qu'il faut, et autant qu'il en faut pour que l'âme voie précisément ce qu'elle peut voir sans se fatiguer, mais qu'elle en voie assez pour s'occuper, elle a cette variété qui la fait regarder avec plaisir.

Il faut que les grandes choses aient de grandes parties: les grands hommes ont de grands bras, les grands arbres de grandes branches, et les grandes montagnes sont composées d'autres montagnes qui sont au-dessus et au-dessous; c'est la nature des choses qui fait cela.

L'architecture grecque, qui a peu de divisions, et de grandes divisions, imite les grandes choses; l'âme sent une certaine majesté qui y règne partout." [22]

However, if one returns now to the chapter *Des Règles*, one discovers in the light of this source material an important point of contact with the doctrines concerning justice, specifically with that area dominated by the difficult tension between invariable ideals and endlessly variable behaviour, between the static pattern of transcendent reality and the chaotic dynamism of the temporal world. Montesquieu launches his treatment of the rules on a parallel with law:

"... comme les lois sont toujours justes dans leur être général, mais presque toujours injustes dans l'application; de même les règles, toujours vraies dans la théorie, peuvent devenir fausses dans l'hypothèse. Les peintres et les sculpteurs ont établi les proportions qu'il faut donner au corps humain, et ont pris pour mesure commune la longueur de la face; mais il faut qu'ils violent à chaque instant les proportions, à cause des différentes attitudes dans lesquelles il faut qu'ils mettent les corps: par exemple, un bras tendu est bien plus long que celui qui ne l'est pas." [23]

The rules of art, like those of justice, are only interpreted through the informed response of artist or legislator to the manifold forms of the physical or social world. The great artist creates a total harmony from the disparate, discordant elements of his subject. Thus, Michaelangelo, steeped in the principles of his art, could play with them as he wished, and rarely produced a building where the proportions were exactly observed; yet so sensitive was he to the pleasures of the eye, that it seems as if each work creates an art of its own. The essential expression of beauty as Montesquieu generally sees it, is a kind of natural rhythm achieved within the limitations of situation and medium. For the moment then, there is a shift of emphasis and the yardstick of sensory response is overshadowed by an appraisal of the aesthetic significance of the relationships of proportion between things.

Over-stylization, complete uniformity, absolute regularity, these are

[22] *Op. cit.,* "Des plaisirs de la variété," Nagel I, pp. 620–621; Pléiade II, pp. 1246–1247.
[23] *Essai sur le Goût,* Nagel III, p. 531; Pléiade II, p. 1260.

characteristic of decadence in art, of the Gothic style that Montesquieu
sees as the antithesis of beauty. He returns to this point time and time
again: in the first reflections on painting and sculpture in the *Spicilège*,
he remarks that too much ornamentation produces a monotonous uniformity, and is very bad taste.[24] Among the fragments added to this
outline in the *Pensées* he includes a note on the necessity of movement
and grace in sculpture:

"Le sculpteur ... n'a que la ressource de mettre du feu et du mouvement
dans ses ouvrages, en mettant ses figures dans de belles attitudes et leur
donnant de beaux airs de tête. Ainsi, quand il a mis les proportions dans ses
figures, que ses draperies sont belles, il n'a rien fait s'il ne les met pas en
action, si la position est dure: car la sculpture est naturellement froide.
    La symétrie dans les attitudes y est insupportable .... Mais les contrastes
trop contrastes souvent le sont autant; comme quand on voit qu'un bras en
contraste fait exactement tout ce que l'autre fait, et qu'on voit qu'on a
étudié de faire précisément l'un comme l'autre."[25]

The same theme reappears in the short sketch *De la Manière Gothique*:

"Lorsque l'art commence à décliner, on ne connaît plus ce qu'on appelle *la
grâce*. Bientôt, on ne sait plus donner de mouvement aux figures. Ensuite, on
ignore la variété des attitudes. On ne songe plus qu'à faire bien ou mal des
figures, et on les met dans une position unique. C'est ce qu'on appelle *la manière gothique*.
    Cette position unique est celle qui se présente d'abord à ceux qui ignorent
l'art: de la raideur, de la dureté, de la symétrie dans les diverses parties du
corps, et comme, pour en venir là, il faut aussi avoir peu de connaissance du
dessin, aucune proportion dans les parties du corps."[26]

All of this naturally finds its way into the *Essai sur le Goût*,[27] but it is
best summarized in an entry in the *Pensées* where Montesquieu
expresses a conception of beauty far removed from that of his early
mentor, le Père Buffier:

"La trop grande régularité, quelquefois et même souvent désagréable. Il n'y
rien de si beau que le ciel; mais il est semé d'étoiles sans ordre. Les maisons
et jardins d'autour de Paris n'ont que le défaut de se ressembler trop: ce
sont des copies continuelles de Le Nôtre. Vous voyez toujours le même air,
qualem decet esse sororum. Si on a eu un terrain bizarre, au lieu de l'employer

[24] *Op. cit.*, 461; manuscript 413–420.
[25] *Op. cit.*, 399 (Bkn. 969); Nagel II, pp. 154–155; Pléiade I, pp. 1259–1260; other
fragments 397 (Bkn. 967) – 407 (Bkn. 977).
[26] This sketch draws largely on Montesquieu's notes on Florence (Nagel III, pp. 1313–
1356; Pléiade I, pp. 923–965); Shackleton dates its composition around 1734, but it received
its title from its first editors in the Bordeaux edition of 1896. Passage quoted, Nagel III, p.
276; Pléiade I, p. 967.
[27] See especially the chapters, "Des plaisirs de la variété," and, "Des contrastes".

tel qu'il est, on l'a rendu régulier, pour faire une maison qui fût comme les autres. Nos maisons sont comme nos caractères."[28]

Much of what Montesquieu has to say on artistic matters is based on observation, but if one attempts to draw theoretical conclusions from his scattered remarks, then an interesting pattern emerges. Side by side with the sensationalist thesis upon which the *Essai sur le Goût* largely hinges and which is epitomized in the assertion:

"Les sources du beau, du bon, de l'agréable, etc., sont donc dans nous-mêmes; et en chercher les raisons, c'est chercher les causes des plaisirs de notre âme"[29]

there is the suggestion of a more complex understanding of the beautiful which involves a deeper consideration of artistic creation in relation to essential proportion. In the *Essai* this essential proportion is not represented simply, as it is in *Pensée* 882,[30] by Greek architecture, considered in isolation from the sensitive constitution of human beings, as a direct translation of natural order; on the contrary, it is impossible to abstract the discussion of proportion from its sensationalist matrix, at least to the extent that the challenge to the artist is seen to consist in the creation of artificial proportion through the reconciliation of natural proportion and the limitations of medium, with the dictates of perception and sensitivity. But the idea does emerge, even though it is only implied through examples, that the most crucial factor in this reconciliation is the successful adaptation of the harmonies epitomized in nature:

"Il faut que les grandes choses aient de grandes parties: les grands hommes ont de grands bras, les grands arbres de grandes branches, et les grandes montagnes sont composées d'autres montagnes qui sont au-dessus et au-dessous; c'est la nature des choses qui fait cela."[31]

There are then, invariable, objective criteria to which beauty is attached, as well as subjective and theoretically variable norms:

"Ainsi l'art donne les règles, et le goût les exceptions."[32]

Indeed, here and there in the analysis of taste, which is based consistently on a stereotype of human sensitivity, the subjective norms being effectively treated as invariable, one encounters clear indi-

[28] *Op. cit.*, 1131 (Bkn. 985), Nagel II, p. 306; Pléiade I, p. 1265.
[29] *Op. cit.*, Nagel I, p. 612; Pléiade II, p. 1240.
[30] See above p. 300.
[31] *Op. cit.*, Nagel I, p. 621; Pléiade II, pp. 1246–1247.
[32] "Des règles," see above p. 296.

cations that the bias of the affections is by no means simply and ar-
bitrarily determined as Montesquieu would have us believe at the
outset. Sensitivity is defined not only by mental constitution and
sensory equipment, but by the content of our perceptions themselves,
and these cannot help but mould it to the structures of the natural
world. Thus, the satisfaction we derive from symmetry can be traced
back to natural forms:

"Il est dans la nature qu'un tout soit achevé, et l'âme qui voit ce tout, veut
qu'il n'y ait point de partie imparfaite. C'est encore pour cela qu'on aime la
symétrie; il faut une espèce de pondération ou de balancement."[33]

The need for contrast which balances this satisfaction is a similar
reflection of natural experience: for example, the stiff, monotonously
regular figures of Gothic art are foreign to nature:

"... la nature ne nous a pas situés ainsi; et comme elle nous a donné du
mouvement, elle ne nous a pas ajustés dans nos actions et nos manières
comme des pagodes."[34]

Taste echoes the proportions of nature; beauty recreates them.
The relationship between concept, attribute and the structure of things
is as intimate as any rational idealist would have them. Montesquieu
himself concedes the existence of natural taste, much as he might that
of natural justice, and defines it as a spontaneous and intuitive faculty
in terms which significantly recall the description of the qualities of
l'homme d'esprit in his *Essai sur les causes*; it consists in "une application
prompte et exquise des règles mêmes que l'on ne connaît pas."[35]
Now the behaviour of the *homme d'esprit* was characterized by the
intuitive interpretation of the rules of moral proportion in terms of his
immediate situation.[36] The question poses itself accordingly: is it fair to
identify Montesquieu's conception of physical proportion with his
understanding of moral proportion, particularly in view of the sensationalist posture he adopts in the *Essai sur le Goût*, and of the absence
of any clear metaphysical allusions? As we know, for Montesquieu, the
rules of justice were not determined by examining the actual relationships of men, but derived from a consideration of what they
ideally should be. In the context of ethics, the nature of things is
double: at once that which is and that which ought to be; and the
challenge facing the just man and legislator alike is to bring the two

---

[33] *Essai sur le Goût*, "Des plaisirs de la symétrie," Nagel I, p. 622; Pléiade II, p. 1247.
[34] *Ibid.*, "Des contrastes," Nagel I, p. 623; Pléiade II, p. 1248.
[35] *Essai sur le Goût*, "Des plaisirs de notre âme," Nagel I, p. 615; Pléiade II, p. 1242.
[36] See above pp. 239–240.

together. There appears to be no comparable dichotomy in aesthetics between the rules of proportion and the structure of the physical world, until one recognizes that the process of abstracting essential proportion from the spectacle of nature inevitably calls *a priori* assumptions about the nature of things into play: it is assumed to be geometric. So the artist too confronts rules conceived as invariable reflections of a necessary order, rather than as true descriptions, and the problem remains for him, as for the moralist, to reconcile them with the variables of a dynamic situation, though, obviously, it poses itself in a tangible and therefore more tractable form.

It is then possible to argue that Montesquieu in his *Essai* chases idealism out of the front door only to let it creep in again at the back. Despite his parade of boldly systematic sensationalism, the content and, on closer inspection, heterogeneous procedures of his work on aesthetics display clear affinites with his moral theory, in that they demonstrate once again his characteristic preoccupation with the rôle of creative intelligence as the mediator between the realm of invariable absolutes and that of infinitely mutable phenomena.

BIBLIOGRAPHY OF WORKS CONSULTED

Abbreviations

Congrès 1955   *Actes du Congrès Montesquieu réuni à Bordeaux du 23 au 26 mai 1955.*

P.I.F.A. 3   "Pierre Bayle: le Philosophe de Rotterdam," éd., P. Dibon, *Publications de l'Institut français d'Amsterdam,* 3, Paris, 1959.

P.M.L.A.   *Publications of the Modern Language Association of America.*

R.H.L.F.   *Revue d'Histoire Littéraire de la France.*

R.M.M.   *Revue de Métaphysique et de Morale.*

R.P.F.E.   *Revue Philosophique de la France et de l'Étranger.*

I. WORKS OF MONTESQUIEU

Oeuvres complètes de Montesquieu, publiées sous la direction de M. André Masson, Paris, Nagel, 3 vols., 1950–55.

Oeuvres complètes de Montesquieu, éd., Roger Caillois, Paris, N.R.F.: Bibliothèque de la Pléiade, 2 vols., 1949 and 1951.

De l'Esprit des Loix, éd. Jean Brethe de la Gressaye, Paris, Société les Belles Lettres, 4 vols., 1950–61.

Lettres Persanes, éd., Élie Carcassonne, Paris, Société les Belles Lettres, 2 vols., 1929.

Lettres Persanes, éd., Paul Vernière, Paris, Garnier, 1960.

II. STUDIES ON MONTESQUIEU

Althusser, L., *Montesquieu, la Politique et l'Histoire,* Paris, P.U.F., 1959.

Barrière, P. F., *Un grand Provincial: Charles-Louis de Secondat, baron de la Brède et de Montesquieu,* Bordeaux, Delmas, 1946.

— "Éléments personnels et éléments bordelais dans les *Lettres Persanes*," in *R.H.L.F.,* Jan., 1951.

Beyer, C. J., "Le Problème du Déterminisme Social dans l'*Esprit des Lois*," in *Romanic Review,* vol. XXXIX, 1948, pp. 102–6.

— "Montesquieu et l'Esprit Cartésien," in *Congrès 1955,* Bordeaux, 1956.

Bonnaire, L. de, *L'Esprit des Loix quintessencié par une Suite de Lettres Analytiques*, s. l., 2 vols., 1751.

Buss, E., "Montesquieu und Cartesius," in *Philosophische Monatshefte*, Band IV, 1869–70, pp. 1–37.

Cabeen, D. C., *Montesquieu: a Bibliography*, New York, Bulletin of New York Public Library, 1947.

— "A Supplementary Montesquieu Bibliography," in *Revue internationale de Philosophie*, vol. IX, 1955, pp. 409–34.

Caillois, R., "Montesquieu et la Révolution Sociologique," in *Les Cahiers de la Pléiade*, automne 1949.

Cotta, S., "Il Problema dell'Ordine Umano e la Necessità nel Pensiero di Montesquieu," in *Rivista di Filosofia*, vol. XXXIX, dec. 1948, pp. 368–80.

— *Montesquieu e la Scienza della Società*, Pubblicazioni dell'Instituto di Scienze politiche dell'Università di Torino, II, Torino, Ramella, 1953.

Crisafulli, A. S., "Parallels to Ideas in the *Lettres Persanes*," in P.M.L.A., vol., LII, 1937.

Davy, G., "Sur la Méthode de Montesquieu," in R.M.M., année 46, 1939.

Desgraves, L., "Notes de Lecture de Montesquieu," in *Revue Historique de Bordeaux et du Département de la Gironde*, avril-juin 1952, pp. 149–51.

— *Catalogue de la Bibliothèque de Montesquieu*, Geneva, Société des Publications Romaines et Françaises 43–45, 1954.

Dimoff, P., "Cicéron, Hobbes et Montesquieu," in *Annales Universitatis Saraviensis*, Philosophie-Lettres 1, 1952, pp. 19–47.

— "La place dans l'Oeuvre de Montesquieu de l'*Essai touchant les Lois Naturelles*," in R.H.L.F., année 57, 1957, pp. 481–93.

Duprat, P., "Les idées économiques de Montesquieu," in *Journal des Économistes*, 3rd. series, vol. 18, no. 51, 1870.

Durkheim, E., *La Contribution de Montesquieu à la Constitution de la Science Sociale*, in *Montesquieu et Rousseau, précurseurs de la Sociologie*, Paris, Libraire Marcel Rivière, 1953.

Groethuysen, B., "Montesquieu et l'Art de rendre les Hommes libres," in *Fontaine*, vol. 10, 1946, pp. 505–19.

— "Le Libéralisme de Montesquieu et la Liberté telle que l'entendent les Républicains," in *Europe*, année 27, no. 37, 1949.

Hubert, R., "Le Devenir historique chez Montesquieu," in R.M.M., année 46, 1939.

Ilbert, C. P., *Montesquieu*, Oxford, Romanes Lecture, 1904.

Jameson, R. P., *Montesquieu et l'Esclavage*, Paris, Hachette, 1911.

Kassem, B., *Décadence et Absolutisme dans l'Oeuvre de Montesquieu*, Geneva and Paris, Droz, Minard, 1960.

Klemperer, V., *Montesquieu*, Heidelberg, 2 vols., 1914–15.

Lanson, G., "Le Déterminisme historique et l'Idéalisme social dans l'*Esprit des Lois*," in R.M.M., année 23, 1916.

Levin, L. M., *The Political Doctrine of Montesquieu's Lois: its Classical Background*, New York, Columbia University Press, 1936.

Martino, P., "De quelques résidus métaphysiques dans l'*Esprit des Lois*," in *Revue d'Histoire de la Philosophie et d'Histoire générale de la Civilisation*, fasc. 43, juillet-sept. 1946.

Meinecke, F., *Die Entstehung des Historismus*, Munich and Berlin, R. Olden-
bourg, 2 vols., 1936.
Mercier, R., "La Notion de la Loi Morale chez Montesquieu," in *Literature
and Science: proceedings of the 6th. Triennial Congress of the International Federa-
tion for Modern Language and Literature*, Oxford, Blackwell, 1955.
Oudin, Ch., *Le Spinozisme de Montesquieu*, Paris, 1911.
Roddier, H., "De la Composition de l'*Esprit des Lois*: Montesquieu et les
Oratoriens de l'Académie de Juilly," in R.H.L.F., 1952.
Rombout, M. W., *La Conception stoïcienne du Bonheur chez Montesquieu et chez
quelques-uns de ses Contemporains*, Leyden, Leidse Romanistische Reeks van
de Rijksuniversiteit de Leiden, deel. IV, 1958.
Saint-Hiliaire, B., "Mémoire sur la Science Politique et particulièrement sur
la Politique de Platon, d'Aristote et de Montesquieu," in *Séances et Travaux
de l'Académie des Sciences morales et politiques*, series 2, vol. 4, 1848.
Shackleton, R., "Montesquieu in 1948," in *French Studies*, vol. III, 1949.
— "La Genèse de l'*Esprit des Lois*," in R.H.L.F., vol. 52, 1952.
— "Les Secrétaires de Montesquieu," in *Oeuvres complètes de Montesquieu*,
Nagel, vol. II, 1953.
— "Montesquieu et les Beaux-Arts," in *Actes du 5e Congrès de la Fédération
internationale des langues et littératures modernes*, Florence, 1954.
— "Bayle and Montesquieu," in P.I.F.A. 3, Paris, 1959.
— *Montesquieu: a Critical Biography*, O.U.P., 1961.
Stark, W., *Montesquieu, Pioneer of the Sociology of Knowledge*, London, Routledge
& Kegan Paul, 1960.
Vian, L., *Histoire de Montesquieu d'après des documents nouveaux et inédits*, Paris,
1879.
Voltaire, F.-M. A., *Commentaire sur quelques maximes de l'Esprit des Lois*, in
Oeuvres complètes de Voltaire, éd. L. Moland, Paris, vol. XXX, 1880.
Wróblewski, J., "La Théorie du Droit de Montesquieu," in *Monteskiusz i
jego dzieło*, Warsaw, Polska Akademia Nauk/Komitet Nauk Prawnych,
1956.

III. CLASSICAL WORKS

Aristotle, *Nichomachean Ethics*, London, Loeb Classical Library, 1926.
— *Politics*, Oxford, Clarendon Press, 1962.
— *Rhetorica*, London, Loeb, 1926.
Cicero, *Les Offices de Cicéron*, trad. Du Bois, Paris, Coignard, 1714.
— *De Officiis*, London, Loeb, 1913.
Herodotus, *History of Herodotus*, London, John Murray, 4 vols., 1875.
Plato, *Timaeus*, London, Loeb, 1929.

IV. DICTIONARIES AND ENCYCLOPEDIAS

Corneille, Thomas, *Le Dictionnaire de l'Académie Française* (Le grand Dictionnaire des Arts et des Sciences), Amsterdam, 4 vols., 1696.

Furetière, Antoine, *Le Dictionnaire Universel,* The Hague and Rotterdam, 1690; and Trévoux, 1704.

Diderot, Denis, *Encyclopédie ou Dictionnaire raisonné des Sciences, des Arts et des Métiers,* Paris, Briasson, David, Le Breton, Durand, 1751–65.

Nicot, Jean, *Thresor de la Langue Françoyse,* Paris, 1606.

Robinet, J. B., etc., *Supplément aux Dictionnaires des Sciences, des Arts et des Métiers,* Paris, Panckoucke, Stoupe, Brunet; Amsterdam, Rey, 4 vols., 1776, 7.

V. AUTHORS OF THE 17TH CENTURY AND EARLIER

Aquinas, *Summa Theologica,* Nicolai, Sylvii, Billuart et C-J. Drioux notis ornata, Paris, Blond et Barral, 8 vols., 1885.

Arnauld, Antoine and Nicole, Pierre, *La Logique ou l'Art de Penser,* Paris, 1869.

Baillet, A., *La Vie de M. Descartes,* Paris, D. Horthemels, 1691.

Bayle, Pierre, *Pensées diverses sur la Comète,* éd. A. Prat, Paris, Société des Textes français modernes, 2 vols., 1911.

— *Dictionnaire Historique et Critique,* Rotterdam, R. Leers, 2 vols., 1697.

— *Oeuvres diverses de Mr. P. Bayle,* The Hague, Husson, Johnson, Gosse etc., 4 vols., 1727–31.

Bossuet, Jacques-Bénigne, *Discours sur l'Histoire Universelle,* Paris, S. Mabre-Cramoisy, 1681.

— *Politique tirée des propres paroles de l'Écriture Sainte,* Paris, 1709.

— *Introduction à la Philosophie ou de la Connaissance de Dieu et de Soi-même,* Paris, 1722.

— *Correspondance,* éd. C. Urbain; E. Levesque, Paris, collection: Les grands Écrivains de la France, 15 vols., 1909.

— *Oeuvres Oratoires de Bossuet,* éd., J. Lebarq, Paris, 7 vols., 1914–26.

Bouhours, D., *La Manière de bien penser dans les Ouvrages d'esprit,* Amsterdam, 1692.

Cudworth, R., *True Intellectual System of the Universe,* London, 1678.

— *Treatise concerning Eternal and Immutable Morality,* London, James & John Knapton, 1731.

Deimier, P., *L'Académie de l'Art Poétique,* Paris, Jean de Bordeaulx, 1610.

Descartes, R., *Regulae ad directionem ingenii,* trad. Georges Le Roy, in *Oeuvres et Lettres,* Paris, N.R.F.: Bibliothèque de la Pléiade, 1937.

— *Discours de la Méthode,* Paris, Garnier, 1960.

— *Le Monde ou Traité de la Lumière et des autres Principaux Objets des Sens,* éd. Clerselier, Paris, Jacques le Gras, 1664.

— *Oeuvres de Descartes,* éd., C. Adam and P. Tannery, Paris, L. Cerf, 11 vols., 1897–1909.

Fénelon, François de Salignac de la Motte, *Lettre à M. Dacier sur les Occupations de l'Académie,* éd. A. Cahen, Paris, Hachette, 1914.

Fleury, Claude, *Traité du Choix et de la Méthode des Études* Paris, 1686.

Gracián, B., *L'Homme Universel,* trad. De Courbeville, Rotterdam, Hofhout, 1729.

Gravina, G. V., *Origines Juris Civilis,* Leipzig, Gleditsch, 1708.

Grotius, H., *De Jure Belli ac Pacis*, Amsterdam, Blaev, 1646.
— *Le Droit de la Guerre et de la Paix*, trad. J. Barbeyrac, Amsterdam, Pierre du Coup, 1724.
Hobbes, Thomas, *Leviathan*, s. l., Collins, 1962.
King, W., *An Essay on the Origin of Evil*, trans. Law, London, 1731.
La Bruyère, Jean de, *Les Caractères*, Paris, Hachette, 1950.
La Mesnardière, H. J. Pilet de, *La Poëtique*, Paris, 1640.
Lamy, B., *Entretiens sur les Sciences*, Brussels, Fricx, 1684.
Le Brun, P., *Histoire critique des Pratiques superstitieuses*, Paris, 1702.
Leibniz, Gottfried Wilhelm, *Essais de Théodicée*, Amsterdam, 1712.
— *The Monadology*, trans. R. Latta, Oxford, 1898.
— *Mitteilungen aus Leibnitzens ungedruckten Schriften*, ed., Mollat, Leipzig, 1893.
— *Oeuvres philosophiques*, éd. P. Janet, Paris, Ladrange, 2 vols., 1866.
Lelevel, H., *La Philosophie moderne par demandes et par réponses*, and *De la vraie et de la fausse Éloquence*, Toulouse, 2 vols., 1697–8.
— *Conférences sur l'Ordre naturel et sur l'Histoire Universelle*, Paris, Mersier, 1698.
— *Entretiens sur ce qui forme l'honnête homme et le vrai savant*, Paris, Couterot, 1690.
Locke, John, *Essays on the Law of Nature*, ed. W. van Leyden, Oxford, 1954.
— *An Essay concerning Human Understanding*, London, Dent, 1961.
— *Two Treatises of Government*, ed. P. Laslett, C.U.P., 1960.
Malebranche, Nicolas, *De la Recherche de la Vérité*, Paris, André Pralard, 1674.
— *Traité de la Nature et de la Grâce*, Rotterdam, 1701.
— *Entretien d'un Philosophe Chrétien et d'un Philosophe Chinois*, éd. A. Le Moine, Paris, 1936.
— *Oeuvres de Malebranche*, Paris, Vrin, Bibliothèque des Textes Philosophiques, 1958–68.
Mariotte, E., *Oeuvres de Mr. Mariotte*, Leyden, 1717.
Méré, A. Gombaud, Chevalier de, *Discours de l'Esprit*, Paris, D. Thierry & C. Barbin, 1677.
— *Les Oeuvres de M. de Méré*, Amsterdam, 2 vols., 1692.
Montaigne, Michel de, *Essais*, Paris, N.R.F.: Bibliothèque de la Pléiade, 1950.
Nicole, Pierre, *Traité de la Vraye et de la Fausse Beauté*, in *Recueil des plus belles épigrammes*, trad. Richelet, Paris, 1698, vol. 1.
Pascal, Blaise, *Pensées*, Paris, Éditions du Seuil, 1962.
Pic, J., *Les Devoirs de la Vie Civile*, Amsterdam, Wolfgangk, 1687.
— *Discours sur la Bienséance*, Paris, S. Mabre-Cramoisy, 1688.
Pufendorf, S., *De Jure Naturae et Gentium*, Lund, Junghans, 1672.
— *Le Droit de la Nature et des Gens*, trad. J. Barbeyrac, Amsterdam, Pierre du Coup, 1712.
Pufendorf, S., *Les Devoirs de l'Homme et du Citoyen*, trad. J. Barbeyrac, Amsterdam, Pierre du Coup, 1715
Rapin, R., *Réflexions sur la Poétique d'Aristote*, Paris, 1674.
— *Réflexions sur la Philosophie ancienne et moderne*, Paris, 1676.
— *Du Grand et du Sublime dans les Moeurs*, Paris, 1686.
Saurin, É., *Traité de l'Amour de Dieu*, Amsterdam, 2 vols., 1700–1.
— *Traité de l'Amour du Prochain*, Utrecht, 1704.

Shaftesbury, Anthony Ashley Cooper, 3rd. Earl of, *Characteristicks*, London, John Darby, 1723.

Soto, D., *De Justitia et Jure*, Salamanca, 2 vols., 1553–4.

Spinoza, Baruch, *Opera*, ed. C. Gebhardt, Heidelberg, 4 vols., 1925.

— *Spinoza: Selections*, ed. J. Wild, London, C. Scribner's Sons, 1930.

Thomassin L., *Méthode d'étudier et d'enseigner les Lettres Humaines par rapport aux Lettres Divines et aux Écritures*, Paris, Muguet, 3 vols., 1681–2.

— *Méthode d'étudier et d'enseigner la Philosophie par rapport à la Religion Chrétienne*, Paris, Muguet, 1685.

— *Méthode d'étudier et d'enseigner les Historiens Profanes par rapport à la Religion Chrétienne et aux Écritures*, Paris, Roulland, 2 vols., 1693.

Trotti de la Chétardie, J., chevalier, *Instructions pour un jeune Seigneur*, Paris, 1683.

Varignon, P., *Nouvelles Conjectures sur la Pesanteur*, Paris, 1690.

Vasquez, G., *Commentatiorum ac Disputationum in Primam Partem et in Primam Secundae Summae Theologiae Sancti Thomae Aquinatis*, Treviso; Venice, 1608–09.

VI. 18TH CENTURY AUTHORS

Argens, J.-B. Boyer, Marquis d', *La Philosophie du Bon Sens*, The Hague, 3 vols., 1747.

Bonnet, C., *Essai analytique sur les Facultés de l'Âme*, Copenhagen and Geneva, 2 vols., 1769.

Buffier, C., *Éléments de Métaphysique*, Paris, 1725.

— *First Truths, and the Origins of our Opinions, Explained*, London, J. Johnson, 1780.

Clarke, Samuel, *De l'Existence et des Attributs de Dieu*, trad. Ricotier, Amsterdam, 1717.

— *A Discourse concerning the Being and Attributes of God, the Obligations of Natural Religion and the Truth and Certainty of the Christian Revelation*, London, 1728.

Des Maizeaux, P., *Recueil de Diverses Pièces sur la Philosophie, la Religion Naturelle, l'Histoire, les Mathématiques etc.*, Amsterdam, 2 vols., 1720.

Du Bos, J.-B., *Réflexions critiques sur la Poésie et sur la Peinture*, Paris, 1719.

Duclos, C. P., *Considérations sur les Moeurs de ce Siècle*, ed. F. C. Green, Cambridge, 1946.

Fontenelle, Bernard Le Bovier de, *De l'Origine des Fables*, éd. J. R. Carré, Paris, 1932.

Fontenelle, Bernard Le Bovier de, *Oeuvres de M. de Fontenelle*, Paris, 11 vols., 1766–.

— *Oeuvres de Fontenelle*, Paris, Bastien, 8 vols., 1790.

Fréret, N., *Oeuvres complettes*, London, 1775.

Hume, David, *A Treatise of Human Nature*, London, 3 vols., 1739–40.

— *An Enquiry concerning the Principles of Morals*, London, 1751.

Le Clerc, J., *La Bibliothèque Universelle et Historique*, Amsterdam, 25 vols., 1686–94.

— *La Bibliothèque Choisie*, Amsterdam and The Hague, 1703–38.

Maupertuis, P.-L. Moreau de, *Oeuvres de Maupertuis*, Lyons, 4 vols., 1768.
Newton, Isaac, *Optics*, trans. S. Clarke, London, W & J. Innys, 1719.
Reid, T., *Essays on the Active Powers of the Human Mind*, in *The Works of Thomas Reid D.D.*, ed. Sir W. Hamilton, Edinburgh, 2 vols., 1872.
Rousseau, Jean-Jacques, *Émile*, Paris, Garnier, 1961.
Saint-Hyacinthe, T. de, *Letters giving an account of Several Conversations upon Important and Entertaining Subjects*, London, 1731.
— *Recherches Philosophiques*, Rotterdam and The Hague, Johnson, 1743.
Terrasson, J., *Dissertation critique sur l'Iliade d'Homère*, Paris, Fournier & Coustelier, 2 vols., 1715.
Turrettini, J. A., *Traité de la Vérité de la Religion Chrétienne*, trad. Vernet, Geneva, 1730–36.
— *Cogitationes et Dissertationes Theoligicae*, Geneva, Barrillot & Fils, 1737.
Vauvenargues, L. de Clapiers, Marquis de, *Introduction à la Connaissance de l'Esprit Humain*, Paris, 1746.
— *Oeuvres complètes*, Paris, 2 vols., 1797.
Voltaire, F.-M. A., *Lettres Philosophiques*, Paris, Garnier, 1956.
— *Oeuvres complètes de Voltaire*, éd. L. Moland, Paris, Garnier, 52 vols., 1877–1885; for *Dictionnaire Philosophique*, vol. XX, and *Traité de Métaphysique*, vol. XXII.

VII. CRITICAL, BIOGRAPHICAL AND HISTORICAL STUDIES

Adry, J., *Notice sur le Collège de Juilly*, Paris à l'Institution des Sourds-Muets, 1807.
Aron, R., *Les Étapes de la Pensée Sociologique*, Paris, N.R.F.: Bibliothèque des Sciences Humaines, 1967.
Ascoli, G., *La Grande Bretagne devant l'Opinion française aux 16e et 17e siècles*, in *Travaux et Mémoires de l'Université de Lille*, new series, fascs. 11 and 13, 1927 and 1930.
Banfi, A., "Malebranche et l'Italie," in R.P.F.E., vol. CXXV, 1938.
Barber, W. H., *Leibniz in France from Arnauld to Voltaire*, Oxford, 1955.
Barnes, A., *Jean Le Clerc 1657–1736, et la République des Lettres*, Paris, 1938.
Bouillier, F., *Histoire de la Philosophie Cartésienne*, Paris, Delagrave, 1868.
Bray, R., *La Formation de la Doctrine Classique en France*, Paris, 1927.
Bréhier, E., *Études de Philosophie Antique*, Paris, P.U.F., 1955.
Briggs, E. R., "Mysticism and Rationalism in the Debate upon Eternal Punishment," in *Studies on Voltaire and the 18th. century*, vols. XXIV-XXVII, 1963.
Brown, D. D., *An edition of selected Sermons of John Tillotson*, University of London Thesis, 1956.
Brunschvicg, L., *Le Progrès de la Conscience dans la Philosophie Occidentale*, Paris, 1927.
— *Spinoza et ses Contemporains*, Paris, 1923.
Carré, J. R., *La Philosophie de Fontenelle*, Paris, 1932.
Cassirer, E., *Logos, Dike, Kosmos in der Entwicklung der griechischen Philosophie*, Göteborgs Högskolas Årsskrift, XLVII, 1941.

— *The Platonic Renaissance in England*, trans. J. P. Pettegrove, London, Nelson 1953.

— *The Philosophy of the Enlightenment*, trans. F. C. A. Koelln and J. P. Pettegrove, Boston, Beacon Press, 1955.

— *Determinism and Indeterminism in Modern Physics*, New Haven, Yale University Press, 1956.

Cloyseault, C. E., *Recueil des Vies de quelques Prêtres de l'Oratoire*, éd. A. M. P. Ingold, Paris, Bibliothèque Oratorienne, vols. 1–3, 1880.

Compayré, G., *Histoire critique des Doctrines de l'Éducation en France depuis le 16e siècle*, Paris, Hachette, 1879.

Comte, A., *Cours de Philosophie Positive*, Paris, 6 vols., 1830–42.

Counillon, J. F., *Fontenelle, Écrivain, Savant, Philosophe*, Fécamp, 1959.

Courtines, L. P., *Bayle's Relations with England and the English*, New York, Columbia University Press, 1938.

Cousin, V., *Fragments de Philosophie Cartésienne*, Paris, 1845.

Dartiques, G., *Le Traité des Études de l'Abbé Claude Fleury*, Paris, 1921.

Delvolvé, J., *Religion, Critique et Philosophie Positive chez Pierre Bayle*, Paris, 1906.

Dibon, P., *Pierre Bayle: le Philosophe de Rotterdam*, Paris, 1959.

Dodge, G. H., *The Political Theory of the Huguenots of the Dispersion*, New York, Columbia University Press, 1947.

Evans, A. W., *Warburton and the Warburtonians*, Oxford, 1932.

Folkierski, W., *Entre le Classicisme et le Romantisme: étude sur l'Esthétique et les Esthéticiens du XVIIIe siècle*, Crakow and Paris, 1925.

Free, J. P., *Rousseau's Use of the "Examen de la Religion" and of the "Lettre de Thrasibule à Leucippe,"* Princeton, 1935.

Gaquère, F., *La Vie et les Oeuvres de Claude Fleury, 1640–1723*, Paris, 1925.

Gierke, O., *Natural Law and the Theory of Society, 1500–1800*, trans. E. Barker, Boston, Beacon Press, 1957.

Gilson, E., *Le Thomisme*, Paris, 1947.

Gohin, F., *Les Transformations de la Langue française pendant la deuxième moitié du 18e siècle, 1740–1789*, Paris, 1903.

Guérin, P., *L'Idée de Justice dans la Conception de l'Univers chez les premiers Philosophes Grecs*, Paris, Alcan, 1934.

Guéroult, M., *Malebranche*, Paris, 3 vols., 1955–59.

Haeghen, V., *Geulinx. Étude sur sa Vie, sa Philosophie et ses Ouvrages*, Gand, 1886.

Hamel, C., *Histoire de l'abbaye et du collège de Juilly*, Paris, 1868.

Hastings, H., *Man and Beast in French Thought*, Baltimore, Johns Hopkins Studies in Romance Literatures and Languages, vol. 27, 1936.

Hazard, P., *La Crise de la Conscience Européenne, 1680–1715*, Paris, 3 vols., 1935.

Ingold, A. M. P., "Mémoire sur le règlement des Études dans les Lettres Humaines par M. Arnauld," in *Revue internationale de l'enseignement*, juillet-août 1886.

Janet, P., *Histoire de la Science Politique dans ses rapports avec la Morale*, Paris, 1872.

Kirkinen, H., *Les Origines de la Conception moderne de l'Homme – Machine*, Helsinki, Suomalaisen Tiedeakatemian Toimituksia, series B, vol. 122, 1960.

Lallemand, P., *Histoire de l'Éducation dans l'ancien Oratoire de France*, Paris, Thorin, 1888.

Lanson, G., "Le rôle de l'Expérience dans la Formation de la Philosophie du 18e siècle en France," in *Revue du Mois*, 1910.

— "L'Influence de la Philosophie Cartésienne sur la Littérature," in R.M.M., année 4, 1896.

Laurila, K. S., *Les premiers Devanciers français de la Théorie du Milieu*, Helsinki, Suomalaisen Tiedeakatemian Toimituksia, series B, vol. 22, 1923.

Lévêque, A., "L'Honnête-Homme et l'Homme de Bien au XVIIe siècle," in P.M.L.A., vol. LXXII, 1957.

L'Isle André, Y.-M. de, *La Vie du R. P. Malebranche ... avec l'histoire de ses Ouvrages*, éd. A. M. P. Ingold, Paris, Bibliothèque Oratorienne, vol. 8, 1881.

Luce, A. A., "Malebranche et le Trinity College de Dublin," in R.P.F.E., vol. CXXV, 1938.

Magendie, M., *La Politesse Mondaine et les Théories de l'Honnêteté en France au XVIIe siècle, de 1600 à 1660.*, Paris, 2 vols., 1925.

Mauzi, R., *L'Idée du Bonheur dans la Littérature et la Pensée françaises au XVIIIe siècle*, Paris, Colin 1960.

Mercier, R., *La Réhabilitation de la Nature Humaine*, Villemonble, 1960.

Michéa, R., "Les Variations de la Raison au XVIIe siècle," in R.P.F.E., vol. CXXVI, 1938.

Monod, A., *De Pascal à Chateaubriand: les défenseurs français du Christianisme, de 1670 à 1802*, Paris, 1916.

Monod, G., "Du Progrès des Études Historiques en France," in *Revue Historique*, année 1, jan.-mars 1876.

Nourrisson, J. F., *La Politique de Bossuet*, Paris, 1867.

Parodi, D., "L'Honnête-Homme et l'Idéal Moral du XVIIe et du XVIIIe siècles.," in *Revue Pédagogique*, new series, vol. LXXVIII, 1921.

Perraud, A. L. A., *L'Oratoire en France au XVIIe et au XIXe siècle*, Paris, 1865.

Peyre, H., *Le Classicisme français*, New York, 1942.

Rochedieu, C. A., *Bibliography of French Translations of English Works, 1700–1800*, Chicago, 1948.

Rosenfield, L. C., *From Beast Machine to Man Machine: Animal Soul in French Letters from Descartes to La Mettrie*, New York, O.U.P., 1941.

Roth, L., *Spinoza*, London, 1929.

Sayous, P. A., *Histoire de la Littérature française à l'Étranger depuis le commencement du XVIIe siècle*, Paris, 2 vols., 1853.

Sée, H., *L'Évolution de la Pensée Politique en France au XVIIIe siècle*, Paris, 1925.

Simon, R., *Henry de Boulainviller, Historien, Politique, Philosophe, Astrologue*, Paris, 1941.

— *Nicolas Fréret*, in *Studies on Voltaire and the 18th. Century*, vol. XVII, 1961.

Spink, J. S., *French Free Thought from Gassendi to Voltaire*, London, Althlone Press, 1960.

Théry, A. E., *Histoire de l'Éducation en France depuis le cinquième siècle jusqu'à nos jours*, Paris, 2 vols., 1858.

Thijssen-Schoute, C. L., "Le Cartésianisme aux Pays-Bas," in *Descartes et le Cartésianisme Hollondais, Études et Documents*, Paris, Amsterdam and the Hague, Institut Français d'Amsterdam, 1950.

Vaughan, C. E., *Studies in the History of Political Philosophy before and after Rousseau*, Manchester University Press, 1925.

Vecchio, G. del, *Justice: an Historical and Philosophical Essay*, trans. Guthrie, Edinburgh University Press, 1952.

Vernière, P., *Spinoza et la Pensée française avant la Révolution*, Paris, Publications de la Faculté des Lettres d'Alger, series 2, no. 20, 1954.

INDEX

Abbadie, J., 38
Adry, J. F., 119; 121
Aguesseau, H.-F. d', 118
Alembert, J. Le Rond d', 127, n. 51
Althusser, L., 113, n. 2; 186
Aquinas, XI; 11; 74; 243
Argens, J.-B. Boyer, Marquis d', 63, n. 101
Aristotle, X–XI; XII; 43; 185; 228; 255, nn. 1, 3
Arnauld, A., 13; 16; 42; 252
Aron, R., 199; 226, n. 31; 240, n. 63
Ascoli, G., 67, n. 1; 70, n. 13
Augustine, Saint, 10; 12; 24; 118; 125

Baillet, A., XIII
Banfi, A., 14, n. 20
Barber, W., 22, nn. 47, 48; 23, n. 49; 29, n. 69
Barbeyrac, J., 38; 69
Barnes, A., 46, n. 37; 47, n. 40
Barrière, P., 70, n. 16; 114; 115; 117, n. 11; 144; n. 3
Basnage, J., 47
Bayle, P., 35; 37; 38; 39; 40; 46; 47; 52; 54–56; 57; 82; 117; 125–127; 128; 132–133; 162; 163; 168; 252
Berkeley, G., 9; 82
Bernard, J. F., 47
Bertault, Père P., 120
Bérulle, Père P. de, 118; 120; 121
Beyer, C. J., 132, n. 66; 148, n. 14; 199, n. 46; 238, n. 60
Boehmer, J. H., 223
Bolingbroke, H. St. John, Viscount, 23
Bonnaire, L. de, 197
Bonnet, C., 184; 185; 234–35
Bossuet, J.-B., bishop of Meaux, 16–21; 22; 31; 33; 38; 39; 40; 98; 103; 108; 143; 195, n. 33; 252
Bossuet, Abbé J.-B., 16
Bouhours, Père D., 43; 92; 94
Bouillier, F., 9, n. 5; 42, n. 21
Boulainviller, H. de, 59; 117; 136; 247
Bourdaloue, Père L., 41

Bray, R., 92; 94
Bréhier, E., 276, n. 76
Briggs, E. R., 40, n. 15
Brown, D., 73, n. 28
Browne, P., 9
Brunschvicg, L., 23, n. 50
Buffier, Père C., 57, n. 77; 63, n. 101; 299–300; 302.
Burnet, T., 71, n. 21
Buss, E., 199, n. 46; 223, n. 29

Caillois, R., 143; 149, n. 16; 163, n. 37
Carcassone, E., 21, n. 44; 171, n. 57
Carré, J. R., 53, n. 64; 129, n. 58
Casati, E., 69, n. 7
Cassirer, E., 148, n. 14; 185; 199; 228, n. 37; 230, n. 42; 240, n. 62; 243, n. 69; 255, n. 1
Charron, P., 37
Chouet, R., 47
Cicero, 45; 122–24; 125; 128; 131; 134; 135; 142; 276, n. 76; 277
Clarke, S., 39; 69; 70; 71; n. 21; 84–87; 160; 182; 204; 243; 244; 268
Cloyseault, Père E., 120, n. 24; 122
Collins, A., 69
Compayré, G., 119, n. 20
Comte, A., 185
Condren, Père C. de, 119; 122
Conti, A., 21
Corneille, T., 3–7
Coste, P., 39; 69; 70; 71
Cotta, S., 148, n. 14; 213; 262, n. 25
Counillon, J. F., 53, n. 64
Courtines, L. P., 126, n. 48
Cousin, V., 13, n. 17
Crisafulli, A. S., 21, n. 44; 78, n. 41; 159, n. 29; 178, n. 80
Cudworth, R., 68; 70; 75; 78; 85; 125–26
Culverwel, N., 74

Dacier, A., 297
Dartigues, G., 138, n. 83
Davy, G., 114, n. 2; 201; 203